SAS/OR®
User's Guide,
Version 5 Edition

SAS SAS Institute Inc.
Box 8000
Cary, North Carolina 27511-8000

The correct bibliographic citation for this manual is as follows: SAS Institute Inc. *SAS/OR® User's Guide, Version 5 Edition.* Cary, NC: SAS Institute Inc., 1985. 347 pp.

SAS/OR® User's Guide, Version 5 Edition

Copyright © 1985 by SAS Institute Inc., Cary, NC, USA.
ISBN 0-917382-64-1

86 4 3 2

Base SAS® software, the foundation of the SAS System, provides data retrieval and management, programming, statistical, and reporting capabilities. Also in the SAS System are SAS/GRAPH® SAS/FSP® SAS/ETS® SAS/IMS-DL/I® SAS/OR® SAS/AF® SAS/IML,™ SAS/DMI,™ SAS/RTERM,™ SAS/REPLAY-CICS,™ SAS/STAT,™ and SAS/QC™ software. These products and SYSTEM 2000® Data Base Management System, including the basic SYSTEM 2000® Multi-User,™ QueX,™ Screen Writer,™ CREATE,™ and CICS interface products, are available from SAS Institute Inc., a private company devoted to the support and further development of the software and related services. *SAS Communications,® SAS Training,® SAS Views,®* and the SASware Ballot® are published by SAS Institute Inc.

Contents

iv

Illustrations

Tables

Acknowledgments

Program development includes design, programming, debugging, support, and documentation. Listed below for each procedure are, first, the developer currently supporting the procedure, then earlier developers.

ASSIGN	Marc-david Cohen
CPM	Radhika Kulkarni, Marc-david Cohen
GANTT	Radhika Kulkarni
LP	Marc-david Cohen
NETFLOW	Marc-david Cohen
TRANS	Marc-david Cohen

For several years, the SASware ballot has shown that SAS users place a high priority on a linear programming procedure. SAS/OR is the result of that request. Although many people have been instrumental in the development of SAS/OR, special mention is due to:

Dr. David Rubin	University of North Carolina at Chapel Hill
Mark Tedone	Reynolds Metals
Sherry Wartelle	Peoples National Bank of Washington
Robert Rice	National Spinning
Agnes Eggleston	Texasgulf
Don Henderson	ORI Consulting Group
Robert Floyd	Bluebell Inc.
Dr. John Stone	North Carolina State University
Barbara Gregoire	Hughes Aircraft Co.
Walter Mahan	Morino Associates Inc.
Franklin Young	United Airlines.

x

Preface

SAS/OR software, together with base SAS software, is a complete package for solving management problems. The *SAS/OR User's Guide* must be read along with the *SAS User's Guide: Basics*, which is the primary description of the SAS language and the procedures in base SAS software.

As you begin, read the first chapter in this manual, "Introduction to SAS/OR Procedures" to review several operations research problems that are solved using SAS/OR software. This chapter may contain an example similar to yours that you can adapt.

Next, read the appendix "Operating System Notes." This information will help you use your operating system's capabilities to get your data into and out of the SAS System.

To start learning more about writing SAS programs, go to the *SAS User's Guide: Basics* chapter entitled "Introduction to the SAS Language." If you are using OS batch or TSO, you can also refer to the *SAS Introductory Guide*.

The *SAS/OR User's Guide, Version 5 Edition* documents a collection of SAS procedures for analyzing data using the tools of operations research. Operations research tools are directed toward the solution of management problems. Each problem is formalized with the construction of a mathematical model to represent it. These models are defined as data in SAS data sets and then analyzed by SAS/OR procedures. Since they are SAS data sets, models can be saved and easily changed or reanalyzed. Many SAS/OR procedures also output SAS data sets containing the results of the analysis.

SAS/OR software contains these procedures:

ASSIGN	assignment problems
CPM	critical path analysis and project management
GANTT	Gantt charts
LP	linear programming methods
NETFLOW	network analysis
TRANS	transportation problems.

Also included is a conversion macro SASMPSX.

SAS/OR procedures are part of the SAS System and behave like other SAS procedures. Before using the procedures in this manual, you should have the following knowledge:

- You should understand the SAS System (documented in the *SAS User's Guide: Basics*) and elementary statistics.
- You should know techniques of operations research at the level discussed, for example, in H.M. Wagner (1975, *Principles of Operations Research*, Prentice Hall).

To help you increase your knowledge in the areas listed above, SAS/OR chapters provide references to textbooks that you can use to learn these techniques.

What is the SAS System?

The SAS System is a software system for data analysis. The goal of SAS Institute is to provide data analysts one system to meet all their computing needs. When your computing needs are met, you are free to concentrate on results rather than on the mechanics of getting them. Instead of learning programming languages, several statistical packages, and utility programs, you only need to learn the SAS System.

The SAS System is an all-purpose data analysis system. To base SAS software, you can add tools for graphics, operations research, forecasting, data entry, and interfaces to other data bases to provide one total system. SAS software runs on IBM 370/30xx/43xx and compatible machines in batch and interactively under OS and TSO, CMS, DOS/VSE, and SSX; on Digital Equipment Corporation VAX™ 11/7xx series under VMS;™ Data General ECLIPSE® series under AOS/VS; MV series under AOS/VS; Prime Series 50 under PRIMOS® and IBM PC AT/370 and XT/370 under VM/PC. Note: not all products are available for all operating systems.

Base SAS software provides tools for

- information storage and retrieval
- data modification and programming
- report writing
- statistical analysis
- file handling.

Information storage and retrieval   The SAS System reads data values in virtually any form from cards, disk, or tape and then organizes the values into a SAS data set. The data can be combined with other SAS data sets using the file-handling operations described below. The data can be analyzed statistically and can be used to produce reports. SAS data sets are automatically self-documenting since they contain both the data values and their descriptions. The special structure of a SAS data library minimizes maintenance.

Data modification and programming   A complete set of SAS statements and functions is available for modifying data. Some program statements perform standard operations such as creating new variables, accumulating totals, and checking for errors; others are powerful programming tools such as DO/END and IF-THEN/ELSE statements. The data-handling features are so valuable that base SAS software is used by many as a data base management system.

Report writing   Just as base SAS software reads data in almost any form, it can write data in almost any form. In addition to the preformatted reports that SAS procedures produce, SAS software users can design and produce printed reports in any form, as well as punched cards and output files.

Statistical analysis   The statistical analysis procedures in the SAS System are among the finest available. They range from simple descriptive statistics to complex multivariate techniques. Their designs are based on our belief that you should never need to tell the SAS System anything it can figure out by itself. Statistical integrity is thus accompanied by ease of use. Especially noteworthy statistical features are the linear model procedures, of which GLM (**G**eneral **L**inear **M**odels) is the flagship.

File handling   Combining values and observations from several data sets is often necessary for data analysis. SAS software has tools for editing, subsetting, concatenating, merging, and updating data sets. Multiple input files can be processed simultaneously, and several reports can be produced in one pass of the data.

Other SAS System Products

With base SAS software and SAS/OR software, you can integrate SAS software products for graphics, data entry, forecasting, and interfaces to other data bases to provide one total system:

- SAS/AF software—a full-screen, interactive applications facility
- SAS/ETS software—expanded tools for business analysis, forecasting, and financial planning
- SAS/FSP software—interactive, menu-driven facilities for data entry, editing, retrieval of SAS files, letter writing, and spreadsheet analysis
- SAS/GRAPH software—device-intelligent color graphics for business and research applications
- SAS/IML software—multi-level, interactive programming language whose data elements are matrices
- SAS/IMS-DL/I software—interface for reading, updating, and writing IMS/VS or CICS DL/I data bases
- SAS/REPLAY-CICS software—interface that allows users of CICS/OS/VS and CICS/DOS/VS to store, manage, and replay SAS/GRAPH displays.

SAS Institute Documentation

Using this manual   The first chapter of this manual provides an overview and describes the capabilities of SAS/OR software. In planning your analyses, refer to this general discussion, which includes how to construct a mathematical model to represent your problem and how to define the model as data in a SAS data set to be analyzed by SAS/OR procedures.

Procedure descriptions follow alphabetically in the next chapters. Each procedure description is self-contained; you need to be familiar with only the most basic features of the SAS System and SAS terminology to use most procedures. The statements and syntax necessary to run each procedure are presented in a uniform format throughout the manual. You can duplicate the examples by using the same statements and data to run a SAS job. The examples are also useful as models for writing your own programs.

Each procedure description is divided into the following major parts:

ABSTRACT: a short paragraph describing what the procedure does.
INTRODUCTION: introductory and background material, including definitions and occasional introductory examples.
SPECIFICATIONS: reference section for the syntax of the control language for the procedure.
DETAILS: expanded descriptions of features, internal operations, output, treatment of missing values, computational methods, required computational resources, and usage notes.
EXAMPLES: examples using the procedure, including data, SAS statements, and printed output. You can reproduce these examples by copying the statements and data and running the job.
REFERENCES: a selected bibliography.

There are five appendices, including a description of the conversion macro SASMPSX; a summary of Version 5 changes and enhancements to SAS/OR software; operating system notes; a guide to the SAS Display Manager System for full-screen terminals; and a discussion of full-screen editing capabilities with the SAS System.

If you have any problems with this manual, please take time to complete the review page at the end of this book and send it to SAS Institute. We will consider your suggestions for future editions. In the meantime, ask your installation's SAS Software Consultant for help.

New SAS/OR Features

Version 5 of SAS/OR software contains many new features, including a new procedure and enhancements to existing procedures. See the appendix, "Version 5 Changes and Enhancements to SAS/OR Software" for a complete description. The TIMEPLOT procedure and the LINPROG subroutine are now documented elsewhere. TIMEPLOT is documented in the *SAS User's Guide: Basics, Version 5 Edition*; the LINPROG subroutine is included in SAS Technical Report P-135, "The MATRIX Procedure."

SAS release?   To find out which release of SAS software you are using, run any SAS job and look at the release number in the notes at the beginning of the SAS log. This user's guide documents Version 5 SAS/OR software. If you have an earlier release (for example, the 82.4 release), you should use the 1983 edition of the *SAS/OR User's Guide*.

Other SAS Institute manuals and technical reports   Below is a list of other manuals that document Version 5 SAS System software:

> *SAS User's Guide: Basics, Version 5 Edition*
> *SAS User's Guide: Statistics, Version 5 Edition*
> *SAS/GRAPH User's Guide, Version 5 Edition*
> *SAS/FSP User's Guide, Version 5 Edition*
> *SAS/ETS User's Guide, Version 5 Edition*
> *SAS/AF User's Guide, Version 5 Edition*
> *SAS/IML User's Guide, Version 5 Edition*

The SAS Technical Report Series documents work in progress, describes new supplemental procedures and covers a variety of applications areas. Some of the features described in these reports are still in experimental form and are not yet available as SAS procedures.

Write to SAS Institute for a current publications catalog, which describes the manuals as well as technical reports and lists their prices.

SAS Services to Users

Technical support   SAS Institute supports users through the Technical Support Department. If you have a problem running a SAS job, you should contact your site's SAS Software Consultant. If the problem cannot be resolved locally, your local support personnel should call the Institute's Technical Support Department at (919) 467-8000 on weekdays between 9:00 a.m. and 5:00 p.m. Eastern Standard Time. A brochure describing the services provided by the Technical Support Department is available from SAS Institute.

Training   SAS Institute sponsors a comprehensive training program, including programs of study for novice data processors, statisticians, applications programmers, systems programmers, and local support personnel. *SAS Training*, a semi-annual training publication, describes the total training program and each course currently being offered by SAS Institute.

News magazine   *SAS Communications* is the quarterly news magazine of SAS Institute. Each issue contains ideas for more effective use of the SAS System, information about research and development underway at SAS Institute, the current training schedule, new publications, and news of the SAS Users Group International (SUGI).

To receive a copy of *SAS Communications* regularly, send your name and complete address to:

SAS Institute Mailing List
SAS Institute Inc.
Box 8000
Cary, NC 27511-8000

Sample library   One of the data sets included on the base product installation tape is called SAS.SAMPLE. This data set contains sample SAS applications to illustrate features of SAS procedures and creative SAS programming techniques that can help you gain an in-depth knowledge of SAS capabilities.

Here are a few examples of programs included:

ANOVA	analyzing a Latin-square split-plot design
ARIMA5	fitting an intervention model to an ozone time series
CENSUS	reading hierarchical files of the U.S. Census Bureau Public Use Sample tapes
CPM1	scheduling a construction project
HARRIS	reading Harris Poll tapes coded in column-binary format
NETFLOW4	finding the shortest path through a network
PDL	fitting a polynomial distributed lag regression model.

Check with your SAS Software Consultant to find out how to access the library since it may have been put on disk at your site.

SUGI

The SAS Users Group International (SUGI) is a nonprofit association of professionals who are interested in how others are using the SAS System. Although SAS Institute provides administrative support, SUGI is independent from the Institute. Membership is open to all users at SAS sites, and there is no membership fee.

Annual conferences are structured to allow many avenues of discussion. Users present invited and contributed papers on various topics, for example:

- computer performance evaluation and systems software
- econometrics and time series
- graphics
- information systems
- interactive techniques
- operations research
- statistics
- tutorials in SAS System software.

Proceedings of the annual conferences are distributed free to SUGI registrants. Extra copies may be purchased from SAS Institute.

SASware Ballot   SAS users provide valuable input toward the direction of future SAS development by ranking their priorities on the annual SASware Ballot. The top vote-getters are announced at the SUGI conference. Complete results of the SASware Ballot are also printed in the *SUGI Proceedings*.

Supplemental library   SAS users at many installations have written their own SAS procedures for a wide variety of specialized applications. Some of these user-written procedures are available through the SUGI supplemental library and are documented in the *SUGI Supplemental Library User's Guide*. The procedures in the supplemental library are sent to each installation that licenses base SAS software, although only a few procedures are supported by SAS Institute staff.

Licensing the SAS System

The SAS System is licensed to customers in the Western Hemisphere from the Institute's headquarters in Cary, NC. To serve the needs of our international customers, the Institute maintains subsidiaries in the United Kingdom, New Zealand, Australia, Singapore, Germany, and France. In addition, agents in other countries are licensed distributors for the SAS System. For a complete list of offices, write or call:

SAS Institute Inc.
SAS Circle
Box 8000
Cary, NC 27511-8000
(919) 467-8000

Chapter 1
Introduction to SAS/OR™ Software

INTRODUCTION

SAS/OR software is a set of programs for analyzing data using the tools of operations research. SAS/OR programs are SAS procedures. If you are familiar with other SAS procedures, you will find the syntax and use of options very similar. All SAS retrieval, data management, reporting, analysis, and other capabilities can be used with SAS/OR.

Operations research tools are directed toward the solution of management problems. Each problem is formalized with the construction of a mathematical model to represent it. These models are defined as data in SAS data sets and then analyzed by SAS/OR procedures. Since they are SAS data sets, models can be saved and easily changed or re-analyzed. Many SAS/OR procedures also output SAS data sets containing the results of the analysis.

SAS/OR software contains these procedures:

ASSIGN	assignment problems
CPM	project planning
GANTT	plotting Gantt charts
LP	linear, integer, and mixed-integer programming methods
NETFLOW	network analysis
TRANS	transportation problems.

Also included is a data conversion macro SASMPSX.

Linear, Integer, and Mixed-Integer Programming Problems

Linear, integer, and mixed-integer programming are optimization techniques that can be applied to a wide range of problems in business and industry. Decisions about allocating work to machines or orders to be filled to plants are problems handled by these techniques.

Management often finds itself in the position of making a decision that would maximize (or minimize) an objective within bounds imposed by secondary factors. Many problems of this type can be posed as linear programs. For example, during a particular month a manufacturer has available 100 machine hours, 700 labor hours, and 8000 pounds of material. Using different combinations of these resources, the plant can produce two kinds of products (types 1 and 2). Product 1 adds $1.00 per unit to profits; product 2 adds $2.00 per unit. What quantity of each product should be produced in order to maximize total profits? The manager can choose from all possible proportions of the two product types. He is limited by his resources and may place other constraints on the problem. For example, he may want to produce at least 25% of each product, or he may want to produce less than a given quantity of one product.

The transportation problem   One application of linear programming techniques is the transportation problem— the need to fill requirements at destination points with the capacity at source points while minimizing the total cost of transportation. A typical transportation problem is that of a firm with n manufacturing plants and m warehouses. Each plant has certain monthly capacities; each warehouse has certain monthly sales requirements. For each plant-to-warehouse combination, there is an associated cost for transporting one unit. The firm must decide the quantities to be shipped from each plant to each warehouse so that transportation costs for the company are minimized.

The assignment problem   In an assignment problem you want to associate objects in one group with objects in a second group in a way that minimizes costs. For example, a foreman has four repairmen that he wants to assign to four different jobs. The different skills of the repairmen mean that they will exhibit different levels of efficiency from one job to another. How can the men be assigned in order to maximize total efficiency (or minimize total man hours and thus costs)?

Networks   Problems in operations research include scheduling problems and those associated with flows and paths through networks. Networks are a series of nodes with arcs or lines connecting each node. Problems that can be formalized as finding a path or flow in a network are often the focus of operations research. SAS/OR procedures for network problems can be used, for example, to determine the optimal flow of products through a manufacturing process, the timing of jobs in a construction job, or traffic flow patterns in a freeway system.

Project Planning

A special type of network problem can be solved with PROC CPM—a way of presenting scheduling information and the relationships between activities. Scheduling a project can be difficult when many activities are involved. It is particularly difficult when the activities must be scheduled to meet given deadlines without exceeding limited resources. PROC CPM solves this type of scheduling problem and saves the schedule in a SAS data set. Resource use can also be monitored with PROC CPM.

A Gantt chart is a tool that is useful for monitoring the progress of a project. The chart graphically displays the calculated schedule and shows the current progress in meeting the schedule. PROC GANTT can be used to produce both line printer and high resolution Gantt charts.

How to Use This Manual

This chapter begins by illustrating how SAS/OR procedures solve two simple linear programming problems and an integer programming problem. The transportation problem and the assignment problem, special cases of linear programming, are discussed as well as shortest path and maximum flow network problems, which can be handled by the NETFLOW procedure and a simple critical-path problem. Next, the SAS/OR procedures are described in alphabetical order. Appendix 1 gives a description of the SASMPSX macro. Go over these examples and then use the procedure descriptions to decide how to set up the statements you need to solve your own SAS/OR problems. Other appendices detail the Version

5 changes to SAS/OR software, operating system information, full-screen editing capabilities, and a description of the SAS Display Manager.

LINEAR PROGRAMMING: AN INTRODUCTION

A Simple Production Problem

This section describes a common linear programming problem through two simple examples. More complicated examples are given in the LP procedure description.

A small candy manufacturer makes two products—chocolates and gum drops. The company's president asks the question: What combination of chocolates and gum drops should we produce in a day in order to maximize the company's profit? He knows that chocolates contribute $.25 per pound to profit and gum drops $.75 per pound. The variables chocolates and gum drops are called *decision variables*.

Four processes are used to manufacture the candy:

1. In Process 1, the basic ingredients for both chocolates and gum drops are combined and cooked.
2. Process 2 adds colors and flavors to the gum drops, then cools and shapes the drops.
3. Process 3 chops and mixes nuts and raisins, adds them to the chocolates, then cools and shapes the candies.
4. Process 4 is packaging: chocolates are placed in individual paper shells; gum drops are wrapped in two-ounce cellophane packages.

During the day there are 7.5 hours (27,000 seconds) available for each process.

Firm time standards have been established for each process. For Process 1, mixing and cooking take 15 seconds for each pound of chocolates and 40 seconds for each pound of gum drops. Process 2 takes 56.25 seconds per pound of gum drops. For Process 3, 18.75 seconds are required for each pound of chocolates; in packaging, a pound of chocolates can be wrapped in 12 seconds, whereas 50 seconds are required for a pound of gum drops. These data are summarized below:

		Time Required per Pound	
Process	available time (sec)	chocolates (sec)	gum drops (sec)
1 Cooking	27,000	15	40
2 Color/Flavor	27,000	.	56.25
3 Condiments	27,000	18.75	.
4 Packaging	27,000	12	50

Stating the Problem Algebraically

The objective function   The profitability of each product can be expressed as an equation, sometimes called the *objective function*, or function to be optimized. The equation representing the objective function for this problem is

$$Z = .25(\text{chocolates}) + .75(\text{gum drops}) \quad .$$

Z represents the company's total profit or the amount you want to maximize.

Constraints   The production of the candy is limited by the time available for each process. These constraints on production can be stated algebraically.

The limits placed on production by Process 1 are expressed by the equation

$$15(\text{chocolates}) + 40(\text{gum drops}) = 27{,}000 \quad .$$

The equation shows that if no gum drops are produced (substituting 0 for gum drops)

$$15(\text{chocolates}) = 27{,}000$$

then 27,000/15=1,800 pounds of chocolates can be produced.

If no chocolates are produced, it would be possible to produce 27,000/40= 675 pounds of gum drops. It is also possible to produce any combination of chocolates and gum drops that satisfy the above equation.

Expressing the relationship above as an **equality** implies that Process 1 must use all its available time. A more realistic approach may be for the company to tolerate some slack in each department and not schedule work for the full 7.5 hours. This is one way to handle any bottlenecks that might occur during any process. An expression that accounts for this inequality is

$$15(\text{chocolates}) + 40(\text{gum drops}) \le 27{,}000 \quad .$$

Process 1 can handle any combination of chocolates and gum drops that satisfies this inequality.

Evaluating the Problem Graphically

You can represent the limits on production of Process 1 in a graph. The point on the graph representing pounds of chocolates when no gum drops are produced (1,800) and the point representing pounds of gum drops when no chocolates are made (675) are joined to form a straight line. This line represents the maximum pounds of chocolates and gum drops that can be mixed and cooked in exactly 27,000 seconds during Process 1. The inequality is represented by the shaded area below the line. This area shows combinations of gum drops and chocolates that can be mixed and cooked by Process 1 in the limit of 7.5 hours.

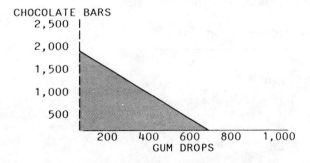

Figure 1.1   Representing Inequalities on a Graph

The inequality described expresses a constraint since it limits the total number of chocolates and gum drops to be produced.

The limits on production by other processes generate constraints described by these inequalities:

Process 2   56.25(gum drops)   ≤ 27,000
Process 3   18.75(chocolates)   ≤ 27,000
Process 4   12(chocolates) + 50(gum drops) ≤ 27,000

The four inequalities are plotted together in **Figure 1.2**.

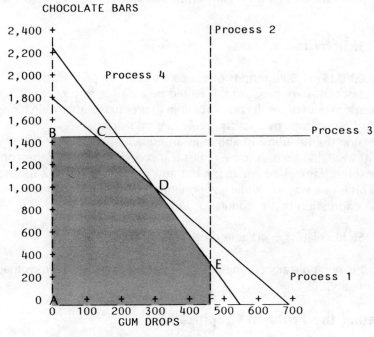

Figure 1.2   Plotting Four Inequalities Together

The four constraints plotted on the same graph form a polygon (shaded in **Figure 1.2**). Any point falling in this shaded area (the intersection of the shaded areas from each of the production inequalities) describes a combination of chocolates and gum drops that can be produced by the company within the production constraints imposed by the available time.

The corners of the polygon are labeled. These corners correspond to the following pounds of chocolates and gum drops:

	chocolates	gum drops
A	0	0
B	1,440	0
C	1,440	135
D	1,000	300
E	250	480
F	0	480

The question now becomes: Which of the possible solutions is optimum in terms of its overall contribution to the profit of the manufacturer? Which best satisfies the objective function?

If you incorporate the objective function

$$Z = .25(\text{chocolates}) + .75(\text{gum drops})$$

into the graph containing the plots of the four constraints, the resulting graph is a series of lines corresponding to possible combinations of chocolates and gum drops (**Figure 1.3**).

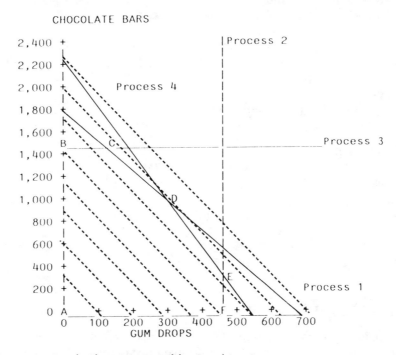

Figure 1.3 Graph Showing Possible Combinations

Each dotted line in the graph corresponds to a different value of Z. For example, the dotted line connecting 200 on the gum drops axis and 600 on the chocolates axis represents a Z value or total profit contribution of $150. (This number is the result of substituting 600 pounds of chocolates, 0 gum drops or 200 pounds of gum drops, 0 chocolates in the objective function equation.)

Dotted lines represent higher Z or total contribution values as they move on the graph from left to right. Thus, the highest possible Z value that meets the constraints is the rightmost point in the polygon shaded in **Figure 1.2**. The rightmost point in the polygon is the point D, where the equation becomes:

$$(1,000 \times .25) + (300 \times .75) = \$475 \quad .$$

Our optimum point of operation is point D, producing 1,000 pounds of chocolates and 300 pounds of gum drops with a profit of $475.

Preparing the Data for PROC LP

The problem must be stored in a SAS data set before the LP procedure can be used to solve it. Each observation in the SAS data set corresponds to either the objective function or a constraint in the statement of the problem above. Variables in the data set correspond to the unknowns (chocolates and gum drops), a type identifier describing the relationship between the left- and right-hand sides of the inequality, and values that form the right-hand side of the equations in the problem definition.

To review, the objective function for the problem is

$$Z = .25(\text{chocolates}) + .75(\text{gum drops}) \quad .$$

You want to maximize Z.

The constraints in the problem generate the following inequalities:

Process 1: 15(chocolates) + 40(gum drops) ≤ 27,000
Process 2:   56.25(gum drops) ≤ 27,000
Process 3: 18.75(chocolates)   ≤ 27,000
Process 4: 12(chocolates) + 50(gum drops) ≤ 27,000 .

The DATA step below creates a SAS data set for the problem described above. Notice that the values of CHOCO and GUMDR in the data set are the coefficients of those variables in the equations corresponding to the objective function and constraints.

The data set of values containing the objective function and constraints becomes the problem matrix that is solved for an optimum Z value.

```
DATA PROBLEM;
   INPUT ROWNAME $ CHOCO GUMDR RELAT $ VALUE;
   CARDS;
OBJECT     .25     .75   MAX   .
PROCESS1 15       40     LE  27000
PROCESS2  0       56.25  LE  27000
PROCESS3 18.75     0     LE  27000
PROCESS4 12       50     LE  27000
;
```

Invoking PROC LP

After invoking the procedure with a PROC statement, you must identify the variables in the data set using procedure information statements. For example, this problem can be solved using these PROC LP statements:

```
PROC LP DATA=PROBLEM;
   ID   ROWNAME;
   VAR  CHOCO GUMDR;
   TYPE RELAT;
   RHS  VALUE;
```

The ID statement identifies the names of the rows in the model. The VAR statement identifies the unknowns in the problem—the number of pounds of chocolates and gum drops to be produced. The RHS statement gives the name of the variable whose values are the constants on the right-hand-side in the problem equations. The TYPE statement identifies a character variable whose values represent the relationship of the left-hand to the right-hand side in each equation.

Analyzing the Procedure Results

Problem summary   The output from PROC LP is divided into four sections. The first section, PROBLEM SUMMARY, (**Output 1.1**), describes the problem by identifying the objective function (defined by the first observation in the data set used as input); the right-hand-side variable; the type variable; and the density of the problem. Simply put, the problem density describes the relative number of elements in the problem matrix that are nonzero. The fewer zeros in the matrix, the higher the problem density.

Output 1.1 Problem Summary

```
                                                                        1

           L I N E A R   P R O G R A M M I N G   P R O C E D U R E

                            PROBLEM  SUMMARY


               MAX OBJECT        OBJECTIVE FUNCTION
               VALUE                   RHS  VARIABLE
               RELAT                  TYPE VARIABLE
               PROBLEM DENSITY             0.417


               VARIABLE TYPE                NUMBER

               STRUCTURAL
                 NONNEGATIVE                   2

               LOGICAL
                 SLACK                         4

               TOTAL                           6


               CONSTRAINT TYPE              NUMBER

               LE                             4
               FREE                           1

               TOTAL                          5
```

Next in the PROBLEM SUMMARY section, the types of variables in the problem are identified. Variables are either structural or logical. *Structural variables* are identified in the VAR statement; they are the unknowns in the equations defining the objective function and constraints. By default, PROC LP assumes that structural variables have the additional constraint that they must be nonnegative. You may also define upper and lower bounds to structural variables.

Logical variables are either slack or surplus. A slack variable is automatically added to each constraint with a type variable equal to LE (less than or equal to). A surplus variable is added to the constraint when the type variable is GE (greater than or equal to). The logical variable takes the name of the constraint for which it is a logical variable. For example, the Process 1 constraint becomes:

PROCESS1 + 15(chocolates) + 40(gum drops) = 27,000   .

Note that at point A in **Figure 1.3** when no chocolates or gum drops are produced the equation becomes:

PROCESS1 = 27,000   .

PROCESS1 represents the unused seconds in Process 1 or slack time in the mixing-cooking phase.

The procedure generates one slack variable for each of the four constraints. Thus there are four slack variables in this problem.

The objective function is considered by the procedure a free constraint; other nonbinding (free) constraints may also be defined.

Output 1.2   Solution Summary

```
                                                                              2

                    LINEAR  PROGRAMMING  PROCEDURE


                              SOLUTION  SUMMARY


                           TERMINATED SUCCESSFULLY

             OBJECTIVE VALUE              475.000

             PHASE 1 ITERATIONS                 0
             PHASE 2 ITERATIONS                 4
             INITIAL B.F. VARIABLES             4
             TIME USED (SECS)               0.00
             NUMBER OF INVERSIONS               1

             MACHINE EPSILON         1.00000E-08
             MACHINE INFINITY        7.23701E+75
             INVERT FREQUENCY               50
             MAX PHASE 1 ITERATIONS        100
             MAX PHASE 2 ITERATIONS        100
             TIME LIMIT (SECS)          120.00
```

Solution summary   This section of the PROC LP output, (**Output 1.2**), tells whether the procedure found a solution to the problem. This example terminated successfully showing an optimum profitability (Z) of \$475, the same solution found earlier by graphing the problem.

When the procedure solves the problem, an iterative process is used. First, the procedure finds a feasible solution, one that satisfies the constraints. The second phase finds the optimum solution from the set of feasible solutions (the shaded polygon in **Figure 1.3**). The SOLUTION SUMMARY gives the number of iterations the procedure took in each of these phases, the number of variables in the initial feasible solution, the time the procedure used to solve the problem, and the number of matrix inversions necessary.

Output 1.3 Variable Summary

```
                                                                          3

          L I N E A R   P R O G R A M M I N G   P R O C E D U R E

                          VARIABLE   SUMMARY

          VARIABLE                                         REDUCED
    COL  NAME      STATUS   TYPE     PRICE    ACTIVITY       COST


      1  CHOCO     BASIC  NON-NEG    0.25    1000.000          0
      2  GUMDR     BASIC  NON-NEG    0.75     300.000          0
      3  PROCESS1         SLACK         0           0      -0.012963
      4  PROCESS2  BASIC  SLACK         0    10125.000         0
      5  PROCESS3  BASIC  SLACK         0     8250.000         0
      6  PROCESS4         SLACK         0           0      -0.00462963
```

Variable summary The VARIABLE SUMMARY (**Output 1.3**), contains details about each variable in the solution. The ACTIVITY column shows that optimum profitability is achieved when 1000 pounds of chocolates and 300 pounds of gum drops are produced. The variables PROCESS1, PROCESS2, PROCESS3, and PRO-CESS4 correspond to the four slack variables in the Process 1, Process 2, Process 3, and Process 4 constraints, respectively. Producing 1000 pounds of chocolate and 300 pounds of gum drops a day leaves 10,125 seconds of slack time in Process 2 (where colors and flavors are added to the gum drops) and 8,250 seconds of slack time in Process 3 (where nuts and raisins are mixed and added to the chocolate).

Output 1.4 Constraint Summary

```
                                                                          4

          L I N E A R   P R O G R A M M I N G   P R O C E D U R E

                          CONSTRAINT SUMMARY

    CONSTRAINT           S/S                                 DUAL
    ROW  ID      TYPE    COL      RHS       ACTIVITY       ACTIVITY


      1  PROCESS1  LE      3    27000.000   27000.000      0.012963
      2  PROCESS2  LE      4    27000.000   16875.000         0
      3  PROCESS3  LE      5    27000.000   18750.000         0
      4  PROCESS4  LE      6    27000.000   27000.000      0.00462963
      5  OBJECT    OBJECTIVE      475.000     475.000         0
```

Constraint summary In the last section, (**Output 1.4**), the ACTIVITY column gives the value of the right-hand side of each equation when the problem is solved using the information given in the previous table.

The DUAL ACTIVITY column tells you that each second in Process 1 (mixing-cooking) is worth $.013; each second in Process 4 (Packaging), $.005. You can use these figures (called *shadow prices*) to decide whether to add to the total available time for Processes 1 and 4. If you can add a second to the total production time in Process 1 for less than $.013, then it would be profitable to do so. The dual activities for Process 1 and 4 are zero since adding time to those processes does not increase profits. Keep in mind that the dual activity gives the marginal improvement to the objective and that adding time to Process 1 changes the original problem and solution.

Another Maximization Problem

Once you introduce more products into a problem like the one above, it becomes impossible to analyze graphically. The following example contains three products. Again, you want to maximize total company profitability given the time constraints of two processes.

A firm has two machines (Machine A and Machine B) used to produce three products (products 1, 2, and 3). Machine A has 120 hours and Machine B has 260 hours of available time during July. One unit of product 1 requires the use of 0.10 hours of Machine A time and 0.20 hours of Machine B time. Product 2 requires 0.25 hours of Machine A time and 0.30 hours of Machine B time for each unit. Product 3 requires 0.40 hours of Machine B time and no time from Machine A. The unit contributions to profits of the three products are \$3, \$4, and \$5, respectively.

The problem: Determine a July production program that maximizes the total contribution to profits.

In this problem you want to maximize the total contribution to profits subject to constraints imposed by the limited capacity of the two machines.

Mathematically, the problem can be stated as:

$$\begin{aligned} \text{Maximize:} \quad & Z = 3X1 + 4X2 + 5X3 \\ \text{Subject to:} \quad & 0.10X1 + 0.25X2 + 0X3 \leq 120 \\ & 0.20X1 + 0.30X2 + 0.40X3 \leq 260 \\ & X1 \geq 0 \\ & X2 \geq 0 \\ & X3 \geq 0 \ . \end{aligned}$$

The first step in solving the problem with PROC LP is to include the problem definition in a SAS data set. The DATA step below creates a SAS data set corresponding to this problem:

```
DATA PROBLEM2;
   INPUT X1 X2 X3 RELAT $ VALUE;
   CARDS;
 3     4     5     MAX    .
0.10  0.25  0     LE    120
0.20  0.30  0.40  LE    260
 ;
```

Remember that by default, PROC LP assumes that lower bounds on variables are 0 so that the last three inequalities above need not be included in the data set.

The LP procedure can now be used to solve the problem represented in SAS data set PROBLEM2:

```
PROC LP DATA=PROBLEM2;
   VAR X1-X3;
   RHS VALUE;
   TYPE RELAT;
```

This problem is similar to the first one except now there are three structural and two slack variables. Also note that in this problem no ID variable was included in the problem data set. As a result PROC LP assigned row names and logical variable names that identify the observation in which the constraint appears.

The objective value at optimality is \$3,850. This amount is realized when 1200 units of Product A and 50 units of Product C are produced. No units of Product

B are produced under this optimum plan. In fact, if any unit of Product B is introduced into the solution, the total profit is reduced by $1. There is no slack time on either Machine A or Machine B. The value to total profit of adding an additional hour on Machine A is $5; on Machine B, $12.50.

Output 1.5   A Maximization Problem

```
                                                                              5

        L I N E A R    P R O G R A M M I N G    P R O C E D U R E

                        PROBLEM  SUMMARY


              MAX _OBS1_           OBJECTIVE FUNCTION
              VALUE                      RHS VARIABLE
              RELAT                     TYPE VARIABLE
              PROBLEM DENSITY               0.700


              VARIABLE TYPE                NUMBER

              STRUCTURAL
                NONEGATIVE                    3

              LOGICAL
                SLACK                         2

              TOTAL                           5


              CONSTRAINT TYPE              NUMBER

              LE                            2
              FREE                          1

              TOTAL                         3
```

```
                                                                              6

        L I N E A R    P R O G R A M M I N G    P R O C E D U R E


                        SOLUTION  SUMMARY


                    TERMINATED SUCCESSFULLY

          OBJECTIVE VALUE            3850.000

          PHASE 1 ITERATIONS               0

          PHASE 2 ITERATIONS               3
          INITIAL B.F. VARIABLES           2
          TIME USED (SECS)              0.00
          NUMBER OF INVERSIONS             1

          MACHINE EPSILON         1.00000E-08
          MACHINE INFINITY        7.23701E+75
          INVERT FREQUENCY                50
          MAX PHASE 1 ITERATIONS         100
          MAX PHASE 2 ITERATIONS         100
          TIME LIMIT (SECS)           120.00
```

```
                                                                          7
            L I N E A R   P R O G R A M M I N G   P R O C E D U R E
                           VARIABLE   SUMMARY

            VARIABLE                                          REDUCED
        COL NAME      STATUS  TYPE      PRICE   ACTIVITY       COST


         1  X1        BASIC NON-NEG       3     1200.000         0
         2  X2              NON-NEG       4        0          -1.000000
         3  X3        BASIC NON-NEG       5     50.000000        0
         4  _OBS2_           SLACK        0        0          -5.000000
         5  _OBS3_           SLACK        0        0          -12.500000
```

```
                                                                          8
            L I N E A R   P R O G R A M M I N G   P R O C E D U R E
                          CONSTRAINT SUMMARY

        CONSTRAINT          S/S                              DUAL
        ROW ID      TYPE    COL      RHS     ACTIVITY      ACTIVITY


         1  _OBS2_  LE       4     120.000    120.000     5.000000
         2  _OBS3_  LE       5     260.000    260.000     12.500000
         3  _OBS1_  OBJECTIVE     3850.000   3850.000        0
```

An Integer Program

Often your model requires that the decision variables only take integer values. Problems with this special additional constraint are called integer programs. An example of such a problem is the knapsack problem.

A shipping firm has received six contracts (labeled A, B, C, D, E, and F) for transporting material on its next ship. The weight of material to be shipped is different for each contract. The profit from accepting each contract also varies. Below is a summary of the information:

CONTRACT	WEIGHT	PROFIT
A	10.6	30
B	22.3	75
C	14.6	45
D	5.9	17
E	6.8	22
F	13.0	13

The firm must decide which contracts to accept in order to maximize its profits without exceeding the ship's capacity of 35. Mathematically, the problem can be stated as:

Maximize: $Z = 30A + 75B + 45C + 17D + 22E + 13F$

Subject to: $10.6A + 22.3B + 14.6C + 5.9D + 6.8E + 13F \leq 35$

$0 \leq A, B, C, D, E,$ and $F \leq 1$

$A, B, C, D, E,$ and F integer

If a decision variable — C for example — takes a 1, then that indicates that the contract should be accepted. If it takes a 0, then that indicates that the contract should be rejected. Since all of the decision variables must be integers and are between 0 and 1, they will either be 0 or 1; as a result, each contract will either be accepted or rejected. The weight constraint requires that the total weight of all the accepted contracts must not exceed the ship's capacity.

The first step in solving the problem with PROC LP is to include the problem definition in a SAS data set. The DATA step below creates a SAS data set corresponding to this problem:

```
DATA PROBLEM3;
   INPUT ROWNAME $ A B C D E F RELAT $ VALUE;
   CARDS;
PROFIT   30   75   45   17   22   13   MAX        .
WEIGHT   10.5 22.3 14.6 5.9  6.8  13.0 LE         35
INTEGER  1    2    3    4    5    6    INTEGER    .
BOUNDS   1    1    1    1    1    1    UPPERBD     .
;
```

There are several differences between this problem data set and those of the last two examples. First, the observation with RELAT equal to INTEGER identifies those variables that must take only integer values. Since all the decision variables have nonmissing and nonzero values, they are all integer constrained. Second, the observation having RELAT equal to UPPERBD tells LP the largest value that each decision variable can take. This is an economical way of specifying individual upper bounds. Finally, remember that by default, PROC LP assumes that lower bounds on variables are 0, so no additional rows are needed in the problem data set.

The LP procedure can now be used to solve the problem represented in SAS data set PROBLEM3.

```
PROC LP DATA=PROBLEM3;
   ID    ROWNAME;
   VAR   A B C D E F;
   RHS   VALUE;
   TYPE  RELAT;
```

Because the problem is an integer program, in addition to the usual PROBLEM SUMMARY, SOLUTION SUMMARY, VARIABLE SUMMARY, and CONSTRAINT SUMMARY, PROC LP prints an INTEGER ITERATION LOG. This describes the progress towards an integer solution and is explained in the chapter on PROC LP.

Output 1.6 An Integer Program

```
                                                                            9

              L I N E A R   P R O G R A M M I N G   P R O C E D U R E

                          PROBLEM  SUMMARY


           MAX PROFIT         OBJECTIVE FUNCTION
           VALUE                    RHS VARIABLE
           RELAT                   TYPE VARIABLE
           PROBLEM DENSITY              1.000


           VARIABLE TYPE                NUMBER

           STRUCTURAL
             INTEGER                         6

           LOGICAL
             SLACK                           1

           TOTAL                             7


           CONSTRAINT TYPE              NUMBER

           LE                              1
           FREE                            1

           TOTAL                           2
```

```
                                                                           10

              L I N E A R   P R O G R A M M I N G   P R O C E D U R E

                          INTEGER ITERATION LOG

     ITER PROBLEM  CONDITION OBJECTIVE BRANCHED VALUE SINFEAS ACTIVE

        1    +0      ACTIVE   115.185 C       .4041 0.40411     2
        2    -1      ACTIVE   113.61  B       .9148 .085202     2
        3    +2      ACTIVE   106     A       .7333 .266667     3
        4    +3      ACTIVE   91.7    F       .5923 .407692     4
        5    -4      ACTIVE   81.7288 D       .1017 .101695     5
        6    -5      ACTIVE   79.8529 E       .2206 .220588     6
        7    -6    INFEASIBLE 79.8529 .        .     .          5
        8    +1    SUBOPTIMAL 114     .        .     0          4
```

```
                                                              11
        L I N E A R   P R O G R A M M I N G   P R O C E D U R E


                        SOLUTION  SUMMARY


                    OPTIMAL INTEGER SOLUTION

            OBJECTIVE VALUE              114.000

            PHASE 1 ITERATIONS                 0
            PHASE 2 ITERATIONS                 2
            PHASE 3 ITERATIONS                 9
            INTEGER ITERATIONS                 8
            INTEGER SOLUTIONS                  1
            INITIAL B.F. VARIABLES             1
            TIME USED (SECS)                0.01
            NUMBER OF INVERSIONS               1

            MACHINE EPSILON          1.00000E-08
            MACHINE INFINITY         7.23701E+75
            INVERT FREQUENCY                  50
            MAX PHASE 1 ITERATIONS           100
            MAX PHASE 2 ITERATIONS           100
            MAX PHASE 3 ITERATIONS      99999999
            MAX INTEGER ITERATIONS           100
            TIME LIMIT (SECS)            120.00
```

```
                                                              12
        L I N E A R   P R O G R A M M I N G   P R O C E D U R E
                        VARIABLE  SUMMARY

           VARIABLE                                    REDUCED
      COL NAME     STATUS    TYPE     PRICE   ACTIVITY    COST

       1 A                 INTEGER      30          0  -0.254237
       2 B                 INTEGER      75   1.000000  10.745763
       3 C                 INTEGER      45          0   2.932203
       4 D         BASIC   INTEGER      17   1.000000          0
       5 E                 INTEGER      22   1.000000   2.406780
       6 F                 INTEGER      13          0 -24.457627
       7 WEIGHT            SLACK         0          0  -2.881356
```

```
                                                              13
        L I N E A R   P R O G R A M M I N G   P R O C E D U R E
                        CONSTRAINT SUMMARY

      CONSTRAINT         S/S                            DUAL
      ROW ID      TYPE   COL      RHS     ACTIVITY    ACTIVITY

       1 WEIGHT   LE      7    35.000000  35.000000   2.881356
       2 PROFIT   OBJECTIVE    114.000    114.000            0
```

The objective value at optimality is 114. This amount is realized when the contracts B, D, and E are accepted. Notice that the slack weight is 0. This means that the ship's full capacity is used.

THE TRANSPORTATION PROBLEM: AN INTRODUCTION

A special case of a linear program is the problem of minimizing costs when a product is produced at n locations and distributed to m locations. Although PROC LP can handle the problem, the TRANS procedure accepts input in a more convenient format, uses a solution technique that is suited to this problem, and is thus easier and more efficient to use.

This section illustrates a simple transportation problem and how to solve it with PROC TRANS and with PROC LP. Both procedure descriptions include other examples.

A Simple Transportation Problem

Your firm has two plants (Plant 1 and Plant 2) and three distribution warehouses (Warehouse 1, Warehouse 2, and Warehouse 3). You want to schedule production at the plants and distribution to the warehouses in a way that minimizes the sum of the plant manufacturing costs and shipping costs from plants to warehouses. Below is a summary of each of these costs for the two plants:

Plant	Unit Variable Manuf. Cost	Monthly Capacity	Shipping Costs To: Warehouse #		
			1	2	3
Plant 1	$17	42 units	$0	$1	$2
Plant 2	$15	37 units	$1	$2	$4

In addition, you know that Warehouse 1 requires 25 units per month; Warehouse 2 requires 30 units per month; and Warehouse 3 requires 12 units.

Stating the Problem Mathematically

Let

UNIT_{ij} =   the number of units shipped from plant i to warehouse j

and

k_{ij} =   the total cost for this transportation (the sum of the unit variable manufacturing cost for plant i plus the shipping cost from plant i to warehouse j).

The data are presented below:

UNIT$_{ij}$	Unit Variable Manufact. Cost	Shipping Cost to j	k_{ij}
UNIT$_{11}$	$17	$0	$17
UNIT$_{12}$	$17	$1	$18
UNIT$_{13}$	$17	$2	$19
UNIT$_{21}$	$15	$1	$16
UNIT$_{22}$	$15	$2	$17
UNIT$_{23}$	$15	$4	$19

Using the TRANS Procedure

You now have the information necessary to solve the problem with PROC TRANS. The DATA step below creates a SAS data set to be analyzed by PROC TRANS. The data are entered in the form of a matrix where rows correspond to supply sources (plants) and columns correspond to destination points (warehouses). The value of MAX is the maximum that can be produced by each plant. The first observation in the data set contains the total number needed at each warehouse.

```
DATA TRANPROB;
   INPUT WRHOUSE1 WRHOUSE2 WRHOUSE3 MAX PLANT $ COMMENT $40.;
   CARDS;
25 30 12 . .            WAREHOUSE REQUIREMENTS
17 18 19 42 PLANT1      TOTAL COSTS & MAX CAPACITY-PLANT1
16 17 19 37 PLANT2      TOTAL COSTS & MAX CAPACITY-PLANT2
;
```

These statements analyze the problem above:

```
PROC TRANS COST=TRANPROB;
   ID PLANT;                    /* Identify supply source */
   VAR WRHOUSE1-WRHOUSE3;       /* Transportation costs */
   SUPPLY MAX;                  /* Capacity requirement */
```

The COST= option in the PROC TRANS statement identifies the SAS data set containing the cost, supply, and demand data for this transportation problem. The ID statement specifies the variable in data set TRANPROB that identifies the supply source. The VAR statement is required by the procedure. It names the variables that contain the cost of transporting one unit from a source to a destination. The SUPPLY statement is also required. It names the variable containing the amount available for shipment from each source.

20   Chapter 1

The following messages are printed on the SAS log:

```
WARNING: OBSERVATION CONTAINING DEMAND HAS NOT BEEN SPECIFIED. IT IS ASSUMED TO BE THE FIRST OBSERVATION.
WARNING: SUPPLY EXCEEDS DEMAND BY 12 UNITS. EXCESS SUPPLY WILL BE IGNORED.
NOTE: MINIMUM COST ROUTING = 1156.
```

The last message gives the transportation cost when the objective function is minimized.

The procedure creates a SAS data set as output. Print the data set using the PRINT procedure with these statements:

```
PROC PRINT;
    TITLE 'TRANSPORTATION EXAMPLE';
```

Output 1.7 The Transportation Problem: Using PROC TRANS

```
                          TRANSPORTATION EXAMPLE                              14

        OBS    PLANT    WRHOUSE1    WRHOUSE2    WRHOUSE3    _DUAL_

         1     _DUAL_      17          18          19         .
         2     PLANT1       0          18          12         0
         3     PLANT2      25          12           0        -1
```

The resulting data set contains the variables listed in the VAR statement, the ID statement, and a new variable _DUAL_. The first observation is the ID observation, which includes the variables WRHOUSE1, WRHOUSE2, and WRHOUSE3 containing the marginal costs of increasing the demand at each destination point. These variables are called *dual variables*.

The second and third observations correspond to Plant 1 and Plant 2, respectively. The values of WRHOUSE1, WRHOUSE2, and WRHOUSE3 in these observations are the optimal flow from the plant to each warehouse. The variable _DUAL_ contains the marginal costs of increasing supply at each supply source. Note that at Plant 1 no cost is incurred by increasing the available supply; at Plant 2, an increase to cost of −$1.00 (a decrease of $1.00) is incurred for each unit of additional supply.

In this problem, transportation costs are minimized when Plant 1 ships 18 units to Warehouse 2 and 12 units to Warehouse 3. It is best to ship no units from Plant 1 to Warehouse 1. From Plant 2, optimal flow is achieved by shipping 25 units to Warehouse 1, 12 to Warehouse 2, and none to Warehouse 3.

Minimum order to a destination   Suppose that in the problem above you want to restrict the demand for Warehouse 3 so that at least five units come from Plant 2. The TRANS procedure can handle the problem if the restriction is placed in a SAS data set. To define the minimum flow to Warehouse 3 from Plant 2, use this DATA step:

```
DATA MINIMUM;
    INPUT WRHOUSE3 PLANT $;
    CARDS;
5 PLANT2
;
```

Then invoke the TRANS procedure and indicate the original data set and the new data set containing the minimum flow data:

```
PROC TRANS COST=TRANPROB MINFLOW=MINIMUM;
    ID PLANT;
    VAR WRHOUSE1-WRHOUSE3;
    SUPPLY MAX;
```

The procedure prints these messages on the SAS log:

```
WARNING: OBSERVATION CONTAINING DEMAND HAS NOT BEEN SPECIFIED. IT IS ASSUMED TO BE THE FIRST OBSERVATION.
NOTE: 1 VARIABLES IN MINFLOW DATA SET MATCH VARIABLES IN THE COST DATA SET.
WARNING: SUPPLY EXCEEDS DEMAND BY 12 UNITS. EXCESS SUPPLY WILL BE IGNORED.

NOTE: MINIMUM COST ROUTING = 1161.
```

Note that the added restriction increases the transportation costs.
Print the data set produced by the procedure:

Output 1.8 The Transportation Problem: Defining the Minimum Flow

```
                          TRANSPORTATION EXAMPLE                                        15

        OBS    PLANT    WRHOUSE1    WRHOUSE2    WRHOUSE3    _DUAL_

         1     _DUAL_      17          18          19          .
         2     PLANT1       0          23           7          0
         3     PLANT2      25           7           5         -1
```

To meet the new minimum flow restrictions, Plant 1 should now ship 23 units
to Warehouse 2 and 7 units to Warehouse 3; 5 of the 12 units originally shipped
from Plant 2 to Warehouse 2 now go to Warehouse 3.

Using the LP Procedure

The objective function   Although PROC TRANS was designed to handle transportation problems like the one above, PROC LP can also be used if you state
the problem in terms of the objective function and a set of constraints. The objective function becomes:

$$\text{Minimize}: \quad Z = \Sigma_{i=1}^{2} \Sigma_{j=1}^{3} k_{ij}\text{UNIT}_{ij} \quad .$$

Expanded with values substituted, this becomes:

$$Z = 17\text{UNIT}_{11} + 18\text{UNIT}_{12} + 19\text{UNIT}_{13} + 16\text{UNIT}_{21} + 17\text{UNIT}_{22} + 19\text{UNIT}_{23} \quad .$$

Constraints   These constraints can be defined:

capacity of Plant 1	$UNIT_{11} + UNIT_{12} + UNIT_{13} \leq 42$
capacity of Plant 2	$UNIT_{21} + UNIT_{22} + UNIT_{23} \leq 37$
demand at Warehouse 1	$UNIT_{11} + UNIT_{21} \geq 25$
demand at Warehouse 2	$UNIT_{12} + UNIT_{22} \geq 30$
demand at Warehouse 3	$P_1W_3 + UNIT_{23} \geq 12$
restriction on shipments between Plant 2 and Warehouse 3	$UNIT_{23} \geq 5$.

The job below creates a data set to be read by PROC LP and then invokes the procedure:

```
DATA TRANPRB1;
   INPUT ID $ UNIT11-UNIT13 UNIT21-UNIT23 TYPE $ RHS;
   CARDS;
OBJ        17 18 19 16 17 19 MIN        .
P1_CAP      1  1  1  .  .  . LE        42
P2_CAP      .  .  .  1  1  1 LE        37
W1_DEM      1  .  .  1  .  . GE        25
W2_DEM      .  1  .  .  1  . GE        30
W3_DEM      .  .  1  .  .  1 GE        12
P2W3_RES    0  0  0  0  0  5 LOWERBD    .
;
PROC LP DATA=TRANPRB1;
   ID ID;
   VAR UNIT11 UNIT12 UNIT13 UNIT21 UNIT22 UNIT23;
   TYPE TYPE;
   RHS RHS;
```

Output 1.9   PROC LP

```
                        TRANSPORTATION EXAMPLE                          16

            LINEAR  PROGRAMMING  PROCEDURE

                        PROBLEM  SUMMARY



              MIN OBJ         OBJECTIVE FUNCTION
              RHS             RHS  VARIABLE
              TYPE            TYPE VARIABLE
              PROBLEM DENSITY          0.309



              VARIABLE TYPE             NUMBER

              STRUCTURAL
                NONEGATIVE                 5
                LOWER BOUNDED              1
```

(continued on next page)

```
(continued from previous page)

                        LOGICAL
                          SLACK                    2
                          SURPLUS                  3

                        TOTAL                      11


                        CONSTRAINT TYPE        NUMBER

                        LE                         2
                        GE                         3
                        FREE                       1

                        TOTAL                      6
```

```
                      TRANSPORTATION EXAMPLE                      17

            L I N E A R   P R O G R A M M I N G   P R O C E D U R E


                            SOLUTION  SUMMARY


                        TERMINATED SUCCESSFULLY

               OBJECTIVE VALUE            1161.000

               PHASE 1 ITERATIONS               4
               PHASE 2 ITERATIONS               3
               INITIAL B.F. VARIABLES           2
               TIME USED (SECS)              0.01
               NUMBER OF INVERSIONS             1

               MACHINE EPSILON         1.00000E-08
               MACHINE INFINITY        7.23701E+75
               INVERT FREQUENCY                50
               MAX PHASE 1 ITERATIONS         100
               MAX PHASE 2 ITERATIONS         100
               TIME LIMIT (SECS)          120.00
```

```
                      TRANSPORTATION EXAMPLE                      18

            L I N E A R   P R O G R A M M I N G   P R O C E D U R E
                            VARIABLE  SUMMARY

          VARIABLE                                        REDUCED
      COL NAME     STATUS  TYPE     PRICE   ACTIVITY         COST

        1 UNIT11   ALTER NON-NEG      17          0             0
        2 UNIT12   BASIC NON-NEG      18  23.000000             0
        3 UNIT13   BASIC NON-NEG      19   7.000000             0
        4 UNIT21   BASIC NON-NEG      16  25.000000             0
        5 UNIT22   BASIC NON-NEG      17   7.000000             0
        6 UNIT23         LOWERBD      19   5.000000      1.000000
        7 P1_CAP   BASIC   SLACK       0  12.000000             0
        8 P2_CAP           SLACK       0          0      1.000000
        9 W1_DEM         SURPLUS       0          0     17.000000
       10 W2_DEM         SURPLUS       0          0     18.000000
       11 W3_DEM         SURPLUS       0          0     19.000000
```

24   Chapter 1

```
                      TRANSPORTATION EXAMPLE                              19

              L I N E A R   P R O G R A M M I N G   P R O C E D U R E

                             CONSTRAINT SUMMARY

        CONSTRAINT          S/S                                  DUAL
        ROW ID       TYPE   COL      RHS      ACTIVITY         ACTIVITY


          1 P1_CAP   LE      7    42.000000   30.000000              0
          2 P2_CAP   LE      8    37.000000   37.000000      -1.000000
          3 W1_DEM   GE      9    25.000000   25.000000      17.000000
          4 W2_DEM   GE     10    30.000000   30.000000      18.000000
          5 W3_DEM   GE     11    12.000000   12.000000      19.000000
          6 OBJ      OBJECTIVE     1161.000    1161.000              0
```

Notice that the objective value given in the SOLUTION SUMMARY agrees with that produced by the TRANS procedure above.

The results given in the VARIABLE SUMMARY also agree. The variable _ROW1_, a slack variable corresponding to the constraint

capacity of Plant 1 $\quad\quad$ UNIT$_{11}$ + UNIT$_{12}$ + UNIT$_{13} \leq 42$

shows in the ACTIVITY column that 12 units remain from Plant 1. (You can verify this by adding the total sent from Plant 1 to each warehouse and subtracting from the maximum produced by Plant 1.) In the REDUCED COST column, the value of $1.00 for UNIT23 is the marginal value of the restriction on shipments between Plant 2 and Warehouse 3. If you decrease (increase) the minimum of 5 by one unit, you decrease (increase) the cost by $1.00.

In the CONSTRAINT SUMMARY, the ACTIVITY column for P1_CAP shows that the plant had a surplus of 12 units. For the next four observations (P2_CAP, W1_DEM, W2_DEM, and W3_DEM) the column shows the same outcome as the right-hand side of the constraint inequality. The last row in the table gives the total transportation cost for the solution.

The DUAL ACTIVITY column shows the marginal cost of increasing supply (or demand) by one unit. For example, an increase in the capacity of Plant 2 by one unit costs $1.00. The DUAL ACTIVITY column for W1_DEM, W2_DEM, and W3_DEM contains the marginal costs of increasing the demand at each warehouse.

THE ASSIGNMENT PROBLEM: AN INTRODUCTION

The assignment problem is similar to the transportation problem with the problem stated as follows: you have *n* tasks that you want to assign to *m* agents in a way that minimizes costs or maximizes flow. Consider the following business problems:

- A company has four machines and four jobs to be done. Although each machine can do each job in one day, the costs vary for each machine-job assignment. How should the company assign jobs to machines to minimize costs and complete all the jobs?
- An electronics company has developed a new product that is assembled from several component parts. The company wants to subcontract the production of some of the parts to outside contractors, who have placed

bids on the production of each part. What is the least expensive way to assign parts to subcontractors?

These typical business problems are called *assignment problems* and can be solved easily using PROC ASSIGN.

A Simple Assignment Problem

Take the first example above. Suppose the costs (in dollars) of doing each job (in dollars) on each machine are as follows:

	Job 1	Job 2	Job 3	Job 4
Machine 1	10	16	12	8
Machine 2	8	12	15	12
Machine 3	15	13	13	11
Machine 4	12	15	10	7

As with other SAS/OR procedures, PROC ASSIGN requires that the data presented above be in a SAS data set. Each observation in the data set should correspond to one of the rows above. For example,

```
TITLE 'ASSIGNMENT EXAMPLE';
DATA JOBPROB;
   INPUT MACHINE $ JOB1-JOB4;
   CARDS;
M1    10    16    12    8
M2    8     12    15    12
M3    15    13    13    11
M4    12    15    10    7
;
```

Using the ASSIGN Procedure

The data are ready to be analyzed by PROC ASSIGN with these statements:

```
PROC ASSIGN;
   COST JOB1-JOB4;
   ID MACHINE;
```

The COST statement identifies the variables in the data set that contain the costs of assigning each job to each machine. The variable given in the ID statement is to be included in the SAS data set output by the procedure.

The procedure prints on the SAS log the value of the objective function when the jobs are optimally assigned to machines:

```
NOTE: MINIMUM COST ASSIGNMENT = 39.
```

The total cost incurred when the optimum assignment is made is $39.00. You can print the resulting data set containing optimum assignments with the PRINT procedure:

Output 1.10   The Assignment Problem: Using PROC ASSIGN

```
                          ASSIGNMENT EXAMPLE                                    20

        OBS     MACHINE     JOB1     JOB2     JOB3     JOB4     _ASSIGN_

         1        M1         10       16       12        8        JOB4
         2        M2          8       12       15       12        JOB1
         3        M3         15       13       13       11        JOB2
         4        M4         12       15       10        7        JOB3
```

The variables in the data set output by the procedure are those identified in the COST statement, the ID variables, and the variable _ASSIGN_. The new _ASSIGN_ variable contains the name of the variable whose values represent the optimal assignment to that machine. Costs are minimized in this example when Job 4 is assigned to Machine 1, Job 1 to Machine 2, Job 2 to Machine 3, and Job 3 to Machine 4.

Note that this problem has the same results if observations in the input data set correspond to jobs, with machines as COST variables.

```
DATA JOBPROB2;
   INPUT JOB M1-M4;
   CARDS;
1 10 8 15 12
2 16 12 13 15
3 12 15 13 10
4 8 12 11 7
;
PROC ASSIGN;
   COST M1-M4;
   ID JOB;
   PROC PRINT;
```

Output 1.11   Using PROC ASSIGN to Minimize Costs

```
                          ASSIGNMENT EXAMPLE                                    21

        OBS     JOB     M1     M2     M3     M4     _ASSIGN_

         1       1      10      8     15     12        M2
         2       2      16     12     13     15        M3
         3       3      12     15     13     10        M4
         4       4       8     12     11      7        M1
```

NETWORKS: AN INTRODUCTION

A directed network consists of a series of nodes (circles) and directed arcs (lines), as shown in **Figure 1.4**.

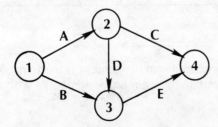

Figure 1.4   A Directed Network

Nodes can represent such things as steps to complete a procedure, intersections or destinations in a highway system, vents in an air-conditioning system, and so on. In such cases, arcs may represent time, highways, or ventilation pipes. Networks are sometimes a convenient way to visualize and formalize problems that involve flow, routing, or scheduling.

Transportation and assignment problems are also network problems. The network shown in **Figure 1.5** represents the transportation problem described earlier: values shown on each arc could be the cost of shipping from plant to warehouse.

SAS/OR software has two procedures designed specifically for solving certain kinds of network problems. The NETFLOW procedure is used for solving shortest path, maximum flow, minimum flow, and transshipment problems. The CPM procedure uses critical path methods to solve networks that represent scheduling problems.

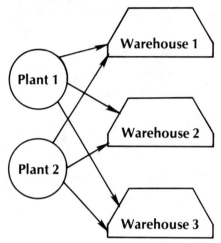

Figure 1.5 A Network Used to Visualize a Problem

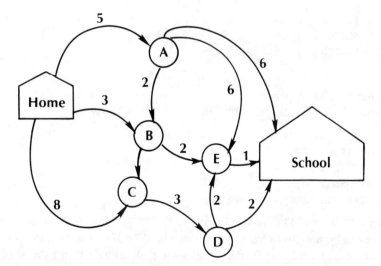

Figure 1.6 A Simple Shortest Path Problem

A Simple Shortest Path Problem

When your problem is one of going from point A to point B in the shortest amount of time, distance, or money, it is called a *shortest path problem* and can be solved using PROC NETFLOW.

Bobby has decided to ride his bicycle instead of the school bus to his new school. He wants to use the shortest route from home to school each day. **Figure 1.6** shows several routes Bobby can use in his ride to school. The numbers on each arc represent the distance in blocks for that route. What is the shortest route from Bobby's house to school?

Preparing the data   To create a SAS data set for NETFLOW to analyze, let each observation represent an arc in **Figure 1.6**; represent an arc with two directions by two observations. The nodes that begin and end each arc and the length of the arc are variables in the data set. The DATA step below creates such a data set for the routes from Bobby's house to school:

```
TITLE 'SHORTEST PATH EXAMPLE';
DATA SCHOOL;
    INPUT FROM $ TO $ DISTANCE;
    CARDS;
HOME A       5
HOME B       3
HOME C       8
A    B       2
A    E       6
B    A       2
B    C       1
B    E       2
C    B       1
C    D       3
D    E       2
A    SCHOOL  6
E    SCHOOL  1
D    SCHOOL  2
;
```

Using the NETFLOW procedure   The following statements ask PROC NETFLOW to analyze the network described in the data set above:

```
PROC NETFLOW DATA=SCHOOL ASOURCENODE=HOME ASINKNODE=SCHOOL
        SHORTPATH;
    TAILNODE FROM;
    HEADNODE TO;
    COST DISTANCE;
```

In the PROC NETFLOW statement, ASOURCENODE= identifies the source node or origination point in the problem, ASINKNODE= identifies the sink node or ending point, and SHORTPATH tells the procedure to find the shortest path from the source to the sink node. The TAILNODE statement identifies the variable containing the node at the tail of each arc. The HEADNODE statement gives the name of the variable in the data set that represents the node at the head of the arc.

The COST statement identifies the variable that contains the value shown on each arc. Often in other examples, this value represents the cost of crossing the arc; here the quantity on each arc is distance. Note that the procedure minimizes cost in the same way that it finds the shortest distance between Bobby's house and the school.

Analyzing the Procedure Results

The SAS log produced when these statements are executed includes a description of the minimum cost flow:

```
NOTE: LENGTH OF SHORTEST PATH = 6.
```

The minimum distance Bobby can travel from home to school is six blocks. NETFLOW's output SAS data set can be printed with PROC PRINT.

Output 1.12   Shortest Path Problem: PROC NETFLOW

```
                        SHORTEST PATH EXAMPLE                              22

      OBS    FROM    TO      DISTANCE    _FLOW1_      _DUAL1_

        1    HOME    A          5           0            0
        2    HOME    B          3           1            0
        3    HOME    C          8           0            4
        4    A       B          2           0            4
        5    A       E          6           0            6
        6    B       A          2           0            0
        7    B       C          1           0            0
        8    B       E          2           1            0
        9    C       B          1           0            2
       10    C       D          3           0            1
       11    D       E          2           0            3
       12    A       SCHOOL     6           0            5
       13    E       SCHOOL     1           1            0
       14    D       SCHOOL     2           0            2
```

The resulting data set contains all the original variables in data set SCHOOL plus these new variables:

FLOW1   describes the optimal flow across arcs in the network.

DUAL1   gives the marginal cost of increasing flow along each arc that is not at a flow bound.

The optimal flow described by the _FLOW1_ variable can best be explained by referring to **Figure 1.7**. The variable has a value of 1 in the observation representing the arc from HOME to node B; place a 1 on that arc in the drawing. For each value of _FLOW1_ that is nonzero, place the value on the corresponding arc in the diagram.

Figure 1.7 shows Bobby's shortest path to school. Those arcs that have been labeled are on the shortest path.

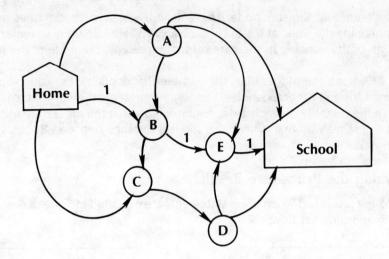

Figure 1.7 Shortest Path Diagram

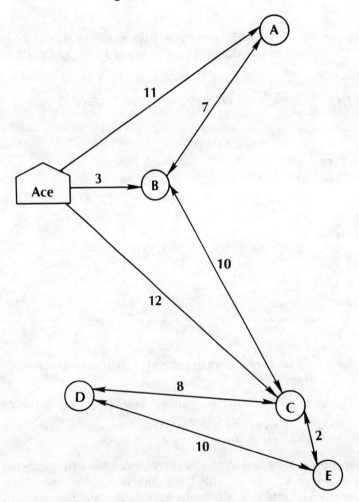

Figure 1.8 Shortest Path Problem with Multiple Sink Nodes

SHORTEST PATH: MULTIPLE SINK NODES

ACE Delivery Service delivers daily to several stores and other businesses in the area. To save gas and time, ACE's managers want their five drivers to use the shortest routes when making deliveries. **Figure 1.8** shows the delivery stops and distances in miles. What is the shortest route from ACE to each of the five delivery points?

Preparing the data   Since the problem contains several sink nodes, variables must be included in the data set to represent for each node whether it is a supply or destination node. The DATA step below creates such a data set for ACE Delivery Service:

```
TITLE 'SHORTEST PATH EXAMPLE: MULTIPLE SINK NODES';
DATA ACE;
   INPUT FROM $ TO $ DISTANCE BEGIN END;
   CARDS;
ACE  A  11  5  1
ACE  B   3  .  1
ACE  C  12  .  1
A    B   7  .  .
B    A   7  .  .
B    C  10  .  .
C    B  10  .  .
C    D   8  .  1
D    C   8  .  .
C    E   2  .  .
E    C   2  .  .
D    E  10  .  1
E    D  10  .  .
;
```

ACE Delivery Service is the supply node or origination point in this problem. Since it is the single supply node for five destinations, 5 is entered as the value of BEGIN in one of the three observations representing arcs leading from ACE. (The sum of the BEGIN values must be equal to the number of sink nodes. Thus, any combination of values that adds to five can be entered in the observations with ACE as the value of FROM.) Nonmissing values for the BEGIN variable denote a supply node.

Each observation with a TO value corresponding to a sink or destination node must be given a nonmissing value for END. The sum of the END values must also be five; END values correspond to destination nodes. Enter a 1 as the value of END in one of the observations with that destination node as the value of TO.

Using the NETFLOW Procedure

The following statements ask PROC NETFLOW to analyze the network described in the data set above:

```
PROC NETFLOW DATA=ACE;
   TAILNODE FROM;
   HEADNODE TO;
   COST DISTANCE;
   SUPPLY BEGIN;
   DEMAND END;
```

The TAILNODE statement identifies the variable containing the node at the tail of each arc; the HEADNODE statement gives the name of the variable in the data set that represents the node at the head of the arc.

The COST statement identifies the variable that contains the value shown on each arc. Although this value often represents the cost of crossing that arc, in this example the quantity represented on each arc is distance. Note that the procedure minimizes cost as it finds the shortest distance between ACE and each delivery point.

The SUPPLY statement names the variable that identifies supply nodes in this problem, and the DEMAND statement names the variable that identifies demand nodes.

Analyzing the procedure results   The SAS log produced when these statements are executed includes a description of the minimum cost flow:

```
NOTE: MINIMUM COST OF FLOW = 59.
```

The minimum distance traveled by ACE to all of its five delivery points is 59 miles. The data set output by the procedure can be printed using PROC PRINT.

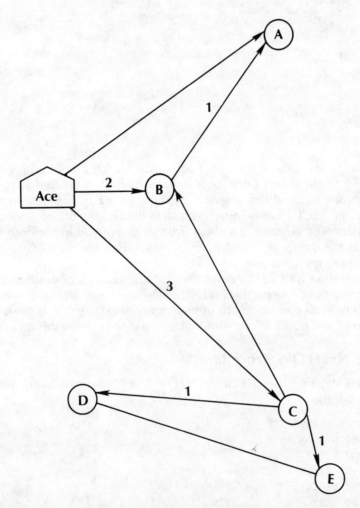

Figure 1.9   Shortest Path with Multiple Sink Nodes

Output 1.13   Solving Shortest Path Problems with Multiple Sink
Nodes Using PROC NETFLOW

```
                      SHORTEST PATH EXAMPLE: MULTIPLE SINK NODES                            23

    OBS    FROM    TO    DISTANCE    BEGIN    END    _FLOW1_    _DUAL1_

     1     ACE     A        11         5       1        0          1
     2     ACE     B         3         .       1        2          0
     3     ACE     C        12         .       1        3          0
     4     A       B         7         .       .        0         14
     5     B       A         7         .       .        1          0
     6     B       C        10         .       .        0          1
     7     C       B        10         .       .        0         19
     8     C       D         8         .       1        1          0
     9     D       C         8         .       .        0         16
    10     C       E         2         .       .        1          0
    11     E       C         2         .       .        0          4
    12     D       E        10         .       1        0         16
    13     E       D        10         .       .        0          4
```

Refer to **Figure 1.9** and describe the optimal flow using the values of _FLOW1_.
The diagram now shows the shortest path to each delivery point.

Maximum Flow Problem

A traffic situation involves a network where nodes are intersections and branches
are roads. You can use the NETFLOW procedure to alleviate traffic congestion
on the opening day of the fair. You know the number of cars that can travel from
one intersection to another in one minute based on the number of traffic lanes
and stop signs and the speed limit.

At the end of the day, you want to direct traffic from the fairgrounds to the
edge of town using the route that will allow maximum traffic flow. **Figure 1.10**
is a network diagram for the problem.

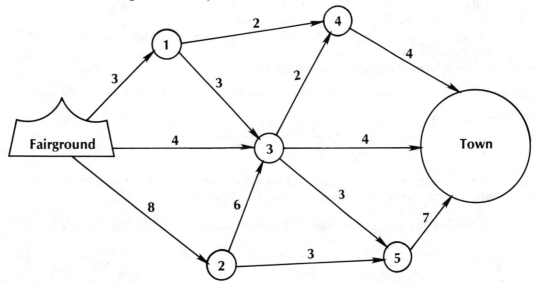

Figure 1.10   Maximum Flow Problem

Preparing the data   The data are entered in a SAS data set by representing each
arc in the diagram as an observation. Each observation contains values for two
variables corresponding to the beginning (BEGIN) and ending (END) nodes of the
arc and the number of cars that can pass in a minute. The DATA step below pre-
pares the data:

```
TITLE 'MAXIMUM FLOW EXAMPLE';
DATA FAIRDAY;
   INPUT BEGIN $ END $ MAXCARS;
   CARDS;
FAIR  1     3
FAIR  2     8
FAIR  3     4
1     3     3
1     4     2
2     3     6
2     5     3
3     4     2
3     5     3
3     TOWN  4
4     TOWN  5
5     TOWN  7
;
```

Using the NETFLOW procedure   PROC NETFLOW analyzes the data with these statements:

```
PROC NETFLOW DATA=FAIRDAY MAXFLOW ASOURCENODE=FAIR ASINKNODE=TOWN;
   TAILNODE BEGIN;
   HEADNODE END;
   CAPACITY MAXCARS;
PROC PRINT;
```

Since NETFLOW by default minimizes costs, you can tell the procedure to maximize flow with the MAXFLOW option in the PROC statement. The options ASOURCENODE= and ASINKNODE= identify the single source and sink nodes in the problem. The TAILNODE and HEADNODE statements give the tail and head nodes for the arc. The CAPACITY statement identifies the variables containing the arc's capacity.

The following message appears on the SAS log:

```
NOTE: MAXIMUM FLOW = 14.
```

In this example the maximum cost flow equals the maximum flow from the fairgrounds to town—in this case, fourteen cars per minute.

Analyzing the procedure results   The data set produced by the procedure is shown below:

Output 1.14   Solving a Maximum Flow Problem Using PROC NETFLOW

```
                        MAXIMUM FLOW EXAMPLE                              24

        OBS    BEGIN    END    MAXCARS    _FLOW1_    _DUAL1_

         1     FAIR     1         3          3          0
         2     FAIR     2         8          7          0
         3     FAIR     3         4          4          0
         4     1        3         3          1          0
         5     1        4         2          2          1
         6     2        3         6          4          0
         7     2        5         3          3          1
         8     3        4         2          2          1
         9     3        5         3          3          1
        10     3        TOWN      4          4          1
        11     4        TOWN      5          4          0
        12     5        TOWN      7          6          0
```

The variable _FLOW1_ gives the flow on each arc at optimality. The first three observations show the traffic pattern for cars leaving the fairground: three go to node 1, seven to node 2, and four to node 3. Of the three going to node 1, one then goes to node 3, and two to node 4, and so on.

In a maximum flow problem like this, dual variables have values of +1, 0, or −1. A dual value of +1 means that an increase in the capacity of the arc (an increase in MAXCARS) may increase the flow through the network. A dual value of 0 means that increasing capacity on the arc may have no effect on total flow. A negative value tells you that if you increase the arc's capacity in the opposite direction, total flow in the network may increase.

PROJECT MANAGEMENT: AN INTRODUCTION

This section describes a simple scheduling problem and how it can be solved using the CPM procedure. The results are displayed in a Gantt chart using PROC GANTT. Additional examples of scheduling problems using the extensive capabilities of the procedure are given in the CPM procedure description.

A Simple Critical Path Problem

A construction project to be completed consists of five tasks. Management has estimated the time needed to complete each task and has also determined which tasks must be complete before the next can begin. The company wants to find out the earliest possible completion date for the project.

Suppose the project consists of the five jobs A, B, C, D, and E. Below is a summary showing the job precedence and days necessary to complete each task.

Job	Jobs That Follow	Completion Time(Days)
A	C,D	4
B	E	6
C	—	8
D	E	3
E		2

It is clear that Job C cannot begin until Job A is finished and that both Jobs B and D must be finished before Job E can begin.

Representing the Problem Schematically

This problem is represented by the network diagram **Figure 1.11**.

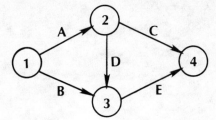

Figure 1.11   Representing a Critical Path Problem Schematically

In **Figure 1.11** the activities are placed on the edges or arcs of the network.

Using the CPM Procedure

In order for the CPM procedure to analyze the problem, you must enter the data into a SAS data set where observations correspond to jobs or other tasks to be completed. Identify in each observation the nodes preceding and following that task and the completion time for the task.

```
TITLE 'PROJECT MANAGEMENT EXAMPLE';
DATA CONST;
   INPUT JOB $ PRECEDE  FOLLOW  TIME;
   CARDS;
A 1 2 4
B 1 3 6
C 2 4 8
D 2 3 3
E 3 4 2
;
```

CPM produces an output data set with no printed output. The DATE= option in the PROC CPM statement gives the starting date for the project.

These statements request a critical path analysis of the construction problem above with the starting date on December 1, 1985:

```
PROC CPM DATE='01DEC85'D;
   ID JOB;
   HEADNODE FOLLOW;
   TAILNODE PRECEDE;
   DURATION TIME;
```

You need the ID statement to include the variable JOB in the output data set. When the network diagram is in the form of the one above, the HEADNODE statement gives the name of the variable containing the name or number of the node following the task, the TAILNODE statement names the variable that represents the preceding node, the DURATION statement names the variable containing the task's duration.

Analyzing the Procedure Results

You can print the data set output by the procedure using the PRINT procedure and the statements below. All the original variables are included in the output data set; these statements request that only the result variables be printed:

```
PROC PRINT;
   ID JOB;
   VAR E_START E_FINISH L_START L_FINISH T_FLOAT F_FLOAT;
```

Output 1.15   Critical Path Analysis: PROC CPM

```
                       PROJECT MANAGEMENT EXAMPLE                                    25

     JOB    E_START    E_FINISH    L_START    L_FINISH    T_FLOAT    F_FLOAT

      A     01DEC85    04DEC85     01DEC85    04DEC85        0          0
      B     01DEC85    06DEC85     05DEC85    10DEC85        4          1
      C     05DEC85    12DEC85     05DEC85    12DEC85        0          0
      D     05DEC85    07DEC85     08DEC85    10DEC85        3          0
      E     08DEC85    09DEC85     11DEC85    12DEC85        3          3
```

These special variables are generated by the procedure and shown above:

E_START   is the earliest time the task can begin.

E_FINISH   is the earliest time the task can end if it begins at E_START.

L_START   is the latest time the task can begin.

L_FINISH   is the completion time if the task begins at L_START.

T_FLOAT   is the total float time or maximum delay that can be tolerated in performing the task and still complete the project on schedule.

F_FLOAT   is the free float time or maximum delay that can be tolerated in the task without affecting the scheduling of a subsequent task.

Plotting the Results

The GANTT procedure can be used to plot the resulting schedule. The procedure uses the data set output from the CPM procedure as input and produces charts on either a line printer or a high resolution graphics device.

```
PROC GANTT;
   ID JOB;
   CHART / NOJOBNUM;
```

Output 1.16   Plotting a Schedule: PROC GANTT

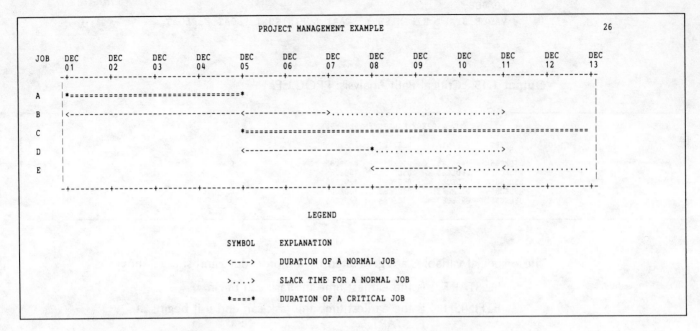

An Alternate Diagram

Some people prefer diagramming the problem by representing the job or activity at each node of the network. For example, consider **Figure 1.12**.

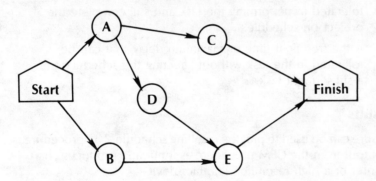

Figure 1.12   Diagram Representing Each Node of the Network

If your network is in the format shown in **Figure 1.12**, then you can use a DATA step to prepare the data for PROC CPM. The data set should include an observation for each task; each observation must identify all subsequent tasks and the length of the task.

```
DATA CONSTR2;
    INPUT JOB $ NEXT1 $ NEXT2 $ LENGTH;
    CARDS;
A C D 4
B E . 6
C . . 8
D E . 3
E . . 2
;
```

The PROC CPM statements you need to schedule the project when described in this format are

```
PROC CPM DATE='01DEC85'D;
    ACTIVITY JOB;
    DURATION LENGTH;
    SUCCESSOR NEXT1 NEXT2;
```

The ACTIVITY statement names the variable containing the name of the node for the current task or activity. The DURATION statement gives the name of the variable containing the time to complete that task. The SUCCESSOR statement gives the names of any variables containing tasks preceded by the current task. To print the data set, use these statements:

```
PROC PRINT;
    ID JOB;
    VAR E_START E_FINISH L_START L_FINISH T_FLOAT F_FLOAT;
```

The results are the same as the results of **Figure 1.11**.

Output 1.17   Critical Path Example: PROC CPM

```
                         PROJECT MANAGEMENT EXAMPLE                              27

    JOB    E_START    E_FINISH    L_START    L_FINISH    T_FLOAT    F_FLOAT

     A     01DEC85    04DEC85     01DEC85    04DEC85        0          0
     B     01DEC85    06DEC85     05DEC85    10DEC85        4          1
     C     05DEC85    12DEC85     05DEC85    12DEC85        0          0
     D     05DEC85    07DEC85     08DEC85    10DEC85        3          0
     E     08DEC85    09DEC85     11DEC85    12DEC85        3          3
```

REFERENCES

Chiang, A.C. (1967), *Fundamental Methods of Mathematical Economics*, New York: McGraw-Hill.

Ford, L.R. and Fulkerson, D.R. (1962), *Flows in Networks*, Princeton: Princeton University Press.

Frazer, J.R. (1968), *Applied Linear Programming*, Englewood Cliffs, N.J.: Prentice-Hall.

Hesse, R. and Woolsey, G., assisted by Swanson, H.S. (1980), *Applied Management Science: A Quick & Dirty Approach*, Chicago: Science Research Associates.

Horowitz, I. (1972), *An Introduction to Quantitative Business Analysis*, Second Edition, New York: McGraw-Hill.

Thompson, W.W., Jr. (1967), *Operations Research Techniques*, Columbus, Ohio: Charles E. Merrill Books, Inc.

Wagner, H.M. (1969), *Principles of Operations Research, With Applications to Managerial Decisions*, Englewood Cliffs, N.J.: Prentice-Hall.

40

Chapter 2
The ASSIGN Procedure

Operating systems: All

ABSTRACT

The ASSIGN procedure finds the minimum or maximum cost assignment of n source nodes or agents to m sink nodes or tasks. The procedure can handle problems where $m=n$, $m<n$, or $m>n$.

INTRODUCTION

The ASSIGN procedure finds the minimum or maximum cost assignment of source nodes to sink nodes. Many practical problems can be formulated in a way that is solvable by PROC ASSIGN. For example, consider assigning five programmers to five programming jobs. Each programmer prefers some programming jobs to others. You can use PROC ASSIGN to assign jobs to programmers in such a way that the total preferences of the group are maximized. Suppose you ask each programmer to rank the jobs according to preference, using 1 for the most preferred and 5 for the least preferred job. PROC ASSIGN maximizes the total preference of the group by minimizing the sum of the preferences. In the matrix that follows, each row represents a programming job and each column represents a programmer. Each entry in the matrix is a preference ranking the programmer gave the programming job.

JOB	PRGMER1	PRGMER2	PRGMER3	PRGMER4	PRGMER5
JOB1	4	2	3	2	4
JOB2	1	1	2	3	2
JOB3	3	3	4	4	3
JOB4	5	4	1	5	1
JOB5	2	5	5	1	5

To solve this problem using ASSIGN, the data must be in a SAS data set; the solution is output to a SAS data set. Each observation corresponds to a programming job and contains the programmer assigned to it. In this way the procedure identifies the assignment of the five jobs to the five programmers. The output from this problem is shown in **Example 1**.

The formal statement of the problem solved by the ASSIGN procedure is

If $n=m$ then:

$$\min (\max) \Sigma_{j=1}^{m} \ \Sigma_{i=1}^{n} \ c_{ij} x_{ij}$$

subject to: $\Sigma_{j=1}^{m} x_{ij} = 1$ for $i=1,...,n$

$\Sigma_{i=1}^{n} x_{ij} = 1$ for $j=1,...,m$

where   for $i=1,...,n \ j=1,...,m$

$$x_{ij} = \begin{cases} 0 \text{ or } 1 \text{ if the assignment of} \\ \qquad \text{node } i \text{ to node } j \text{ is allowed,} \\ 0 \text{ otherwise.} \end{cases}$$

If $n<m$ then:

$$\min (\max) \Sigma_{j=1}^{m} \ \Sigma_{i=1}^{n} \ c_{ij} x_{ij}$$

subject to: $\Sigma_{j=1}^{m} x_{ij} = 1$ for $i=1,...,n$

$\Sigma_{i=1}^{n} x_{ij} \leq 1$ for $j=1,...,m$

where   for $i=1,...,n \ j=1,...,m$

$$x_{ij} = \begin{cases} 0 \text{ or } 1 \text{ if the assignment of} \\ \qquad \text{node } i \text{ to node } j \text{ is allowed,} \\ 0 \text{ otherwise.} \end{cases}$$

If $n>m$ then:

$$\min (\max) \Sigma_{j=1}^{m} \ \Sigma_{i=1}^{n} \ c_{ij} x_{ij}$$

subject to: $\Sigma_{j=1}^{m} x_{ij} \leq 1$ for $i=1,...,n$

$\Sigma_{i=1}^{n} x_{ij} = 1$ for $j=1,...,m$

where   for $i=1,...,n \ j=1,...,m$

$$x_{ij} = \begin{cases} 0 \text{ or } 1 \text{ if the assignment of} \\ \qquad \text{node } i \text{ to node } j \text{ is allowed,} \\ 0 \text{ otherwise.} \end{cases}$$

SPECIFICATIONS

The following statements are used in PROC ASSIGN:

PROC ASSIGN *options*;
   BY *variables*;
   COST *variables*;
   ID *variables*;

The COST statement is required.

PROC ASSIGN Statement

PROC ASSIGN *options*;

The options below can appear in the PROC ASSIGN statement:

DATA=*SASdataset*
> names the SAS data set that contains the network specification. If DATA= is omitted, the most recently created SAS data set is used.

MAXIMUM
> specifies that the objective is to find an assignment that maximizes the sum of the costs. By default, PROC ASSIGN minimizes the sum of the costs.

OUT=*SASdataset*
> specifies a name for the output data set. If OUT= is omitted, SAS creates a data set and automatically names it according to the DATA*n* naming convention. See "SAS Files" in the *SAS User's Guide: Basics* for more information.

BY Statement

BY *variables*;

A BY statement can be used with PROC ASSIGN to obtain separate analyses on observations in groups defined by the BY variables. When a BY statement appears, the procedure expects the input data to be sorted in order of the BY variables. If your input data set is not sorted, use the SORT procedure with a similar BY statement to sort the data, or, if appropriate, use the BY statement options NOTSORTED or DESCENDING. For more information, see the discussion of the BY statement in "Statements Used in the PROC Step" in the *SAS User's Guide: Basics*.

COST Statement

COST *variables*;

The COST statement identifies the variables in the input data set that contain the costs of assigning each source node to each sink node. If the value of a COST variable is missing, then that particular assignment between source and sink node is infeasible.

To find an assignment that maximizes profit instead of minimizing cost, include the MAXIMUM option in the PROC ASSIGN statement and let the COST variables represent profit instead of cost. The COST variables must be numeric.

ID Statement

ID *variables*;

The ID statement identifies variables in the input data set not given in the COST statement that are to be included in the output data set. ID variables can be character or numeric.

DETAILS

Output Data Set

The output data set contains the *m* cost variables in the input data set, any variables identified in the ID statement, and a new variable named _ASSIGN_. This new variable is a character variable containing the names of the variables assigned to the source nodes.

The Objective Value

If the problem is infeasible, a note is printed on the SAS log. Otherwise, the value of the objective function,

$$\sum_{j=1}^{m} \sum_{i=1}^{n} c_{ij} x_{ij}$$

under the optimal assignment is reported on the SAS log.

Missing Values

Since the value of a cost variable is interpreted as the cost of an assignment, a missing value for a cost variable is assumed to mean that the assignment is not allowed.

EXAMPLES

Assigning Programming Jobs to Programmers: Example 1

To solve the assignment problem described above, read the preference data into a SAS data set and then call PROC ASSIGN, identifying the cost variables in the input data set. The solution is output by PROC ASSIGN to a SAS data set and printed with PROC PRINT as in the following program:

```
TITLE 'ASSIGNING PROGRAMMING JOBS TO PROGRAMMERS';

DATA PREFER;                  * STORE THE DATA ;
  INPUT JOB $ PRGMER1-PRGMER5;
  CARDS;
JOB1 4 2 3 2 4
JOB2 1 1 2 3 2
JOB3 3 3 4 4 3
JOB4 5 4 1 5 1
JOB5 2 5 5 1 5
;
PROC ASSIGN DATA=PREFER;   * SOLVE THE PROBLEM;
  COST PRGMER1-PRGMER5;
  ID JOB;

PROC PRINT;                * PRINT THE SOLUTION;
```

The following note is printed on the SAS log.

```
NOTE: MINIMUM COST ASSIGNMENT = 8.
```

The solution data set printed by PROC PRINT looks like this:

Output 2.1   Assigning Programming Jobs to Programmers

```
                    ASSIGNING PROGRAMMING JOBS TO PROGRAMMERS                        1

     OBS    JOB    PRGMER1    PRGMER2    PRGMER3    PRGMER4    PRGMER5    _ASSIGN_

      1    JOB1       4          2          3          2          4       PRGMER2
      2    JOB2       1          1          2          3          2       PRGMER1
      3    JOB3       3          3          4          4          3       PRGMER5
      4    JOB4       5          4          1          5          1       PRGMER3
      5    JOB5       2          5          5          1          5       PRGMER4
```

The solution shows how each programming job should be assigned to each worker in order to minimize the assignment cost, which is equivalent to maximizing the worker preferences.

Assigning Subcontractors to Construction Jobs: Example 2

This example shows how PROC ASSIGN can be used to maximize an objective function. Consider a construction project that consists of nine jobs. Because of the nature of the project each job must be performed by a different subcontractor. Each job is bid upon by twelve subcontractors. The matrix that follows shows the expected profit to the contractor if each job is given to each subcontractor. Each row in the matrix represents a different job, and each column represents a different subcontractor.

SUBCONTRACTOR	1	2	3	4	5	6	7	8	9	10	11	12
JOB1	79	24	13	53	47	66	85	17	92	47	46	13
JOB2	43	59	33	95	55	97	34	55	84	94	26	56
JOB3	29	52	0	27	13	33	0	11	71	86	6	76
JOB4	88	83	64	72	0	67	27	47	83	62	35	38
JOB5	65	90	56	62	53	91	48	23	6	89	49	33
JOB6	44	79	86	93	71	7	86	59	0	56	45	59
JOB7	35	51	-9	91	39	32	3	12	79	25	79	81
JOB8	50	12	59	32	23	64	20	94	97	14	11	97
JOB9	25	17	39	.	38	63	87	14	4	18	11	45

The negative profit in the third column means that if job 7 is awarded to subcontractor 3, the contractor loses money. The missing value in the fourth column means that subcontractor 4 did not bid on job 9. PROC ASSIGN treats a missing value differently from the way it treats a 0. While it is possible that an optimal assignment could include a 0 (or even a negative) contribution to profit, the missing value is never included in an assignment. In this case subcontractor 4 is never awarded job 9, regardless of the profit structure.

You can use PROC ASSIGN to find how the contractor should award the jobs to the subcontractors to maximize his profit. First, put the data in a SAS data set. Then call PROC ASSIGN using the MAXIMUM option.

Consider this SAS program:

```
TITLE 'ASSIGNING SUBCONTRACTORS TO CONSTRUCTION JOBS';

DATA PROFIT;                        * READ THE DATA ;
  INPUT JOB $ SUBCON1-SUBCON12;
  CARDS;
JOB1 79 24 13 53 47 66 85 17 92 47 46 13
JOB2 43 59 33 95 55 97 34 55 84 94 26 56
JOB3 29 52  0 27 13 33  0 11 71 86  6 76
JOB4 88 83 64 72  0 67 27 47 83 62 35 38
JOB5 65 90 56 62 53 91 48 23  6 89 49 33
JOB6 44 79 86 93 71  7 86 59  0 56 45 59
JOB7 35 51 -9 91 39 32  3 12 79 25 79 81
JOB8 50 12 59 32 23 64 20 94 97 14 11 97
JOB9 25 17 39  . 38 63 87 14  4 18 11 45
;
PROC ASSIGN MAXIMUM DATA=PROFIT;    * SOLVE THE PROBLEM;
  COST SUBCON1-SUBCON12;
  ID JOB;

PROC PRINT;                         * PRINT THE SOLUTION;
```

The cost of the optimal assignment printed on the SAS log is

```
NOTE: MAXIMUM COST ASSIGNMENT = 814.
```

This means that the contractor can expect a profit of $814 if he follows the optimal assignment.

Output 2.2   Assigning Subcontractors to Construction Jobs

```
                      ASSIGNING SUBCONTRACTORS TO CONSTRUCTION JOBS                                           2

OBS JOB  SUBCON1 SUBCON2 SUBCON3 SUBCON4 SUBCON5 SUBCON6 SUBCON7 SUBCON8 SUBCON9 SUBCON10 SUBCON11 SUBCON12 _ASSIGN_

  1 JOB1    79      24      13      53      47      66      85      17      92      47       46       13     SUBCON9
  2 JOB2    43      59      33      95      55      97      34      55      84      94       26       56     SUBCON6
  3 JOB3    29      52       0      27      13      33       0      11      71      86        6       76     SUBCON10
  4 JOB4    88      83      64      72       0      67      27      47      83      62       35       38     SUBCON1
  5 JOB5    65      90      56      62      53      91      48      23       6      89       49       33     SUBCON2
  6 JOB6    44      79      86      93      71       7      86      59       0      56       45       59     SUBCON3
  7 JOB7    35      51      -9      91      39      32       3      12      79      25       79       81     SUBCON4
  8 JOB8    50      12      59      32      23      64      20      94      97      14       11       97     SUBCON12
  9 JOB9    25      17      39       .      38      63      87      14       4      18       11       45     SUBCON7
```

Note that three subcontractors, SUBCON5, SUBCON8, and SUBCON11, are not assigned to any jobs.

Assigning Construction Jobs to Subcontractors: Example 3

Suppose the data from **Example 2** are arranged so that variables are jobs. Then each observation contains the profit from awarding each job to a single subcontractor. The following program finds the maximum profit assignment.

```
TITLE 'ASSIGNING CONSTRUCTION JOBS TO SUBCONTRACTORS';

DATA PROFIT;                                    *READ THE DATA;
  INPUT SUBCONT $ JOB1-JOB9;
  CARDS;

SUBCON1    79    43    29    88    65    44    35    50    25
SUBCON2    24    59    52    83    90    79    51    12    17
SUBCON3    13    33     0    64    56    86    -9    59    39
SUBCON4    53    95    27    72    62    93    91    32     .
SUBCON5    47    55    13     0    53    71    39    23    38
SUBCON6    66    97    33    67    91     7    32    64    63
SUBCON7    85    34     0    27    48    86    32     0    87
SUBCON8    17    55    11    47    23    59    12    94    14
SUBCON9    92    84    71    83     6     0    79    97     4
SUBCON10   47    94    86    62    89    56    25    14    18
SUBCON11   46    26     6    35    49    45    79    11    11
SUBCON12   13    56    76    38    33    59    81    97    45
;

PROC ASSIGN MAXIMUM DATA=PROFIT;    * SOLVE THE PROBLEM;
  COST JOB1-JOB9;
  ID SUBCONT;

PROC PRINT;                                     * PRINT THE SOLUTION;
```

The cost of the optimal assignment printed on the SAS log is

```
NOTE: NUMBER OF SOURCE NODES EXCEEDS NUMBER OF SINK NODES.
NOTE: MAXIMUM COST ASSIGNMENT = 814.
```

This means that the contractor can expect a profit of $814 if he follows the optimal assignment. The output data set includes the same results as in **Example 2**.

Output 2.3   Assigning Construction Jobs to Subcontractors

```
                       ASSIGNING CONSTRUCTION JOBS TO SUBCONTRACTORS                                3

   OBS   SUBCONT    JOB1   JOB2   JOB3   JOB4   JOB5   JOB6   JOB7   JOB8   JOB9   _ASSIGN_

     1   SUBCON1     79     43     29     88     65     44     35     50     25    JOB4
     2   SUBCON2     24     59     52     83     90     79     51     12     17    JOB5
     3   SUBCON3     13     33      0     64     56     86     -9     59     39    JOB6
     4   SUBCON4     53     95     27     72     62     93     91     32      .    JOB7
     5   SUBCON5     47     55     13      0     53     71     39     23     38    .
     6   SUBCON6     66     97     33     67     91      7     32     64     63    JOB2
     7   SUBCON7     85     34      0     27     48     86     32      0     87    JOB9
     8   SUBCON8     17     55     11     47     23     59     12     94     14    .
     9   SUBCON9     92     84     71     83      6      0     79     97      4    JOB1
    10   SUBCON10    47     94     86     62     89     56     25     14     18    JOB3
    11   SUBCON11    46     26      6     35     49     45     79     11     11    .
    12   SUBCON12    13     56     76     38     33     59     81     97     45    JOB8
```

Chapter 3

The CPM Procedure

Operating systems: All

ABSTRACT

The CPM procedure performs critical path analysis, a method for project scheduling when the activities in the project are subject to technological (precedence) and time constraints. The schedule obtained by PROC CPM is saved in an output data set. In addition to precedence constraints, PROC CPM also allows you to schedule project activities subject to constraints on resource availabilities. Resource utilization can be summarized and saved in an output data set.

INTRODUCTION

The CPM procedure is used to schedule activities that compose a project. In many projects there are precedence relationships among activities that make efficient scheduling difficult. The CPM procedure finds a schedule that completes a project in the shortest time. The procedure calculates early and late start times, early and late finish times, total float, and free float for each activity in the network and saves these values in an output data set.

In addition to precedence constraints on the activities, you can also specify start or finish dates for the different activities in the project, and CPM will schedule the project subject to these restrictions. Precedence relationships among activities can be conveniently represented by a network diagram. Two representations are popular: one shows activities on the vertices or nodes of the network, and the other shows activities on the edges or arcs of the network (arrow notation). See **Figure 3.1** and **Figure 3.2** in **Example 1** for examples of these two representations. The data set analyzed by PROC CPM can define the network in either format. Each observation in the data set contains information about an activity (on either an arc or a node) in the network.

Quite often the resources needed to perform the activities in a project are available only in limited quantities and may cause certain activities to be postponed due to unavailability of the required resources. You can use CPM to schedule the activities in a project subject to resource constraints. In addition to obtaining a resource-constrained schedule in an output data set, you can save the resource utilization summary in another output data set.

SPECIFICATIONS

The following statements are used in PROC CPM:

> **PROC CPM** *options*;
> **ALIGNDATE** *variable*;
> **ALIGNTYPE** *variable*;
> **DURATION** *variable*;
> **HEADNODE** *variable*;
> **HOLIDAY** *variables*;
> **ID** *variables*;
> **RESOURCE** *variables / resource options*;

TAILNODE *variable*;

or

PROC CPM *options*;
  ACTIVITY *variable*;
  ALIGNDATE *variable*;
  ALIGNTYPE *variable*;
  DURATION *variable*;
  HOLIDAY *variables*;
  ID *variables*;
  RESOURCE *variables / resource options*;
  SUCCESSOR *variables*;

If the network is defined with activities on the arcs, then HEADNODE and TAILNODE statements are required. If the network is defined with activities on the nodes, then ACTIVITY and SUCCESSOR statements are required. In either case, the DURATION statement is required. The ALIGNDATE and ALIGNTYPE statements are required if several activities in the network are constrained to start or finish on specific dates. The HOLIDAY statement is required if the activities are to be scheduled around holidays. The RESOURCE statement is required if a resource utilization summary is required or if the project is to be scheduled subject to resource constraints.

PROC CPM Statement

PROC CPM *options*;

The options below can appear in the PROC CPM statement:

Data set options

DATA=*SASdataset*
    names the SAS data set that contains the network specification. If DATA= is omitted, the most recently created SAS data set is used.

HOLIDATA=*SASdataset*
    identifies a SAS data set that contains variables whose values are holidays. These variables should be formatted as SAS date variables. HOLIDATA= must be used with a HOLIDAY statement that lists the variables in the SAS data set containing the list of holidays.

RESOURCEIN=*SASdataset*
RESIN=*SASdataset*
RIN=*SASdataset*
RESLEVEL=*SASdataset*
    names the SAS data set that contains the levels available for the different resources used by the activities in the project. This data set also contains information about the type of resource (replenishable or consumable) and the priority for each resource. The specification of the RESIN= data set indicates to PROC CPM that the schedule of the project is to be determined subject to resource constraints. For details about the format of this data set, see the section **RESOURCEIN= Input Data Set**.

    If this option is specified, you must also use the RESOURCE statement to identify the variable names for the resources to be used for resource-constrained scheduling. In addition, you must specify the name of the variable in this data set (using the PERIOD= option in the RESOURCE statement) that contains the dates from which the resource availabilities in each observation are valid. Further, the data set must be sorted in order of increasing values of this period variable.

RESOURCEOUT=*SASdataset*
RESOUT=*SASdataset*
ROUT=*SASdataset*
RESUSAGE=*SASdataset*

names the SAS data set where you can save resource usage profiles for each of the resources specified in the RESOURCE statement. In this data set you can save the resource usage by time period for the early start, late start, and resource-constrained schedules and for the surplus level of resources remaining after resource allocation is performed. By default it provides the usage profiles for the early and late start schedules if resource allocation is not performed.

If resource allocation is performed, this data set also provides usage profiles for the resource-constrained schedule and a profile of the level of remaining resources.

You can control the types of profiles to be saved by using the ESPROFILE (early start usage), LSPROFILE (late start usage), RCPROFILE (resource-constrained usage), or AVPROFILE (resource availability after resource allocation) options in the RESOURCE statement. Any combination of these four options can be specified. You can also specify the option ALL to indicate that all four options (ESPROFILE, LSPROFILE, RCPROFILE, AVPROFILE) are to be in effect. For details about variable names and the interpretation of the values in this data set, see the section **RESOURCEOUT= Data Set**.

OUT=*SASdataset*

specifies a name for the output data set that contains the schedule determined by PROC CPM. If CPM is used to determine an unconstrained schedule (that is, without any limitations on resource availability), then this data set contains the early and late start schedules; otherwise, if CPM is used to obtain a resource-constrained schedule, this data set contains the resource-constrained schedule. See the section **OUT= Output Data Set** for details about the names of the new variables in the data set. If OUT= is omitted, the SAS System still creates a data set and names it according to the DATA*n* convention. See "SAS Files" in *SAS User's Guide: Basics* for more information.

Duration control options

DAYLENGTH=*daylength*

specifies the length of the workday. The DAYLENGTH= value should be a SAS time value. When DAYLENGTH= is used with INTERVAL=DTDAY, the procedure schedules work on non-holidays and through weekends. Work is scheduled starting at the beginning of the day as specified in the DATE= option and ending *daylength* hours later.

INTERVAL=*interval*

requests that each unit of duration be measured in *interval* units. Possible values for *interval* are DAY, WEEK, WEEKDAYS, WORKDAY, MONTH, QTR, YEAR, HOUR, MINUTE, SECOND, DTDAY, DTWRKDAY, DTWEEK, DTMONTH, DTQTR, DTYEAR, DTHOUR, DTMINUTE, and DTSECOND. If DATE= is specified then

the default is DAY. See the section **Specifying the INTERVAL=
Option** for further details regarding this option.

INTPER=*period*

    requests that each unit of duration be equivalent to *period* units of
duration. The default is 1.

Align options

AACTIVITY=*a*

    identifies the name of an activity that either starts or finishes by the
date specified in the DATE= option. The AACTIVITY= option is
used when the network is input in activity-on-node format and the
ACTIVITY variable has values that are valid SAS names. If
AACTIVITY= is specified, the ALIGN= option must also appear.

AHEADNODE=*a*

    identifies the number of the headnode of an activity that either starts
or finishes by the date specified in the DATE= option. The
AHEADNODE= option is used when the network is input in activity-
on-arc format and the HEADNODE variable is a valid SAS name. If
AHEADNODE= is used, the ATAILNODE= and ALIGN= options
must also appear.

ALIGN=ES,LS,EF,LF

    specifies how the activity identified by the NACTIVITY=
(AACTIVITY=) or NTAILNODE=/NHEADNODE=
(ATAILNODE=/AHEADNODE=) options is to be aligned. If
ALIGN=ES, the activity is aligned so that its early start time is the
date specified in the DATE= option. If ALIGN=LS, EF, or LF, the
activity is aligned so that its late start time, early finish time, or late
finish time is the date specified in the DATE= option.

ATAILNODE=*a*

    identifies the number of the tailnode of an activity that either starts
or finishes by the date specified in the DATE= option. The
ATAILNODE= option is used when the network is input in activity-
on-arc format, and the TAILNODE variable is a valid SAS name. If
ATAILNODE= is used, the AHEADNODE= option must also appear.

DATE=*d*

    requests that all start and finish times be evaluated as SAS date
values, SAS time values, or SAS datetime values, beginning with the
SAS date, time, or datetime *d*. If neither the FINISHBEFORE option
nor any other alignment options are specified, then CPM schedules
the project to start on *d*.

FINISHBEFORE

    specifies that the project be scheduled to complete before the date
given in the DATE= option.

NACTIVITY=*n*

    identifies the number of an activity that either starts or finishes by
the date specified in the DATE= option. The NACTIVITY= option is
used when the network is input in activity-on-node format and the
ACTIVITY variable is numeric. If NACTIVITY= is used, the ALIGN=
option must also appear.

NHEADNODE=*m*

    identifies the number of the headnode of an activity that either starts
or finishes by the date specified in the DATE= option. The

NHEADNODE= option is used if the network is input in activity-on-arc format and the HEADNODE variable is numeric. If NHEADNODE= is used, the NTAILNODE= option must also appear.

NTAILNODE=*n*

identifies the number of the tailnode of an activity that either starts or finishes by the date specified in the DATE= option. The NTAILNODE= option is used when the network is input in activity-on-arc format and the TAILNODE variable is numeric. If NTAILNODE= is used, the NHEADNODE= option must also appear.

Miscellaneous option

COLLAPSE

creates only one observation per activity in the output data set when the input data set for a network in activity-on-vertex format contains multiple observations for the same activity. Note that this option is allowed only if the network is in activity-on-vertex format.

ACTIVITY Statement

ACTIVITY *variable*;

The ACTIVITY statement is required when data are input in an activity-on-node format, and it identifies the variable that contains the names of the nodes in the network. The activity associated with each node has a duration equal to the value of the DURATION variable. The ACTIVITY variable can be character or numeric since it is treated symbolically. However, each node in the network must be uniquely defined.

ALIGNDATE Statement

ALIGNDATE *variable*;

The ALIGNDATE statement identifies the variable in the DATA= input data set that specifies the dates to be used to constrain each activity to start or finish on a particular date. The ALIGNDATE statement is used in conjunction with the ALIGNTYPE statement, which specifies the type of alignment. A missing value for this variable indicates that the particular activity has no restriction imposed on it. This is a generalization of the DATE= and ALIGN= options on the PROC CPM statement, which can be used to impose a date restriction on one activity or on the start or finish dates of the project as a whole. If the DATE= and ALIGN= options are used in addition to the ALIGNDATE statement, then any conflict between the imposed dates on an activity is resolved in favor of the date given by the ALIGNDATE variable.

PROC CPM requires that if the ALIGNDATE statement is used, then all start activities (activities with no predecessors) have nonmissing values for the ALIGNDATE variable. If any start activity has a missing ALIGNDATE value, it is assumed to start on the date specified in the PROC CPM statement (if such a date is given), or, if no date is given, on the earliest specified start date of all start activities. If none of the start activities has a start date specified and a project start date is not specified in the PROC CPM statement, it is treated as an input error and the procedure stops execution and returns an error message.

ALIGNTYPE Statement

ALIGNTYPE *variable*;

This statement is used to specify whether the date value in the ALIGNDATE state-ment is the earliest start date, the latest finish date, and so forth, for the activity in the observation. The allowed values of the variable specified are SEQ, SGE, SLE, FEQ, FGE, and FLE. If an ALIGNDATE statement is specified and no ALIGNTYPE statement is given, all the activities are assumed to have an aligntype of 'SGE'. If an activity has a nonmissing value for the ALIGNDATE variable and a missing value for the ALIGNTYPE variable, then the aligntype is assumed to be 'SGE'.

The following explanation best illustrates the restrictions imposed on the start or finish times of an activity by the above mentioned types of alignment. Let D denote the value of the ALIGNDATE variable for a particular activity and let DUR be its duration. If MINSDATE and MAXFDATE are used to denote the earliest allowed start date and the latest allowed finish date, respectively, for the activity, then **Table 3.1** illustrates the values of MINSDATE and MAXFDATE as a function of the value of the ALIGNTYPE variable.

Table 3.1 Determining Alignment Date Values with the ALIGNTYPE Statement: PROC CPM

ALIGNTYPE	MINSDATE	MAXFDATE
SEQ	D	D + DUR
SGE	D	+ INFINITY
SLE	− INFINITY	D + DUR
FEQ	D − DUR	D
FGE	D − DUR	+ INFINITY
FLE	− INFINITY	D

Once the above dates have been calculated for all the activities in the project, the values of MINSDATE are used in the computation of the early start schedule and those of MAXFDATE are used in the computation of the late start schedule. The early start time (E_START) of an activity is computed during a forward pass through the network as the maximum of its MINSDATE and the early finish times (E_FINISH) of all its predecessors (E_FINISH = E_START + DUR).

If a target completion date is not specified (using the FINISHBEFORE option), the project completion time is determined as the maximum value of E_FINISH over all the activities in the project. The late finish time (L_FINISH) for each of the finish activities (those with no successors) is computed as the minimum of its MAXFDATE and the project completion date; late start time (L_START) is com-puted as L_FINISH − DUR. L_FINISH for each of the other activities in the net-work is computed as the minimum of its MAXFDATE and the L_START times of all its successors.

Note that it is possible for the L_START time of an activity to be less than its E_START if there are constraints on the start times of certain activities in the net-work that make the target completion date (or constraints on the finish times of some successor activities) infeasible. In such cases, some of the activities in the network have negative values for T_FLOAT, indicating that these activities are 'super-critical'. See **Example 9** for a demonstration of this situation.

DURATION Statement

> DURATION *variable;*

The DURATION statement identifies the variable in the input data set that contains the length of time necessary to complete the activity. If the network is input in activity-on-arc format, then the variable identifies the duration of the activity denoted by the arc joining the TAILNODE and the HEADNODE. If the network is input in activity-on-node format, then the variable identifies the duration of the activity at the node specified in the ACTIVITY statement. The variable specified must be numeric. The DURATION statement must be specified.

HEADNODE Statement

> HEADNODE *variable;*

The HEADNODE statement is required when data are input in activity-on-arc format. It specifies the variable in the input data set that contains the name of the node on the head of an arrow in the project network. This node is identified with the event that signals the end of an activity on that arc. The variable specified can be either a numeric or character variable since the procedure treats this variable symbolically. Each node must be uniquely defined.

HOLIDAY Statement

> HOLIDAY *variables;*

The HOLIDAY statement lists the names of variables used to describe non-workdays in a SAS data set. The HOLIDAY statement must be used with the HOLIDATA= option in the PROC CPM statement. The HOLIDATA= option identifies the SAS data set that contains a list of the holidays and non-workdays around which you schedule your project. Holiday variables must be formatted as SAS date variables. Since holidays are required to be date values, CPM accounts for holidays only when the INTERVAL= option has one of the following values: DAY, WORKDAY, WEEKDAY, DTDAY, or DTWRKDAY.

ID Statement

> ID *variables;*

The ID statement identifies variables not specified in the TAILNODE, HEADNODE, ACTIVITY, SUCCESSOR, or DURATION statements that are to be included in the OUT= output data set.

RESOURCE Statement

> RESOURCE *variables / resource options;*

The RESOURCE statement identifies the variables in the DATA= input data set, which contains the levels of the various resources required by the different activities. This statement is required when the activities in the network use limited resources and a schedule is to be determined subject to resource constraints in addition to precedence constraints.

This statement is also necessary if the procedure is required to summarize resource utilization for various resources. The resources required by the different activities and the amounts required are specified in the DATA= input data set.

The levels of the various resources available are obtained from the RESOURCEIN= data set, which need not contain all the variables listed in the RESOURCE statement. If any resource variable specified in the RESOURCE statement is not also found in the RESOURCEIN= data set, it is assumed to be available in unlimited quantity and is not used in determining the constrained schedule.

The following options are available with the RESOURCE statement to help control scheduling the activities subject to resource constraints.

Resource allocation control options

ACTIVITYPRTY=*variable*
ACTPRTY=*variable*

> required if resource-constrained scheduling is to be performed and the scheduling rule specified is ACTPRTY. This option identifies the variable in the input data set that contains the priority of each activity. If SCHEDRULE=ACTPRTY, then all activities waiting for resources are ordered by increasing values of the ACTPRTY variable. Missing values of the priority variable are treated as + INFINITY.

DELAY=*delay*

> specifies the maximum amount by which an activity can be delayed due to lack of resources. If E_START of an activity is 1JUN85 and L_START is 5JUN85 and DELAY is specified as 2, CPM first tries to schedule the activity to start on 1JUN85. If there are not enough resources to schedule the activity CPM postpones the activity's start time. However it does not postpone it beyond 7JUN85 (since DELAY=2 and L_START=5JUN85).
>
> If the activity cannot be scheduled even on 7JUN85 then CPM tries to schedule it by using supplementary levels of resources, if available. If resources are still not sufficient, the procedure stops with an error message. The default value of DELAY is assumed to be + INFINITY.

OBSTYPE=*variable*

> specifies a character variable in the RESOURCEIN= data set that contains the type identifier for each observation. Valid values for this variable are RESLEVEL, RESTYPE, RESPRTY, or SUPLEVEL. If OBSTYPE= is not specified, then all observations in the data set are assumed to denote the levels of the resources, and all resources are assumed to be replenishable.

PERIOD=*variable*

> specifies the variable in the RESOURCEIN= data set that specifies the date from which a specified level of the resource is available for each observation containing levels of the resources. It is an error if the PERIOD= variable has a missing value for any observation specifying the levels of the resources or if the RESOURCEIN= data set is not sorted in increasing order of the PERIOD= variable.

SCHEDRULE=*rule*
RULE=*rule*

> specifies the rule to be used to order the list of activities whose predecessor activities have been completed while scheduling activities subject to resource constraints. Valid values for *rule* are LST, LFT, SHORTDUR, ACTPRTY, and RESPRTY. (For details see the section **Scheduling Rules**.) The default value of SCHEDRULE is LST. If a wrong specification is given for the SCHEDRULE= option, the

default value is used, and a message is printed on the log to this effect.

Options controlling RESOURCEOUT= data set

ALL

is equivalent to specifying both options ESPROFILE and LSPROFILE when an unconstrained schedule is obtained and equivalent to specifying all four options, AVPROFILE (AVP), ESPROFILE (ESP), LSPROFILE (LSP), and RCPROFILE (RCP), when a resource-constrained schedule is obtained. If none of the four options (AVP, ESP, LSP, RCP) is specified and a RESOUT= data set is specified, by default the ALL option is assumed to be in effect.

AVPROFILE
AVP
AVL

creates one variable in the RESOURCEOUT= data set corresponding to each variable in the RESOURCE statement. These new variables denote the amount of resources remaining after resource allocation. This option is ignored if resource allocation is not done.

ESPROFILE
ESP
ESS

creates one variable in the RESOURCEOUT= data set corresponding to each variable in the RESOURCE statement. Each new variable denotes the resource usage based on the early start schedule for the corresponding resource variable.

LSPROFILE
LSP
LSS

creates one variable in the RESOURCEOUT= data set corresponding to each variable in the RESOURCE statement. Each new variable denotes the resource usage based on the late start schedule for the corresponding resource variable.

MAXOBS=*max*

specifies an upper limit on the number of observations that the RESOURCEOUT= data set can contain. If the values specified for ROUTINTERVAL= and ROUTINTPER= are such that the data set will contain more than *max* observations, then CPM does not create the output data set; it stops with an error message.

The MAXOBS= option is useful as a check to ensure that a very large data set (with several thousands of observations) is not created due to a wrong specification of the ROUTINTERVAL= parameter. For example, if INTERVAL=DTYEAR and ROUTINTERVAL=DTHOUR and the project extends over 2 years, the number of observations would exceed 15,000 observations. The default value of MAXOBS= is 1000.

RCPROFILE
RCP
RCS

creates one variable in the RESOURCEOUT= data set corresponding to each variable in the RESOURCE statement. Each new variable denotes the resource usage based on the resource-constrained schedule for the corresponding resource variable. This option is ignored if resource allocation is not done.

ROUTINTERVAL=*routinterval*
STEPINT=*routinterval*

> specifies the units to be used to determine the time interval between two successive values of the variable _TIME_ in the RESOURCEOUT= data set. It can be used in conjunction with the ROUTINTPER= option to control the amount of information to be presented in the data set. Valid values for ROUTINTERVAL= are DAY, WORKDAY, WEEK, MONTH, WEEKDAY, QTR, YEAR, DTDAY, DTWRKDAY, DTWEEK, DTMONTH, DTQTR, DTYEAR, DTSECOND, DTMINUTE, DTHOUR, SECOND, MINUTE, or HOUR.
>
> The default value is chosen by the procedure in an appropriate manner. For example, if the E_START times are formatted as DATE values, then ROUTINTERVAL is set to be DAY; if they are unformatted numeric values, ROUTINTERVAL is ' ' and _TIME_ is incremented in steps of one. The value of this parameter must be chosen carefully; a massive amount of data could be generated by a bad choice.

ROUTINTPER=*number*
STEPSIZE=*number*
STEP=*number*

> specifies the number of *routinterval* units between successive observations in the RESOURCEOUT= data set when ROUTINTERVAL=*routinterval* is specified. For example, if ROUTINTERVAL=MONTH and ROUTINTPER=2, the time interval between each pair of observations in the RESOURCEOUT= data set is two months. The default value of ROUTINTPER is 1. If the value of ROUTINTERVAL is ' ', then ROUTINTPER can be used to specify the exact numeric interval between two successive values of the variable _TIME_ in the RESOURCEOUT= data set.

Options controlling OUT= data set

E_START

> requests that the OUT= data set also include the early start schedule, namely, the E_START and E_FINISH variables. Note that if resource allocation is not done, these variables are always included in the output data set.

L_START

> requests that the OUT= data set also include the late start schedule, namely, the L_START and L_FINISH variables. Note that if resource allocation is not done, these variables are always included in the output data set.

RESOURCEVARS
RESVARSOUT

> requests that the variables specified in the RESOURCE statement also be included in the OUT= data set.

SUCCESSOR Statement

SUCCESSOR *variables*;

The SUCCESSOR statement is required when data are input in an activity-on-node format. It specifies the variables that contain the names of the immediate successor nodes (activities) to the ACTIVITY node. These variables must be of the same type as those defined in the ACTIVITY statement.

TAILNODE Statement

   TAILNODE *variable*;

The TAILNODE statement is required when data are input in activity-on-arc (arrow notation) format. It specifies the variable that contains the name of each node on the tail of an arc in the project network. This node is identified with the event that signals the start of the activity on that arc. The variable specified can be either a numeric or character variable since the procedure treats this variable symbolically. Each node must be uniquely defined.

DETAILS

Specifying the INTERVAL= Option

The INTERVAL= option enables you to define a standard workday (8 hours) and to schedule only within those hours. When you use INTERVAL=WORKDAY, the procedure schedules work on weekdays and non-holidays starting at 9 a.m. and ending at 5 p.m. If you use INTERVAL=DTWRKDAY, the procedure also schedules work only on weekdays and non-holidays. In this case, however, the procedure assumes the DATE= option equals a SAS datetime value, and the procedure interprets the start of the workday from the time portion of that option. To change the length of the workday, use the DAYLENGTH= option in conjunction with INTERVAL=DTWRKDAY. If you use INTERVAL=DTHOUR, INTERVAL= DTMINUTE, or INTERVAL=DTSECOND, the value of the DATE= option is interpreted as a SAS datetime value and gives the length of one unit of duration. For example, if INTERVAL=DTMINUTE, each unit of duration is assumed to be one minute.

   If the value of INTERVAL is specified as YEAR, MONTH, QTR, WEEK, DTYEAR, DTMONTH, DTQTR, or DTWEEK, and none of the durations are fractional, then the start and finish times are specified as the **beginning** of the appropriate period. Thus, if INTERVAL is DTQTR, all the start and finish times are specified as midnight of the first day of the appropriate quarter.

Resource Allocation

Often the activities in a project use several resources. If you assume that these resources are available in unlimited quantities, then the only restrictions on the start and finish times of the activities in the project are those imposed by the precedence constraints and dates specified for alignment of the activities. In most practical situations, however, there are limitations on the availability of resources; as a result, neither the early start schedule nor the late start schedule (nor any intermediate schedule for that matter) may be feasible. In such cases, the project manager is faced with the task of scheduling the activities in the project subject to constraints on resource availability, in addition to precedence constraints and constraints on the start and finish times of certain activities in the project. This problem is known as Resource Allocation.

   You can use PROC CPM to schedule the activities in a project subject to resource constraints. To perform resource allocation you must specify the resource requirements for each activity in the project, and also specify the amount of resources available on each day under consideration. The resource requirements are specified in the input data set, with the variable names identified to PROC CPM through the RESOURCE statement. The levels of resources available on different dates, as well as other information regarding the resources, such as the type of resource, the priority of the resource, and so forth, are obtained from the RESOURCEIN= data set.

Specifying resource requirements is described in detail in the section **Specification of Resource Requirements**, and the description of the format of the RESOURCEIN= data set is given in the section **RESOURCEIN= Input Data Set**. The section **Scheduling Method** describes how you can use the SCHEDRULE= and DELAY= options in conjunction with certain special observations in the RESOURCEIN= data set to control the process of resource allocation to suit your needs.

RESOURCEIN= input data set This data set contains all the necessary information about the resources that are to be used by PROC CPM to schedule the project. Typically, the RESOURCEIN= data set contains the resource variables (numeric), a type identifier variable (character) that identifies the type of information in each observation, and a period variable (numeric and usually a SAS time, date, or datetime variable). The value of the type identifier variable in each observation tells CPM how to interpret that observation. Valid values for this variable are RESLEVEL, RESTYPE, RESPRTY, and SUPLEVEL. If the value of the type identifier variable in a particular observation is RESLEVEL, then that observation contains the levels available for each resource from the time specified in the period variable. Missing values are not allowed for the period variable in an observation containing the levels of the resources.

Each resource can be classified as either consumable or replenishable. A consumable resource is one that is used up by the job (like brick, money, and so forth), while a replenishable resource becomes available again once a job using it is over (such as manpower, machinery, and so forth). If the value of the type identifier variable is RESTYPE, then that observation identifies the nature (consumable or replenishable) of the resource—the observation contains a value '1' for a replenishable resource and a value '2' for a consumable one. A missing value in this observation is treated as '1'. In fact, if there is no observation in the RESOURCEIN= data set with the type identifier variable equal to RESTYPE, then all resources are assumed to be replenishable.

One of the scheduling rules that can be specified in the SCHEDRULE= option is RESPRTY, which requires ordering the resources according to some priority (details are given in the section **Scheduling Rules**). If this option is used, there must be an observation in the RESOURCEIN= data set with the type identifier variable taking the value RESPRTY. This observation then specifies the ordering of the resources.

If the type identifier variable is given as SUPLEVEL, the observation denotes the amount of 'extra' resource that is available for use throughout the duration of the project. This extra resource is used only if the activity cannot be delayed any further. See the section **Secondary Levels of Resources** for details about the use of supplementary levels of resources.

The period variable must have nonmissing values for observations specifying the levels of the resources (that is, with type identifier equal to RESLEVEL). However, the period variable does not have any meaning when the type identifier variable has values RESTYPE, RESPRTY, or SUPLEVEL; if the period variable has nonmissing values in these observations, it is ignored. It is assumed that the data set is sorted in order of increasing values of the period variable. You can specify only one observation of each of the types RESTYPE, RESPRTY, and SUPLEVEL; if you specify more than one observation of any of these three types, only the first one is used.

A resource is available at the specified level from the time given in the first observation with a nonmissing value for the level of the resource. Its level changes to a new one whenever a new observation is encountered with a nonmissing value of level for this resource, and the date of change to this new level is the date specified in this new observation.

The following example illustrates the details about the RESOURCEIN= data set. Consider the following data:

```
OBSTYPE    DATE      WORKERS    BRICKS

RESTYPE       .          1         2
RESPRTY       .         10        10
SUPLEVEL      .          1         .
RESLEVEL   1JUL85        .      1000
RESLEVEL   5JUL85        4         .
RESLEVEL   9JUL85        .      1500
```

In this example there are two resources, 'WORKERS' and 'BRICKS'. The variable named OBSTYPE is the type identifier, and the variable named DATE is the period variable. The first observation (since OBSTYPE has value RESTYPE) indicates that WORKERS is a replenishable resource and BRICKS is a consumable resource. The second observation indicates that both resources have equal priority. In the third observation, a '1' under WORKERS indicates that a supplementary level of 1 'worker' is available if necessary, while no reserve is available for the resource BRICKS.

The next three observations indicate the resource availability profile. The resource WORKERS is unavailable until July 5, 1985 when the level jumps from 0 to 4 and remains at that level through the end of the project. The resource BRICKS is available from July 1, 1985 at level 1000. On July 9 an additional 500 bricks are made available to increase the total availability to 1500. Note that missing values in observations 5 and 6 indicate that there is no change in the availability for the respective resources.

Specification of resource requirements   To perform resource allocation or to summarize the resource utilization, it is necessary to specify the amount of resources required by each activity. In this section we describe the format for this specification. The amount required by each activity, for each of the resources listed in the RESOURCE statement, is specified in the DATA= input data set. The requirements for each activity are assumed to be constant throughout the activity's duration. A missing value for a resource variable in the input data set indicates that the particular resource is not required for the activity in that observation.

The interpretation of the specification depends on whether or not the resource is replenishable. Suppose that the value for a given resource variable in a particular observation is x. If the resource is replenishable, it indicates that x units of the resource are required throughout the duration of the activity specified in that observation. On the other hand, if the resource is consumable, it indicates that the specified resource is consumed at the rate of x units per unit *interval*, where *interval* is the value specified in the INTERVAL= option in the PROC CPM statement. For example, consider the following specification:

```
ACTIVITY    DUR    WORKERS    BRICKS

a            5         .        100
b            4         2          .
```

Here ACTIVITY denotes the activity under consideration, DUR is the duration in days (that is, INTERVAL=DAY), and the resource variables are WORKERS and

BRICKS. A missing value for WORKERS in observation 1 indicates that activity a does not need the resource WORKERS while the same is true for the resource BRICKS and activity b. Here we assume that the resource WORKERS has been identified as replenishable, and the resource BRICKS has been identified as consumable in a RESOURCEIN= data set. Thus, a value 100 for the consumable resource BRICKS indicates that 100 bricks per day are required for each of the 5 days of a's duration, and a value 2 for the replenishable resource WORKERS indicates that 2 workers are required throughout the duration (4 days) of activity b.

Scheduling method CPM uses the serial-parallel (serial in time and parallel in activities) method of scheduling. This method proceeds through the following steps:

Step 1   An initial tentative schedule describing the early and late start and finish times is determined without taking any resource constraints into account. This schedule does, however, reflect any restrictions placed on the start and finish times by the use of the ALIGNDATE and ALIGNTYPE statements (or the use of DATE= and ALIGN= options in the PROC CPM statement). As far as possible CPM tries to schedule each activity to start at its E_START time (as calculated in this step). Set TIME=*min*(E_START), where the minimum is taken over all activities in the network.

Step 2   All the activities whose E_START coincide with TIME are arranged in a waiting list that is sorted according to the rule specified in the SCHEDRULE= option. (See the section **Scheduling Rules** for details on the valid values of this option.) CPM tries to schedule the activities in the same order as on this list. For each activity the procedure checks to see if the required amount of each resource will be available throughout the activity's duration; if enough resources are available the activity is scheduled to start at TIME, otherwise it is postponed. If TIME is equal to or greater than the value of L_START + DELAY and not enough resources are available, the procedure tries to obtain supplementary resources (if there was an observation in the RESOURCEIN= data set specifying supplementary levels of resources). If the procedure is still unable to schedule the activity, it stops with an error message, giving a partial schedule.

Note that if the DELAY= option is unspecified, it is assumed to be +INFINITY and, hence, supplementary resources will never be used (since supplementary resources are used only if the activity has not been scheduled to start before L_START + DELAY). Further, once the activity that uses a supplementary level of a **replenishable** resource is over, the supplementary level that was used is returned to the 'reservoir' and is not used again until needed.

For consumable resources, if supplementary levels were used on a particular date, PROC CPM attempts to bring the 'reservoir' back to the original level at the earliest possible time; in other words, the next time the primary availability of the resource increases, it is first used to replenish the supplementary level of the resource (see **Example 6**). Adjustment is made to the resource availability profile to account for any activity that is scheduled to start at TIME.

Step 3   All the activities in the waiting list that were unable to be scheduled in Step 2 are postponed and are tentatively scheduled to start at the time when the next change takes place in the resource availability profile (that is, their E_START is set to the next change date in the availability of resources). An updated schedule of E_START, E_FINISH, L_START, and L_FINISH is determined for all the activities that are yet to be scheduled. TIME is advanced to the minimum E_START time of all unscheduled activities, and Steps 1, 2, and 3 are repeated until all activities are scheduled or the procedure stops with an error message.

Some important points to keep in mind are

- Holidays are automatically accounted for in the process of resource allocation. Do not specify zero availabilities for the resources on holidays; CPM skips holidays and weekends if needed during resource allocation just as in the unrestricted case.
- It is assumed that the activities cannot be interrupted once they are started. If you wish to allow an activity, A, to be split, you can divide it into component parts A1, A2, A3, for instance, with A3 as an immediate successor to A2 and A2 as an immediate successor to A1. Then CPM attempts to schedule the three parts, one after another, if resources permit.

Scheduling rules   The SCHEDRULE= option specifies the criterion to use for determining the order in which activities are to be considered while scheduling them subject to resource constraints. As described in the section **Scheduling Method**, at a time given by TIME, all activities whose tentative E_START coincides with TIME are arranged in a list ordered according to *rule*. The five valid values of *rule* are listed below along with a brief description of their respective effects:

LST
    specifies that the activities in the waiting list are sorted in the order of increasing L_START time. Thus, this option causes activities that are closer to being critical to be scheduled first.

LFT
    specifies that the activities in the waiting list are sorted in the order of increasing L_FINISH time.

SHORTDUR
    specifies that the activities in the waiting list are sorted in the order of increasing durations. Thus, CPM tries to schedule activities with shorter durations first.

ACTPRTY
    specifies that CPM sort the activities in the waiting list in the order of increasing values of the variable specified in the ACTIVITYPRTY= option in the RESOURCE statement. This variable specifies a user-

assigned priority to each activity in the project (low value of the variable indicates high priority).

Note that if SCHEDRULE is specified as ACTPRTY, the RESOURCE statement **must** contain the specification of the variable in the input data set that assigns priorities to the activities; if the variable name is not specified through the ACTIVITYPRTY= option, then CPM ignores the specification for the SCHEDRULE= option and uses the default scheduling rule of LST instead.

RESPRTY

specifies that CPM should expect an observation in the RESOURCEIN= data set identified by the value RESPRTY for the type identifier variable and specifying priorities for the resources. CPM uses these priority values (once again low values indicate high priority) to order the activities; the activities are ordered according to the highest priority resource that they use. In other words, CPM uses the resource priorities to assign priorities to the activities in the project; these activity priorities are then used to order the activities in the waiting list (in increasing order). If this option is specified and there is no observation in the RESOURCEIN= data set specifying the resource priorities, CPM ignores the specification for the SCHEDRULE= option and uses the default scheduling rule of LST instead.

Secondary levels of resources and the DELAY= option   These are two features that you can use to control the process of scheduling subject to resource constraints. In some applications time is an important factor and you may be willing to use extra resources in order to meet project deadlines; on the other hand, there may be cases where you are willing to allow the project completion to be delayed by an arbitrary amount if insufficient resources warrant doing so. In the first case you can specify the availability of supplementary resources in the RESOURCEIN= data set and set DELAY=0. In the latter case, set DELAY equal to some very large number or leave it unspecified (in which case it is assumed to be + INFINITY). You can achieve a combination of both effects (using supplementary levels and setting a limit on the delay allowed) by specifying an intermediate value for the DELAY= option and including an observation in the RESOURCEIN= data set with supplementary levels.

OUT= Output Data Set

The output data set always contains the variables in the input data set that are listed in the TAILNODE, HEADNODE, ACTIVITY, SUCCESSOR, DURATION, or ID statements. If the INTPER= option is specified in the PROC CPM statement, then the values of the DURATION variable in the output data set are obtained by multiplying the corresponding values in the input data set by INTPER. Thus, the values in the output data set are the durations used by CPM to compute the schedule. If the procedure was used without specifying a RESOURCEIN= data set and only the unconstrained schedule was obtained, then the output data set contains six new variables named E_START, L_START, E_FINISH, L_FINISH, T_FLOAT, and F_FLOAT.

If a resource-constrained schedule was obtained, however, the output data set contains only two new variables named S_START and S_FINISH. If you want the early start or late start schedule to be included in the data set in addition to S_START and S_FINISH, you can request them by specifying the E_START and L_START options in the RESOURCE statement. If you want the variables listed in the RESOURCE statement to be included in the output data set, use the

RESOURCEVARS option in the RESOURCE statement. Except for T_FLOAT and F_FLOAT, the format of the new variables in this data set is consistent with the format of the DATE= option in the PROC CPM statement. Since each observation in the input data set identifies a new activity either on a node or on an arc, each observation in the output data set is also associated with an activity. For each activity, the variables have the following meanings:

E_FINISH
> completion time if the activity is started at the early start time.

E_START
> earliest time the activity can be started.

F_FLOAT
> free float time, which is the difference between the early finish time of the activity and the early start time of the activity's immediate successors. Consequently, it is the maximum delay that can be tolerated in the activity without affecting the scheduling of a successor activity.

L_FINISH
> completion time if the activity is started at the late start time.

L_START
> latest time the activity can be started.

S_FINISH
> the completion time for the activity under the resource-constrained schedule.

S_START
> the resource-constrained start time of the activity.

T_FLOAT
> the total float time, which is the difference between the activity late start time and early start time. Consequently, it is the maximum delay that can be tolerated in performing the activity and still complete the project on schedule. If the activity is on the critical path, then T_FLOAT=0.

RESOURCEOUT= Data Set

This data set contains information about the resource usage for the resources specified in the RESOURCE statement. The options ALL, AVPROFILE, ESPROFILE, LSPROFILE, and RCPROFILE (each is defined above in the section **RESOURCE Statement**) control the number of variables that are to be created in this data set. The options ROUTINTERVAL and ROUTINTPER control the number of observations that this data set is to contain. Of the options listed above, AVPROFILE and RCPROFILE are allowed only if the procedure is used to obtain a resource-constrained schedule.

   The data set always contains a variable named _TIME_ that specifies the date for which the resource usage or availability in the observation is valid. For each of the variables specified in the RESOURCE statement, one, two, three, or four new variables are created depending on how many of the four options AVPROFILE, ESPROFILE, LSPROFILE, and RCPROFILE are in effect. If none of these four options is specified, the ALL option is assumed to be in effect. Recall that the ALL option is equivalent to specifying ESPROFILE and LSPROFILE when CPM is used to obtain an unconstrained schedule and is equivalent to specifying all four options (AVPROFILE, ESPROFILE, LSPROFILE, and RCPROFILE) when CPM is used to obtain a resource-constrained schedule.

The new variables are named according to the following convention:

- The prefix A is used for the variable describing the resource availability profile.
- E is used for the variable denoting the early start usage.
- L is used for the variable denoting the late start usage.
- R is used for the variable denoting the resource-constrained usage.

The suffix is the name of the resource variable if the name is less than 8 characters; if the name is 8 characters long, the suffix is formed by concatenating the first 4 and last 3 characters of the variable name. The user must ensure that this naming convention results in unique variable names in the RESOURCEOUT= data set.

ROUTINTERVAL=*routinterval* and ROUTINTPER=*n* specify that two successive values of the _TIME_ variable differ by *n* number of *routinterval* units. If the value of ROUTINTERVAL is not specified, CPM chooses a default value depending on the format of the start and finish variables in the OUT= data set. The value of ROUTINTERVAL (STEPINT) used is indicated in a message written to the SAS log. Note that holidays used during the computation of the schedule are skipped in the RESOURCEOUT= data set. In other words, if ROUTINTERVAL=DAY and July 4, 1985 is specified as a holiday, the RESOURCEOUT= data set does not contain an observation with _TIME_ =4JUL85.

Interpretation of new variables   The availability profile indicates the amount of resources available at the **beginning** of the time interval specified in the _TIME_ variable after accounting for the resources used through the previous time period. For replenishable resources, the usage profiles indicate the amount of resource used, while for consumable resources they indicate the rate of usage per unit *routinterval* at the start of the time interval specified in the _TIME_ variable. The following example illustrates the interpretation.

Suppose that for the data given earlier, activities a and b have S_START equal to 1JUL85 and 5JUL85, respectively. If the RESOURCE statement had the options AVPROFILE and RCPROFILE, the RESOURCEOUT= data set would have these five variables, _TIME_, RWORKERS, AWORKERS, RBRICKS, and ABRICKS. Suppose further that ROUTINTERVAL=DAY and ROUTINTPER=1. The RESOURCEOUT= data set would contain the following observations:

TIME	RWORKERS	AWORKERS	RBRICKS	ABRICKS
1JUL85	0	0	100	1000
2JUL85	0	0	100	900
3JUL85	0	0	100	800
4JUL85	0	0	100	700
5JUL85	2	2	100	600
6JUL85	2	2	0	500
7JUL85	2	2	0	500
8JUL85	2	2	0	500
9JUL85	0	4	0	1000

On each day of activity a's duration, the resource BRICKS is consumed at the rate of 100 bricks per day. At the beginning of the first day (July 1, 1985), all 1000 bricks are still available. Note that each day the availability drops by 100 bricks, which is the rate of consumption. On July 5 activity b is scheduled to start. On the four days starting with July 5 the value of RWORKERS is 2, indicating that 2 workers are used on each of those days leaving an available supply of 2 workers (AWORKERS is equal to 2 on all 4 days). If, in this example, ROUTINTPER is set to 2, then the observations would be as below:

TIME	RWORKERS	AWORKERS	RBRICKS	ABRICKS
1JUL85	0	0	100	1000
3JUL85	0	0	100	800
5JUL85	2	2	100	600
7JUL85	2	2	0	500
9JUL85	0	4	0	1000

Note that the value of RBRICKS remains 100 in the first 3 observations since RBRICKS denotes the rate of consumption of the resource BRICKS per **day** on the days specified by the variable _TIME_ in the respective observations.

On a day when supplementary levels of resources were used through the beginning of the day, the value for the availability profile for the relevant resources is negative; the absolute magnitude of this value denotes the amount of supplementary resource that was used through the beginning of the day. For instance, if ABRICKS is −100 on 11JUL85, it indicates that 100 bricks from the supplementary 'reservoir' were used through the end of July 10, 1985.

Missing Values

In the DATA= input data set, missing values for the variables listed in the SUCCESSOR statement, the ALIGNDATE statement, the ID statement, and the RESOURCE statement are treated as missing. Missing values are not allowed for the variables in the DURATION statement, the HEADNODE statement, the TAILNODE statement, and the ACTIVITY statement. A missing value for the variable in the ALIGNTYPE statement is treated as missing if the corresponding value for the ALIGNDATE variable is also missing; otherwise, the alignment is assumed to be of the type 'SGE'. A missing value for the ACTIVITYPRTY variable is treated as + INFINITY.

In the RESOURCEIN= input data set, for variables in the RESOURCE statement, the treatment of missing values in an observation depends on the value of the type identifier variable (the OBSTYPE= variable) in that observation. If the observation denotes levels of resources, a missing value indicates that the level for that resource is unchanged from the previous change date (initially the levels are assumed to be 0). If the observation denotes type of resource, missing values default to 1 (indicating that the resource is replenishable); if the observation denotes resource priority, missing values default to + INFINITY; and if the observation indicates supplementary levels of resources, missing values are treated as 0. A missing value for the OBSTYPE= variable is treated as 'RESLEVEL'. The PERIOD variable cannot have missing values in observations denoting levels of resources.

EXAMPLES

Introduction

This section contains twelve examples that illustrate several of the features of PROC CPM. **Example 1** shows how to use PROC CPM to find the critical path in a network using either the activity-on-arc format or the activity-on-node format. **Example 2** shows how you can exhibit the output from PROC CPM on a calendar, while **Example 3** illustrates the use of PROC GANTT to display the schedule. **Example 4** shows one way of including uncertainty about durations while scheduling.

In **Example 5**, the HOLIDATA= option is used in conjunction with the HOLIDAY statement to schedule the project around holidays. **Example 6** shows you how to use the DAYLENGTH= option with the specification of INTERVAL= WORKDAY or DTWRKDAY to schedule work only on weekdays during a selected part of the day. In **Example 7** the HOLIDAY statement is used to schedule work on a 6-day week. **Example 8** illustrates the use of the FINISHBEFORE option to schedule the project to finish before a specified date; it also shows how the ALIGN= option can be used to align any given activity to start or finish on a particular date. In **Example 9** the ALIGNDATE and ALIGNTYPE statements are used to impose restrictions on the start times of two activities simultaneously.

Example 10 uses the RESOURCEOUT= option together with the RESOURCE statement to summarize resource utilization and save the summary information in an output data set. **Example 11** illustrates the use of PROC CPM to schedule the activities in the network subject to resource limitations. In **Example 12** the DELAY= option is used to illustrate the use of a supplementary level of resources.

Scheduling a Construction Project: Example 1

This example shows how to use CPM to find the critical path in a small network when data are input in both the activity-on-arc format and the activity-on-node format. The problem is one of scheduling the times to begin several tasks in a construction project. Because of the nature of the project, some of the tasks must be completed before others can be started.

Table 3.2 summarizes the relationship among the tasks and gives the duration in days to complete each task. The table shows the relationship among tasks by listing the immediate successors to each task—the activities that can be started only upon completion of the predecessor task. For example, since the well must be drilled before the pump house can be constructed, the task DRILL WELL has as its immediate successor the task PUMP HOUSE.

Table 3.2   Summary of Task Relationships and Task Completion Times

TASK	DURATION	IMMEDIATE SUCCESSORS
DRILL WELL	4	PUMP HOUSE
PUMP HOUSE	3	INSTALL PIPE
POWER LINE	3	INSTALL PIPE
EXCAVATE	5	INSTALL PIPE, INSTALL PUMP, FOUNDATION
DELIVER MATERIAL	2	ASSEMBLE TANK
ASSEMBLE TANK	4	ERECT TOWER
FOUNDATION	4	ERECT TOWER
INSTALL PIPE	2	
INSTALL PUMP	6	
ERECT TOWER	6	

INSTALL PIPE, INSTALL PUMP, and ERECT TOWER have no activities as successors since completion of these tasks completes the project. These activities are included in this list in order to specify their durations.

The relationship among the tasks can be represented by the following network.

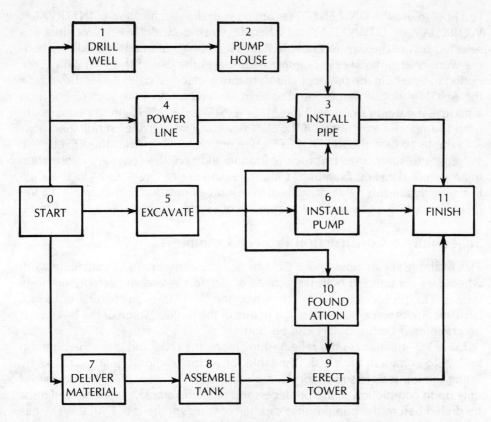

Figure 3.1 Network Showing Task Relationships as Represented in Activity-on-Node Format

The project is represented in activity-on-node format. The following DATA step reads the network in this activity-on-node format into a SAS data set.

```
DATA EXMP1;
   INPUT TASK      $ 1-16
      DURATION
      SUCCESR1 $ 21-35
      SUCCESR2 $ 36-50
      SUCCESR3 $ 51-65;
   CARDS;
DRILL WELL        4  PUMP HOUSE
PUMP HOUSE        3  INSTALL PIPE
POWER LINE        3  INSTALL PIPE
EXCAVATE          5  INSTALL PIPE     INSTALL PUMP    FOUNDATION
DELIVER MATERIAL  2  ASSEMBLE TANK
ASSEMBLE TANK     4  ERECT TOWER
FOUNDATION        4  ERECT TOWER
INSTALL PUMP      6
INSTALL PIPE      2
ERECT TOWER       6
;
```

To find the critical path for this network, call CPM with the statements:

```
TITLE 'SCHEDULING A CONSTRUCTION PROJECT';
TITLE2 'ACTIVITY-ON-NODE FORMAT';
```

```
PROC CPM;
    ACTIVITY TASK;
    DURATION DURATION;
    SUCCESSOR SUCCESR1 SUCCESR2 SUCCESR3;
```

CPM produces the data set in **Output 3.1**.

Output 3.1   Using PROC CPM to Schedule Problems in Activity-on-Node Format

```
                          SCHEDULING A CONSTRUCTION PROJECT                                    1
                              ACTIVITY-ON-NODE FORMAT

OBS TASK            SUCCESR1      SUCCESR2      SUCCESR3    DURATION E_START E_FINISH L_START L_FINISH T_FLOAT F_FLOAT

  1 DRILL WELL      PUMP HOUSE                                 4       0       4       6      10       6       0
  2 PUMP HOUSE      INSTALL PIPE                               3       4       7      10      13       6       0
  3 POWER LINE      INSTALL PIPE                               3       0       3      10      13      10       4
  4 EXCAVATE        INSTALL PIPE  INSTALL PUMP FOUNDATION      5       0       5       0       5       0       0
  5 DELIVER MATERIAL ASSEMBLE TANK                             2       0       2       3       5       3       0
  6 ASSEMBLE TANK   ERECT TOWER                                4       2       6       5       9       3       3
  7 FOUNDATION      ERECT TOWER                                4       5       9       5       9       0       0
  8 INSTALL PUMP                                               6       5      11       9      15       4       4
  9 INSTALL PIPE                                               2       7       9      13      15       6       6
 10 ERECT TOWER                                                6       9      15       9      15       0       0
```

The data set output by CPM contains the solution in days. It shows that the early start time for DRILL WELL is the beginning of day 0, and the early finish time is the beginning of day 4. Alternatively, if you know that the project is to start on the first of July 1985, then you might want to solve the problem using the following statements:

```
PROC CPM DATE='1JUL85'D;
    ACTIVITY TASK;
    DURATION DURATION;
    SUCCESSOR SUCCESR1 SUCCESR2 SUCCESR3;
    TITLE2 'DATED SCHEDULE';
```

The additional specification of the DATE= parameter results in the output data set shown in **Output 3.2**.

Output 3.2   Finding the Critical Path in a Small Network with the DATE= Parameter Specified

```
                          SCHEDULING A CONSTRUCTION PROJECT                                    2
                                  DATED SCHEDULE

OBS TASK            SUCCESR1      SUCCESR2      SUCCESR3    DURATION E_START   E_FINISH  L_START   L_FINISH T_FLOAT F_FLOAT

  1 DRILL WELL      PUMP HOUSE                                 4    01JUL85  04JUL85  07JUL85  10JUL85    6       0
  2 PUMP HOUSE      INSTALL PIPE                               3    05JUL85  07JUL85  11JUL85  13JUL85    6       0
  3 POWER LINE      INSTALL PIPE                               3    01JUL85  03JUL85  11JUL85  13JUL85   10       4
  4 EXCAVATE        INSTALL PIPE  INSTALL PUMP FOUNDATION      5    01JUL85  05JUL85  01JUL85  05JUL85    0       0
  5 DELIVER MATERIAL ASSEMBLE TANK                             2    01JUL85  02JUL85  04JUL85  05JUL85    3       0
  6 ASSEMBLE TANK   ERECT TOWER                                4    03JUL85  06JUL85  06JUL85  09JUL85    3       3
  7 FOUNDATION      ERECT TOWER                                4    06JUL85  09JUL85  06JUL85  09JUL85    0       0
  8 INSTALL PUMP                                               6    06JUL85  11JUL85  10JUL85  15JUL85    4       4
  9 INSTALL PIPE                                               2    08JUL85  09JUL85  14JUL85  15JUL85    6       6
 10 ERECT TOWER                                                6    10JUL85  15JUL85  10JUL85  15JUL85    0       0
```

In this case the early start time for DRILL WELL is the beginning of 01JUL85, and the early completion time is the end of 04JUL85.

The same problem can be described in an activity-on-arc format. The network representation is shown in **Figure 3.2**.

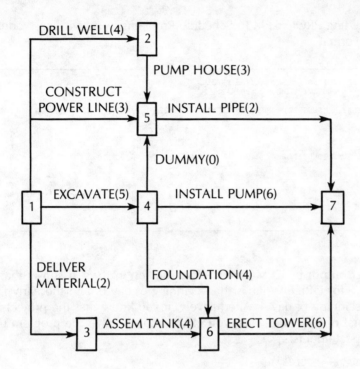

Figure 3.2   Network Showing Task Relationships as Represented in Activity-on-Arc Format

The number in brackets following each activity is the activity's duration in days. The arc labeled DUMMY is used to capture the precedence relationship between the tasks EXCAVATE and INSTALL PIPE. Dummy arcs are often needed when representing scheduling problems in activity-on-arc format. The following DATA statement saves the network description in a SAS data set.

```
DATA CONST1;
   INPUT ACTIVITY $ 1-20 TAIL 22 DUR 24 HEAD 26;
   CARDS;
DRILL WELL            1 4 2
PUMP HOUSE            2 3 5
INSTALL PIPE          5 2 7
CONSTRUCT POWER LINE 1 3 5
EXCAVATE             1 5 4
INSTALL PUMP          4 6 7
DELIVER MATERIAL      1 2 3
ASSEMBLE TANK         3 4 6
ERECT TOWER           6 6 7
FOUNDATION            4 4 6
DUMMY                4 0 5
   ;
```

To find the critical path for this network when you know that the project is to start on July 1, 1985, invoke CPM with these statements:

```
PROC CPM DATE='1JUL85'D OUT=SAVE;
    TAILNODE TAIL;
    DURATION DUR;
    HEADNODE HEAD;
    ID ACTIVITY;
    TITLE2 'ACTIVITY-ON-ARC FORMAT';
```

The data set from CPM, named SAVE, is shown in **Output 3.3**.

Output 3.3   Using PROC CPM to Schedule Problems in Activity-on-Arc Format

```
                              SCHEDULING A CONSTRUCTION PROJECT                                    3
                                    ACTIVITY-ON-ARC FORMAT

OBS    TAIL    HEAD    DUR    ACTIVITY             E_START    E_FINISH    L_START    L_FINISH    T_FLOAT    F_FLOAT

  1      1       2      4     DRILL WELL           01JUL85    04JUL85     07JUL85    10JUL85        6          0
  2      2       5      3     PUMP HOUSE           05JUL85    07JUL85     11JUL85    13JUL85        6          0
  3      5       7      2     INSTALL PIPE         08JUL85    09JUL85     14JUL85    15JUL85        6          6
  4      1       5      3     CONSTRUCT POWER LINE 01JUL85    03JUL85     11JUL85    13JUL85       10          4
  5      1       4      5     EXCAVATE             01JUL85    05JUL85     01JUL85    05JUL85        0          0
  6      4       7      6     INSTALL PUMP         06JUL85    11JUL85     10JUL85    15JUL85        4          4
  7      1       3      2     DELIVER MATERIAL     01JUL85    02JUL85     04JUL85    05JUL85        3          0
  8      3       6      4     ASSEMBLE TANK        03JUL85    06JUL85     06JUL85    09JUL85        3          3
  9      6       7      6     ERECT TOWER          10JUL85    15JUL85     10JUL85    15JUL85        0          0
 10      4       6      4     FOUNDATION           06JUL85    09JUL85     06JUL85    09JUL85        0          0
 11      4       5      0     DUMMY                06JUL85    06JUL85     14JUL85    14JUL85        8          2
```

Printing the Schedules on Calendars: Example 2

This example shows how you can use the output from CPM to print calendars containing the critical path schedule, the late start schedule, and the early start schedule. The example uses the network described in the last example and assumes that SAVE contains the solution as printed above. The following statements print the three calenders:

```
DATA CRIT; SET SAVE;
    IF T_FLOAT>0 THEN DELETE;   /* KEEP ONLY THE CRITICAL ACTIVITIES */

PROC SORT DATA=CRIT;
    BY E_START;
RUN;

TITLE 'CALENDAR OF CRITICAL ACTIVITIES';
PROC CALENDAR SCHEDULE;         /* PRINT THE CRITICAL ACT. CALENDAR  */
    ID E_START;
    VAR ACTIVITY;
    DUR DUR;
RUN;

PROC SORT DATA=SAVE;            /* SORT DATA FOR LATE START CALENDAR */
    BY L_START;

TITLE 'LATE START CALENDAR';
PROC CALENDAR SCHEDULE;         /* PRINT THE LATE START CALENDAR     */
```

```
        ID L_START;
        VAR ACTIVITY;
        DUR DUR;
     RUN;

     PROC SORT DATA=SAVE;           /* SORT DATA FOR EARLY START CALENDAR*/
        BY E_START;


     TITLE 'EARLY START CALENDAR';
     PROC CALENDAR SCHEDULE;        /* PRINT THE EARLY START CALENDAR    */
        ID E_START;
        VAR ACTIVITY;
        DUR DUR;
     RUN;
```

This program produces the calendars in **Output 3.4**.

Output 3.4   Printing Schedule Calendars

```
+--------------------------------------------------------------------------------------------------------------------+
|                                          CALENDAR OF CRITICAL ACTIVITIES                                          1 |
| +------------------------------------------------------------------------------------------------------------------+
| |                                                                                                                  |
| |                                                   JULY   1985                                                    |
| +------------+------------+------------+------------+------------+------------+------------+                        |
| |   SUNDAY   |   MONDAY   |  TUESDAY   | WEDNESDAY  |  THURSDAY  |   FRIDAY   |  SATURDAY  |                        |
| +------------+------------+------------+------------+------------+------------+------------+                        |
| |            |     1      |     2      |     3      |     4      |     5      |     6      |                        |
| |            |            |            |            |            |            |            |                        |
| |            |            |            |            |            |            |            |                        |
| |            +============================EXCAVATE========================================+ +==FOUNDATION==>      |
| |     7      |     8      |     9      |    10      |    11      |    12      |    13      |                        |
| |            |            |            |            |            |            |            |                        |
| | <==================FOUNDATION==================+ +=============================ERECT TOWER========================> |
| |    14      |    15      |    16      |    17      |    18      |    19      |    20      |                        |
| |            |            |            |            |            |            |            |                        |
| | <=========ERECT TOWER==========+                                                        |                        |
| |    21      |    22      |    23      |    24      |    25      |    26      |    27      |                        |
| |            |            |            |            |            |            |            |                        |
| +------------+------------+------------+------------+------------+------------+------------+                        |
| |    28      |    29      |    30      |    31      |            |            |            |                        |
| |            |            |            |            |            |            |            |                        |
| +------------+------------+------------+------------+------------+------------+------------+                        |
+--------------------------------------------------------------------------------------------------------------------+
```

```
                        LATE START CALENDAR                                      2

+----------------------------------------------------------------------------------------------+
|                                                                                              |
|                                      JULY  1985                                               |
|                                                                                              |
+-------------+-------------+-------------+-------------+-------------+-------------+-------------+
|   SUNDAY    |   MONDAY    |   TUESDAY   |  WEDNESDAY  |  THURSDAY   |   FRIDAY    |  SATURDAY   |
+-------------+-------------+-------------+-------------+-------------+-------------+-------------+
|             |      1      |      2      |      3      |      4      |      5      |      6      |
|             |             |             |             |             |             |             |
|             |             |             |             |+=======DELIVER MATERIAL=========+|+==FOUNDATION===>|
|             |+===================================EXCAVATE===================================+|+ASSEMBLE TANK=>|
+-------------+-------------+-------------+-------------+-------------+-------------+-------------+
|      7      |      8      |      9      |     10      |     11      |     12      |     13      |
|             |             |             |             |+==============CONSTRUCT POWER LINE==============+|
|+==========================DRILL WELL============================+|+==================PUMP HOUSE===================+|
|<===================FOUNDATION===================+|+============================ERECT TOWER===============================>|
|<===================ASSEMBLE TANK================+|+===========================INSTALL PUMP================================>|
+-------------+-------------+-------------+-------------+-------------+-------------+-------------+
|     14      |     15      |     16      |     17      |     18      |     19      |     20      |
|             |             |             |             |             |             |             |
|+=========INSTALL PIPE==========+|                                                             |
|<==========ERECT TOWER==========+|                                                             |
|<==========INSTALL PUMP=========+|                                                             |
+-------------+-------------+-------------+-------------+-------------+-------------+-------------+
|     21      |     22      |     23      |     24      |     25      |     26      |     27      |
|             |             |             |             |             |             |             |
|             |             |             |             |             |             |             |
+-------------+-------------+-------------+-------------+-------------+-------------+-------------+
|     28      |     29      |     30      |     31      |             |             |             |
|             |             |             |             |             |             |             |
|             |             |             |             |             |             |             |
+-------------+-------------+-------------+-------------+-------------+-------------+-------------+
```

```
|                                                                                                      |
|                                            JULY  1985                                                |
|                                                                                                      |
|------------------------------------------------------------------------------------------------------|
|   SUNDAY    |    MONDAY    |   TUESDAY    |  WEDNESDAY   |   THURSDAY   |    FRIDAY    |   SATURDAY    |
|-------------|--------------|--------------|--------------|--------------|--------------|---------------|
|             |      1       |      2       |      3       |      4       |      5       |       6       |
|             |              |              |              |              |              |               |
|             +==============CONSTRUCT POWER LINE===============+              | +==========PUMP HOUSE===========>  +=INSTALL PUMP=>
|             +====================================DRILL WELL==============================+ +==========PUMP HOUSE===========>
|             +=======DELIVER MATERIAL========+ +======================================ASSEMBLE TANK============================+
|             +===================================EXCAVATE======================================+ +==FOUNDATION==>
|-------------|--------------|--------------|--------------|--------------|--------------|---------------|
|      7      |      8       |      9       |     10       |     11       |     12       |      13       |
|             |              |              |              |              |              |               |
|<====================================INSTALL PUMP=====================================+               |
|<====================FOUNDATION===================+                                                   |
|<==PUMP HOUSE==+ +=========INSTALL PIPE==========+ +============================ERECT TOWER===========================>
|-------------|--------------|--------------|--------------|--------------|--------------|---------------|
|     14      |     15       |     16       |     17       |     18       |     19       |      20       |
|             |              |              |              |              |              |               |
|<==========ERECT TOWER==========+                                                                     |
|-------------|--------------|--------------|--------------|--------------|--------------|---------------|
|     21      |     22       |     23       |     24       |     25       |     26       |      27       |
|             |              |              |              |              |              |               |
|             |              |              |              |              |              |               |
|-------------|--------------|--------------|--------------|--------------|--------------|---------------|
|     28      |     29       |     30       |     31       |              |              |               |
|             |              |              |              |              |              |               |
|             |              |              |              |              |              |               |
|------------------------------------------------------------------------------------------------------|
```

Printing a Gantt Chart: Example 3

This example prints a Gantt chart of the schedule obtained from PROC CPM. The example uses the network described in Example 1 (activity-on-arc format) and assumes that the data set SAVE contains the schedule sorted by the variable E_START. First, the dummy activity is deleted in a DATA step and PROC GANTT is invoked to print the Gantt chart in **Output 3.5**.

```
DATA;
   SET SAVE;
   IF DUR=0 THEN DELETE;

TITLE 'GANTT CHART OF THE SCHEDULE';
PROC GANTT;
   ID ACTIVITY;
```

Output 3.5   Printing a Gantt Chart

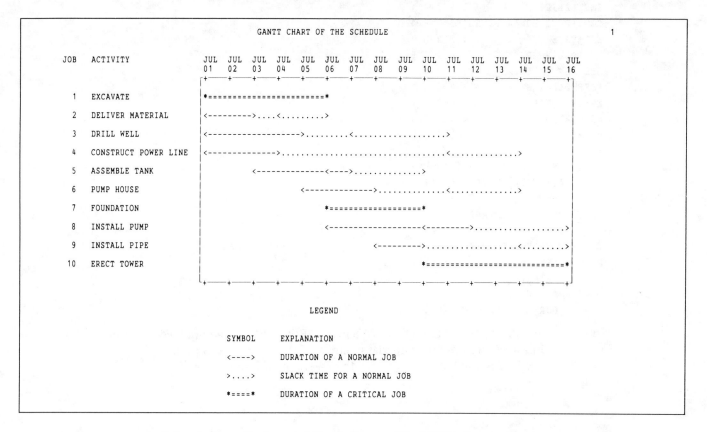

Scheduling Only on Weekdays with PERT: Example 4

This example uses CPM to perform Program Evaluation Review Technique (PERT) analysis on a project. The PERT technique is used to include uncertainty about durations in scheduling.

You must provide three estimates of project duration: a pessimistic estimate (TP), an optimistic estimate (TO), and a median estimate (TM). The PERT approach uses a weighted average of these estimates as the activity duration. The average usually used is

(TP + (4*TM) + TO)/ 6

This average may result in nonintegral durations, where some jobs take part of a day. Although CPM does not require integral durations, they are needed to print the schedule on a calendar. To demonstrate the WEEKDAYS option, round off the weighted average durations using the ROUND function. The following program saves the network from **Example 1** with three estimates of project duration in a SAS data set. The DATA step also calculates the weighted average duration.

```
TITLE 'SCHEDULING ONLY ON WEEKDAYS';
DATA;
    INPUT ACTIVITY $ 1-20 TAIL 22 TM 24 HEAD 26 TP 28 TO 30;
    DUR=ROUND((TP+(4*TM)+TO)/6,1);
    CARDS;

DRILL WELL            1 4 2 5 2
```

```
        PUMP HOUSE           2 3 5 5 2
        INSTALL PIPE         5 2 7 3 1
        CONSTRUCT POWER LINE 1 3 5 6 1
        EXCAVATE             1 5 4 6 4
        INSTALL PUMP         4 6 7 7 5
        DELIVER MATERIAL     1 2 3 4 1
        ASSEMBLE TANK        3 4 6 6 1
        ERECT TOWER          6 6 7 9 4
        FOUNDATION           4 4 6 5 3
        DUMMY                4 0 5 0 0
        ;
        PROC CPM DATE='1JUL85'D INTERVAL=WEEKDAYS;
            ID ACTIVITY; TAILNODE TAIL; DUR DUR; HEADNODE HEAD;

        PROC SORT; BY E_START;

        TITLE2 'CALENDAR OF SCHEDULE';
        PROC CALENDAR SCHEDULE WEEKDAYS;
            ID E_START;
            VAR ACTIVITY;
            DUR DUR;
```

Note that specifying INTERVAL=WEEKDAYS in the PROC CPM statement tells CPM to schedule activities only on weekdays. Similarly, the WEEKDAYS option in the PROC CALENDAR statement produces the calendar with only weekdays in **Output 3.6**.

Output 3.6   Scheduling Only on Weekdays with PERT

```
                              SCHEDULING ONLY ON WEEKDAYS                                    1
                                 CALENDAR OF SCHEDULE

|                                                                                           |
|                                       JULY  1985                                          |
|                                                                                           |
| MONDAY          | TUESDAY        | WEDNESDAY       | THURSDAY        | FRIDAY             |
|      1          |      2         |       3         |       4         |      5             |
|                 |                |                 |                 |                    |
| +=============DELIVER MATERIAL==============+ +=========================ASSEMBLE TANK==========================>
| +===================================================EXCAVATE==========================================+
| +===================CONSTRUCT POWER LINE======================+
| +=============================DRILL WELL===============================+ +=====PUMP HOUSE=====>
|      8          |      9         |      10         |      11         |     12             |
|                 |                |                 |                 |                    |
| +====================================FOUNDATION===========================+
| +===================================================INSTALL PUMP=====================>
| <==============PUMP HOUSE==============+
| <===ASSEMBLE TANK====+            | +==============INSTALL PIPE===============+ +====ERECT TOWER=====>
|     15          |     16         |      17         |      18         |     19             |
|                 |                |                 |                 |                    |
| <===========================================ERECT TOWER========================================+
| <====INSTALL PUMP====+
|     22          |     23         |      24         |      25         |     26             |
|                 |                |                 |                 |                    |
|                 |                |                 |                 |                    |
|                 |                |                 |                 |                    |
|     29          |     30         |      31         |                 |                    |
|                 |                |                 |                 |                    |
|                 |                |                 |                 |                    |
|                 |                |                 |                 |                    |
```

Scheduling around Holidays: Example 5

This example shows how you can schedule around holidays with PROC CPM. First, save a list of holidays in a SAS data set as SAS date variables. Then, use the HOLIDATA= option in the PROC CPM statement to identify the data set, and list the names of the variables in the data set in a HOLIDAY statement. For example, suppose you want to schedule the project in **Example 1** to start on July 1, 1985.

Suppose in your scheduling plans you want to assign work on all days of the week, allowing a day off on July 4, 1985. The following DATA step saves the 4th of July and five Sundays starting from June 30, 1985 in a SAS data set:

```
DATA HOLIDAYS;
   RETAIN SUNDAYS '30JUN85'D;
   DO I=1 TO 5;
      OUTPUT; SUNDAYS=SUNDAYS+7;
      END;
   VACTN='4JUL85'D; OUTPUT;
```

80   Chapter 3

Using PROC CPM, you can schedule the project to start on July 1, as follows:

```
TITLE 'SCHEDULING AROUND HOLIDAYS';
PROC CPM DATA=EXMP1 OUT=SAVE
        HOLIDATA=HOLIDAYS DATE='1JUL85'D;
    HOLIDAY VACTN;
    ACTIVITY TASK;
    DURATION DURATION;
    SUCCESSOR SUCCESR1 SUCCESR2 SUCCESR3;
```

The schedule shown in **Output 3.7** is printed with PROC PRINT.

Output 3.7 Holiday Scheduling

```
                                    SCHEDULING AROUND HOLIDAYS                                              1

OBS TASK            SUCCESR1        SUCCESR2      SUCCESR3    DURATION E_START  E_FINISH L_START  L_FINISH T_FLOAT F_FLOAT

  1 DRILL WELL      PUMP HOUSE                                   4     01JUL85 05JUL85 08JUL85 11JUL85    6      0
  2 PUMP HOUSE      INSTALL PIPE                                 3     06JUL85 08JUL85 12JUL85 14JUL85    6      0
  3 POWER LINE      INSTALL PIPE                                 3     01JUL85 03JUL85 12JUL85 14JUL85   10      4
  4 EXCAVATE        INSTALL PIPE    INSTALL PUMP FOUNDATION      5     01JUL85 06JUL85 01JUL85 06JUL85    0      0
  5 DELIVER MATERIAL ASSEMBLE TANK                               2     01JUL85 02JUL85 05JUL85 06JUL85    3      0
  6 ASSEMBLE TANK   ERECT TOWER                                  4     03JUL85 07JUL85 07JUL85 10JUL85    3      3
  7 FOUNDATION      ERECT TOWER                                  4     07JUL85 10JUL85 07JUL85 10JUL85    0      0
  8 INSTALL PUMP                                                 6     07JUL85 12JUL85 11JUL85 16JUL85    4      4
  9 INSTALL PIPE                                                 2     09JUL85 10JUL85 15JUL85 16JUL85    6      6
 10 ERECT TOWER                                                  6     11JUL85 16JUL85 11JUL85 16JUL85    0      0
```

Scheduling on Workdays: Example 6

You can use the INTERVAL= option to schedule only on weekdays during a part of the day; for example, only on weekdays from 9 a.m. to 5 p.m. To do this you specify the option INTERVAL=WORKDAY (DTWRKDAY) in the PROC CPM statement. If all of the activity durations are in integral units of days, then INTERVAL=WORKDAY is equivalent to INTERVAL=WEEKDAYS. However, if some of the activity durations require fractions of days and you want to schedule only during a portion of the workday, you should use INTERVAL=WORKDAY when DATE= is a SAS date value and INTERVAL=DTWRKDAY when DATE= is a SAS datetime value.

In the following example, suppose you want to schedule the job specified in **Example 1**, but you have revised the durations of two activities. You plan for DRILL WELL to take 3.5 days and EXCAVATE to take 4.75 days. To schedule this job use the INTERVAL=WORKDAY option rather than the default INTERVAL= DAY. The default setting would schedule work only on a daily basis. The workday option causes CPM to schedule only on weekdays from 9 a.m. to 5 p.m. One unit of duration is interpreted as 8 hours of work. To schedule the construction project to start on July 1, you can call PROC CPM with the following program:

```
TITLE 'SCHEDULING ON WORKDAYS';
TITLE2 'DAY STARTS AT 9 A.M.';
PROC CPM INTERVAL=WORKDAY
     DATA=EX DATE='1JUL85'D
     HOLIDATA=HOLIDAYS;
   HOLIDAY VACTN;
   ACTIVITY TASK;
   DURATION DURATION;
   SUCCESSOR SUCCESR1 SUCCESR2 SUCCESR3;
```

The schedule is printed with PROC PRINT and shown in **Output 3.8**.

Output 3.8   Workday Scheduling

```
                              SCHEDULING ON WORKDAYS                                        1
                              DAY STARTS AT 9 A.M.

OBS  TASK             DURATION    E_START           E_FINISH          L_START           L_FINISH          T_FLOAT  F_FLOAT

 1   DRILL WELL          3.50   01JUL85:09:00:00  05JUL85:12:59:59  10JUL85:11:00:00  15JUL85:14:59:59    6.25     0.00
 2   PUMP HOUSE          3.00   05JUL85:13:00:00  10JUL85:12:59:59  15JUL85:15:00:00  18JUL85:14:59:59    6.25     0.00
 3   POWER LINE          3.00   01JUL85:09:00:00  03JUL85:16:59:59  15JUL85:15:00:00  18JUL85:14:59:59    9.75     3.50
 4   EXCAVATE            4.75   01JUL85:09:00:00  08JUL85:14:59:59  01JUL85:09:00:00  08JUL85:14:59:59    0.00     0.00
 5   DELIVER MATERIAL    2.00   01JUL85:09:00:00  02JUL85:16:59:59  03JUL85:15:00:00  08JUL85:14:59:59    2.75     0.00
 6   ASSEMBLE TANK       4.00   03JUL85:09:00:00  09JUL85:16:59:59  08JUL85:15:00:00  12JUL85:14:59:59    2.75     2.75
 7   FOUNDATION          4.00   08JUL85:15:00:00  12JUL85:14:59:59  08JUL85:15:00:00  12JUL85:14:59:59    0.00     0.00
 8   INSTALL PUMP        6.00   08JUL85:15:00:00  16JUL85:14:59:59  12JUL85:15:00:00  22JUL85:14:59:59    4.00     4.00
 9   INSTALL PIPE        2.00   10JUL85:13:00:00  12JUL85:12:59:59  18JUL85:15:00:00  22JUL85:14:59:59    6.25     6.25
10   ERECT TOWER         6.00   12JUL85:15:00:00  22JUL85:14:59:59  12JUL85:15:00:00  22JUL85:14:59:59    0.00     0.00
```

If you want to change the length of the workday, use the DAYLENGTH=
option in the PROC CPM statement. For example, if you want an 8.5-hour workday instead of the 8-hour default workday, you should include DAYLENGTH=
'08:30'T in the PROC CPM statement. In the example, you can invoke PROC
CPM with the following statements:

```
PROC CPM DAYLENGTH='08:30'T
     INTERVAL=WORKDAY DATA=EX DATE='1JUL85'D
     HOLIDATA=HOLIDAYS;
   HOLIDAY VACTN;
   ACTIVITY TASK;
   DURATION DURATION;
   SUCCESSOR SUCCESR1 SUCCESR2 SUCCESR3;
   TITLE2 'DAY STARTS AT 9 A.M. AND IS 8.5 HOURS LONG';
```

You might also want to change the start of the workday. By default the workday
starts at 9 a.m. To change the default, you use the INTERVAL=DTWRKDAY
option. This tells CPM that the DATE= option is a SAS datetime value and that
the time given is the start of the workday. The example that follows schedules
the project to start at 7 a.m. on July 1. The project is scheduled on 8.5-hour workdays each starting at 7 a.m. The schedule produced by PROC CPM is shown in
Output 3.9.

```
PROC CPM DAYLENGTH='08:30'T INTERVAL=DTWRKDAY
     DATE='1JUL85:07:00'DT DATA=EX
     HOLIDATA=HOLIDAYS;
   HOLIDAY VACTN;
   ACTIVITY TASK;
   DURATION DURATION;
   SUCCESSOR SUCCESR1 SUCCESR2 SUCCESR3;
   TITLE2 'DAY STARTS AT 7 A.M. AND IS 8.5 HOURS LONG';
```

Output 3.9   Scheduling on Workdays with Nonstandard Hours

```
                                    SCHEDULING ON WORKDAYS                                              2
                             DAY STARTS AT 9 A.M. AND IS 8.5 HOURS LONG

OBS    TASK              DURATION     E_START           E_FINISH          L_START           L_FINISH        T_FLOAT   F_FLOAT

  1    DRILL WELL          3.50    01JUL85:09:00:00   05JUL85:13:14:59   10JUL85:11:07:30   15JUL85:15:22:29    6.25      0.00
  2    PUMP HOUSE          3.00    05JUL85:13:15:00   10JUL85:13:14:59   15JUL85:15:22:30   18JUL85:15:22:29    6.25      0.00
  3    POWER LINE          3.00    01JUL85:09:00:00   03JUL85:17:29:59   15JUL85:15:22:30   18JUL85:15:22:29    9.75      3.50
  4    EXCAVATE            4.75    01JUL85:09:00:00   08JUL85:15:22:29   01JUL85:09:00:00   08JUL85:15:22:29    0.00      0.00
  5    DELIVER MATERIAL    2.00    01JUL85:09:00:00   02JUL85:17:29:59   03JUL85:15:22:30   08JUL85:15:22:29    2.75      0.00
  6    ASSEMBLE TANK       4.00    03JUL85:09:00:00   09JUL85:17:29:59   08JUL85:15:22:30   12JUL85:15:22:29    2.75      2.75
  7    FOUNDATION          4.00    08JUL85:15:22:30   12JUL85:15:22:29   08JUL85:15:22:30   12JUL85:15:22:29    0.00      0.00
  8    INSTALL PUMP        6.00    08JUL85:15:22:30   16JUL85:15:22:29   12JUL85:15:22:30   22JUL85:15:22:29    4.00      4.00
  9    INSTALL PIPE        2.00    10JUL85:13:15:00   12JUL85:13:14:59   18JUL85:15:22:30   22JUL85:15:22:29    6.25      6.25
 10    ERECT TOWER         6.00    12JUL85:15:22:30   22JUL85:15:22:29   12JUL85:15:22:30   22JUL85:15:22:29    0.00      0.00
```

```
                                    SCHEDULING ON WORKDAYS                                              3
                             DAY STARTS AT 7 A.M. AND IS 8.5 HOURS LONG

OBS    TASK              DURATION     E_START           E_FINISH          L_START           L_FINISH        T_FLOAT   F_FLOAT

  1    DRILL WELL          3.50    01JUL85:07:00:00   05JUL85:11:14:59   10JUL85:09:07:30   15JUL85:13:22:29    6.25      0.00
  2    PUMP HOUSE          3.00    05JUL85:11:15:00   10JUL85:11:14:59   15JUL85:13:22:30   18JUL85:13:22:29    6.25      0.00
  3    POWER LINE          3.00    01JUL85:07:00:00   03JUL85:15:29:59   15JUL85:13:22:30   18JUL85:13:22:29    9.75      3.50
  4    EXCAVATE            4.75    01JUL85:07:00:00   08JUL85:13:22:29   01JUL85:07:00:00   08JUL85:13:22:29    0.00      0.00
  5    DELIVER MATERIAL    2.00    01JUL85:07:00:00   02JUL85:15:29:59   03JUL85:13:22:30   08JUL85:13:22:29    2.75      0.00
  6    ASSEMBLE TANK       4.00    03JUL85:07:00:00   09JUL85:15:29:59   08JUL85:13:22:30   12JUL85:13:22:29    2.75      2.75
  7    FOUNDATION          4.00    08JUL85:13:22:30   12JUL85:13:22:29   08JUL85:13:22:30   12JUL85:13:22:29    0.00      0.00
  8    INSTALL PUMP        6.00    08JUL85:13:22:30   16JUL85:13:22:29   12JUL85:13:22:30   22JUL85:13:22:29    4.00      4.00
  9    INSTALL PIPE        2.00    10JUL85:11:15:00   12JUL85:11:14:59   18JUL85:13:22:30   22JUL85:13:22:29    6.25      6.25
 10    ERECT TOWER         6.00    12JUL85:13:22:30   22JUL85:13:22:29   12JUL85:13:22:30   22JUL85:13:22:29    0.00      0.00
```

Scheduling on the 6-Day Week: Example 7

This example shows how you can schedule the job over a nonstandard day and a nonstandard week. As in the last example, suppose you want to schedule the project to start on July 1 at 7 a.m. and you want to work 8.5-hour workdays. However, unlike the previous example where weekends were off, in this case you want to take off only Sundays and the 4th of July. Use INTERVAL=DTDAY, indicating a 7-day work week, but specify the Sundays over the planning horizon as holidays with the HOLIDATA= option to indicate the HOLIDAYS data set and the HOLIDAY list to identify the appropriate variables in that data set. The resulting schedule is shown in **Output 3.10**.

```
TITLE 'SCHEDULING ON THE 6-DAY WEEK';
PROC CPM DAYLENGTH='08:30'T INTERVAL=DTDAY
     DATE='1JUL85:07:00'DT DATA=EX
        HOLIDATA=HOLIDAYS;
   HOLIDAY SUNDAYS VACTN;
   ACTIVITY TASK;
   DURATION DURATION;
   SUCCESSOR SUCCESR1 SUCCESR2 SUCCESR3;
```

Output 3.10   Scheduling a Job with Nonstandard Days and Weeks

```
                           SCHEDULING ON THE 6-DAY WEEK                                           1

OBS   TASK              DURATION    E_START         E_FINISH        L_START         L_FINISH      T_FLOAT   F_FLOAT

 1    DRILL WELL          3.50    01JUL85:07:00:00  05JUL85:11:14:59  09JUL85:09:07:30  12JUL85:13:22:29    6.25    0.00
 2    PUMP HOUSE          3.00    05JUL85:11:15:00  09JUL85:11:14:59  12JUL85:13:22:30  16JUL85:13:22:29    6.25    0.00
 3    POWER LINE          3.00    01JUL85:07:00:00  03JUL85:15:29:59  12JUL85:13:22:30  16JUL85:13:22:29    9.75    3.50
 4    EXCAVATE            4.75    01JUL85:07:00:00  06JUL85:13:22:29  01JUL85:07:00:00  06JUL85:13:22:29    0.00    0.00
 5    DELIVER MATERIAL    2.00    01JUL85:07:00:00  02JUL85:15:29:59  03JUL85:13:22:30  06JUL85:13:22:29    2.75    0.00
 6    ASSEMBLE TANK       4.00    03JUL85:07:00:00  08JUL85:15:29:59  06JUL85:13:22:30  11JUL85:13:22:29    2.75    2.75
 7    FOUNDATION          4.00    06JUL85:13:22:30  11JUL85:13:22:29  06JUL85:13:22:30  11JUL85:13:22:29    0.00    0.00
 8    INSTALL PUMP        6.00    06JUL85:13:22:30  13JUL85:13:22:29  11JUL85:13:22:30  18JUL85:13:22:29    4.00    4.00
 9    INSTALL PIPE        2.00    09JUL85:11:15:00  11JUL85:11:14:59  16JUL85:13:22:30  18JUL85:13:22:29    6.25    6.25
10    ERECT TOWER         6.00    11JUL85:13:22:30  18JUL85:13:22:29  11JUL85:13:22:30  18JUL85:13:22:29    0.00    0.00
```

Aligning the Schedule: Example 8

This example shows you how to use the FINISHBEFORE option and the ALIGN=
option. Suppose you want to schedule the project given in **Example 1**, but instead
of starting work on July 1, 1985, you want to schedule it for completion before
that date. The activity-on-arc format is used. In that case you call CPM with the
option FINISHBEFORE:

```
TITLE 'USE OF THE FINISHBEFORE OPTION';
PROC CPM DATA=CONST1 FINISHBEFORE DATE='1JUL85'D;
   TAILNODE TAIL;
   DURATION DUR;
   HEADNODE HEAD;
   ID ACTIVITY;
```

CPM produces the data set in **Output 3.11**.

Output 3.11   Using the FINISHBEFORE Option in Scheduling

```
                          USE OF THE FINISHBEFORE OPTION                                          1

OBS  TAIL  HEAD  DUR   ACTIVITY              E_START    E_FINISH   L_START    L_FINISH   T_FLOAT   F_FLOAT

 1    1     2     4    DRILL WELL            16JUN85    19JUN85    22JUN85    25JUN85       6         0
 2    2     5     3    PUMP HOUSE            20JUN85    22JUN85    26JUN85    28JUN85       6         0
 3    5     7     2    INSTALL PIPE          23JUN85    24JUN85    29JUN85    30JUN85       6         6
 4    1     5     3    CONSTRUCT POWER LINE  16JUN85    18JUN85    26JUN85    28JUN85      10         4
 5    1     4     5    EXCAVATE              16JUN85    20JUN85    16JUN85    20JUN85       0         0
 6    4     7     6    INSTALL PUMP          21JUN85    26JUN85    25JUN85    30JUN85       4         4
 7    1     3     2    DELIVER MATERIAL      16JUN85    17JUN85    19JUN85    20JUN85       3         0
 8    3     6     4    ASSEMBLE TANK         18JUN85    21JUN85    21JUN85    24JUN85       3         3
 9    6     7     6    ERECT TOWER           25JUN85    30JUN85    25JUN85    30JUN85       0         0
10    4     6     4    FOUNDATION            21JUN85    24JUN85    21JUN85    24JUN85       0         0
11    4     5     0    DUMMY                 21JUN85    21JUN85    29JUN85    29JUN85       8         2
```

Note that all the activities are completed before July 1, 1985.
Instead of requiring the entire project to be completed before July 1, suppose
you have a constraint on the earliest time to start construction of the PUMP
HOUSE and that this activity cannot be started until July 1. To specify this, you
must identify the activity PUMP HOUSE and note that you want to schedule the
task to begin on July 1. You do that with the NTAILNODE=, NHEADNODE=,
DATE=, and ALIGN= options in the PROC CPM statement. Since the network
is in activity-on-arc format and the TAILNODE= and HEADNODE= variables
are numeric, you use the NTAILNODE= and NHEADNODE= options to identify
the PUMP HOUSE activity. The ALIGN= option tells CPM to align the PUMP

HOUSE activity with the date specified in the DATE= option. Since you want the early start time of the PUMP HOUSE activity to be on July 1, you set ALIGN equal to ES. The following statements show the call to PROC CPM:

```
TITLE 'ALIGNING THE START TIME OF ONE ACTIVITY';
PROC CPM DATE='1JUL85'D DATA=CONST1
      NTAILNODE=2 NHEADNODE=5 ALIGN=ES;
   TAILNODE TAIL;
   DURATION DUR;
   HEADNODE HEAD;
   ID ACTIVITY;
```

The procedure produces the data set in **Output 3.12**.

Output 3.12 Aligning the Start Time

```
                     ALIGNING THE START TIME OF ONE ACTIVITY                                    2

 OBS   TAIL   HEAD   DUR   ACTIVITY              E_START   E_FINISH   L_START   L_FINISH   T_FLOAT   F_FLOAT

   1     1      2     4    DRILL WELL            27JUN85   30JUN85    03JUL85   06JUL85       6         0
   2     2      5     3    PUMP HOUSE            01JUL85   03JUL85    07JUL85   09JUL85       6         0
   3     5      7     2    INSTALL PIPE          04JUL85   05JUL85    10JUL85   11JUL85       6         6
   4     1      5     3    CONSTRUCT POWER LINE  27JUN85   29JUN85    07JUL85   09JUL85      10         4
   5     1      4     5    EXCAVATE              27JUN85   01JUL85    27JUN85   01JUL85       0         0
   6     4      7     6    INSTALL PUMP          02JUL85   07JUL85    06JUL85   11JUL85       4         4
   7     1      3     2    DELIVER MATERIAL      27JUN85   28JUN85    30JUN85   01JUL85       3         0
   8     3      6     4    ASSEMBLE TANK         29JUN85   02JUL85    02JUL85   05JUL85       3         3
   9     6      7     6    ERECT TOWER           06JUL85   11JUL85    06JUL85   11JUL85       0         0
  10     4      6     4    FOUNDATION            02JUL85   05JUL85    02JUL85   05JUL85       0         0
  11     4      5     0    DUMMY                 02JUL85   02JUL85    10JUL85   10JUL85       8         2
```

Note that the PUMP HOUSE has an early start time of 01JUL85 and that the remaining jobs in the project are scheduled according to the scheduling of that job.

Multiple Alignment: Example 9

Suppose that for the construction project of the previous examples, restrictions are imposed on two of the activities: DRILL WELL has to start on July 1, and DELIVER MATERIAL cannot start before July 5, 1985. The data set EXMP9, printed below, has two variables, ADATE and ATYPE, which allow you to specify these restrictions. DRILL WELL has ATYPE equal to 'SEQ' for 'start equal to', and DELIVER MATERIAL has ATYPE equal to 'SGE' for 'start greater than or equal to'. Suppose also that you want the project to be completed by the end of July 15, 1985.

The statements needed to schedule the project subject to these restrictions are shown below. The resulting data set is printed using PROC PRINT and shown in **Output 3.13**. Note that the floats corresponding to the activities are different from the unconstrained schedule. In particular, some of the activities have negative values for T_FLOAT, indicating that if the project deadline has to be met these activities must be started earlier. Examining the constraints indicates that the activity DELIVER MATERIAL is responsible for the negative floats since it is constrained to start on or after July 5, 1985; however, for the project to be completed on time it must start no later than July 4.

```
TITLE 'MULTIPLE ALIGNMENT OF ACTIVITIES';
TITLE2 'DATA EXMP9';
DATA EXMP9;
    INPUT ACTIVITY $ 1-20 TAIL 22 DUR 24 HEAD 26 ADATE DATE9.
         ATYPE $ 36-38;
    CARDS;
DRILL WELL           1 4 2  1JUL85 SEQ
PUMP HOUSE           2 3 5  .
INSTALL PIPE         5 2 7  .
CONSTRUCT POWER LINE 1 3 5  .
EXCAVATE             1 5 4  .
INSTALL PUMP         4 6 7  .
DELIVER MATERIAL     1 2 3  5JUL85 SGE
ASSEMBLE TANK        3 4 6  .
ERECT TOWER          6 6 7  .
FOUNDATION           4 4 6  .
DUMMY                4 0 5  .
;

PROC PRINT DATA=EXMP9;
   FORMAT ADATE DATE7.;
   RUN;

TITLE2 'ALIGNED SCHEDULE';
PROC CPM DATA=EXMP9 DATE='16JUL85'D FINISHBEFORE;
   TAILNODE TAIL;
   DURATION DUR;
   HEADNODE HEAD;
   ALIGNDATE ADATE;
   ALIGNTYPE ATYPE;
   ID ACTIVITY;
```

Output 3.13   Multiple Alignment

```
                    MULTIPLE ALIGNMENT OF ACTIVITIES                        1
                              DATA EXMP9

     OBS    ACTIVITY              TAIL    DUR    HEAD    ADATE    ATYPE

      1     DRILL WELL              1      4      2     01JUL85    SEQ
      2     PUMP HOUSE              2      3      5       .
      3     INSTALL PIPE            5      2      7       .
      4     CONSTRUCT POWER LINE    1      3      5       .
      5     EXCAVATE                1      5      4       .
      6     INSTALL PUMP            4      6      7       .
      7     DELIVER MATERIAL        1      2      3     05JUL85    SGE
      8     ASSEMBLE TANK           3      4      6       .
      9     ERECT TOWER             6      6      7       .
     10     FOUNDATION              4      4      6       .
     11     DUMMY                   4      0      5       .
```

```
                          MULTIPLE ALIGNMENT OF ACTIVITIES                                    2
                               ALIGNED SCHEDULE

  OBS    TAIL    HEAD    DUR    ACTIVITY              E_START    E_FINISH    L_START    L_FINISH    T_FLOAT    F_FLOAT
   1      1       2       4     DRILL WELL            01JUL85    04JUL85     01JUL85    04JUL85        0          0
   2      2       5       3     PUMP HOUSE            05JUL85    07JUL85     11JUL85    13JUL85        6          0
   3      5       7       2     INSTALL PIPE          08JUL85    09JUL85     14JUL85    15JUL85        6          6
   4      1       5       3     CONSTRUCT POWER LINE  01JUL85    03JUL85     11JUL85    13JUL85       10          4
   5      1       4       5     EXCAVATE              01JUL85    05JUL85     01JUL85    05JUL85        0          0
   6      4       7       6     INSTALL PUMP          06JUL85    11JUL85     10JUL85    15JUL85        4          4
   7      1       3       2     DELIVER MATERIAL      05JUL85    06JUL85     04JUL85    05JUL85       -1          0
   8      3       6       4     ASSEMBLE TANK         07JUL85    10JUL85     06JUL85    09JUL85       -1          0
   9      6       7       6     ERECT TOWER           11JUL85    16JUL85     10JUL85    15JUL85       -1         -1
  10      4       6       4     FOUNDATION            06JUL85    09JUL85     06JUL85    09JUL85        0          1
  11      4       5       0     DUMMY                 06JUL85    06JUL85     14JUL85    14JUL85        8          2
```

Summarizing Resource Utilization: Example 10

This example shows how you can use the RESOURCE statement in conjunction
with the RESOURCEOUT= option to summarize resource utilization. The following program assumes that the project network and the activity costs are in a SAS
data set:

```
OBS  ACTIVITY              TAIL  DUR  HEAD  COST

 1   DRILL WELL              1    4    2    1.5
 2   PUMP HOUSE              2    3    5    2.3
 3   INSTALL PIPE            5    2    7    2.1
 4   CONSTRUCT POWER LINE    1    3    5    1.1
 5   EXCAVATE                1    5    4    5.3
 6   INSTALL PUMP            4    6    7    1.2
 7   DELIVER MATERIAL        1    2    3    0.5
 8   ASSEMBLE TANK           3    4    6    3.2
 9   ERECT TOWER             6    6    7   15.0
10   FOUNDATION              4    4    6    1.2
11   DUMMY                   4    0    5    .
```

The program saves the cost information in a data set named ROUT, which is
printed using PROC PRINT. Two variables, ECOST and LCOST, denote the usage
of the resource COST corresponding to the early and late start schedules, respectively. The summary information is then presented in two ways: on a calendar
and in a chart. Charts as shown in **Output 3.14** can be used to compare different
schedules with respect to resource usage.

```
TITLE 'SUMMARIZING RESOURCE UTILIZATION';
PROC CPM DATE='1JUL85'D RESOURCEOUT=ROUT;
    ID ACTIVITY COST;
    TAILNODE TAIL;
    DURATION DUR;
    HEADNODE HEAD;
    RESOURCE COST;

PROC FORMAT;                    /* FORMAT THE COST VARIABLES */
    PICTURE EFMT OTHER='009.99 E' (PREFIX='$');
    PICTURE LFMT OTHER='009.99 L' (PREFIX='$');

PROC CALENDAR LEGEND;           /* PRINT THE COSTS ON A CALENDAR */
    ID _TIME_;
    VAR  ECOST LCOST;
    FORMAT ECOST EFMT.
```

```
            LCOST LFMT.;
        LABEL ECOST='E = EARLY START COSTS'
          LCOST='L = LATE START COSTS';

    PROC CHART;                      /* PLOT THE COSTS IN A BAR CHART */
      HBAR _TIME_/SUMVAR=ECOST DISCRETE;
      HBAR _TIME_/SUMVAR=LCOST DISCRETE;
```

Output 3.14 Summarizing Resource Utilization

```
                    SUMMARIZING RESOURCE UTILIZATION                        1

            OBS     _TIME_     ECOST    LCOST

              1    01JUL85      8.4      5.3
              2    02JUL85      8.4      5.3
              3    03JUL85     11.1      5.3
              4    04JUL85     10.0      5.8
              5    05JUL85     10.8      5.8
              6    06JUL85      7.9      4.4
              7    07JUL85      4.7      5.9
              8    08JUL85      4.5      5.9
              9    09JUL85      4.5      5.9
             10    10JUL85     16.2     17.7
             11    11JUL85     16.2     19.6
             12    12JUL85     15.0     19.6
             13    13JUL85     15.0     19.6
             14    14JUL85     15.0     18.3
             15    15JUL85     15.0     18.3
             16    16JUL85      0.0      0.0
```

```
                    SUMMARIZING RESOURCE UTILIZATION                        2
```

	JULY 1985					
SUNDAY	MONDAY	TUESDAY	WEDNESDAY	THURSDAY	FRIDAY	SATURDAY
	1	2	3	4	5	6
	$8.40 E $5.30 L	$8.40 E $5.30 L	$11.10 E $5.30 L	$10.00 E $5.80 L	$10.80 E $5.80 L	$7.90 E $4.40 L
7	8	9	10	11	12	13
$4.70 E $5.90 L	$4.50 E $5.90 L	$4.50 E $5.90 L	$16.20 E $17.70 L	$16.20 E $19.60 L	$15.00 E $19.60 L	$15.00 E $19.60 L
14	15	16	17	18	19	20
$15.00 E $18.30 L	$15.00 E $18.30 L	$0.00 E $0.00 L				
21	22	23	24	25	26	27
28	29	30	31			

```
                    LEGEND
          E = EARLY START COSTS
          L = LATE START COSTS
```

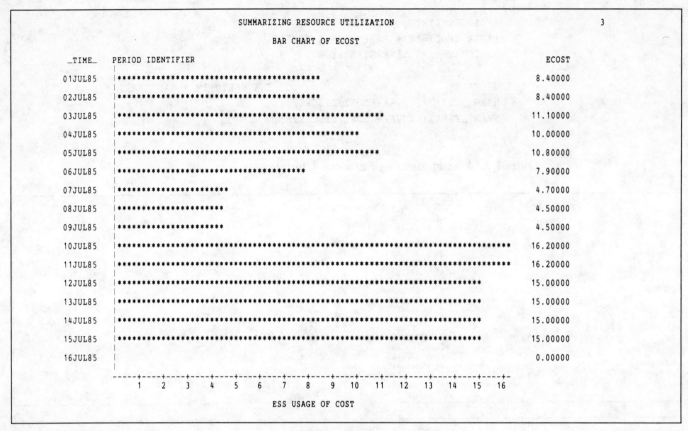

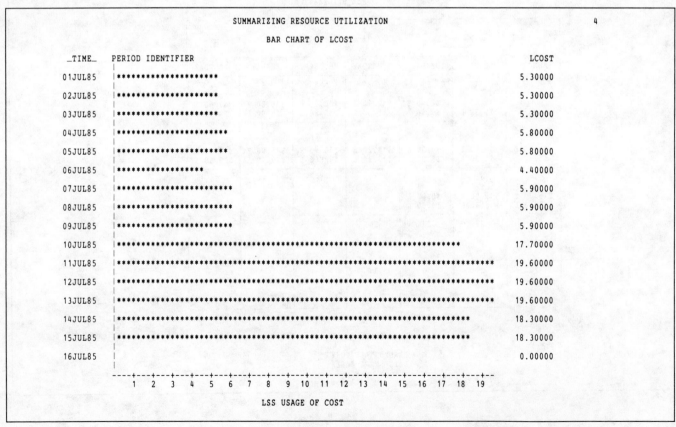

Resource Allocation: Example 11

In the previous example a summary of the resource utilization was obtained. Suppose that you want to schedule the project subject to constraints on the availability of money. The data, as in **Example 10**, are assumed to be in a data set named EXMP10. The resource variable, COST, specifies the rate of consumption of dollars per day by each activity in the project. Now suppose that the availability of money is saved in a data set named RESINF printed below:

```
TITLE 'DATA RESINF';
DATA RESINF;
   INPUT PER DATE7. OTYPE $ COST;
   CARDS;
   .       RESTYPE   2
   .       SUPLEVEL  40
1JUL85     RESLEVEL  40
6JUL85     RESLEVEL  90
11JUL85    RESLEVEL  130
16JUL85    RESLEVEL  180
;
PROC PRINT;
RUN;
```

Output 3.15   Resource Allocation

```
                     DATA RESINF                                    1

        OBS     PER      OTYPE     COST

         1       .       RESTYPE      2
         2       .       SUPLEVEL    40
         3    01JUL85    RESLEVEL    40
         4    06JUL85    RESLEVEL    90
         5    11JUL85    RESLEVEL   130
         6    16JUL85    RESLEVEL   180
```

In the data set RESINF the first observation indicates that COST is a consumable resource, the second observation indicates that a supplementary level of forty dollars is available, if necessary. The remaining observations indicate the availability profile from July 1, 1985. PROC CPM is then used to schedule the project to start on July 1, 1985 subject to the availability, as specified. Here the DELAY= option is not specified and therefore the supplementary level of resource is not used.

The E_START option in the RESOURCE statement requests that the early start schedule also be included in the OUT= output data set. Thus the data set contains four new variables: S_START, S_FINISH, E_START, and E_FINISH. Note that the project is delayed by 3 days due to lack of sufficient resources (the maximum value of S_FINISH is 18JUL85, while the maximum value of E_FINISH is 15JUL85). The data set ROUT contains variables RCOST and ACOST; RCOST denotes the usage of the resource COST corresponding to the resource-constrained schedule, and ACOST denotes the remaining level of the resource after resource allocation. Both output data sets are printed below using PROC PRINT.

```
TITLE 'RESOURCE CONSTRAINED SCHEDULE';
PROC CPM DATA=EXMP10 DATE='1JUL85'D RESOURCEIN=RESINF
     OUT=SCHED RESOURCEOUT=ROUT;
   TAILNODE TAIL;
   DURATION DUR;
   HEADNODE HEAD;
   RESOURCE COST / PERIOD=PER OBSTYPE=OTYPE RCP AVP E_START;
   ID ACTIVITY COST;
   TITLE 'RCPROFILE AND AVPROFILE FOR CONSTRAINED SCHEDULE';
RUN;
```

Output 3.16 Scheduling a Project Subject to Availability of Resources

```
                          RESOURCE CONSTRAINED SCHEDULE                                    1

   OBS    TAIL    HEAD    DUR    ACTIVITY              COST    S_START   S_FINISH   E_START   E_FINISH

    1       1       2      4     DRILL WELL            1.5     01JUL85   04JUL85    01JUL85   04JUL85
    2       2       5      3     PUMP HOUSE            2.3     06JUL85   08JUL85    05JUL85   07JUL85
    3       5       7      2     INSTALL PIPE          2.1     09JUL85   10JUL85    08JUL85   09JUL85
    4       1       5      3     CONSTRUCT POWER LINE  1.1     01JUL85   03JUL85    01JUL85   03JUL85
    5       1       4      5     EXCAVATE              5.3     01JUL85   05JUL85    01JUL85   05JUL85
    6       4       7      6     INSTALL PUMP          1.2     06JUL85   11JUL85    06JUL85   11JUL85
    7       1       3      2     DELIVER MATERIAL      0.5     01JUL85   02JUL85    01JUL85   02JUL85
    8       3       6      4     ASSEMBLE TANK         3.2     05JUL85   08JUL85    03JUL85   06JUL85
    9       6       7      6     ERECT TOWER          15.0     13JUL85   18JUL85    10JUL85   15JUL85
   10       4       6      4     FOUNDATION            1.2     06JUL85   09JUL85    06JUL85   09JUL85
   11       4       5      0     DUMMY                  .      06JUL85   06JUL85    06JUL85   06JUL85
```

```
                   RCPROFILE AND AVPROFILE FOR CONSTRAINED SCHEDULE                         2

                         OBS    _TIME_     RCOST    ACOST

                          1     01JUL85     8.4     40.0
                          2     02JUL85     8.4     31.6
                          3     03JUL85     7.9     23.2
                          4     04JUL85     6.8     15.3
                          5     05JUL85     8.5      8.5
                          6     06JUL85     7.9     50.0
                          7     07JUL85     7.9     42.1
                          8     08JUL85     7.9     34.2
                          9     09JUL85     4.5     26.3
                         10     10JUL85     3.3     21.8
                         11     11JUL85     1.2     58.5
                         12     12JUL85     0.0     57.3
                         13     13JUL85    15.0     57.3
                         14     14JUL85    15.0     42.3
                         15     15JUL85    15.0     27.3
                         16     16JUL85    15.0     62.3
                         17     17JUL85    15.0     47.3
                         18     18JUL85    15.0     32.3
                         19     19JUL85     0.0     17.3
```

Using Supplementary Resources: Example 12

In this example the same project as in **Example 11** is scheduled with a specification of DELAY=0. This indicates to PROC CPM that a supplementary level of resources is to be used if an activity cannot be scheduled to start on or before its latest start time (as computed in the unrestrained case). Once again the RCPROFILE and AVPROFILE options are used to save the resource-constrained usage profile and the resource availability profile in a data set named ROUT1.

The negative values for RCOST in observation numbers 14 and 15 of the data set ROUT1 indicate the amount of supplementary resource that was used through the beginning of the day specified in the respective observations. Thus ACOST= −2.7 in observation 14, indicating that the primary level fell to 0 and 2.7 dollars were used from the supplementary level through the end of July 13, 1985.

Similarly, by the beginning of July 14 the supplementary level was depleted by 17.7 dollars. Since the rate of consumption is 15 dollars per day on July 15, the level is further depleted by 15 dollars so that ACOST at the end of July 15 is −32.7. At the beginning of July 16, the value of ACOST increases to 17.3 dollars since 50 dollars are added to the primary availability on this day (see DATA RESINF), of which 32.7 dollars are allotted to bring the supplementary level back to forty dollars.

```
TITLE 'USE OF SUPPLEMENTARY RESOURCES';
PROC CPM DATA=EXMP10 DATE='1JUL85'D RESOURCEIN=RESINF
     OUT=SCHED1 RESOURCEOUT=ROUT1;
   TAILNODE TAIL;
   DURATION DUR;
   HEADNODE HEAD;
   RESOURCE COST / DELAY=0 PERIOD=PER OBSTYPE=OTYPE RCP AVP;
   ID ACTIVITY COST;
```

Output 3.17 Using Supplementary Resources

```
                        USE OF SUPPLEMENTARY RESOURCES                              1

       OBS   TAIL   HEAD   DUR    ACTIVITY               COST    S_START    S_FINISH

        1      1      2     4     DRILL WELL              1.5    01JUL85    04JUL85
        2      2      5     3     PUMP HOUSE              2.3    06JUL85    08JUL85
        3      5      7     2     INSTALL PIPE            2.1    09JUL85    10JUL85
        4      1      5     3     CONSTRUCT POWER LINE    1.1    01JUL85    03JUL85
        5      1      4     5     EXCAVATE                5.3    01JUL85    05JUL85
        6      4      7     6     INSTALL PUMP            1.2    06JUL85    11JUL85
        7      1      3     2     DELIVER MATERIAL        0.5    01JUL85    02JUL85
        8      3      6     4     ASSEMBLE TANK           3.2    05JUL85    08JUL85
        9      6      7     6     ERECT TOWER            15.0    10JUL85    15JUL85
       10      4      6     4     FOUNDATION              1.2    06JUL85    09JUL85
       11      4      5     0     DUMMY                    .     06JUL85    06JUL85
```

```
                        USE OF SUPPLEMENTARY RESOURCES                              2

                   OBS    _TIME_    RCOST    ACOST

                    1    01JUL85     8.4     40.0
                    2    02JUL85     8.4     31.6
                    3    03JUL85     7.9     23.2
                    4    04JUL85     6.8     15.3
                    5    05JUL85     8.5      8.5
                    6    06JUL85     7.9     50.0
                    7    07JUL85     7.9     42.1
                    8    08JUL85     7.9     34.2
                    9    09JUL85     4.5     26.3
                   10    10JUL85    18.3     21.8
                   11    11JUL85    16.2     43.5
                   12    12JUL85    15.0     27.3
                   13    13JUL85    15.0     12.3
                   14    14JUL85    15.0     -2.7
                   15    15JUL85    15.0    -17.7
                   16    16JUL85     0.0     17.3
```

REFERENCES

Clough, R. and Sears, G. (1979), *Construction Project Management*, New York: John Wiley & Sons.

Elmaghraby, S.E. (1977), *Activity Networks: Project Planning and Control by Network Models*, New York: John Wiley & Sons.

Horowitz, E. and Sahni, S. (1976), *Fundamentals of Data Structures*, Potomac, MD: Computer Science Press, Inc.

Minieka, E. (1978), *Optimization Algorithms for Networks and Graphs*, New York: Marcel Dekker, Inc.

Moder, J.J. and Phillips, C.R. (1964), *Project Management* with *CPM and PERT*, New York: Reinhold Publishing Co.

Nunnally, S. (1980), *Construction Methods and Management*, Englewood Cliffs, NJ: Prentice-Hall, Inc.

Chapter 4

The GANTT Procedure

Operating systems: All

ABSTRACT

The GANTT procedure represents graphically the progress of activities in a project such as may be scheduled by the CPM method. In addition to the early and late start schedules, PROC GANTT can plot the actual schedule and depict, on the chart, other important times associated with a project, such as project deadlines and holidays. It is a useful tool for monitoring projects as they progress.

The chart produced by PROC GANTT can be of high resolution quality rather than line printer quality if you specify the GRAPHICS option in the PROC GANTT statement. **(You must have SAS/GRAPH software if you want to produce Gantt charts of high resolution quality using the GRAPHICS option.)** See the section **Graphics Version of PROC GANTT** for more information on producing high-quality Gantt charts.

INTRODUCTION

The GANTT procedure recognizes several options and statements for tailoring Gantt charts to suit your needs. Each option and statement is explained in detail in the **Specifications** section, and examples illustrate most features. There are several distinctive features:

- The input data set is expected to be similar to the OUT= output data set produced by PROC CPM, with each observation representing an activity in the network.
- It is possible to obtain a detailed Gantt chart by specifying the single statement

    `PROC GANTT DATA=SASdataset;`

  where the data set specified is the output data set from PROC CPM.
- Each observation in the data set is plotted on a separate line of the chart; the horizontal axis represents time, the vertical axis represents the sequence of observations in the data set.
- Both axes can be plotted across more than one page.
- The procedure automatically provides extensive labeling of the time axis allowing you to determine easily the exact time of events plotted on the chart. The labels are determined on the basis of the formats of the times being plotted.
- By default the procedure produces Gantt charts of line-printer quality. You can specify the GRAPHICS option on the PROC GANTT statement to obtain high resolution quality Gantt charts.

The first part of this chapter describes all the options for producing line-printer Gantt charts. Options needed for producing high resolution charts are described later, starting with the section **Graphics Version of PROC GANTT**.

SPECIFICATIONS

The following statements are used in PROC GANTT:

    PROC GANTT options;
      BY variables;
      CHART specifications / options;
      ID variables;

PROC GANTT Statement

> PROC GANTT *options*;

The following options can appear in the PROC GANTT statement when you want a chart of line-printer quality:

DATA=*SASdataset*

> names the SAS data set to be used by PROC GANTT. If DATA= is omitted, the most recently created SAS data set is used. This data set contains all the time variables (early, late, and actual times and any other variables to be specified on a CHART statement) that are to be plotted on the chart.

HOLIDATA=*SASdataset*

> names the SAS data set that contains variables whose values are holidays. These variables should be formatted as SAS date or datetime variables depending on the format of the times on the schedule to be plotted. If the holiday variables are SAS date values and the times in the DATA= data set are formatted as SAS datetime variables, then the holiday values are converted to SAS datetime values. The holidays that are to be plotted on the chart must be specified in the HOLIDAYS= option on the CHART statement.

MAXDEC=*n*
M=*n*

> indicates the maximum number of decimal positions printed for a number. A decimal specification in a format overrides a MAXDEC= specification. The default is MAXDEC=2.

BY Statement

> BY *variable*;

A BY statement can be used with PROC GANTT to obtain separate Gantt charts for observations in groups defined by the BY variables. When a BY statement appears, the procedure expects the input data to be sorted in order of the BY variables. If your input data set is not sorted, use the SORT procedure with a similar BY statement to sort the data. The chart for each BY group is formatted separately based only on the observations within that group.

CHART Statement

> CHART *specifications / options*;

The CHART statement controls the format of the Gantt chart and specifies additional variables (other than the early, late, and actual start and finish times) to be plotted on the chart. This statement is not needed if default options are to be used for plotting the Gantt chart. For example, a variable that can be specified in the CHART statement is one that contains the target finish date for each activity in a project. That is, if FDATE is a variable in the input data set containing the desired finish date for each activity, the CHART statement can be used to mark the value of FDATE on the chart for each activity. A CHART specification can be one of the following types:

> *variable1...variablen*
> *variable1=symbol1...variablen=symboln*
> *(variables)=symbol1...(variables)=symboln.*

Variable1...variablen
>   indicates that each variable is to be plotted using the default symbol, the first character of the variable name. For example, the statement

```
CHART SDATE FDATE;
```

>   causes the values of SDATE to be plotted with an S and the values of FDATE with an F.

Variable1=symbol1...variablen=symboln
>   indicates that each variable is to be plotted using the symbol specified. The symbol must be a single character enclosed in quotes.

(variables)=symbol1...(variables)=symboln
>   indicates that each variable within the parentheses is to be plotted using the symbol associated with that group. The symbol must be a single character enclosed in single quotes. For example, the statement

```
CHART (ED SD)='*'
      (FD LD)='+';
```

>   plots the values of the variables in the first group using an asterisk(*) and the values of the variables in the second group using a plus(+).

A single CHART statement can contain specifications in more than one of these forms.

Note: it is not necessary to specify a CHART statement if default values are to be used to draw the Gantt chart.

The following options can appear in the CHART statement:

A_FINISH=*variable*
AF=*variable*
>   specifies the variable containing the actual finish time of each activity in the input data set. This option is not required if the default variable name A_FINISH is used.

A_START=*variable*
AS=*variable*
>   specifies the variable containing the actual start time of each activity in the input data set. This option is not required if the default variable name A_START is used.

CRITFLAG
FLAG
>   indicates that critical jobs be flagged as being critical or 'super_critical'. An activity is said to be critical if its total float is zero. If the total float is negative, the activity is said to be supercritical. Critical activities are marked 'CR', and supercritical activities are marked 'SC' on the left side of the chart.

E_FINISH=*variable*
EF=*variable*
>   specifies the variable containing the early finish time of each activity in the input data set. This option is not required if the default variable name E_FINISH is used.

E_START=*variable*
ES=*variable*
>   specifies the variable containing the early start time of each activity in the input data set. This option is not required if the default variable name E_START is used.

FILL

> causes each page of the Gantt chart to be filled as completely as possible before a new page is started (when the size of the project requires the Gantt chart to be split across several pages). If the FILL option is not specified, the pages are constrained to contain an approximately equal number of activities.

FORMCHAR[*index list*]='*string*'

> defines the characters to be used for constructing the table outlines and dividers. The value is a string 11 characters long defining the two bar characters, vertical and horizontal, and the nine corner characters: upper left, upper middle, upper right, middle left, middle middle (cross), middle right, lower left, lower middle, and lower right. The default value is FORMCHAR=' |---- | + | ---'. Any character or hexadecimal string can be substituted to customize the table appearance. Use an index list to specify which default form character each supplied character replaces; or replace the entire default string by specifying the full 11 character replacement string with no index list. For example, change the four corners to asterisks by using

```
FORMCHAR( 3 5 9 11)= '****'    .
```

> Specifying

```
FORMCHAR='            ' (11 blanks)
```

produces tables with no outlines or dividers. If you have your printout routed to an IBM 6670 printer using an extended font (typestyle 27 or 225) with input character set 216, we recommend that you specify

```
FORMCHAR='FABFACCCBCEB8FECABCBBB'X    .
```

> If you are printing on a printer with a TN (text) print train, we recommend that you specify

```
FORMCHAR='4FBFACBFBC4F8F4FABBFBB'X    .
```

> See "The CALENDAR Procedure" in the *SAS User's Guide: Basics* for an illustration of these characters.

HOLICHAR='*c*'

> indicates the character to print for holidays. Note that GANTT prints only those holidays that fall within the duration or the slack time of an activity. The default symbol used for holidays is '!'.

HOLIDAY=(*variables*)
HOLIDAYS=(*variables*)

> specifies the variables in the HOLIDATA data set that identify holidays to be marked on the schedule.

INCREMENT=*increment*

> specifies the increment for labeling the time axis of the Gantt chart. If INCREMENT= is not specified, a value is chosen that provides the maximum possible labeling.

JOINCHAR='*string*'

> defines a string 6 characters long, identifying nonblank characters to be used for drawing the schedule. The first two symbols are used to plot the schedule of an activity with positive total float. The first symbol denotes the duration of such an activity while the second symbol denotes the slack present in the activity's schedule. The third

symbol is used to plot the duration of a *critical* activity (with zero total float).

The next two symbols are used to plot the schedule of a *super_critical* activity (one with negative float). Thus, the fourth symbol is used to plot the negative slack of such an activity starting from the late start time (to early start time), and the fifth symbol is used to plot the duration of the activity (from early start to early finish). The sixth symbol is used to plot the actual schedule of an activity if the A_START and A_FINISH variables are specified. The default value is JOINCHAR='-.=-*-'.

L_FINISH=*variable*
LF=*variable*

specifies the variable containing the late finish time of each activity in the input data set. This option is not required if the default variable name L_FINISH is used.

L_START=*variable*
LS=*variable*

specifies the variable containing the late start time of each activity in the input data set. This option is not required if the default variable name L_START is used.

MAXDATE=*maxdate*

specifies the finish time for the time axis of the chart. The default value is the largest value of the times being plotted.

MINDATE=*mindate*

specifies the starting time for the time axis of the chart. The default value is the smallest value of the times being plotted.

MININTERVAL=*mininterval*

specifies the smallest interval to be identified on the chart. For example, if MININTERVAL=*day*, then one day is represented on the chart by *scale* (see the SCALE= option) number of columns. The default value of MININTERVAL is chosen on the basis of the formats of the times being plotted, as explained in the section **Specification of Mininterval**. See also the section **Page Format** for further explanation on how to use MININTERVAL= in conjunction with the SCALE= option.

NOJOBNUM

suppresses printing of an identifying job number for each activity; the job number is printed by default to the left of the Gantt chart.

NOLEGEND

suppresses printing the concise default legend at the end of each page of the Gantt chart.

OVERLAPCH='*c*'
OVLPCHAR='*c*'

indicates the overprint character to be printed when more than one of the early, late, or actual times (that is, the AF, AS, EF, ES, LS, LF variables) are to be plotted in the same column. The default character is '*'.

OVPCHAR='*c*'

indicates the character to be printed if one of the variables specified in the CHART statement is to be plotted in the same column as one of the start or finish times. If no OVPCHAR= option is given, @ is used. Note that if one of the E_START, E_FINISH, L_START, or

L_FINISH times coincides with another, the overprint character to be printed can be specified separately using the OVERLAPCH= option.

PADDING=*padding*

FINPAD=*padding*

requests that finish times on the chart be increased by one *padding* unit. This allows the procedure to mark the finish times as the end of the last time period instead of the beginning. Possible values for *padding* are DTSECOND, DTMINUTE, DTHOUR, DTWEEK, DTMONTH, DTQTR, DTYEAR, SECOND, MINUTE, HOUR, DAY, WEEK, MONTH, QTR, YEAR. The default value is chosen on the basis of the format of the times being plotted. See the section **Specification of the PADDING Option** for further explanation of this option.

PAGELIMIT=*pages*

PAGES=*pages*

specifies an upper limit on the number of pages allowed for the Gantt chart. The default value of *pages* is 100. This option is useful for preventing a voluminous amount of output being generated by a wrong specification of the MININTERVAL= or SCALE= options.

REF=*values*

indicates the position of one or more vertical reference lines in the chart section. The values allowed are constant values. Only those reference lines that fall within the scope of the chart are printed. The reference lines are printed using the character specified in the REFCHAR= option (or |, if none is specified). If a time variable value is to be printed in the column where a REF= value goes, the plotting symbol for the time variable is printed instead of the REFCHAR= value. Similarly, the HOLICHAR= symbol has precedence over the REFCHAR= value.

Examples 5 and **6** show some of the ways to specify a list of values for reference lines.

REFCHAR='c'

indicates the character to print for reference lines. If no REFCHAR= option is given, the vertical bar(|) is used.

SCALE=*scale*

requests that *scale* number of columns on the chart be equal to one unit of *mininterval*. Default is SCALE=1 if the time axis of the chart is too wide to fit on one page. If the time axis fits on less than one page, then a default value is chosen that expands the time axis as much as possible but still fits the time axis on one page.

SKIP=*skip*

S=*skip*

requests that *skip* number of lines be skipped between the plots of the schedules of two activities. The SKIP= option is allowed to take integer values between 0 and 4, inclusive. The default value of *skip* is 1.

SUMMARY

requests that a detailed description of all symbols and joining characters used in the Gantt chart be printed before the first page of the chart. This description includes examples of some strings that could occur in the body of the Gantt chart.

SYMCHAR=*'string'*

> defines the symbols to be used for plotting the early start, late start, early finish, late finish, actual start, and actual finish times, in that order. The default value is '<<>>**'. If any of the above times coincide, the symbol plotted is the one specified in the OVERLAPCH= option (or *, if none is specified). If the actual times are not plotted on the chart, you can specify only the first four symbols. If fewer than the required number of symbols are specified, nonspecified symbols are obtained from the default string.

ID Statement

ID *variables*;

The ID statement specifies the variables to be printed that further identify each activity. If two or more consecutive observations have the same combination of values for all the ID variables, only the first of these observations is plotted. If the ID variables do not all fit on one page, they are omitted and a message explaining the omission is printed on the log.

DETAILS

Input Data Set

Typically the input data set is the output data set produced by PROC CPM, sometimes with some additional variables added. Note that for a given observation in the output data set from PROC CPM, the finish times (E_FINISH, L_FINISH, and S_FINISH) denote the end of the time period specified. For instance, if an activity has E_START=2JUN85 and E_FINISH=4JUN85, then the earliest start time for the activity is the beginning of June 2, 1985, and the earliest finish time is the end of June 4, 1985. Thus, PROC GANTT assumes that the early, late, or actual finish time of an activity is at the **end** of the time interval specified for the respective variable.

All start and finish times and additional variables specified in the CHART statement must be numeric and have the same formats. The ID and BY variables can be either numeric or character. Although the data set does not have to be sorted, the output may be more meaningful if the data are in order of increasing early start time.

Labeling on the Time Axis

If the variables being plotted in the chart are unformatted numeric values, the time axis is labeled by the corresponding numbers in increments specified by the INCREMENT= option. However, if the variables have DATE, DATETIME, or TIME formats, then the time axis is labeled with two lines. Each line is determined by the value of MININTERVAL, which in turn is determined by the format. The following table illustrates the label corresponding to different values of MININTERVAL:

MININTERVAL	First Line	Second Line
DAY, DTDAY, WEEK, DTWEEK	Month	Day
MONTH, QTR, YEAR, DTMONTH, DTQTR, DTYEAR	Year	Month
SECOND, DTSECOND	Minute	Second
MINUTE, HOUR, DTMINUTE, DTHOUR	Hour	Minute

Missing Values

Missing values of plotting variables are not plotted. A missing value of an ID variable is considered to be a valid value and is treated like any other value of the variable.

Page Format

The GANTT procedure divides the observations (activities) into a number of subgroups of approximately equal numbers. The size of each group is determined by the PAGESIZE system option. Similarly, the time axis is divided into a number of approximately equal divisions depending on the LINESIZE system option.

If the FILL option is specified, however, each page is filled as completely as possible before plotting on a new page. If both axes are split, the pages are ordered with the chart for each group of activities being plotted completely (the time axis occupying several consecutive pages, if needed) before proceeding to the next group.

If a BY statement is used, each BY group is formatted separately.

Two options that can be used effectively to control the format of the chart are the MININTERVAL and SCALE options. MININTERVAL is the smallest time interval unit to be identified on the chart, and SCALE is the number of columns to be used to denote one unit of MININTERVAL. For example, if MININTERVAL=MONTH and SCALE=10, the chart is formatted so that 10 columns denote the period of one month. The first of these 10 columns denotes the start of the month and the last denotes the end, with each column representing approximately 3 days. Further, the INCREMENT option can be used to control the labeling. In the above example, if INCREMENT=2, then the time axis would have labels for alternate months.

Printed Output

PROC GANTT produces one or more pages of printed values and a plot of the schedule. If the SUMMARY option is specified, the chart is preceded by a detailed description of the symbols used. A legend is printed at the foot of the chart on each page unless suppressed by the NOLEGEND option. The main body of the output consists of columns of the ID values and the Gantt chart of the schedule.

Each activity is identified by a job number (unless the NOJOBNUM option is used), which by default is printed to the left of the ID values. If the time axis of the chart is very wide, causing it to be divided across more than one page, this job number is printed to the left of the respective activity on succeeding pages. ID values are not printed on continuation pages.

Column headings for ID variables consist of either variable labels (if they are present and if space permits) or variable names. To suppress variable labels in column headings, use the NOLABEL system option. (See the OPTIONS statement in "SAS Statements Used Anywhere," *SAS User's Guide: Basics*, for a description of the NOLABEL option.) If the ID variable is formatted, the value is printed using that format. If the ID variables occupy too much space, leaving no room for the chart to be started on the first page, they are omitted and a warning message is printed on the log.

If the CRITFLAG option is specified, a flag is printed to the right of the ID values which indicates how critical the activity is. This flag is also repeated on continuation pages if the time axis occupies more than one page. The body of the chart starts to the right of this flag.

The chart itself displays the schedule and any variables specified in the CHART statement. If the AS= and AF= options are specified in the CHART statement or if the input data set has the default variable names A_START and A_FINISH, then an additional line depicting the actual schedule is plotted for each activity in the project. Holidays and reference lines are also marked appropriately. It is important to note that all the times are plotted at the **start** of the appropriate time period. Thus, if the chart starts on June 1st in column 15 of the page and the value of E_START is 2JUN85, MININTERVAL=DAY and SCALE=5, then the early start time is plotted in column 20.

Specification of Mininterval

If the time values being plotted are SAS date values, the valid values for MININTERVAL are DAY, WEEK, QTR, or YEAR. If the values are SAS datetime values, valid values for the option are DTDAY, DTWEEK, DTMONTH, DTQTR, DTYEAR, DTHOUR, DTMINUTE, or DTSECOND. If they are SAS time values, then valid values for MININTERVAL are HOUR, MINUTE, or SECOND. Note that if the times being plotted are SAS datetime values and MININTERVAL is specified as DTHOUR, DTMINUTE, or DTSECOND, the output generated could run into several thousands of pages. Therefore, be careful when choosing the value of MININTERVAL.

The following table shows the default values of MININTERVAL corresponding to different values of the format of the times being plotted on the chart:

FORMAT	MININTERVAL
DATEw.	DAY
DATETIMEw.d	DTDAY
HHMMw.d	HOUR
MONYYw.	MONTH
TIMEw.d	HOUR
YYMMDDw.	MONTH
YYQw.	MONTH

Specification of the PADDING Option

As explained in the section **Input Data Set**, the finish times in the output data set from PROC CPM denote the final time interval of an activity's duration; that is, the activity finishes at the end of the time interval specified as the finish time. Thus, a plot of the activity's duration should continue through the end of the final interval.

However, as explained in the section **Printed Output**, PROC GANTT plots all times at the beginning of the time period specified. So, if the duration of the activity is to be plotted correctly (through the **end** of the final interval), you must tell the GANTT procedure how to pad the finish times. This information is available to the procedure through the data set label of the output data set from PROC CPM (if used as the input data set for PROC GANTT).

For example, if the finish times are to be increased by one day, the data set label is set by PROC CPM as FINISH TIMES SHOW START OF LAST DAY. (See "SAS Files" in the *SAS User's Guide: Basics* for a description of the data set label option). PROC GANTT then uses this information to set the value of the PADDING option. Internally, the finish times are increased by one day. For instance, if the value of the variable E_FINISH is 4JUN85 and PADDING=DAY, then the value is increased to 5JUN85 (by one DAY), so that the activity's early finish is plotted at the start of 5JUN85 indicating that the early finish time is the **end** of 4JUN85.

It should be noted, however, that the data set label is lost if any operations are performed on the output data set from PROC CPM. If the label field of the input data set to PROC GANTT is blank, the procedure sets the value of the PADDING= option on the basis of the format of the times being plotted. Default values for this option corresponding to the different values of the format of the times being plotted are shown in the following table:

FORMAT	PADDING
DATEw.	DAY
DATETIMEw.d	DTSECOND
TIMEw.d	SECOND
HHMMw.d	MINUTE
MONYYw.	MONTH
YYMMDDw.	YEAR
YYQw.	QTR

If the default value is not appropriate, then the user must specify the correct value using the PADDING= option. Valid values of this option are SECOND, MINUTE, HOUR, DAY, WEEK, MONTH, QTR, YEAR, DTSECOND, DTMINUTE, DTHOUR, DTWEEK, DTMONTH, DTQTR, and DTYEAR. Note that if the PADDING= option is specified and the data set label is available, the value specified overrides the information in the data set label.

Since finish times are adjusted by the value of the PADDING= option, it is recommended that activities with 0 duration be deleted from the data set input to PROC GANTT. If this is not done, an activity with 0 duration is shown on the chart as having a positive duration because finish times are padded to show the **end** of the last time interval.

EXAMPLES

Introduction

The following eight examples illustrate several of the options available with PROC GANTT. **Example 1** shows how to obtain a basic Gantt chart using the default options. The second example demonstrates how to use various options to customize the Gantt chart for the same project. In **Example 3** an extra input data set containing holiday information is used to mark the holidays used in computing the schedule by PROC CPM. The same example also illustrates the use of the CHART statement to specify additional variables to be plotted on the chart.

In **Example 4** the actual schedule for each activity is plotted on a separate line, in addition to the early and late start schedules. **Example 5** illustrates the use of the MININTERVAL and SCALE options to control the width of the chart; this also shows how the chart is divided and continued on the succeeding page when the time axis extends beyond one page. In **Example 6** the MINDATE and MAXDATE options are used to permit viewing of only the desired portion of the schedule in greater detail. **Example 7** illustrates the use of the BY statement to obtain Gantt charts for different projects in a multi-project environment. In **Example 8** PROC GANTT is used after some data manipulation steps to produce Gantt charts for individuals, each working on different subsets of activities in the project.

In all the examples presented the early and late start schedules are specified in the data set by means of the variables, E_START, E_FINISH, L_START, and L_FINISH; hence, the ES=, EF=, LS=, and LF= options are not needed in the CHART statement.

Printing a Gantt Chart: Example 1

This example shows how to use the GANTT procedure to obtain a basic Gantt chart using the default options. The data shown below describe the precedence relationships among the tasks involved in the construction of a typical floor in a multi-story building. The first step saves the precedence relationships in a SAS data set. The variable ACTIVITY names each task, the variable DUR specifies the time it takes to complete the task in days, and the variables SUCCESS1 to SUCCESS4 specify tasks that are immediate successors to the task identified by the ACTIVITY variable.

PROC CPM determines the shortest schedule for the project that finishes before September 1, 1985. The solution schedule, saved in a SAS data set, is sorted before PROC GANTT plots the schedule. Since the DATA= option is not specified, PROC GANTT uses the latest data set, which happens to be the sorted version of the output data set from PROC CPM. The Gantt chart is plotted on two pages because there are too many observations (29) to fit on one page. Note that the observations are split into two groups containing 15 and 14 observations, respectively, so that the chart size on each page is approximately equal. The time axis is labeled from June 21, 1985 to September 1, 1985 since these are the minimum and maximum dates in the input data set. A legend is printed at the bottom of the chart on each page.

```
TITLE 'GANTT EXAMPLE 1';
TITLE2 'PRINTING A GANTT CHART';

DATA;
    FORMAT ACTIVITY $20. SUCCESS1 $20. SUCCESS2 $20. SUCCESS3 $20.
                     SUCCESS4 $20.;
    INPUT ACTIVITY DUR SUCCESS1-SUCCESS4;
    CARDS;
FORM                  4 POUR . . .
POUR                  2 CORE . . .
CORE                 14 STRIP SPRAY_FIREPROOF INSULATE_WALLS .
STRIP                 2 PLUMBING CURTAIN_WALL RISERS DOORS
STRIP                 2 ELECTRICAL_WALLS BALANCE_ELEVATOR . .
CURTAIN_WALL          5 GLAZE_SASH . . .
GLAZE_SASH            5 SPRAY_FIREPROOF INSULATE_WALLS . .
SPRAY_FIREPROOF       5 CEIL_DUCTS_FIXTURE . . .
CEIL_DUCTS_FIXTURE    5 TEST . . .
PLUMBING             10 TEST . . .
TEST                  3 INSULATE_MECHANICAL . . .
INSULATE_MECHANICAL   3 LATH . . .
INSULATE_WALLS        5 LATH . . .
RISERS               10 CEIL_DUCTS_FIXTURE . . .
DOORS                 1 PORT_MASONRY . . .
PORT_MASONRY          2 LATH FINISH_MASONRY . .
ELECTRICAL_WALLS     16 LATH . . .
BALANCE_ELEVATOR      3 FINISH_MASONRY . . .
FINISH_MASONRY        3 PLASTER MARBLE_WORK . .
LATH                  3 PLASTER MARBLE_WORK . .
PLASTER               5 FLOOR_FINISH TILING ACOUSTIC_TILES .
MARBLE_WORK           3 ACOUSTIC_TILES . . .
ACOUSTIC_TILES        5 PAINT FINISH_MECHANICAL . .
TILING                3 PAINT FINISH_MECHANICAL . .
FLOOR_FINISH          5 PAINT FINISH_MECHANICAL . .
PAINT                 5 FINISH_PAINT . . .
FINISH_MECHANICAL     5 FINISH_PAINT . . .
FINISH_PAINT          2 CAULKING_CLEANUP . . .
CAULKING_CLEANUP      4 FINISHED . . .
;

* INVOKE CPM TO FIND THE OPTIMAL SCHEDULE;

PROC CPM FINISHBEFORE DATE='1SEP85'D;
    ACTIVITY ACTIVITY;
    DURATION DUR;
    SUCCESSORS SUCCESS1-SUCCESS4;

* SORT THE SCHEDULE BY THE EARLY START DATE;

PROC SORT; BY E_START;

* INVOKE PROC GANTT TO PRINT THE SCHEDULE;

PROC GANTT;
RUN;
```

Output 4.1   Printing a Gantt Chart

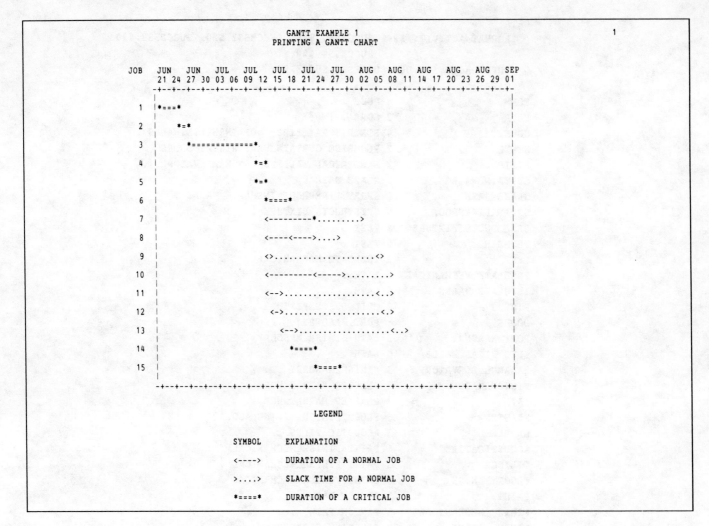

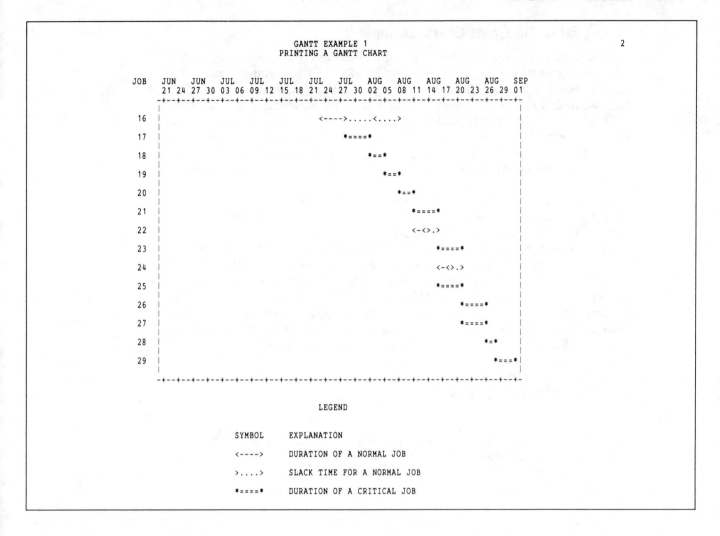

```
JOB   JUN  JUN  JUL  JUL  JUL  JUL  JUL  AUG  AUG  AUG  AUG  AUG  SEP
      21 24  27 30  03 06  09 12  15 18  21 24  27 30  02 05  08 11  14 17  20 23  26 29  01
     -+--+--+--+--+--+--+--+--+--+--+--+--+--+--+--+--+--+--+--+--+--+--+--+--+-
      |                                                                       |
  16  |                               <---->.....<....>                       |
      |
  17  |                               *====*                                  |
      |
  18  |                                  *==*                                 |
      |
  19  |                                   *==*                                |
      |
  20  |                                     *=*                               |
      |
  21  |                                      *====*                           |
      |
  22  |                                      <-<>.>                            |
      |
  23  |                                         *====*                        |
      |
  24  |                                         <-<>.>                         |
      |
  25  |                                         *====*                        |
      |
  26  |                                           *====*                      |
      |
  27  |                                           *====*                      |
      |
  28  |                                              *=*                       |
      |
  29  |                                               *===*|
      |
     -+--+--+--+--+--+--+--+--+--+--+--+--+--+--+--+--+--+--+--+--+--+--+--+--+-
```

                              LEGEND

              SYMBOL   EXPLANATION

              <---->   DURATION OF A NORMAL JOB

              >....>   SLACK TIME FOR A NORMAL JOB

              ====   DURATION OF A CRITICAL JOB

Customizing the Gantt Chart: Example 2

This example shows how to control the format of the Gantt chart using CHART statement options. The input data set used by PROC GANTT is the same as that used in **Example 1**. The output is on four pages; the first two pages contain a detailed description of the various symbols used by the procedure to plot the schedule. This description is produced by using the SUMMARY option. The next two pages contain the chart. The FILL option causes the first page to be filled as completely as possible before the second page is started. Thus, the first page of the chart contains 16 activities while the second page contains only 12 activities.

The SKIP=2 option causes 2 lines to be skipped between observations. The NOLEGEND option suppresses printing of the legend while the NOJOBNUM option causes job numbers to be omitted. The CRITFLAG option is used to produce the flag to the left of the main chart indicating if an activity is critical. The REF= option produces the reference lines shown on the chart on the specified dates. INCREMENT=5 indicates to the procedure that labels are to be printed in increments of 5 units of MININTERVAL, which, by default, is DAY. The ID statement is used to print the activity names to the left of the chart. The ID statement also causes the activity, STRIP, to appear only once in the chart. Thus, there are only 28 activities in this chart instead of 29 as in **Example 1**.

```
TITLE 'GANTT EXAMPLE 2';
TITLE2 'CUSTOMIZING THE GANTT CHART';

PROC GANTT;
   CHART / REF='10JUN85'D TO '30AUG85'D BY 15 SUMMARY FILL NOLEGEND
           INCREMENT=5 SKIP=2 CRITFLAG NOJOBNUM;
   ID ACTIVITY;
RUN;
```

Output 4.2   Customizing the Gantt Chart

```
                          GANTT EXAMPLE 2                              1
                       CUSTOMIZING THE GANTT CHART

                               SUMMARY


           SYMBOLS USED FOR DIFFERENT TIMES ON THE SCHEDULE

                       VARIABLE    SYMBOL

                       E_START        <

                       L_START        <

                       E_FINISH       >

                       L_FINISH       >



                        MISCELLANEOUS SYMBOLS

        SYMBOL     EXPLANATION

          |        REFERENCE LINE

          *        OVERPRINT CHARACTER WHEN START OR
                   FINISH TIMES COINCIDE


        SYMBOLS USED FOR JOINING START AND/OR FINISH TIMES

        SYMBOL     EXPLANATION

          -        DURATION OF NON-CRITICAL JOB

          .        SLACK TIME FOR A NON-CRITICAL JOB

          =        DURATION OF JOB ON CRITICAL PATH

          -        SLACK TIME(NEG.) FOR SUPERCRITICAL JOB

          *        DURATION OF SUPERCRITICAL JOB
```

```
                          GANTT EXAMPLE 2                              2
                       CUSTOMIZING THE GANTT CHART

                              SUMMARY(CONTD.)



                      SOME EXAMPLES OF TYPICAL STRINGS

        STRING              DESCRIPTION

        <--->...<...>       DURATION FOLLOWED BY SLACK TIME:
                            EARLY FINISH BEFORE LATE START

        <---<--->...>       DURATION FOLLOWED BY SLACK TIME:
                            EARLY FINISH AFTER LATE START

        <---*...>           DURATION FOLLOWED BY SLACK TIME:
                            EARLY FINISH EQUALS LATE START

        *=======*           DURATION OF JOB ON CRITICAL PATH

        <--->---<***>       DURATION PRECEDED BY NEGATIVE SLACK TIME
                            FOR A SUPERCRITICAL JOB: LATE FINISH
                            BEFORE EARLY START

        <---<***>***>       DURATION PRECEDED BY NEGATIVE SLACK TIME
                            FOR A SUPERCRITICAL JOB: LATE FINISH
                            AFTER EARLY START

        <---****>           DURATION PRECEDED BY NEGATIVE SLACK TIME
                            FOR A SUPERCRITICAL JOB: LATE FINISH
                            EQUALS EARLY START
```

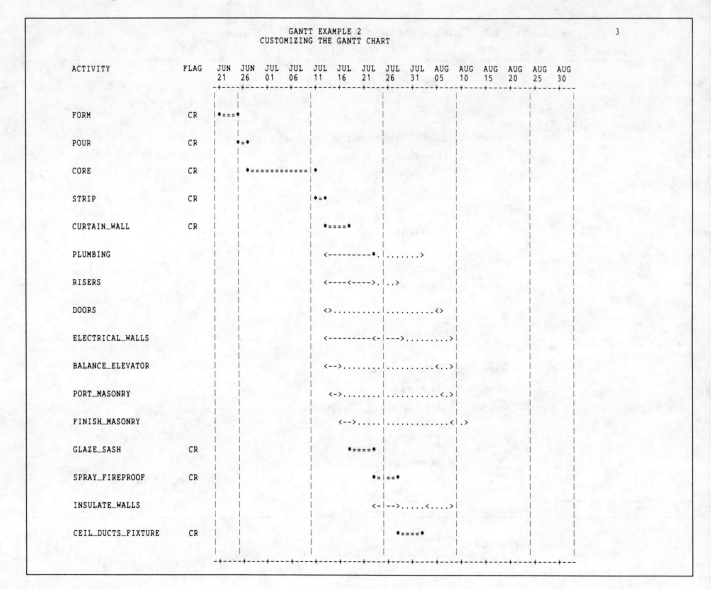

```
                                    GANTT EXAMPLE 2                                          3
                                 CUSTOMIZING THE GANTT CHART


    ACTIVITY            FLAG   JUN  JUN  JUL  JUL  JUL  JUL  JUL  JUL  JUL  AUG  AUG  AUG  AUG  AUG  AUG
                               21   26   01   06   11   16   21   26   31   05   10   15   20   25   30
                              -+----+----+----+----+----+----+----+----+----+----+----+----+----+----+---
                               |         |         |         |         |
    FORM                 CR   |*===*     |         |         |         |
                               |         |         |         |         |
    POUR                 CR   |    *=*   |         |         |         |
                               |         |         |         |         |
    CORE                 CR   |    *============|*        |         |         |
                               |         |         |         |         |
    STRIP                CR   |         |         *=*      |         |         |
                               |         |         |         |         |
    CURTAIN_WALL         CR   |         |         *====*   |         |         |
                               |         |         |         |         |
    PLUMBING                   |         |         <---------*.|.......>     |         |
                               |         |         |         |         |
    RISERS                     |         |         <----<---->.|..>    |         |
                               |         |         |         |         |
    DOORS                      |         |         <>..........|.........<>   |
                               |         |         |         |         |
    ELECTRICAL_WALLS           |    |.   |         <---------<-|--->.........>|
                               |         |         |         |         |
    BALANCE_ELEVATOR           |         |         <-->.......|.........<..>|
                               |         |         |         |         |
    PORT_MASONRY               |         |          <->.......|...........<.>
                               |         |         |         |         |
    FINISH_MASONRY             |         |          <-->.....|............<|.>
                               |         |         |         |         |
    GLAZE_SASH           CR   |         |         |   *====*   |         |
                               |         |         |         |         |
    SPRAY_FIREPROOF      CR   |         |         |         *=|==*     |
                               |         |         |         |         |
    INSULATE_WALLS             |         |         |         <-|-->.....<....>|
                               |         |         |         |         |
    CEIL_DUCTS_FIXTURE   CR   |         |         |         *====*   |
                               |         |         |         |         |
                              -+----+----+----+----+----+----+----+----+----+----+----+----+----+----+---
```

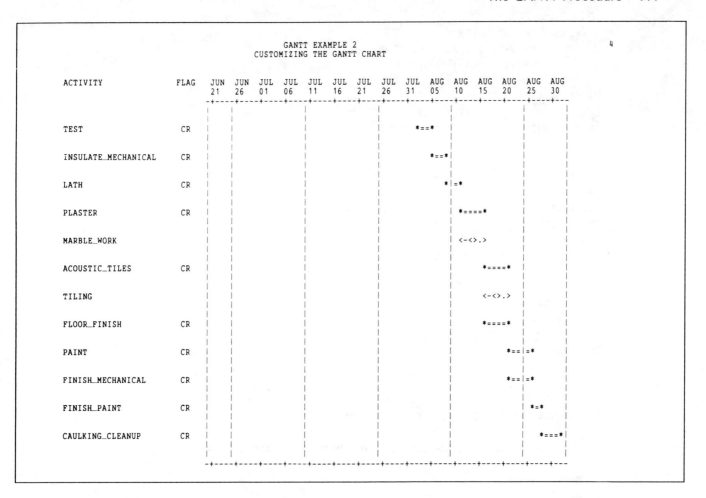

```
                          GANTT EXAMPLE 2                                              4
                       CUSTOMIZING THE GANTT CHART

ACTIVITY              FLAG   JUN  JUN  JUL  JUL  JUL  JUL  JUL  JUL  JUL  AUG  AUG  AUG  AUG  AUG  AUG
                             21   26   01   06   11   16   21   26   31   05   10   15   20   25   30
                           -+----+----+----+----+----+----+----+----+----+----+----+----+----+----+--
                            |    |         |         |         |         |              |         |
TEST                   CR   |    |         |         |         |       *==*             |         |
                            |    |         |         |         |         |              |         |
INSULATE_MECHANICAL    CR   |    |         |         |         |       *==*|            |         |
                            |    |         |         |         |         |              |         |
LATH                   CR   |    |         |         |         |      *  | =*           |         |
                            |    |         |         |         |         |              |         |
PLASTER                CR   |    |         |         |         |         |*====*         |         |
                            |    |         |         |         |         |              |         |
MARBLE_WORK                 |    |         |         |         |         <-<>.>          |         |
                            |    |         |         |         |         |              |         |
ACOUSTIC_TILES         CR   |    |         |         |         |         |   *=====*      |         |
                            |    |         |         |         |         |              |         |
TILING                      |    |         |         |         |         |   <-<>.>       |         |
                            |    |         |         |         |         |              |         |
FLOOR_FINISH           CR   |    |         |         |         |         |   *=====*      |         |
                            |    |         |         |         |         |              |         |
PAINT                  CR   |    |         |         |         |         |            *==|=*        |
                            |    |         |         |         |         |              |         |
FINISH_MECHANICAL      CR   |    |         |         |         |         |            *==|=*        |
                            |    |         |         |         |         |              |         |
FINISH_PAINT           CR   |    |         |         |         |         |              | *=*      |
                            |    |         |         |         |         |              |         |
CAULKING_CLEANUP       CR   |    |         |         |         |         |              |  *====*| |
                            |    |         |         |         |         |              |         |
                           -+----+----+----+----+----+----+----+----+----+----+----+----+----+----+--
```

Marking Holidays and Target Completion Dates: Example 3

The following data describe a construction project, the representation being in activity-on-edge format. In addition to variables specifying the activity name, tail node, head node, and duration of each activity in the network, the data also contain a variable specifying the target dates for some of the activities in the project. Another DATA step saves July 4, 1985 as a holiday in a holiday data set. PROC CPM then schedules the project to start on July 1, 1985 and saves the schedule in an output data set named SAVE. Using the ID statement in PROC CPM, the variables ACTIVITY and TARGET are passed to the output data set.

Following this, a DATA step deletes activities with 0 duration; the resulting data set SAVE1 does not contain the dummy activity. (See the section **Specification of the PADDING Option**, above, for reasons to delete activities of 0 duration.) Next, PROC GANTT is invoked with the specification of HOLIDATA=HOLDATA in the PROC statement and the HOLIDAY= option in the CHART statement causing the holidays to be marked on the chart. Note that the procedure marks the **duration** of the holiday with the symbol specified in the HOLICHAR= option. Specifying the variable TARGET in the CHART statement causes the target dates to be marked on the chart with the symbol 'T'.

```
TITLE 'GANTT EXAMPLE 3';
TITLE2 'MARKING HOLIDAYS AND TARGET COMPLETION DATES';

DATA CONST1;
```

```
      FORMAT TARGET DATE9.;
      INPUT ACTIVITY $ 1-20 TAIL 22 DUR 24 HEAD 26
           TARGET DATE9.;
      CARDS;
DRILL WELL             1 4 2 .
PUMP HOUSE             2 3 5 .
INSTALL PIPE          5 2 7 10JUL85
CONSTRUCT POWER LINE 1 3 5  7JUL85
EXCAVATE              1 5 4  9JUL85
INSTALL PUMP          4 6 7 .
DELIVER MATERIAL      1 2 3 .
ASSEMBLE TANK         3 4 6 .
ERECT TOWER           6 6 7 .
FOUNDATION            4 4 6 12JUL85
DUMMY                 4 0 5 .
;

DATA HOLDATA;
   FORMAT HOL DATE7.;
   INPUT HOL DATE7.;
   CARDS;
3JUL85
;

* SCHEDULE THE PROJECT SUBJECT TO HOLIDAYS;

PROC CPM DATA=CONST1 DATE='1JUL85'D HOLIDATA=HOLDATA OUT=SAVE;
   TAILNODE TAIL;
   DURATION DUR;
   HEADNODE HEAD;
   ID ACTIVITY TARGET;
   HOLIDAY HOL;

* DELETE ACTIVITIES WITH 0 DURATION;

DATA SAVE1;
   SET SAVE;
   IF DUR=0 THEN DELETE;

* SORT THE SCHEDULE BY THE EARLY START DATE;

PROC SORT OUT=SCHED; BY E_START;

* PLOT THE SCHEDULE;

PROC GANTT HOLIDATA=HOLDATA DATA=SCHED;
   CHART TARGET='T' / HOLICHAR='H' HOLIDAY=(HOL)
                   SCALE=4;
   ID ACTIVITY;
RUN;
```

Output 4.3   Marking Holidays and Target Completion Dates on the Gantt Chart

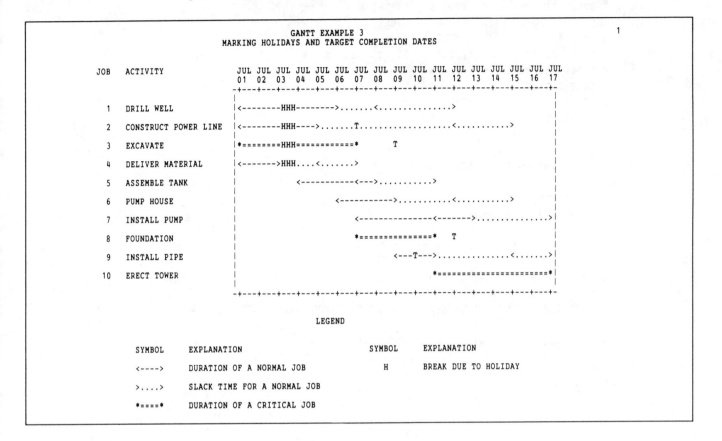

Plotting the Actual Schedule: Example 4

Suppose that the project is complete and you wish to compare the actual progress of the activities with the schedule computed by PROC CPM. The following DATA step stores actual start and finish times of each activity in a data set named ACTUAL. A data set named UPDATE is then created that contains both the schedule obtained from PROC CPM (the data set SAVE1 is used because it does not contain the dummy activity) and the actual schedule. The resulting data set is sorted by early start time.

PROC GANTT is then used to plot computed and actual schedules for each activity on separate lines. The A_START= and A_FINISH= options in the CHART statement specify the variables containing the actual start and finish times for each activity. SYMCHAR='<<>>SF' causes the symbols 'S' and 'F' to be used to print actual start and finish times instead of the default symbol '*'. OVERLAPCH='@' indicates that the symbol '@' is to be used when any of the start or finish times coincide.

```
TITLE 'GANTT EXAMPLE 4';
TITLE2 'PLOTTING ACTUAL START AND FINISH TIMES ON THE CHART';

DATA ACTUAL;
   FORMAT FDATE DATE9. SDATE DATE9.;
   INPUT ACTIVITY $ 1-20 FDATE DATE9. SDATE DATE9.;
   CARDS;
DRILL WELL           5JUL85    1JUL85
```

```
        PUMP HOUSE           9JUL85    7JUL85
        INSTALL PIPE        12JUL85   10JUL85
        CONSTRUCT POWER LINE 4JUL85    1JUL85
        EXCAVATE             7JUL85    2JUL85
        INSTALL PUMP        12JUL85    8JUL85
        DELIVER MATERIAL     4JUL85    2JUL85
        ASSEMBLE TANK        7JUL85    5JUL85
        ERECT TOWER         17JUL85   13JUL85
        FOUNDATION          12JUL85    8JUL85
        ;

   * MERGE THE COMPUTED SCHEDULE WITH THE ACTUAL SCHEDULE;

   DATA UPDATE;
      MERGE SAVE1 ACTUAL;

   * SORT THE DATA;

   PROC SORT; BY E_START;

   * PLOT THE COMPUTED AND ACTUAL SCHEDULES USING PROC GANTT;

   PROC GANTT DATA=UPDATE HOLIDATA=HOLDATA;
      CHART / SYMCHAR='<<>>SF' OVERLAPCH='@' HOLIDAY=(HOL)
             A_START=SDATE A_FINISH=FDATE;
      ID ACTIVITY;

   RUN;
```

Output 4.4   Plotting the Actual Schedule on the Gantt Chart

```
                                    GANTT EXAMPLE 4                                         1
                         PLOTTING ACTUAL START AND FINISH TIMES ON THE CHART

   JOB   ACTIVITY               JUL  JUL  JUL  JUL  JUL  JUL  JUL  JUL  JUL  JUL  JUL  JUL  JUL  JUL  JUL  JUL  JUL  JUL
                                01   02   03   04   05   06   07   08   09   10   11   12   13   14   15   16   17   18
                             -+----+----+----+----+----+----+----+----+----+----+----+----+----+----+----+----+----+--
                             |
     1   DRILL WELL          |<----------!!!!---------->.........<.................>                                  |
                             |S----------!!!!----------F                                                             |
                             |
     2   CONSTRUCT POWER LINE |<----------!!!!----->...........................<..............>                      |
                             |S----------!!!!-----F                                                                  |
                             |
     3   EXCAVATE            |ə==========!!!!==============ə                                                          |
                             |        S-----!!!!--------------------F                                                |
                             |
     4   DELIVER MATERIAL    |<--------->!!!!.....<........>                                                          |
                             |        S-----!!!!-----F                                                                |
                             |
     5   ASSEMBLE TANK       |              <-------------<---->.............>                                        |
                             |                   S--------------F                                                     |
                             |
     6   PUMP HOUSE          |                 <------------->............<............>                             |
                             |                      S--------------F                                                  |
                             |
     7   INSTALL PUMP        |                 <------------------<--------->.................>                       |
                             |                      S----------------------F                                          |
                             |
     8   FOUNDATION          |                 ə===================ə                                                  |
                             |                      S----------------------F                                          |
                             |
     9   INSTALL PIPE        |                        <--------->.................<........>                          |
                             |                             S--------------F                                           |
                             |
    10   ERECT TOWER         |                             ə===========================ə   |
                             |                                  S-----------------------F|
                             -+----+----+----+----+----+----+----+----+----+----+----+----+----+----+----+----+----+--


                                                LEGEND


         SYMBOL      EXPLANATION                         SYMBOL      EXPLANATION

         <---->      DURATION OF A NORMAL JOB              !         BREAK DUE TO HOLIDAY

         >....>      SLACK TIME FOR A NORMAL JOB         S----F      ACTUAL DURATION

         ə====ə      DURATION OF A CRITICAL JOB
```

Using the MININTERVAL and SCALE Options: Example 5

The construction project described in **Example 3** is scheduled using PROC CPM with INTERVAL=WEEK so that durations are in units of weeks instead of days. The start date for the project is specified as June 30, 1985. The output data set obtained from PROC CPM is sorted, thus causing the data set label to be erased. From the description in the **Specification of the PADDING Option** section, you can see that the default value of the PADDING= option (DAY in this example) is not the right choice. Thus, the PADDING= option should be specified as WEEK.

The specifications MININTERVAL=WEEK and SCALE=10 cause PROC GANTT to use 10 columns to denote one week. Note that this choice also causes the chart to become too wide to fit on one page. Thus, PROC GANTT splits the chart into two pages. The first page contains the ID variable as well as the job number while the second page contains only the job number. The chart is split so that the printed area on each page is approximately equal.

The specification REF='1JUL85'D TO '15OCT85'D BY MONTH causes PROC GANTT to draw reference lines at the start of every month.

```
        TITLE 'GANTT EXAMPLE 5';
        TITLE2 'USE OF MININTERVAL AND SCALE OPTIONS';

        * SCHEDULE USING INTERVAL=WEEK;

        PROC CPM DATA=CONST1 DATE='30JUN85'D INTERVAL=WEEK
                OUT=SAVE;
           TAILNODE TAIL;
           DURATION DUR;
           HEADNODE HEAD;
           ID ACTIVITY;

        *DELETE ACTIVITIES WITH 0 DURATION;

        DATA SAVE;
           SET SAVE;
           IF DUR=0 THEN DELETE;

        PROC SORT DATA=SAVE; BY E_START;

        PROC GANTT DATA=SAVE;
           CHART / PADDING=WEEK MININTERVAL=WEEK SCALE=10 NOLEGEND
                   REF='1JUL85'D TO '15OCT85'D BY MONTH;
           ID ACTIVITY;
        RUN;
```

Output 4.5   Using the MININTERVAL and SCALE Options on a Gantt Chart

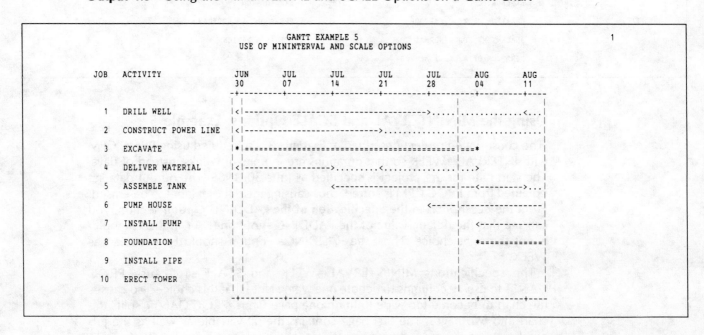

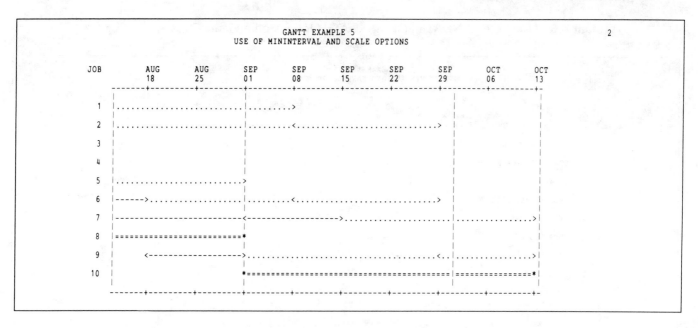

Using the MINDATE and MAXDATE Options: Example 6

In this example the data set SAVE from **Example 5** is used to display the schedule of the project over a limited time period, the start date being specified by MINDATE and the end date by MAXDATE.

```
TITLE 'GANTT EXAMPLE 6';
TITLE2 'USE OF MINDATE AND MAXDATE OPTIONS';
PROC GANTT DATA=SAVE;
   CHART / PADDING=WEEK MINDATE='1AUG85'D MAXDATE='31AUG85'D
           NOLEGEND REF='5AUG85'D TO '25AUG85'D BY 5;
   ID ACTIVITY;
RUN;
```

Output 4.6 Using the MINDATE and MAXDATE Options on a Gantt Chart

```
                                    GANTT EXAMPLE 6                                          1
                                USE OF MINDATE AND MAXDATE OPTIONS

        JOB    ACTIVITY             AUG AUG AUG AUG AUG AUG AUG AUG AUG AUG AUG AUG AUG AUG AUG AUG
                                    01  03  05  07  09  11  13  15  17  19  21  23  25  27  29  31
                                    -+---+---+---+---+---+---+---+---+---+---+---+---+---+---+---+-
                                     |   |   |   |   |   |   |   |   |   |   |   |   |   |   |   |
         1    DRILL WELL             |........|..........|.<.........|...........|..........|...........|
         2    CONSTRUCT POWER LINE   |........|..........|...........|...........|..........|...........|
         3    EXCAVATE               |======* |          |           |           |          |           |
         4    DELIVER MATERIAL       |......> |           |           |           |          |           |
         5    ASSEMBLE TANK          |-------<-|----------|->.......|...........|..........|...........|
         6    PUMP HOUSE             |--------|----------|----------|----->...|..........|...........|
         7    INSTALL PUMP           |     <-|----------|----------|-----------|----------|---------|
         8    FOUNDATION             |     *=|=========|==========|=========|=========|============|
         9    INSTALL PIPE           |       |         |          |   <---|----------|------------|
        10    ERECT TOWER            |       |         |          |       |          |           |
                                     |       |         |          |       |          |           |
                                    -+---+---+---+---+---+---+---+---+---+---+---+---+---+---+---+-
```

BY Processing: Example 7

Suppose that the construction is divided into three sub-projects, A, B, and C, and you want separate Gantt charts for each project. The data set CONST2, printed below, contains project information in a variable named PROJECT. After scheduling the master project using PROC CPM with ACTIVITY and PROJECT as ID variables, the output data set is sorted by project name and early start time. Then PROC GANTT is invoked with the variable PROJECT specified in the BY statement to obtain individual Gantt charts for each project.

```
TITLE 'GANTT EXAMPLE 7';
TITLE2 'BY PROCESSING';
PROC CPM DATA=CONST2 DATE='1JUL85'D;
   TAILNODE TAIL;
   DURATION DUR;
   HEADNODE HEAD;
   ID ACTIVITY PROJECT;

DATA PROJ;
   SET _LAST_;
   IF DUR=0 THEN DELETE;

PROC SORT; BY PROJECT E_START;

PROC GANTT DATA=PROJ;
   CHART / SCALE=4 INCREMENT=2;
   BY PROJECT;
   ID ACTIVITY;
RUN;
```

Output 4.7   Using BY Processing for Separate Gantt Charts

```
                                GANTT EXAMPLE 7                                    1
                                DATA CONST2

        OBS    ACTIVITY                TAIL    DUR    HEAD      PROJECT

         1     DRILL WELL                1      4      2           A
         2     PUMP HOUSE                2      3      5           B
         3     INSTALL PIPE              5      2      7           B
         4     CONSTRUCT POWER LINE      1      3      5           C
         5     EXCAVATE                  1      5      4           A
         6     INSTALL PUMP              4      6      7           B
         7     DELIVER MATERIAL          1      2      3           C
         8     ASSEMBLE TANK             3      4      6           C
         9     ERECT TOWER               6      6      7           C
        10     FOUNDATION                4      4      6           A
        11     DUMMY                     4      0      5
```

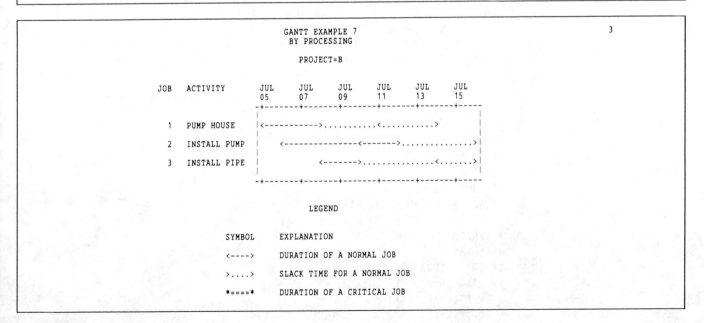

```
                                GANTT EXAMPLE 7                                    2
                                BY PROCESSING

                                   PROJECT=A


        JOB    ACTIVITY      JUL      JUL      JUL      JUL      JUL      JUL
                             01       03       05       07       09       11
                            -+-------+-------+-------+-------+-------+-------+-
                             |                                               |
         1     DRILL WELL    |<--------------->.......<..............>|
                             |                                               |
         2     EXCAVATE      |*==================*                           |
                             |                                               |
         3     FOUNDATION    |                   *================*          |
                             |                                               |
                            -+-------+-------+-------+-------+-------+-------+-



                                      LEGEND


                             SYMBOL    EXPLANATION

                             <---->    DURATION OF A NORMAL JOB

                             >....>    SLACK TIME FOR A NORMAL JOB

                             *====*    DURATION OF A CRITICAL JOB
```

```
                                GANTT EXAMPLE 7                                    3
                                BY PROCESSING

                                   PROJECT=B


        JOB    ACTIVITY      JUL      JUL      JUL      JUL      JUL      JUL
                             05       07       09       11       13       15
                            -+-------+-------+-------+-------+-------+-------+-----
                             |                                               |
         1     PUMP HOUSE    |<----------->..........<...........>           |
                             |                                               |
         2     INSTALL PUMP  |    <--------------<------->..............>|
                             |                                               |
         3     INSTALL PIPE  |            <------->..............<.......>|
                             |                                               |
                            -+-------+-------+-------+-------+-------+-------+-----


                                      LEGEND


                             SYMBOL    EXPLANATION

                             <---->    DURATION OF A NORMAL JOB

                             >....>    SLACK TIME FOR A NORMAL JOB

                             *====*    DURATION OF A CRITICAL JOB
```

120   Chapter 4

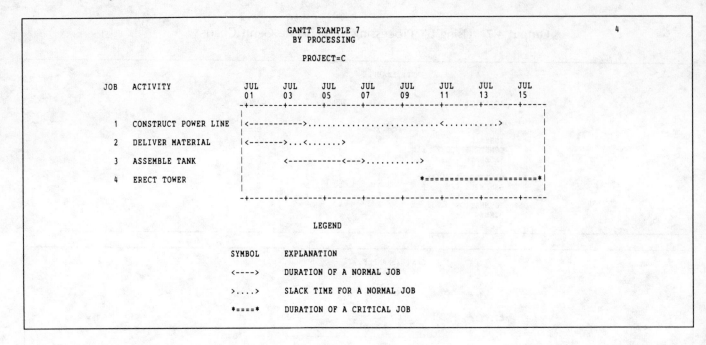

```
                        GANTT EXAMPLE 7                                    4
                         BY PROCESSING

                          PROJECT=C

JOB   ACTIVITY              JUL    JUL    JUL    JUL    JUL    JUL    JUL    JUL
                           01     03     05     07     09     11     13     15
                         -+-------+------+-------+------+------+------+------+-----
                          |
 1    CONSTRUCT POWER LINE |<---------->..........................<..........>   |
                          |
 2    DELIVER MATERIAL     |<------->...<....... >                              |
                          |
 3    ASSEMBLE TANK        |       <-----------<--->...........>                |
                          |
 4    ERECT TOWER          |                              *=====================*|
                          |
                         -+-------+------+-------+------+------+------+------+-----

                              LEGEND

              SYMBOL      EXPLANATION

              <---->      DURATION OF A NORMAL JOB

              >....>      SLACK TIME FOR A NORMAL JOB

              *====*      DURATION OF A CRITICAL JOB
```

Gantt Charts by Persons: Example 8

Now suppose that you want to obtain individual Gantt charts for two people (Thomas and William) working on the construction project. The data set CONST3, printed below, contains two new variables, THOMAS and WILLIAM. Each variable has a value 1 for activities in which the person is involved; a missing value otherwise. Thus, a value 1 for the variable THOMAS in observation number 1 indicates that Thomas is working on the activity DRILL WELL.

PROC CPM is used to schedule the project to start on July 1, 1985. A data set named PERSONS is created containing one observation per activity per person working on that activity and a new variable named PERSON containing the name of the person to which the observation pertains. For example, this new data set contains two observations for the activity INSTALL PUMP, one with PERSON= 'THOMAS' and the other with PERSON='WILLIAM', and no observation for the activity CONSTRUCT POWER LINE. This data set is printed in order by PERSON and E_START. Then, PROC GANTT is used to obtain individual charts for each person.

```
     TITLE 'GANTT EXAMPLE 8';

PROC CPM DATA=CONST3 DATE='1JUL85'D;
     TAILNODE TAIL;
     DURATION DUR;
     HEADNODE HEAD;
     ID ACTIVITY THOMAS WILLIAM;

DATA PERSONS;
     SET _LAST_;
     IF DUR=0 THEN DELETE;
     IF WILLIAM¬=. THEN DO;
        PERSON='WILLIAM';
        OUTPUT;
        END;
     IF THOMAS¬=. THEN DO;
```

```
                PERSON='THOMAS';
                OUTPUT;
                END;
             DROP THOMAS WILLIAM;

     PROC SORT DATA=PERSONS;
        BY PERSON E_START;

     TITLE2 'DATA PERSONS';
     PROC PRINT DATA=PERSONS;
     RUN;

     TITLE2 'PERSONALIZED GANTT CHARTS';
     PROC GANTT DATA=PERSONS;
        CHART / SCALE=4 INCREMENT=2;
        BY PERSON;
        ID ACTIVITY;
```

Output 4.8   Gantt Charts by Person

```
                                    GANTT EXAMPLE 8                                                    1
                                     DATA CONST3

             OBS    ACTIVITY              TAIL    DUR    HEAD    THOMAS    WILLIAM

              1     DRILL WELL             1       4      2        1         .
              2     PUMP HOUSE             2       3      5        .         .
              3     INSTALL PIPE           5       2      7        1         1
              4     CONSTRUCT POWER LINE   1       3      5        .         .
              5     EXCAVATE               1       5      4        .         1
              6     INSTALL PUMP           4       6      7        1         1
              7     DELIVER MATERIAL       1       2      3        1         1
              8     ASSEMBLE TANK          3       4      6        .         1
              9     ERECT TOWER            6       6      7        1         .
             10     FOUNDATION             4       4      6        1         .
             11     DUMMY                  4       0      5        .         .
```

```
                                    GANTT EXAMPLE 8                                                    2
                                     DATA PERSONS

   OBS   TAIL   HEAD   DUR   ACTIVITY          E_START    E_FINISH   L_START    L_FINISH   T_FLOAT   F_FLOAT   PERSON

    1      1      2     4    DRILL WELL        01JUL85    04JUL85    07JUL85    10JUL85       6         0      THOMAS
    2      1      3     2    DELIVER MATERIAL  01JUL85    02JUL85    04JUL85    05JUL85       3         0      THOMAS
    3      4      7     6    INSTALL PUMP      06JUL85    11JUL85    10JUL85    15JUL85       4         4      THOMAS
    4      4      6     4    FOUNDATION        06JUL85    09JUL85    06JUL85    09JUL85       0         0      THOMAS
    5      5      7     2    INSTALL PIPE      08JUL85    09JUL85    14JUL85    15JUL85       6         6      THOMAS
    6      6      7     6    ERECT TOWER       10JUL85    15JUL85    10JUL85    15JUL85       0         0      THOMAS
    7      1      4     5    EXCAVATE          01JUL85    05JUL85    01JUL85    05JUL85       0         0      WILLIAM
    8      1      3     2    DELIVER MATERIAL  01JUL85    02JUL85    04JUL85    05JUL85       3         0      WILLIAM
    9      3      6     4    ASSEMBLE TANK     03JUL85    06JUL85    06JUL85    09JUL85       3         3      WILLIAM
   10      4      7     6    INSTALL PUMP      06JUL85    11JUL85    10JUL85    15JUL85       4         4      WILLIAM
   11      5      7     2    INSTALL PIPE      08JUL85    09JUL85    14JUL85    15JUL85       6         6      WILLIAM
```

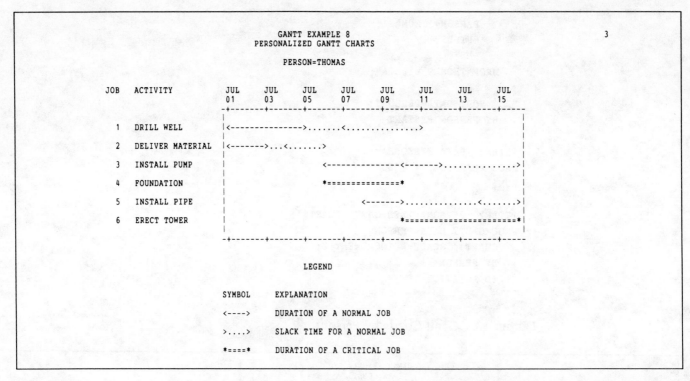

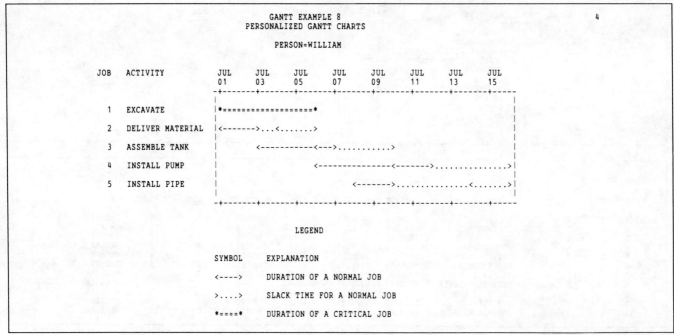

GRAPHICS VERSION OF PROC GANTT

This section describes the options that can be used in conjunction with the GRAPHICS option in a PROC GANTT statement to obtain high resolution quality Gantt charts. Most of the options described earlier for line-printer quality charts are also valid with the GRAPHICS option, with similar interpretations. A table of valid options is provided listing any change in interpretation for the graphics version. Another table lists the line-printer options that are **invalid** with the

GRAPHICS option; for each such option the corresponding option for high resolution charts is listed, where applicable. A third table lists, for each GRAPHICS
option described in this section, the corresponding line-printer option, if one
exists.

SPECIFICATIONS

PROC GANTT Statement

PROC GANTT *options*;

The following options in the PROC GANTT statement are specifically for graphics
quality Gantt charts:

ANNOTATE=*SASdataset*
ANNO=*SASdataset*
          specifies the input data set which must be an ANNOTATE= type
          data set containing the appropriate ANNOTATE variables. (See the
          chapter, "The ANNOTATE= Option" in the *SAS/GRAPH User's
          Guide* for details.)

GOUT=*graphics catalog*
          specifies the name of the graphics catalog used to save the output
          produced by GANTT for later replay. See the chapter "SAS/GRAPH
          Graphics Output" in the *SAS/GRAPH User's Guide* for more details.

GRAPHICS
          indicates that the Gantt chart produced be of high resolution
          quality. If you specify the GRAPHICS option but you do not have
          SAS/GRAPH software at your site, the procedure stops and issues an
          error message.

CHART Statement

CHART *specifications/options*;

As before, the CHART statement controls the format of the Gantt chart and specifies additional variables (other than the early, late, and actual start and finish
times) to be plotted on the chart. The same forms for the specification of CHART
variables (as in the line-printer version) are allowed although the interpretation
is somewhat different. Each form of specification is repeated here with a corresponding description of the interpretation. Note that the symbols for any activity
are plotted on a line **above** the one corresponding to that activity. In addition
to plotting the required symbol, PROC GANTT draws a vertical line below the
symbol in the same color as the symbol. The length of the line is the same as
the height of the bars (referred to as bar height) used to represent the durations
of the activities on the Gantt chart. This line helps identify the exact position of
the plotted value.

Variable1...variablen
          indicates that each variable is to be plotted using symbols specified
          in SYMBOL statements. The *i*th variable in the list is plotted using
          the plot symbol, color, and font specified in the *i*th SYMBOL
          statement. The height specified in the SYMBOL statement is
          multiplied by the bar height to obtain the height of the symbol that
          is plotted. Thus, if H=0.5 in the first SYMBOL statement and the bar
          height is 5 percent of the screen area, then the first symbol is plotted

with a height of 2.5 percent. For example, suppose the following two SYMBOL statements are in effect:

```
SYMBOL1 V=STAR C=RED    H=1;
SYMBOL2 V=V    C=GREEN H=0.5 F=GREEK;
```

Then the statement

```
CHART SDATE FDATE;
```

causes values of SDATE to be plotted with a red star that is as high as each bar and the values of FDATE with an inverted green triangle that is half as high as the bar height.

Variable1=symbol1...variablen=symboln
indicates that each variable is to be plotted using the symbol specified. The symbol must be a single character enclosed in quotes. The font used for the symbol is the same as the font used for the text.

(variables)=symbol1...(variables)=symboln
indicates that each variable in parentheses is to be plotted using the symbol associated with that group. The symbol must be a single character enclosed in single quotes. For example, the statement

```
CHART (ED SD)='*'
      (FD LD)='+';
```

plots the values of variables in the first group using an asterisk (*) and the values of variables in the second group using a plus (+).

A single CHART statement can contain requests in more than one of these forms.

Note: it is not necessary to specify a CHART statement if only default values are to be used to draw the Gantt chart.

The following options that can appear in the CHART statement are specifically for the production of high resolution quality Gantt charts:

ANNOTATE=*SASdataset*
ANNO=*SASdataset*
specifies the input data set which must be an ANNOTATE= type data set containing the appropriate ANNOTATE variables. (See the chapter, "The ANNOTATE= Option" in the *SAS/GRAPH User's Guide* for details.)

CAXIS=*color*
CAXES=*color*
CA=*color*
specifies the color to use for printing axes for the Gantt chart. If CAXIS= is omitted, the first color in the COLORS= list of the GOPTIONS statement is used.

CFRAME=*color*
CFR=*color*
specifies the color to use for filling the axis area. This option is ignored if the NOFRAME option is specified.

CREF=*color*
specifies the color to use for drawing vertical lines on the chart requested by the REF= option. If CREF= is not specified, the axis color is used.

CTEXT=*color*
CT=*color*
> specifies the color to use for printing text that appears on the chart, including variable names or labels, tick mark values, values of ID variables, and so on. If CTEXT= is omitted, PROC GANTT uses the first color in the COLORS= list of the GOPTIONS statement.

DESCRIPTION='*string*'
DES='*string*'
> specifies a descriptive string, up to 40 characters in length, that appears in the description field of PROC GREPLAY's master menu. If DESCRIPTION= is omitted, the description field of PROC GREPLAY's master menu is blank.

FONT=*name*
> specifies the font to use for printing job numbers, ID variables, legend, labels on the time axis, and so forth. If this option is not specified, the hardware character set is used unless the global options NOCHARACTERS is in effect, in which case the SIMPLEX font is used.

LREF=*linetype*
> specifies the line style (1-32) used for drawing the reference lines. (See the **SYMBOL Statements** description in the chapter "Global Statements" in the *SAS/GRAPH User's Guide*, for examples of the various line styles.) The default line style is 1, a solid line.

NOFRAME
NOFR
> suppresses drawing the vertical boundaries to the left and right of the Gantt chart; only the top axis and a parallel line at the bottom are drawn. If this option is not specified, the entire chart area is framed.

DETAILS

Formatting the Chart

If necessary, PROC GANTT divides the Gantt chart into several pages. The amount of information contained on each page is determined by the values of the global parameters HPOS and VPOS. The height of each bar of the Gantt chart is computed as (1/v)% of the screen height where VPOS=v. Thus, the larger the value of VPOS, the narrower the bar. The height of the characters in the text is the same as the height of each bar. The value of HPOS determines the width of the chart. The screen is assumed to be divided into *h* columns where HPOS=*h*; thus, each column is assumed to be as wide as (1/h)% of the screen width. Hence SCALE=10 and MININTERVAL=WEEK implies that a duration of one week is denoted by a bar of length (10/h)% of the screen width.

PROC GANTT uses hardware text whenever possible, unless the global option NOCHARACTERS is in effect, in which case the SIMPLEX font is used. You can specify any other font for the text and the labeling of the time axis by using the FONT= option in the CHART statement. Global PATTERN statements are used to control the fill pattern to be used for the bars depending on whether the activity is critical or not. See the section **Using PATTERN Statements** for details.

Using PATTERN Statements

PROC GANTT uses a maximum of seven different patterns to denote various phases in an activity's duration. Patterns are specified in PATTERN statements.

If you do not specify PATTERN statements, SAS/GRAPH software uses default patterns depending on the colors available for the device. See the section **PATTERN Statements** in the chapter "Global Statements" in the *SAS/GRAPH User's Guide* for details about specifying fill patterns. The following table lists the use of each PATTERN statement:

PATTERN Statement	Used to denote
1	Duration of a non-critical activity
2	Slack time for a non-critical activity
3	Duration of a critical activity
4	Slack time for a supercritical activity
5	Duration of a supercritical activity
6	Actual duration of an activity
7	Break due to a holiday

Valid Options for Line-Printer and Graphics Charts

All the options that are valid for both line-printer and graphics Gantt charts are explained in detail in the **Specifications** section for the line-printer case. With few exceptions these options have the same interpretation for the graphics version. Below is a list of the options that have the same effect in both line-printer and graphics versions of PROC GANTT.

Options in the GANTT statement
DATA=*SASdataset*
HOLIDATA=*SASdataset*
MAXDEC=*n*

Options in the CHART statement
A_FINISH=*variable*
A_START=*variable*
CRITFLAG
E_FINISH=*variable*
E_START=*variable*
FILL
HOLIDAY=(*variables*)
INCREMENT=*increment*
L_FINISH=*variable*
L_START=*variable*
MAXDATE=*maxdate*
MINDATE=*mindate*
MININTERVAL=*mininterval*
NOJOBNUM
NOLEGEND
PADDING=*padding*
PAGES=*pages*
REF=*values*

The following table lists those line-printer options that have a different interpretation for the graphics version of PROC GANTT.

Line-Printer Option	Corresponding Graphics Interpretation
SCALE=*scale*	one column is denoted by (1/*h*)% of the screen width where HPOS=*h*
SKIP=*skip*	*skip* number of bar heights are skipped between the bars for two consecutive activities. 0 is not a valid value in the graphics case
SUMMARY	lists all the patterns and symbols that are used with the corresponding interpretation.

Graphics Options Not Valid for a Line-Printer Chart

Below is a table listing, in alphabetical order, options meant to be used in conjunction with the GRAPHICS option. For each option, the corresponding option (where applicable) to be used for line-printer charts is also listed.

Graphics Option/Statement	Corresponding Line-Printer Option
ANNOTATE=*SASdataset*	N/A
CAXIS=*color*	N/A
CFRAME=*color*	N/A
CREF=*color*	N/A
CTEXT=*color*	N/A
DESCRIPTION=*string*	N/A
FONT=*name*	N/A
GOUT=*graphics catalog*	N/A
GRAPHICS	Line-printer chart is the default
LREF=*linetype*	REFCHAR='*c*'
NOFRAME	FORMCHAR='*string*'
PATTERN Statement	JOINCHAR='*string*' and SYMCHAR='*string*'
SYMBOL Statement	First character of variable name is plotted (See description of CHART specifications)

Line-Printer Options Not Valid with the GRAPHICS Option

Line-Printer Option	Corresponding Graphics Option
FORMCHAR='*string*'	NOFRAME
HOLICHAR='*c*'	PATTERN Statement number 7 is used
JOINCHAR='*string*'	PATTERN Statement numbers 1-6 are used
OVERLAPCH='*c*'	N/A
OVPCHAR='*c*'	N/A
REFCHAR='*c*'	LREF=*linetype* and CREF=*color*
SYMCHAR='*string*'	PATTERN Statement numbers 1-6 are used

EXAMPLES

Previous examples 3, 4, 5 and 6 are repeated here to illustrate the use of PATTERN and SYMBOL statements and other graphics options to produce a graphics quality Gantt chart.

Marking Holidays and Target Completion Dates: Example 9

The data set for the Gantt chart is created in the same manner as in Example 3. Before invoking PROC GANTT, you specify the required fill patterns and symbols using PATTERN and SYMBOL statements. Next, PROC GANTT is invoked with the GRAPHICS option. You specify the HOLIDATA=HOLDATA option in the PROC statement and the HOLIDAY= option in the CHART statement, causing the holidays to be marked on the chart. Note that the procedure marks the **duration** of the holiday with the fill pattern specified in the seventh PATTERN statement. Specifying the variable TARGET in the CHART statement causes target dates to be marked on the chart with the symbol specified in the SYMBOL statement, a PLUS symbol in black. The duration and slack of the activities are indicated by the use of the appropriate fill patterns as explained in the legend.

Colors for the axis, text, and frame fill are specified using the options CAXIS=, CTEXT=, and CFRAME=, respectively. The global options HPOS and VPOS are set to 100 and 40, respectively. The SIMPLEX font is used for all text.

```
TITLE C=WHITE F= SIMPLEX 'GANTT EXAMPLE 9';
TITLE2 C=WHITE F=SIMPLEX' MARKETING HOLIDAYS AND TARGET COMPLETION DATES';

DATA CONST1;
   FORMAT TARGET DATE9.;
   INPUT ACTIVITY $ 1-20 TAIL 22 DUR 24 HEAD 26
         TARGET DATE9.;
   CARDS;
DRILL WELL            1 4 2 .
PUMP HOUSE            2 3 5 .
INSTALL PIPE         5 2 7 10JUL85
CONSTRUCT POWER LINE 1 3 5  7JUL85
EXCAVATE             1 5 4  9JUL85
INSTALL PUMP         4 6 7 .
DELIVER MATERIAL     1 2 3 .
ASSEMBLE TANK        3 4 6 .
ERECT TOWER          6 6 7 .
FOUNDATION           4 4 6 12JUL85
DUMMY                4 0 5 .
;

DATA HOLDATA;
   FORMAT HOL DATE7.;
   INPUT HOL DATE7.;
   CARDS;
3JUL85
;

* SCHEDULE THE PROJECT SUBJECT TO HOLIDAYS;

PROC CPM DATA=CONST1 DATE='1JUL85'D HOLIDATA=HOLDATA OUT=SAVE;
   TAILNODE TAIL;
```

```
      DURATION DUR;
      HEADNODE HEAD;
      ID ACTIVITY TARGET;
      HOLIDAY HOL;

* DELETE ACTIVITIES WITH 0 DURATION;

DATA SAVE1;
   SET SAVE;
   IF DUR=0 THEN DELETE;

* SORT THE SCHEDULE BY THE EARLY START DATE;

PROC SORT OUT=SCHED; BY E_START;

* SPECIFY THE DEVICE ON WHICH YOU WANT THE CHART PRINTED;

GOPTIONS VPOS=40 HPOS=100;

* SET UP REQUIRED PATTERN AND SYMBOL STATEMENTS;

PATTERN1 C=GREEN V=S;
PATTERN2 C=GREEN V=E;
PATTERN3 C=RED   V=S;
PATTERN4 C=RED   V=E;
PATTERN5 C=RED   V=R2;
PATTERN6 C=RED   V=L2;
PATTERN7 C=WHITE V=E;

SYMBOL   C=RED V=PLUS;

* PLOT THE SCHEDULE;

PROC GANTT GRAPHICS HOLIDATA=HOLDATA DATA=SCHED;
   CHART TARGET / HOLIDAY=(HOL) CFRAME=YELLOW FONT=SIMPLEX
               CAXIS=WHITE CTEXT=WHITE;
   ID ACTIVITY;
RUN;
```

Output 4.9   Using the GRAPHICS Option to Mark Holidays and Target
Completion Dates

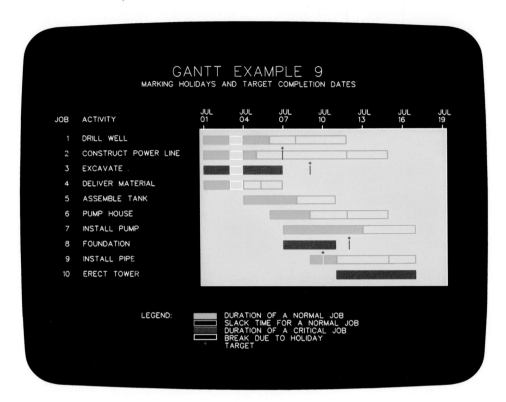

Plotting the Actual Schedule: Example 10

As in **Example 9** fill patterns are specified using PATTERN statements. PROC
GANTT is used with the GRAPHICS option to plot computed as well as actual
schedules on separate lines for each activity. The A_START= and A_FINISH=
options in the CHART statement are used to specify the variables containing the
actual start and finish times for each activity. The actual schedule is plotted with
the fill pattern specified in the sixth PATTERN statement.

The value of VPOS= is set to 50 using a GOPTIONS statement to enable PROC
GANTT to draw the entire chart on one page.

```
TITLE C=WHITE 'GANTT EXAMPLE 10';
TITLE2 C=WHITE F=SIMPLEX 'PLOTTING ACTUAL START AND FINISH TIMES ON THE
   CHART';

DATA ACTUAL;
   FORMAT FDATE DATE9. SDATE DATE9.;
   INPUT ACTIVITY $ 1-20 FDATE DATE9. SDATE DATE9.;
   CARDS;
DRILL WELL            5JUL85     1JUL85
PUMP HOUSE            9JUL85     7JUL85
INSTALL PIPE          12JUL85    10JUL85
CONSTRUCT POWER LINE  4JUL85     1JUL85
EXCAVATE              7JUL85     2JUL85
INSTALL PUMP          12JUL85    8JUL85
DELIVER MATERIAL      4JUL85     2JUL85
ASSEMBLE TANK         7JUL85     5JUL85
ERECT TOWER           17JUL85    13JUL85
```

```
FOUNDATION          12JUL85  8JUL85
;

* MERGE THE COMPUTED SCHEDULE WITH THE ACTUAL SCHEDULE;

DATA UPDATE;
   MERGE SAVE1 ACTUAL;

* SORT THE DATA;

PROC SORT; BY E_START;

* SET VPOS TO 50 AND HPOS TO 100;

GOPTIONS VPOS=50 HPOS=100;

* SET UP REQUIRED PATTERN STATEMENTS;

PATTERN1 C=GREEN V=S;
PATTERN2 C=GREEN V=E;
PATTERN3 C=RED   V=S;
PATTERN4 C=RED   V=E;
PATTERN5 C=RED   V=R2;
PATTERN6 C=YELLOW V=S;
PATTERN7 C=WHITE V=E;
* PLOT THE COMPUTED AND ACTUAL SCHEDULES USING PROC GANTT;

PROC GANTT GRAPHICS DATA=UPDATE HOLIDATA=HOLDATA;
   CHART / HOLIDAY=(HOL)
           A_START=SDATE A_FINISH=FDATE
           CAXIS=WHITE CTEXT=WHITE;
   ID ACTIVITY;

RUN;
```

Output 4.10   Using the GRAPHICS Option to Plot Actual Schedules

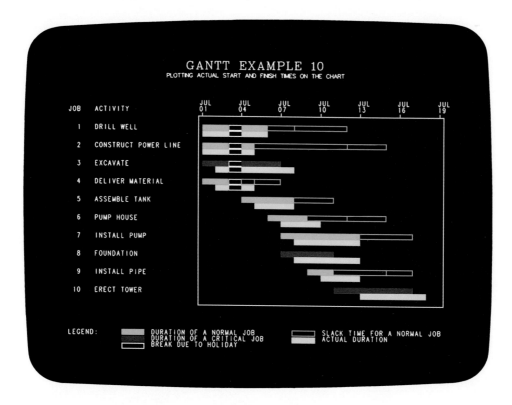

Using the MININTERVAL and SCALE Options: Example 11

This example uses the same data as **Example 5** of the line-printer section. The PATTERN statements are the same as in **Example 10**. Here the SCALE= option is set to 7 so that the chart fits on two pages. Since MININTERVAL=WEEK and SCALE=7, PROC GANTT uses (7/h)% of the screen width to denote one week, where h is the value of HPOS.

```
TITLE F=XSWISS C=WHITE 'GANTT EXAMPLE 11';
TITLE2 F=XSWISS C=WHITE 'USE OF MININTERVAL AND SCALE OPTIONS';

* SCHEDULE USING INTERVAL=WEEK;

PROC CPM DATA=CONST1 DATE='30JUN85'D INTERVAL=WEEK
        OUT=SAVE;
   TAILNODE TAIL;
   DURATION DUR;
   HEADNODE HEAD;
   ID ACTIVITY;

*DELETE ACTIVITIES WITH 0 DURATION;

DATA SAVE;
   SET SAVE;
   IF DUR=0 THEN DELETE;

*SORT THE SCHEDULE BY THE EARLY START DATE;

PROC SORT; BY E_START;
```

```
GOPTIONS VPOS=40 HPOS=85;

PROC GANTT GRAPHICS;
   CHART / PADDING=WEEK MININTERVAL=WEEK SCALE=7 NOLEGEND
           REF='1JUL85'D TO '15OCT85'D BY MONTH
           FONT=XSWISS CAXIS=WHITE CTEXT=WHITE;
   ID ACTIVITY;
RUN;
```

Output 4.11   Using the GRAPHICS Option to Produce a Gantt Chart Using
the MININTERVAL and SCALE Options

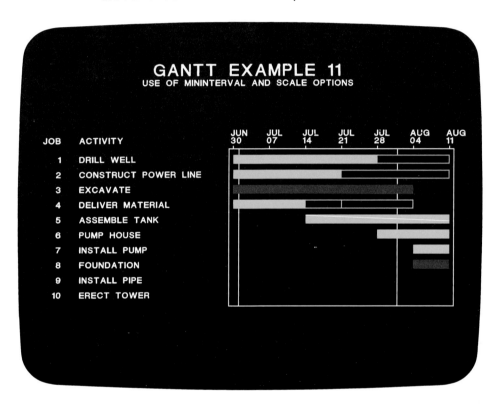

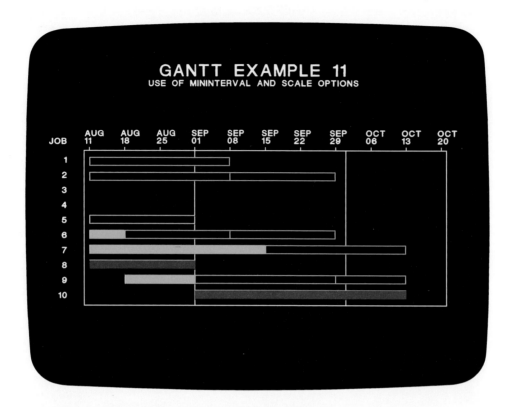

Using the MINDATE and MAXDATE Options: Example 12

This example uses the same data as **Example 6** and illustrates the LREF= option.

```
TITLE C=WHITE 'GANTT EXAMPLE 12';
TITLE2 C=WHITE 'USE OF MINDATE AND MAXDATE OPTIONS';

GOPTIONS VPOS=40 HPOS=100;

PROC GANTT GRAPHICS DATA=SAVE;
   CHART / PADDING=WEEK MINDATE='1AUG85'D MAXDATE='31AUG85'D
           NOLEGEND REF='5AUG85'D TO '25AUG85'D BY 5
           CTEXT=WHITE CAXIS=WHITE FONT=SIMPLEX
           CREF=WHITE LREF=2;
   ID ACTIVITY;
RUN;
```

Output 4.12   Using the GRAPHICS Option to Produce a Gantt Chart Using
the MINDATE and MAXDATE Options

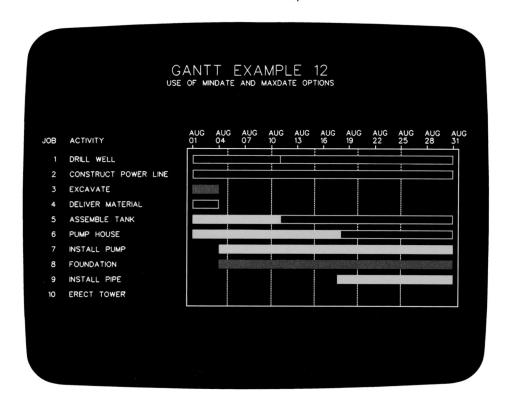

136

Chapter 5
The LP Procedure

Operating systems: All

ABSTRACT

The LP procedure solves linear programs, integer programs, and mixed-integer programs. It also performs parametric programming, range analysis, and reports on solution sensitivity to changes in the right-hand-side constants and price coefficients.

The LP procedure can be used interactively. You can tell the procedure to stop at intermediate stages in the iterative solution process. When one of these stopping points is reached the procedure waits for further input. Then, intermediate results can be printed, options reset, and the procedure instructed to continue execution.

INTRODUCTION

The LP procedure is used to optimize a linear function subject to linear and integer constraints. Specifically, LP solves the general mixed integer program of the form

$$\max (\min) \; \mathbf{c'x}$$

$$\text{subject to: } \mathbf{Ax} \begin{array}{c} \leq \\ = \\ \geq \end{array} \mathbf{b} \qquad\qquad (mip)$$

$$\ell_i \leq x_i \leq u_i \qquad i=1,...,n$$

$$x_i \text{ is integer for } i\varepsilon \mathbf{S}$$

where

$\mathbf{A}$ is an m x n matrix of technological coefficients,

$\mathbf{b}$ is an m x 1 matrix of right-hand-side (rhs) constants,

$\mathbf{c}$ is an n x 1 matrix of price coefficients,

$\mathbf{x}$ is an n x 1 matrix of structural variables,

ℓ_i is a lower bound on x_i,

u_i is an upper bound on x_i, and

$\mathbf{S}$ is a subset of the set of indices $\{\, 1,...,n \,\}$.

Linear programs, when $\mathbf{S}$ is empty, are denoted by (lp). For these problems the procedure employs the two-phase revised simplex method, which uses the Bartels-Golub update of the LU decomposed basis matrix to pivot between feasible solutions (see Bartels 1971). In phase 1, PROC LP finds a basic feasible solution to (lp), while in phase 2, PROC LP finds an optimal solution, $\mathbf{x}^{opt}$. The procedure implicitly handles unrestricted variables, lower-bounded variables, upper-bounded variables, and ranges on constraints. When no explicit lower bounds are specified, PROC LP assumes that all variables are bounded below by zero.

When a variable is specified as an integer, variable $\mathbf{S}$ has at least one element. Then the procedure uses the branch and bound technique for optimization. The relaxed problem (the problem with no integer constraints) is solved initially using the primal algorithm described above. Constraints are added in defining the subsequent descendent problems in the branch and bound tree. These problems are then solved using the dual simplex algorithm. Dual pivots are referred to as phase 3 pivots.

The procedure can also analyze the sensitivity of the solution $\mathbf{x}^{opt}$ to changes in both the objective function and the right-hand-side constants. There are three techniques available for this analysis: sensitivity analysis, parametric programming, and range analysis. Sensitivity analysis enables you to examine the size of a perturbation to the right-hand-side or objective vector by an arbitrary change vector for which the basis of the current optimal solution remains optimal.

Parametric programming, on the other hand, enables you to specify the size of the perturbation beforehand then examine how the optimal solution changes as the desired perturbation is realized. With this technique, the procedure pivots to maintain optimality as the right-hand-side or objective vector is perturbed beyond the point for which the current solution is optimal. Range analysis is used to examine the range of each right-hand-side value or objective coefficient for which the basis of the current optimal solution remains optimal.

The LP procedure can also save both primal and dual solutions, the current tableau, and the branch and bound tree in SAS data sets. This enables you to generate solution reports and perform additional analyses with the SAS System. Although LP reports solutions, this feature is particularly useful for reporting solutions in formats tailored to your specific needs. Saving computational results in a data set also enables you to continue executing a problem not solved because of insufficient time or other computational problems.

Outline of Use

PROC LP expects the definition of one or more linear, integer, or mixed integer programs in an input data set. In the remaining discussion these are referred to as mathematical programs. Each variable in the data set is either a structural variable, an id variable, a right-hand-side constant, a type identifier, a constant for right-hand-side sensitivity analysis, or a range variable. The value of the type identifier variable named in the TYPE statement in each observation tells LP how to interpret the observation as a part of the mathematical programming problem. PROC LP recognizes these keywords as values for the type identifier variable: MAX, MIN, EQ, LE, GE, UNRSTRCT, UPPERBD, LOWERBD, BASIC, PRICESEN, FREE, and INTEGER. A later section describes how the procedure interprets an observation having each of these keywords.

Although order is not important, an input data set normally has the first n variables as the structural variables, for example, $x_1...x_n$, the next variable as the type identifier, and the last variable as the right-hand-side constant. Each observation in the data set is a row in the linear program. For example,

```
DATA PROBLEM;
   INPUT X1 X2 X3 T $ R;
   CARDS;
1.5 2.1 3  MAX .
1  -1 0  EQ 0
1   1 1  LE 1
;
```

defines a SAS data set that PROC LP interprets as the problem

$$\max \quad 1.5x_1 + 2.1x_2 + 3x_3$$

$$\text{subject to:} \quad \begin{aligned} x_1 - x_2 &= 0 \\ x_1 + x_2 + x_3 &\leq 1 \\ x_1 &\geq 0 \\ x_2 &\geq 0 \\ x_3 &\geq 0 \end{aligned}.$$

Note that if lower bounds on the variables are not explicitly specified, PROC LP assumes they are 0. To solve this problem with PROC LP, you must identify the variables in the data set to the procedure. This is done with the VAR, RHS, and TYPE statements. For this example, you call PROC LP using

```
PROC LP DATA=PROBLEM;
   VAR  X1-X3;
   RHS  R;
   TYPE T;
```

If you specify more than one variable in the RHS statement or if the problem data set contains more than one observation with either MIN or MAX as type identifier, then LP considers the data set as defining more than one linear program and solves each problem. In solving multiple problems, LP iterates first by objective function and then by right-hand sides. Once an optimal solution for the first problem is known, the introduction of a new objective function results only in pivots to obtain dual feasibility while maintaining primal feasibility. Similarly, the introduction of a new right-hand-side vector results only in pivots to obtain primal feasibility while maintaining dual feasibility.

The interactive use of the procedure is best understood by considering the types of statements that are used with PROC LP. The ID, VAR, RHS, TYPE, RHSSEN, and RANGE statements are problem definition statements. They tell PROC LP how to interpret the variables in the input data set in terms of solving the mathematical program defined there. After you have entered these statements you can enter a QUIT, PIVOT, (IPIVOT if the problem has integer variables), or a RUN statement. These statements cause an immediate action: QUIT terminates the LP procedure; PIVOT (IPIVOT) executes one simplex (branch and bound) pivot; and RUN is the usual RUN statement. Because of options you may have set or an error condition, the procedure can return control to you before completing execution. When this happens you can reset options using the RESET statement, examine the current solution with the PRINT and SHOW statements, and continue execution of the procedure using the PIVOT (IPIVOT) or RUN statements.

SPECIFICATIONS

The following statements are used in PROC LP:

> **PROC LP** *options;*
>   **ID** *variable;*
>   **VAR** *variables;*
>   **RHS** *variable;*
>   **TYPE** *variable;*
>   **RHSSEN** *variables;*
>   **RANGE** *variable;*
>   **QUIT;**
>   **PIVOT;**
>   **IPIVOT;**
>   **RESET** *options;*
>   **SHOW** *show options;*
>   **PRINT** *print options;*

The RHS, TYPE, ID, RHSSEN, RANGE, RESET, SHOW, PRINT, QUIT, PIVOT, and IPIVOT statements are optional. The RHS and TYPE statements are not needed if the input SAS data set contains variables _RHS_ and _TYPE_; otherwise, they must be used. The VAR statement is optional. When it is not specified, PROC LP uses as structural variables all numeric variables not explicitly or implicitly in other statement lists.

The SHOW, PRINT, PIVOT, IPIVOT, QUIT, and RESET statements are useful when executing PROC LP interactively. However, they can also be used in batch mode. The SHOW, PRINT, QUIT, and RESET statements can be executed only after the first RUN, PIVOT, or IPIVOT statement has been executed.

PROC LP Statement

   PROC LP *options*;

The options below can appear in the PROC LP statement:

Data sets

ACTIVEIN=*SASdataset*
>   names the SAS data set containing the active nodes in a branch and bound tree that is to be used to restart an integer program.

ACTIVEOUT=*SASdataset*
>   names the SAS data set in which to save the current branch and bound tree of active nodes.

DATA=*SASdataset*
>   names the SAS data set containing the problem data. If DATA= is not specified, LP uses the most recently created SAS data set.

DUALOUT=*SASdataset*
>   names the SAS data set that contains the current dual solution (shadow prices) on termination of LP. This data set contains the current dual solution only if LP terminates successfully.

PRIMALIN=*SASdataset*
>   names the SAS data set that contains a feasible solution to the problem defined by the DATA= data set. The data set specified in the PRIMALIN= option should have the same format as a data set saved using the PRIMALOUT= option. Specifying PRIMALIN= is particularly useful for continuing iteration on a problem previously attempted. It is also useful for performing sensitivity analysis on a previously solved problem.

PRIMALOUT=*SASdataset*
>   names the SAS data set that contains the current primal solution when LP terminates.

TABLEAUOUT=*SASdataset*
>   names the SAS data set in which to save the final tableau.

Print control options

FLOW
>   requests that a journal (the ITERATION LOG) of pivot information be printed at each PRINTFREQ= iteration. This includes the number of the columns entering and leaving the basis, the reduced cost of the entering column, and the current objective value.

FUZZ=*f*
>   prints all numbers within *f* of zero as zeros. The default is $1.0E-10$.

NOFLOW
>   is the inverse of the FLOW option.

NOPARAPRINT
>   is the inverse of the PARAPRINT option.

NOPRINT
>   suppresses printing of the VARIABLE, CONSTRAINT, and SENSITIVITY ANALYSIS SUMMARIES. This option is equivalent to the PRINTLEVEL=0 option.

NOTABLEAUPRINT
>   is the inverse of the TABLEAUPRINT option.

PARAPRINT
>   indicates that the solution be printed at each pivot when performing
>   parametric programming.

PRINT
>   is the inverse of the NOPRINT option.

PRINTFREQ=i
>   indicates at each ith iteration a line in the (INTEGER) ITERATION
>   LOG be printed.

PRINTLEVEL=i
>   indicates the amount of printing that the procedure should perform.
>   When $i=-2$, only messages to the SAS log are printed. When
> $i=-1$, the option is equivalent to NOPRINT unless the problem is
>   infeasible. If it is infeasible, the infeasible rows are printed in the
>   CONSTRAINT SUMMARY along with the INFEASIBLE
>   INFORMATION SUMMARY. When $i=0$, this option is identical to
>   NOPRINT. When $i=1$, all output is printed.

TABLEAUPRINT
>   indicates that the final tableau be printed.

Interactive control options

ENDPAUSE
>   requests that LP pause before printing the solution. When this pause
>   occurs, you can enter the RESET, SHOW, or PRINT statements.

FEASIBLEPAUSE
>   requests that LP pause after a feasible (not necessarily integer
>   feasible) solution has been found.

IFEASIBLEPAUSE=m
>   requests that LP pause after every m integer feasible solutions.
>   Default is 99999999.

IPAUSE=n
>   requests that LP pause after n integer iterations. At a pause you can
>   enter the RESET, SHOW, PRINT, IPIVOT, QUIT, and PIVOT
>   statements. The default value is 99999999.

NOENDPAUSE
>   is the inverse of the ENDPAUSE option.

NOFEASIBLEPAUSE
>   is the inverse of the FEASIBLEPAUSE option.

PAUSE=n
>   requests that LP pause after n iterations. At a pause you can enter
>   the RESET, SHOW, PRINT, IPIVOT, QUIT, and PIVOT statements.
>   The default value is 99999999.

Branch and bound algorithm control options

BACKTRACK=LIFO, FIFO, OBJ, PROJECT, PSEUDOC, ERROR
>   specifies the rule used to choose the next active problem when
>   CANSELECT=LIFO and backtracking is required. The default value is
>   OBJ. See the **Details** section for further discussion.

CANSELECT=LIFO, FIFO, OBJ, PROJECT, PSEUDOC, ERROR
> specifies the rule used to choose the next active problem when solving an integer or mixed integer program. The default value is LIFO. See the **Details** section for further discussion.

DOBJECTIVE=d
> specifies that LP should discard active nodes unless the node will lead to an integer solution with objective at least as large (small for minimizations) as the the objective of the relaxed problem minus (plus) d.

IEPSILON=e
> requests that LP consider an integer variable x as having an integer value if x is within e units of an integer. The default value is 1.0E−7.

IMAXIT=m
> performs at most m integer iterations. Default is 100.

IOBJECTIVE=o
> specifies that LP should discard active nodes unless the node will lead to an integer solution with objective at least as large (small for minimizations) as o.

PENALTYDEPTH=n
> requests that LP examine n variables as branching candidates when the VARSELECT=PENALTY. If PENALTYDEPTH is not specified when VARSELECT=PENALTY, then all the variables are considered branching candidates. See the **Details** section for a more complete description.

POBJECTIVE=p
> specifies that LP should discard active nodes unless the node will lead to an integer solution with objective at least as large (small for minimizations) as p times the objective of the relaxed non-integer-constrained problem.

VARSELECT=CLOSE, PRIOR, PSEUDOC, FAR, PRICE, PENALTY
> specifies the rule used to choose the branching variable on an integer iteration. Default is FAR. See the **Details** section for further discussion.

Sensitivity/parametric/ranging control options

NORANGEPRICE
> is the inverse of the RANGEPRICE option.

NORANGERHS
> is the inverse of the RANGERHS option.

PRICEPHI=Φ
> specifies the limit for parametric programming when perturbing the price vector. See the **Details** section for a more complete description.

RANGEPRICE
> indicates that range analysis is to be performed on the price coefficients. See the **Details** section.

RANGERHS
> indicates that range analysis is to be performed on the right-hand-side vector. See the **Details** section.

RHSPHI=Φ
> specifies the limit for parametric programming when perturbing the right-hand-side vector. See the **Details** section.

Simplex algorithm control options

BLAND

specifies that LP use the Bland (Bland 1977) anti-cycling scheme when cycling has been detected to determine which column to bring into the basis. When specified, the column with the smallest index that improves the objective is brought into the basis.

DEVEX

indicates that the devex method of weighting the reduced costs be used in pricing (Harris 1975).

ENTERFIRST

specifies that LP bring into the basis the first column it finds that improves the objective. Since LP spends much of its execution time in pricing, this option provides a heuristic that may shorten computing time.

EPSILON=e
EPS=e

specifies a number close to zero. EPSILON is used in the following several ways:

During phase 1 if the sum of the infeasibilities is within EPSILON of 0, the current solution is considered feasible. If this sum is not exactly zero, then there are artificial variables within EPSILON of zero in the current solution. In this case a note is printed on the SAS log.

During phase 1 if all reduced costs are ($\geq$ EPSILON) and the sum of infeasibilities is greater than EPSILON, then the problem is considered infeasible. If the minimum reduced cost is within EPSILON of 0, a note is printed on the SAS log.

During phase 2 if all reduced costs are ($\geq$ EPSILON), then the current solution is considered optimal. If the minimum reduced cost is between 0 and $-$EPSILON, a note is printed on the SAS log.

During phase 2 if the problem is found to be unbounded and there is at least one basic variable that is within EPSILON of becoming a leaving variable, then a note to that effect is printed on the SAS log.

The default value of EPSILON is 1.0E$-$8 .

INFINITY=s

specifies the largest number PROC LP uses in computation. INFINITY= is used to determine when a problem has an unbounded objective function. The default value is 7.2E75. *

INVFREQ=m

reinverts the current basis matrix after m major and minor iterations. The default value of m is 50.

INVTOL=t

reinverts the current basis matrix if the largest element in absolute value in the decomposed basis matrix is greater than t. If after reinversion this condition still holds, then INVTOL is increased by a factor of 10 and a note indicating this modification is printed on the SAS log. When INVTOL is frequently exceeded, this may be an indication of a numerically unstable problem. By default (see the SCALE= option) LP scales the constraint matrix coefficients and the

---

* This value is system dependent.

objective coefficients so that they are less than or equal to 1 in absolute value. Consequently, a default value of 10 for t is sufficient for maintaining stability in most problems.

MAXIT=m
> performs at most m iterations.

MAXIT1=m
> performs at most m phase 1 iterations. The default value of m is 100.

MAXIT2=m
> performs at most m phase 2 iterations. If $m<0$, then only phase 1 is entered so that on successful termination LP will have found a feasible, but not necessarily optimal, solution. The default value of m is 100.

MAXIT3=m
> performs at most m phase 3 iterations. All dual pivots are counted as phase 3 pivots. The default value of m is 99999999.

NOBLAND
> is the inverse of the BLAND option.

NODEVEX
> is the inverse of the DEVEX option.

NOENTERFIRST
> is the inverse of the ENTERFIRST option.

PRICING=k
PRICE=k
> specifies multiple pricing in selecting the column to enter the basis (Greenberg 1978). The type of suboptimization used is determined by the PRICETYPE= option. The value of k must be less than 21. See the **Details** section for a description of this process.

PRICETYPE=COMPLETE, DYNAMIC, NONE, PARTIAL
> specifies the type of multiple pricing to be performed. If this option is specified and the PRICE option is not specified, then PRICE is assumed to be 5. The default value is DYNAMIC. See the **Details** section for a description of this process.

SCALE=ROW, NONE
> specifies whether or not the coefficient matrix and price vector are to be scaled.

SPARSE=s
> requests that the sparse implementation of the inversion and update routines be used and that the routines use $s*n$, where n is the number of nonzero elements in the constraint matrix, for storing the LU decomposed basis matrix. The default is SPARSE=3. See the **Details** section for further discussion.

STARTPHASE=PRIMAL, DUAL
> specifies whether the procedure should start with the primal or dual revised simplex algorithm. If the dual algorithm is chosen, the procedure first checks for dual feasibility. If the problem is not dual feasible, the procedure terminates with an error message. The default is PRIMAL.

TIME=t
> checks at each iteration to see if t seconds have elapsed since LP began. If more than t seconds have elapsed, the procedure

terminates and prints the current solution. The default value of TIME is 120 seconds.

U=u

allows the user to control the choice of pivots during LU decomposition and updating the basis matrix. The variable u should take values between EPSILON and 1.0 because small values of u bias the algorithm toward maintaining sparsity at the expense of numerical stability and vice versa. The more sparse the decomposed basis the less time each iteration takes. The default is 1.0. See the **Details** section for further discussion.

ID Statement

ID *variable*;

The ID statement specifies a variable in the problem data set that contains an id name for each row of constraint coefficients and for each row of objective coefficients. If ID is not included, LP looks for the default variable name, _ID_. If this is not a variable in the problem data set, LP uses the default name _OBSxx_, where *xx* specifies the number of the observation in the problem data set.

IPIVOT Statement

IPIVOT;

The IPIVOT statement causes the LP procedure to execute one integer branch and bound pivot.

PIVOT Statement

PIVOT;

The PIVOT statement causes the LP procedure to execute one simplex pivot.

PRINT Statement

PRINT *print options*;

The PRINT statement is useful for printing part of a solution summary, examining intermediate tableaus, performing sensitivity analysis, and parametric programming. The options that can be used with this statement are

COLUMN(*colnames*)/SENSITIVITY

prints a VARIABLE SUMMARY containing the logical and structural variables listed in the *colnames* list. If /SENSITIVITY is included, then sensitivity analysis is performed on the price coefficients for the listed *colnames* structural variables.

MATRIX(*rownames,colnames*)/PICTURE

prints the submatrix of the matrix of constraint coefficients defined by the *rownames* and *colnames* lists. If /PICTURE is included, then the formatted submatrix is printed. The format used is summarized in the following table.

Condition on the Coefficient x					Symbols Printed
		ABS(x)	=	0	" "
0	<	ABS(x)	<	.000001	SGN(x) "Z"
.000001	≤	ABS(x)	<	.00001	SGN(x) "Y"
.00001	≤	ABS(x)	<	.0001	SGN(x) "X"
.0001	≤	ABS(x)	<	.001	SGN(x) "W"
.001	≤	ABS(x)	<	.01	SGN(x) "V"
.01	≤	ABS(x)	<	.1	SGN(x) "U"
.1	≤	ABS(x)	<	1	SGN(x) "T"
		ABS(x)	=	1	SGN(x) "1"
1	≤	ABS(x)	<	10	SGN(x) "A"
10	≤	ABS(x)	<	100	SGN(x) "B"
100	≤	ABS(x)	<	1000	SGN(x) "C"
1000	≤	ABS(x)	<	10000	SGN(x) "D"
10000	≤	ABS(x)	<	100000	SGN(x) "E"
100000	≤	ABS(x)	<	1.0E06	SGN(x) "F"

.   .

.   .

.   .

INTEGER
    prints a VARIABLE SUMMARY containing only the integer variables.

NONINTEGER
    prints a VARIABLE SUMMARY containing only the continuous
    variables.

PRICESEN
    prints the results of parametric programming for the current value of
    PRICEPHI, the price coefficients, and all the price change vectors.

RHSSEN
    prints the results of parametric programming for the current value of
    RHSPHI, the right-hand-side coefficients, and all the right-hand-side
    change vectors.

ROW(rownames)/SENSITIVITY
    prints a CONSTRAINT SUMMARY containing the rows listed in the
    rowname list. If /SENSITIVITY is included, then sensitivity analysis is
    performed on the right-hand-side coefficients for the listed
    rownames.

RANGEPRICE
    performs range analysis on the price coefficients.

RANGERHS
    performs range analysis on the right-hand-side vector.

SOLUTION
    prints the SOLUTION SUMMARY, including the VARIABLE
    SUMMARY and the CONSTRAINT SUMMARY.

TABLEAU
    prints the current tableau.

QUIT Statement

QUIT *quit options;*

The QUIT statement causes the LP procedure to terminate processing immediately. No further printing is performed and no output data sets are created. To save the output data sets defined in the PROC LP statement or in the RESET statement, use the option /SAVE, which causes the procedure to terminate immediately after saving output data sets.

RANGE Statement

RANGE *variable;*

The RANGE statement identifies the variable in the problem data set that contains the range coefficients. These coefficients enable you to specify the feasible range of a row. For example, if the ith row is

$$\mathbf{a}'\mathbf{x} \leq b_i$$

and the range coefficient for this row is $r_i > 0$, then all values of $\mathbf{x}$ that satisfy

$$b_i - r_i \leq \mathbf{a}'\mathbf{x} \leq b_i$$

are feasible for this row. The following table shows the bounds on a row as a function of the row type and the sign on a nonmissing range coefficient r.

Table 5.1 Using the RANGE Statement to Specify Bounds on a Row: PROC LP

		Bounds	
r	_TYPE_	Lower	Upper
$\neq 0$	LE	$b - \|r\|$	b
$\neq 0$	GE	b	$b + \|r\|$
>0	EQ	b	$b+r$
<0	EQ	$b+r$	b

If you include the RANGE statement and have a missing value or zero for the range variable in a constraint row, then that constraint is treated as if no range variable had been included.

If the RANGE statement is omitted, LP assumes that the variable named _RANGE_ contains the range coefficients.

RESET Statement

RESET *options;*

The RESET statement is used to change options after the procedure has started execution. All of the options that can be set in the PROC LP statement can also be reset with the RESET statement except for those that reference input data sets, namely the DATA=, PRIMALIN=, and ACTIVEIN= data sets.

RHS Statement

RHS *variables*;

The RHS statement identifies variables in the problem data set that contain the constant right-hand side of the linear program. Only numeric variables can be specified. If more than one variable is included in the RHS statement, the procedure assumes that several linear programs' problems are defined by the problem data set. A new linear program is defined for each variable in the RHS list. If the RHS statement is omitted, LP assumes that the variable named _RHS_ contains the right-hand-side constants.

RHSSEN Statement

RHSSEN *variables*;

The RHSSEN statement identifies variables in the problem data set that define change vectors for examining the sensitivity of the optimal solution to changes in the RHS constants. See the **Right-Hand-Side Sensitivity Analysis** and **Right-Hand-Side Parametric Programming** sections below.

SHOW Statement

SHOW *show options*;

The SHOW statement specifies that LP print on the SAS log either the current options or the current solution status.

OPTIONS	requests that the options be printed on the SAS log.
STATUS	requests that the status of the current solution be printed on the SAS log.

TYPE Statement

TYPE *variables*;

The TYPE statement specifies a character variable in the problem data set that contains the type identifier for each observation. This variable has keyword values that specify how LP should interpret the observation. If the TYPE statement is omitted, LP assumes that the variable named _TYPE_ contains the type keywords.

The following are valid values for the TYPE variable in an observation:

MAX	contains the price coefficients of an objective row, for example, **c** in the problem *(mip)*, to be maximized. A total of 10 objective rows may appear in any problem data set.
MIN	contains the price coefficients of an objective row, for example, **c**, to be minimized. A total of 10 objective rows may appear in any problem data set.
EQ (=)	contains coefficients of an equality constrained row.
LE (≤)	contains coefficients of an inequality, less than or equal to, constrained row.
GE (≥)	contains coefficients of an inequality, greater than or equal to, constrained row.

UNRSTRCT   identifies those structural variables to be considered as unrestricted variables. These are variables for which $\ell_i = -\text{INFINITY}$ and $u_i = +\text{INFINITY}$. Any variable that has a nonzero value in this observation is considered an unrestricted variable.

UPPERBD   identifies upper bounds u_i on the structural variables. For each structural variable that is to have an upper bound $u_i = +\text{INFINITY}$, the observation must contain a missing value or the current value of INFINITY. All other values are interpreted as upper bounds, including 0. Upper bounds can be specified explicitly in constraint rows. However, using the UPPERBD keyword and implicitly specifying upper bounds on the structural variables is more efficient computationally.

LOWERBD   identifies lower bounds on the structural variables. If all structural variables are to be nonnegative, that is $\ell_i = 0$, then do not include an observation with the LOWERBD keyword in a variable specified on the TYPE statement. Using LOWERBD causes LP to treat implicitly the lower bounds on the structural variables, which results in computational efficiencies that could not be realized when explicitly defining the lower bounds in constraint rows.

Note: a variable with lower or upper bounds cannot also be unrestricted.

INTEGER   identifies variables that are integer constrained. In a feasible solution these variables must have integer values. A missing value or a zero in a row with INTEGER type keyword indicates that that variable is not integer constrained. The value of variables in the INTEGER row gives an ordering to the integer constrained variables that is used when the VARSELECT option equals PRIOR. (See **Controlling the Branch and Bound Search** in the **Details** section below.)

BASIC   identifies variables that form an initial basic feasible solution.

PRICESEN   identifies a vector that is used to evaluate the sensitivity of the optimal solution to changes in the objective function.

FREE   identifies a nonbinding constraint. Any number of FREE constraints can appear in a problem data set.

VAR Statement

   VAR *variables*;

The VAR statement identifies variables in the problem data set that are to be interpreted as structural variables, x, in the linear program. Only numeric variables can be specified. If no VAR statement is specified, the procedure uses as structural variables all numeric variables not included in an RHS or RHSSEN statement.

DETAILS

Missing Values

The LP procedure treats missing values as 0 in all observations except in an observation that identifies the upper bounds of the structural variables. In this case, the type identifier is UPPERBD, and LP treats missing values as +INFINITY.

Sensitivity Analysis

Sensitivity analysis is a technique for examining the effect of changes in model parameters on the optimal solution. The analysis enables you to examine the size of a perturbation to the right-hand-side or objective vector by an arbitrary change vector for which the basis of the current optimal solution remains optimal. When sensitivity analysis is performed on integer constrained problems, the integer variables are fixed at the value they obtained in the integer solution. Care must be used when interpreting the results of such analyses.

Right-hand-side sensitivity analysis   Consider the problem

$$\max \ (\min) \ \mathbf{c'x}$$

$$\text{subject to: } \mathbf{Ax} \begin{array}{c} \geq \\ = \\ \leq \end{array} \mathbf{b} + \varphi\mathbf{r} \qquad\qquad (lpr(\varphi))$$

$$\ell_i \leq x_i \leq u_i \qquad i=1,...,n \ .$$

Let $\mathbf{x}^{opt}(\varphi)$ denote an optimal basic feasible solution to $(lpr(\varphi))$. LP can be used to examine the effects of changes in φ on the solution $\mathbf{x}^{opt}(0)$ of problem $(lpr(0))$. For the basic solution $\mathbf{x}^{opt}(0)$, let $\mathbf{B}$ be the matrix composed of the basic columns of $\mathbf{A}$, and let $\mathbf{N}$ be the matrix composed of the nonbasic columns of $\mathbf{A}$. For the basis matrix $\mathbf{B}$ the basic components of $\mathbf{x}^{opt}(0)$, written as $\mathbf{x}^{opt}(0)_{\mathbf{B}}$ can be expressed as

$$\mathbf{x}^{opt}(0)_{\mathbf{B}} = \mathbf{B}^{-1}(\mathbf{b} - \mathbf{N}\mathbf{x}^{opt}(0)_{\mathbf{N}}) \quad .$$

Furthermore, since $\mathbf{x}^{opt}(0)$ is feasible

$$\ell_{\mathbf{B}} \leq \mathbf{B}^{-1}(\mathbf{b} - \mathbf{N}\mathbf{x}^{opt}(0)_{\mathbf{N}}) \leq \mathbf{u}_{\mathbf{B}}$$

where $\ell_{\mathbf{B}}$ is a column vector of the lower bounds on the structural variables, and $\mathbf{u}_{\mathbf{B}}$ is a column vector of the upper bounds on the structural variables.

For each right-hand-side change vector $\mathbf{r}$ identified in the RHSSEN statement, LP finds an interval $[\varphi_{min}, \varphi_{max}]$ such that

$$\ell_{\mathbf{B}} \leq \mathbf{B}^{-1}(\mathbf{b} + \varphi\mathbf{r} - \mathbf{N}\mathbf{x}^{opt}(0)_{\mathbf{N}}) \leq \mathbf{u}_{\mathbf{B}}$$

for $\varphi\epsilon[\varphi_{min}, \varphi_{max}]$. Furthermore, since changes in the right-hand side do not affect the reduced costs, for $\varphi\epsilon[\varphi_{min}, \varphi_{max}]$

$$\mathbf{x}^{opt}(\varphi)' = (\ (\mathbf{B}^{-1}(\mathbf{b} + \varphi\mathbf{r} - \mathbf{N}\mathbf{x}^{opt}(0)_{\mathbf{N}}))', \ \mathbf{x}^{opt}(0)_{\mathbf{N}}'\ )$$

is optimal in $(lpr(\varphi))$.

For $\varphi=\varphi_{min}$ and $\varphi=\varphi_{max}$, LP reports the following:

- the name of the leaving variables
- the value of the optimal objective in the modified problems
- the optimal solution in the modified problems.

The leaving variable identifies the basic variable i that first reaches either the lower bound ℓ_i or the upper bound u_i as φ reaches φ_{min} and φ_{max}. This is the basic variable that would leave the basis to maintain primal feasibility.

Multiple RHSSEN variables can appear in a problem data set.

Price sensitivity analysis   Consider the problem

$$\max \ (\min) \ (\mathbf{c} + \varphi\mathbf{r})'\mathbf{x}$$

$$\text{subject to: } \mathbf{Ax} \begin{array}{c} \geq \\ = \\ \leq \end{array} \mathbf{b} \qquad\qquad (lpp(\varphi))$$

$$\ell_i \leq x_i \leq u_i \qquad i=1,...,n \ .$$

Let $\mathbf{x}^{opt}(\varphi)$ denote an optimal basic feasible solution to $(lpp(\varphi))$. LP can be used to examine the effects of changes in φ on the solution $\mathbf{x}^{opt}(0)$ of problem $(lpp(0))$. For the basic solution $\mathbf{x}^{opt}(0)$ let $\mathbf{B}$ be the matrix composed of the basic columns of $\mathbf{A}$, and let $\mathbf{N}$ be the matrix composed of the nonbasic columns of $\mathbf{A}$. For basis matrix $\mathbf{B}$ the reduced cost associated with the ith variable can be written as

$$rc_i(\varphi) = ((\mathbf{c}+\varphi\mathbf{r})'_\mathbf{N}-(\mathbf{c}+\varphi\mathbf{r})'_\mathbf{B}\mathbf{B}^{-1}\mathbf{N})_i$$

where $(\mathbf{c}+\varphi\mathbf{r})_\mathbf{N}$ and $(\mathbf{c}+\varphi\mathbf{r})_\mathbf{B}$ is a partition of the vector of price coefficients into basic and nonbasic components. Since $\mathbf{x}^{opt}(0)$ is optimal in $(lpp(0))$, the reduced costs satisfy

$$rc_i(0) \geq (\leq) \ 0$$

if the nonbasic variable in column i is at its upper bound and

$$rc_i(0) \leq (\geq) \ 0$$

if the nonbasic variable in column i is at its lower bound.

For each price coefficient change vector $\mathbf{r}$ identified with the keyword PRICESEN in the TYPE variable, LP finds an interval $[\varphi_{min},\varphi_{max}]$ such that for $\varphi\epsilon[\varphi_{min},\varphi_{max}]$

$$rc_i(\varphi) \geq (\leq) \ 0$$

if the nonbasic variable in column i is at its upper bound and

$$rc_i(\varphi) \leq (\geq) \ 0$$

if the nonbasic variable in column i is at its lower bound. Since changes in the price coefficients do not affect feasibility, for $\varphi\epsilon[\varphi_{min},\varphi_{max}]$, $\mathbf{x}^{opt}(0)$ is optimal in $(lpp(\varphi))$. For $\varphi=\varphi_{min}$ and $\varphi=\varphi_{max}$, LP reports the following:

- name of entering variables
- value of the optimal objective in the modified problems
- price coefficients in the modified problems
- reduced costs in the modified problems.

The entering variable identifies the variable whose reduced costs first go to zero as φ reaches φ_{min} and φ_{max}. This is the nonbasic variable that would enter the basis to maintain optimality (dual feasibility).

Multiple PRICESEN variables may appear in a problem data set.

Range Analysis

Range analysis is sensitivity analysis for specific change vectors. When range analysis is performed on integer constrained problems, integer variables are fixed at the value they obtained during the branch and bound iterations. Care must be used in interpreting the results of such analyses.

Right-hand-side range analysis   The effects on the optimal solution of changes in each right-hand-side value can be studied using the RANGERHS option on the PROC LP or RESET statements. This option results in sensitivity analysis for the m right-hand-side change vectors specified by the columns of the m x m identity matrix.

Price range analysis   The effects on the optimal solution of changes in each price coefficient can be studied using the RANGEPRICE option on the PROC LP or RESET statements. This option results in sensitivity analysis for the n price change vectors specified by the rows of the n x n identity matrix.

Parametric Programming

Sensitivity analysis and range analysis examine how the optimal solution behaves with respect to perturbations of model parameter values. These approaches assume that the basis at optimality will not be allowed to change. When greater flexibility is desired and a change of basis is acceptable, parametric programming can be used.

When parametric programming is performed on integer constrained problems, integer variables are fixed at the value they obtained during the branch and bound iterations. Care must be used in interpreting the results of such analyses.

Right-hand-side parametric programming   As discussed in the section on right-hand-side sensitivity analysis, for each right-hand-side change vector $\mathbf{r}$, PROC LP finds an interval $[\varphi_{min}, \varphi_{max}]$ such that for $\varphi \varepsilon [\varphi_{min}, \varphi_{max}]$

$$\mathbf{x}^{opt}(\varphi)' = (\ (\mathbf{B}^{-1}(\mathbf{b} + \varphi\mathbf{r} - \mathbf{N}\mathbf{x}^{opt}(0)_\mathbf{N}))', \mathbf{x}^{opt}(0)_\mathbf{N}'\ )$$

is optimal in ($lpr(\varphi)$) for the fixed basis $\mathbf{B}$. Leaving variables, which inhibit further changes in φ without a change in the basis $\mathbf{B}$, are associated with the quantities φ_{min} and φ_{max}. By specifying RHSPHI=Φ in either the PROC LP statement or in the RESET statement, you can examine the solution $\mathbf{x}^{opt}(\varphi)$ as φ increases or decreases from 0 to Φ.

When RHSPHI=Φ is specified, the procedure first finds the interval $[\varphi_{min}, \varphi_{max}]$ as described above. Then, if $\Phi \varepsilon [\varphi_{min}, \varphi_{max}]$ no further investigation is needed. However, if $\Phi > \varphi_{max}$ or $\Phi < \varphi_{min}$ the procedure attempts to solve the new problem ($lpr(\Phi)$). To accomplish this it pivots the leaving variable out of the basis while maintaining dual feasibility. If this new solution is primal feasible in ($lpr(\Phi)$) no further investigation is needed; otherwise the procedure identifies the new leaving variable and pivots it out of the basis, again maintaining dual feasibility. Dual pivoting continues in this manner until a solution that is primal feasible in $(lpr(\Phi))$ is identified. Because dual feasibility is maintained at each pivot, the $(lpr(\Phi))$ primal feasible solution is optimal.

At each pivot the procedure reports on the variables that enter and leave the basis, the current range of φ, and the objective value. When $\mathbf{x}^{opt}(\Phi)$ is found it is printed. If you want the solution $\mathbf{x}^{opt}(\varphi)$ at each pivot, then specify the PARAPRINT option on either the PROC LP or RESET statement.

Price parametric programming   As discussed in the section on price sensitivity analysis, for each price change vector $\mathbf{r}$, PROC LP finds an interval $[\varphi_{min}, \varphi_{max}]$ such that for each $\varphi \varepsilon [\varphi_{min}, \varphi_{max}]$

$$rc_i(\varphi) = ((\mathbf{c} + \varphi\mathbf{r})'_{\mathbf{N}} - (\mathbf{c} + \varphi\mathbf{r})'_{\mathbf{B}}\mathbf{B}^{-1}\mathbf{N})_i$$

satisfies the conditions for optimality in $(lpp(\varphi))$ for the fixed basis $\mathbf{B}$. Entering variables, which inhibit further changes in φ without a change in the basis $\mathbf{B}$, are associated with the quantities φ_{min} and φ_{max}. By specifying PRICEPHI$=\Phi$ on either the PROC LP statement or on the RESET statement, you can examine the solution $\mathbf{x}^{opt}(\varphi)$ as φ increases or decreases from 0 to Φ.

When PRICEPHI$=\Phi$ is specified, the procedure first finds the interval $[\varphi_{min}, \varphi_{max}]$ as described above. Then, if $\Phi\varepsilon[\varphi_{min}, \varphi_{max}]$, no further investigation is needed. However, if $\Phi>\varphi_{max}$ or $\Phi<\varphi_{min}$ the procedure attempts to solve the new problem $(lpp(\Phi))$. To accomplish this it pivots the leaving variable out of the basis while maintaining primal feasibility. If this new solution is dual feasible in $(lpp(\Phi))$ no further investigation is needed; otherwise the procedure identifies the new leaving variable and pivots it out of the basis, again maintaining primal feasibility. Pivoting continues in this manner until a solution that is dual feasible in $(lpp(\Phi))$ is identified. Because primal feasibility is maintained at each pivot, the $(lpp(\Phi))$ dual feasible solution is optimal.

At each pivot the procedure reports on the variables that enter and leave the basis, the current range of φ, and the objective value. When $\mathbf{x}^{opt}(\Phi)$ is found, it is printed. If you want the solution $\mathbf{x}^{opt}(\varphi)$ at each pivot, then specify the PARAPRINT option in either the PROC LP or RESET statement.

Integer Programming

Formulations of mathematical programs often require that some of the decision variables take only integer values. Consider the formulation of (mip) presented in the **Introduction**.

$$\max \ (\min) \ \mathbf{c}'\mathbf{x}$$

$$\text{subject to: } \mathbf{A}\mathbf{x} \begin{array}{c} \geq \\ = \\ \leq \end{array} \mathbf{b} \qquad\qquad\qquad (mip)$$

$$\ell_i \leq x_i \leq u_i \qquad i=1,...,n$$

$$\{ x_i \mid i \varepsilon \mathbf{S} \} \text{ are integer} \quad .$$

The set of indices $\mathbf{S}$ identifies those variables that must only take integer values. When $\mathbf{S}$ does not contain all the integers between 1 and n, inclusive, problem *(mip)* is called a mixed integer program. Otherwise it is known as an integer program. Let $\mathbf{x}^{opt}(mip)$ denote an optimal solution to *(mip)*.

Specifying the problem   An integer or mixed integer problem can be solved with PROC LP. To solve this problem you must identify the integer variables. You can do this with a row in the input data set that has the keyword INTEGER for the type variable. Any variable that has a nonmissing and nonzero value for this row is interpreted as an integer variable. It is important to note that integer variables must have upper bounds explicitly defined using the UPPERBD keyword. The values in the INTEGER row not only identify those variables that must be integral, but they also give an ordering to the integer variables that can be used in the solution technique.

The branch and bound technique   The branch and bound approach is used to solve integer and mixed integer problems. The following discussion outlines the approach and explains how to use several options to control the procedure.

The branch and bound technique solves an integer program by solving a sequence of linear programs. The sequence can be represented by a tree, each node in the tree being identified with a linear program that is derived from the problems on the path leading to the root of the tree. The root of the tree is identified with a linear program that is identical to *(mip)* except that **S** is empty. This relaxed version of *(mip)* can be written as

$$\max \ (\min) \quad \mathbf{c'x}$$

$$\text{subject to: } \mathbf{Ax} \ \substack{\geq \\ = \\ \leq} \ \mathbf{b} \qquad\qquad\qquad (lp(0))$$

$$\ell_i \leq x_i \leq u_i \qquad i=1,...,n \ \ .$$

The branch and bound approach generates linear programs along the nodes of the tree using the following schema. Consider $\mathbf{x}^{opt}(0)$, the optimal solution to *lp(0)*. If $\mathbf{x}^{opt}(0)_i$ is integer for all $i \varepsilon S$, then $\mathbf{x}^{opt}(0)$ is optimal in *(mip)*. Suppose for some $i \varepsilon S$, $x^{opt}(0)_i$ is nonintegral. In that case, define two new problems *(lp(1))* and *(lp(2))*, descendents of the parent problem *(lp(0))*. *(lp(1))* is identical to *(lp(0))* except for the additional constraint $x_i \leq \lfloor x^{opt}(0)_i \rfloor$, and *(lp(2))* is identical to *(lp(0))* except for the additional constraint $x_i \geq \lceil x^{opt}(0)_i \rceil$. The notation $\lceil y \rceil$ means the smallest integer greater than or equal to y, and the notation $\lfloor y \rfloor$ means the largest integer less than or equal to y. Note that the two new problems do not have $\mathbf{x}^{opt}(0)$ as a feasible solution, but because the solution to *(mip)* must satisfy one of the above constraints, $x^{opt}(mip)_i$ must satisfy one of the new constraints. The two problems thus defined are called *active nodes* in the branch and bound tree, and the variable *i* is called the *branching variable*.

Next, the algorithm chooses one of the problems associated with an active node and attempts to solve it using the dual algorithm. The problem may be infeasible, in which case the problem is dropped. If it can be solved, and it in turn does not have an integer solution, then it defines two new problems. These new problems contain all the constraints of the parent problems plus the appropriate additional one.

Branching continues in this manner until either there are no active problems or an integer solution is found. When an integer solution is found, its objective value provides a bound for the objective of *(mip)*. In particular, if z^* is the objective value of the current best integer solution, then any active problems whose parent problem has objective $\leq z^*$ can be discarded (that is assuming that the problem is a maximization). This can be done because all problems that descend from this parent will also have objective $\leq z^*$.

When there are no active problems remaining to be solved, the current integer solution is optimal in *(mip)*. If no integer solution has been found, then *(mip)* is infeasible.

The INTEGER ITERATION LOG   To help monitor the growth of the branch and bound tree, the procedure reports on the status of each problem that is solved. The report, printed in the INTEGER ITERATION LOG, can be used to reconstruct the branch and bound tree. Each row in the report describes the results of the attempted solution of the linear program at a node in the tree. In the following discussion a problem on a given line in the log is called the current problem. The following eight columns are printed in the report:

ITER
: identifies the number of the branch and bound iteration.

PROBLEM
: identifies how the current problem fits in the branch and bound tree.

CONDITION
: reports the result of the attempted solution of the current problem. Values for CONDITION are

> ACTIVE
> : the current problem was solved successfully
>
> INFEASIBLE
> : the current problem is infeasible
>
> FATHOMED
> : the current problem cannot lead to an improved integer solution so it is dropped
>
> SUBOPTIMAL
> : the current problem is an integer feasible solution.

OBJECTIVE
: reports the objective value of the current problem.

BRANCHED
: names the variable that is branched in subtrees defined by the descendants of this problem.

VALUE
: gives the current value of the variable named in the column labeled BRANCHED.

SINFEAS
: gives the sum of the integer infeasibilities in the current problem.

ACTIVE
: reports the total number of nodes currently active in the branch and bound tree.

To reconstruct the branch and bound tree from this report, consider the interpretation of iteration *j*. If ITER=*j* and PROBLEM=*k*, then the problem solved on iteration *j* is identical to the problem solved on iteration $|k|$ with an additional constraint. If $k>0$ then the constraint is an upper bound on the variable named in the BRANCH column on iteration *j*. On the other hand, if $k<0$ then the constraint is a lower bound on that variable. The value of the bound can be obtained from the value of VALUE in iteration $|k|$ as described in the previous section. **Example 9** in the **Examples** section shows an INTEGER ITERATION LOG in its output.

Controlling the branch and bound search There are several options you can use to control branching. This is accomplished by controlling the program's choice of the branching variable and of the next active problem to solve. In the discussion that follows let

$$f_i(k) = x^{opt}(k)_i - \lfloor x^{opt}(k)_i \rfloor$$

where $x^{opt}(k)$ is the optimal solution to the problem solved on iteration k.

The CANSELECT= option directs the choice of next active problem to be solved. Valid keywords for this option include LIFO, FIFO, OBJ, PROJECT, PSEUDOC, and ERROR. The following list describes the action that each of these causes when the procedure must choose for solution a problem from the list of active problems.

LIFO chooses the last problem added to the tree of active problems. This search has the effect of a depth first search of the branch and bound tree. If at the current node the two descendant problems are not added to the active tree, then the procedure must backtrack. The BACKTRACK= option controls the search for the next problem. This option can take the same values as the CANSELECT= option.

FIFO chooses the first problem added to the tree of active problems. This search has the effect of a breadth first search of the branch and bound tree.

OBJ chooses the problem whose parent has the largest (least if the problem is a minimization) objective value.

PROJECT chooses the problem with the largest (least if the problem is a minimization) projected objective value. The projected objective value is evaluated using the sum of integer infeasibilities, s(k), associated with an active problem (lp(k)), defined by

$$s(k) = \Sigma_{i \in S} \min \{ f_i(k), (1 - f_i(k)) \} .$$

An empirical measure of the rate of decrease (increase) in the objective value is defined as

$$\lambda = (z(0) - z^*) / s(0)$$

where

z(k) is the optimal objective value for (lp(k)), and

z* is the objective value of the current best integer solution.

The projected objective value for problems (lp(k+1)) and (lp(k+2)) is defined as

$$z(k) - \lambda s(k) .$$

PSEUDOC chooses the problem with the largest (least if the problem is a minimization) projected pseudocost. The projected pseudocost is evaluated using the weighted sum of infeasibilities, $s_w(k)$, associated with an active problem $(lp(k))$ defined by

$$s_w(k) = \Sigma_{i \in S} \min \{ d_i f_i(k), u_i(1 - f_i(k)) \}$$

and the weights u_i and d_i are initially equal to the absolute value of the ith objective coefficient and are updated whenever an integer feasible solution is encountered. They are modified by examining the empirical marginal change in the objective as additional constraints are placed on the variables in S along the path from $(lp(0))$ to the node associated with the integer feasible solution. In particular, if the definition of problems $(lp(k+1))$ and $(lp(k+2))$ from parent $(lp(k))$ involve the addition of constraints $x_i \leq \lfloor x^{opt}(k)_i \rfloor$ and $x_i \geq \lceil x^{opt}(k)_i \rceil$, respectively, and one of them is on the path to an integer feasible solution, then either

$$d_i = (z(k) - z(k+1)) / f_i(k)$$

or

$$u_i = (z(k) - z(k+2)) / (1 - f_i(k)) \quad .$$

Note the similarity between $s_w(k)$ and $s(k)$. The weighted quantity $s_w(k)$ accounts to some extent for the influence of the objective function. The projected pseudocost for problems $(lp(k+1))$ and $(lp(k+2))$ is defined as

$$z_w(k) \equiv z(k) - s_w(k) \quad .$$

ERROR   chooses the problem with the largest (least if the problem is a minimization) error. The error associated with problems $(lp(k+1))$ and $(lp(k+2))$ is defined as

$$(z_w(k) - z^*)/(z(k) - z^*) \quad .$$

The VARSELECT= option directs the choice of branching variable. Valid keywords for this option include CLOSE, FAR, PRIOR, PSEUDOC, PRICE, and PENALTY. The following table describes the action that each of these causes when $x^{opt}(k)$, an optimal solution of problem $(lp(k))$, is used to define active problems $(lp(k+1))$ and $(lp(k+2))$.

CLOSE   chooses as branching variable the variable i that minimizes

$$\{\min \{f_i(k), (1-f_i(k))\} \mid i \in S; \text{IEPSILON} \leq f_i(k) \leq 1 - \text{IEPSILON} \} \quad .$$

FAR   chooses as branching variable the variable i that maximizes

$$\{\min \{f_i(k), (1-f_i(k))\} \mid i \in S; \text{IEPSILON} \leq f_i(k) \leq 1 - \text{IEPSILON} \} \quad .$$

PRIOR   chooses as branching variable $i \in S$ such that $x^{opt}(k)_i$ is nonintegral and variable i has the minimum value in the INTEGER row in the input data set. This choice for VARSELECT= is recommended when you have enough insight into the model to identify those integer variables that have the most significant effect on the objective value.

PENALTY   chooses as branching variable $i \varepsilon S$ such that a bound on the decrease in the objective of $(lp(k))$ (penalty) resulting from adding the constraint $x_i \leq \lfloor x^{opt}(k)_i \rfloor$ or $x_i \geq \lceil x^{opt}(k)_i \rceil$ is maximized. The bound is calculated without pivoting using techniques of sensitivity analysis (Garfinkel and Nemhauser 1972). Because the cost of calculating the maximum penalty can be large if **S** is large, you may want to limit the number of variables in **S** for which the penalty is calculated. The penalty is calculated for PENALTYDEPTH= variables in **S**.

PRICE   chooses as branching variable $i \varepsilon S$ such that $x^{opt}(k)_i$ is nonintegral and variable i has the maximum price coefficient.

PSEUDOC   chooses as branching variable the variable i that maximizes

$$\{\min \{d_j f_j(k), u_j(1 - f_j(k))\} \mid j \varepsilon S; \text{IEPSILON} \leq f_j(k) \leq 1 - \text{IEPSILON} \} .$$

The weights u_j and d_j are initially equal to the absolute value of the jth objective coefficient and are updated whenever an integer feasible solution is encountered. See the discussion on the CANSELECT= option for details on the method of updating the weights.

Customizing search heuristics   Often a good heuristic for searching the branch and bound tree of a problem can be found. You are tempted to continue using this heuristic when the problem data changes but the problem structure remains constant. The ability to reset procedure options interactively enables you to experiment with search techniques in an attempt to identify approaches that perform well. Then you can easily reapply these techniques to subsequent problems.

For example, the PIP branch and bound strategy (Crowder, Johnson, and Padberg 1983) describes one such heuristic. The following program uses a similar strategy. Here the OBJ rule (choose the active problem with largest parent objective function) is used for selecting the next active problem to be solved until an integer feasible solution is found. Once such a solution is found, the search procedure is changed to the LIFO rule—choose the problem most recently placed in the list of active problems.

```
PROC LP CANSELECT=OBJ IFEASIBLEPAUSE=1;
RUN;
    RESET CANSELECT=LIFO IFEASIBLEPAUSE=9999999;
RUN;
```

Saving and restoring the list of active nodes   The list of active nodes can be saved in a SAS data set for use at a subsequent invocation of PROC LP. The ACTIVEOUT= option on the PROC LP statement names the data set into which the current list of active problems is saved when the procedure terminates due to an error termination condition. Examples of such conditions are time limit exceeded, integer iterations exceeded, or phase 3 iterations exceeded. The

ACTIVEIN= option on the PROC LP statement names a data set that can be used to initialize the list of active problems. To achieve the greatest benefit when restarting PROC LP, use the PRIMALOUT= and PRIMALIN= options in conjunction with the ACTIVEOUT= and ACTIVEIN= options.

The Reduced Costs, Dual Activities, and CURRENT TABLEAU

The evaluation of reduced costs and the dual activities are independent of problem structure. For a basic solution $\mathbf{x}^{opt}$, let $\mathbf{B}$ be the matrix composed of the basic columns of $\mathbf{A}$ and let $\mathbf{N}$ be the matrix composed of the nonbasic columns of $\mathbf{A}$. The reduced cost associated with the ith variable is

$$(\mathbf{c}' - \mathbf{c_B}'\mathbf{B}^{-1}\mathbf{A})_i$$

and the dual activity of the jth row is

$$(\mathbf{c_B}\mathbf{B}^{-1})_j \quad .$$

The CURRENT TABLEAU is a section printed when either you specify the TABLEAUPRINT option on the PROC LP statement or you specify TABLEAU on the PRINT statement. The output contains a row for each basic variable and a column for each nonbasic variable. In addition, there is a row for the reduced costs and a column for the product

$$\mathbf{B}^{-1}\mathbf{b} \quad .$$

This column is labeled INV(B)*R. The body of the tableau contains the matrix

$$\mathbf{B}^{-1}\mathbf{N} \quad .$$

Interactive Facilities

The interactive features of the LP procedure allow you to examine intermediate results; perform sensitivity analysis, parametric programming, and range analysis; and control the solution process.

Controlling interactive features   You can gain control of the LP procedure for interactive processing when certain error conditions are encountered or by setting a break point:

- when a feasible solution is found
- at each pivot of the simplex algorithm
- at each integer pivot of the branch and bound algorithm
- before results are printed.

When an error condition is encountered the procedure enables you to gain control. Error conditions include time limit exceeded, phase 1 iterations exceeded, phase 2 iterations exceeded, phase 3 iterations exceeded, and integer iterations exceeded. At these points you can enter any of the interactive statements including RESET, PIVOT, IPIVOT, PRINT, QUIT, and RUN. You can use the RESET statement to reset the option that caused the error condition.

Break points are set using the options FEASIBLEPAUSE, PAUSE, IFEASIBLEPAUSE, IPAUSE, and ENDPAUSE. The LP procedure prints a message on the SAS log when it gives you control because of encountering one of these break points. At that point you can enter any of the interactive statements.

Some statements result in immediate execution. PIVOT, IPIVOT, QUIT, PRINT, and SHOW are examples of these. The PIVOT and IPIVOT statements result in control being returned to you after a single simplex algorithm pivot and integer pivot, respectively. On the other hand, the QUIT statement requests that you leave the LP procedure immediately. If you want to quit but save output data sets, then type QUIT/SAVE. The PRINT and SHOW statements print current solution information before returning control to you.

Printing intermediate results   Once you have control of the procedure you can examine the current values of the options and the status of the problem being solved using the SHOW statement. All printing done by the SHOW statement goes to the SAS log.

Details about the current status of the solution are obtained using the PRINT statement. The various print options enable you to examine parts of the variable and constraint summaries, print the current tableau, perform sensitivity analysis on the current solution, and perform range analysis.

Sensitivity analysis   Two features that enhance the ability to perform sensitivity analysis need further explanation. When you specify /SENSITIVITY with the print options on the PRINT statement the procedure defines a new change row (change column if /SENSITIVITY is on a PRINT ROW(rowname) statement) to use in sensitivity analysis and parametric programming. This new change row (change column) has a +1 for each variable (right-hand-side coefficient) listed in the PRINT statement. This enables you to define new change rows interactively.

In addition, you can interactively change the RHSPHI= and PRICEPHI= options using the RESET statement. This enables you to perform parametric programming interactively.

Interactive facilities in batch mode   All of the interactive statements can be used when processing in batch mode. This is particularly convenient when the interactive facilities are used to control the search of the branch and bound tree when you are solving integer problems.

Pricing

PROC LP performs multiple pricing when determining which variable to enter the basis at each pivot (see Greenberg 1978). This heuristic can shorten execution time in many problems. The specifics of the multiple pricing algorithm depend on the value of the PRICETYPE= option. However, in general, when some form of multiple pricing is used, during the first iteration LP places the PRICE=k nonbasic columns yielding the greatest marginal improvement to the objective function in a candidate list. This list identifies a subproblem of the original. On subsequent iterations only the reduced costs for the nonbasic variables in the candidate list are calculated. This accounts for the potential time savings. When either the candidate list is empty or the subproblem is optimal, a new candidate list must be identified and the process repeats. Since identification of the subproblem requires pricing the complete problem, an iteration in which this occurs is called a *major iteration*. An iteration when only the subproblem need be priced is called a *minor iteration*.

The value of the PRICETYPE= option determines the type of multiple pricing that is to be used. The choices include partial suboptimization (PRICETYPE= PARTIAL), complete suboptimization (PRICETYPE=COMPLETE), complete suboptimization with dynamically varying k (PRICETYPE=DYNAMIC).

When partial suboptimization is used, in each minor iteration the nonbasic column in the subproblem yielding the greatest marginal improvement to the objective is brought into the basis and removed from the candidate list. The candidate list now has one less entry. At each subsequent iteration, another column from the subproblem is brought into the basis and removed from the candidate list.

When there are either no remaining candidates, or the remaining candidates do not improve the objective, the subproblem is abandoned and a major iteration is performed. If the objective cannot be improved on a major iteration, the current solution is optimal and LP terminates.

Complete suboptimization is identical to partial suboptimization with one exception. When a nonbasic column from the subproblem is brought into the basis, it is replaced in the candidate list by the basic column that is leaving the basis. As a result the candidate list does not diminish at each iteration.

When PRICETYPE=DYNAMIC, complete suboptimization is performed, but the value of k changes so that the ratio of minor to major iterations is within two units of k.

These heuristics can shorten execution time for small values of k (typically less than 10). Care should be exercised in choosing k since too large a value can use more time than if pricing were not used. If you do not invoke the PRICE= option but you do invoke the PRICETYPE= option, PROC LP uses PRICE=5 by default.

Sparse Implementation

The two options specific to the sparse implementation of revised simplex method used by PROC LP are SPARSE= and U=. They have default values of 3 and 1, respectively. The SPARSE option tells LP how large a work area to use in saving and updating the decomposed basis matrix. If the area used is too small, LP must spend time compressing this matrix, which defeats the time savings obtained with the sparse implementation. If LP must compress the decomposed basis matrix more than 20 times in a single update, the basis is reinverted. Since inverting the basis matrix is slower than updating it, this process further degrades the performance of LP. If the work area is not large enough to invert the basis, an error return occurs. To aid you in setting the size of the work area, LP prints the average number of compresses per iteration.

The size of the decomposed basis is also affected by the value of the option U. U ranges between EPSILON and 1. When searching for a pivot in updating and inverting, any element less than U times the largest element in its row is excluded. A small U biases the algorithm toward maintaining sparsity at the expense of numerical stability and vice versa. Values of 0.1 and .01 have been reported in the literature as satisfactory (Reid 1976). However, since a satisfactory value depends on the problem data, LP's default (=1) is to opt for numerical stability at the expense of sparsity.

Scaling

Before iterating, the procedure scales both the constraint and objective rows. They are scaled so that the largest element in absolute value in each row equals 1. This technique can improve the numerical stability of an ill-conditioned problem. If you want to bypass the matrix scaling, use the SCALE=NONE option on the PROC LP statement.

Computer Resources

Memory   The memory requirements for LP vary with the size of the problem. In addition to the memory that the code of the LP procedure takes, significant portions of memory are needed for the base product and problem data. The memory requirement for data is approximately $64n + 64m + (4*s + 8)*k$ bytes, where n is the number of variables in the model, m is the number of constraints in the model, s is the value of the SPARSE= option (by default 3), and k is the number of nonzero and nonmissing elements in the constraint matrix **A**.

CPU time   The time needed to solve a problem of a given size varies significantly with problem structure, pricing strategy, and other parameter settings.

Problem size limitations   In principle, there are no limitations to the number of constraints or number of variables in a problem that LP can solve. However, there is a limitation on the number of variables in a SAS data set. This limit depends on where the data set resides. If it resides on disk, then the sum of the lengths of the variables in the data set cannot exceed the maximum blocksize of the disk. PROC CONTENTS can be used to determine the maximum blocksize for the disks at your site. If the data set resides on tape, then the sum of the lengths of the variables in the data set cannot exceed 32,768. *For example, a tape data set can have approximately 4,000 variables if their lengths are the default 8. However, if the precision of the data is such that a shorter length variable is adequate, then you can accommodate models with a greater number of variables. For example, if the variables have length 4, then approximately 8,000 variables can be used. If the variables have length 2, then approximately 16,000 variables are possible.

Note that the length of the variable in the SAS data set does not affect the precision of arithmetic used by PROC LP. Regardless of a variable's length, PROC LP uses double precision arithmetic for all calculations. As a result, using short length formats for variables not needing much precision can be an economic use of mass storage even for small models.

Output Data Sets

The procedure can optionally produce four output data sets. These are the ACTIVEOUT, PRIMALOUT, DUALOUT, and TABLEAUOUT data sets. Each contains two variables that identify the particular problem in the input data set. These variables are

_OBJ_ID_   identifies the objective function ID.

_RHS_ID_   identifies the right-hand-side variable.

Additionally, each data set contains other variables, which are discussed below.

ACTIVEOUT= data set   The ACTIVEOUT= data set contains a representation of the current active branch and bound tree. You can use this data set to initialize the branch and bound tree to continue iterations on an incompletely solved problem. Each active problem in the tree generates two observations in this data set. The first is a LOWERBD observation that is used to reconstruct the lower bound constraints on the currently described active problem, and the second is an UPPERBD observation that is used to reconstruct the upper bound constraints on the currently described active problem. In addition to these, an observation that describes the current best integer solution is included. The data set contains the following variables:

STATUS
    contains the keywords LOWERBD, UPPERBD, and INTBEST for identifying the type of observation.

PROB
    contains the problem number for the current observation.

OBJECT
    contains the objective value of the parent problem that generated the current problem.

---
* This value is system dependent.

SINFEA

contains the sum of the integer infeasibilities of the current problem.

The Integer Constrained Structural Variables

each integer constrained structural variable is also included in the ACTIVEOUT data set. For each observation these contain values for defining the active problem in the branch and bound tree.

PRIMALOUT = data set   The PRIMALOUT = data set contains the current primal solution. If the problem has integer constrained variables, the PRIMALOUT data set contains the current best integer feasible solution. If none have been found, the PRIMALOUT data set contains the relaxed solution. In addition to the _OBJ_ID_ and the _RHS_ID_ variables, the data set contains:

TYPE	identifies the type of variable as specified in the input data set.
STATUS	identifies whether the variable is basic, nonbasic, or at an upper bound in the current solution. The variable also identifies artificial variables that are basic; these are labeled _ARTFCL_.
VAR	identifies the variable name.
VALUE	identifies the value of the variable in the current solution.
_R_COST_	identifies the value of the reduced cost in the current solution.
PRICE	contains the input price coefficient of the variable.
LBOUND	contains the input lower bound on the variable unless an integer solution is given. In this case _LBOUND_ contains the lower bound on the variable needed to realize the integer solution on subsequent calls to PROC LP when using the PRIMALIN = option.
UBOUND	contains the input upper bound on the variable unless an integer solution is given. In this case _UBOUND_ contains the upper bound on the variable needed to realize the integer solution on subsequent calls to PROC LP when using the PRIMALIN = option.

Example 2 shows a typical data set. Note that it is necessary to include the information on objective function, type identifier, and right-hand side in order to distinguish problems in multiple problem data sets.

DUALOUT = data set   The DUALOUT = data set contains the dual solution for the current solution. In addition to _OBJ_ID_ and _RHS_ID_, it contains the following variables:

TYPE	identifies the type of row as specified in the input data set.
_ROW_ID_	identifies the row or constraint name.
RHS	gives the value of the right-hand side on input.
_L_RHS_	gives the lower bound for the row evaluated from the input right-hand-side value, the TYPE of the row, and the value of the RANGE variable for the row.
VALUE	gives the value of the row at optimality, excluding logical variables.

_U_RHS_   gives the upper bound for the row evaluated from the input right-hand-side value, the TYPE of the row, and the value of the RANGE variable for the row.

DUAL   gives the value of the dual variable associated with the row.

TABLEAUOUT= data set   The TABLEAUOUT= data set contains the current tableau. The tableau is output so that the basic variables in the solution are variables in the data set and each observation, except for the first, corresponds to a nonbasic variable in the solution. The observation labeled INV(B)*R contains $B^{-1}b$ in the variables named for the basic variables and $c_B B^{-1}b$ in the variable named R_COSTS. In addition to the _OBJ_ID_ and the _RHS_ID_ variables, it contains the following:

NBASIC
the names of the nonbasic variables in the solution.

R_COSTS
the values of the reduced costs.

The Basic Variables
the values in the tableau, namely $B^{-1}N$.

Input Data Sets

In addition to the DATA= input data set, LP recognizes the ACTIVEIN= and the PRIMALIN= data sets.

ACTIVEIN= data set   The ACTIVEIN= data set contains a representation of the current active tree. The format is identical to the ACTIVEOUT= data set.

PRIMALIN= data set   The PRIMALIN= data set's format is identical to the PRIMALOUT= data set. PROC LP uses the PRIMALIN= data set to identify

• variables at their upper bounds in the current solution
• variables that are basic in the current solution.

You can add observations to the end of the problem data set if they define cost sensitivity change vectors and have TYPE=PRICESEN. You can also add variables that define right-hand-side sensitivity change vectors. This enables you to solve a problem, save the solution in a SAS data set, and perform sensitivity analysis later. You can also use the PRIMALIN= data set to restart problems that have not been completely solved or to which new variables have been added.

Printed Output

The output from the LP procedure is presented in five sections: the PROBLEM SUMMARY; the SOLUTION SUMMARY including a VARIABLE SUMMARY and a CONSTRAINT SUMMARY; the INFEASIBLE INFORMATION SUMMARY; the RHS SENSITIVITY ANALYSIS SUMMARY including the RHS RANGE ANALYSIS SUMMARY; and the PRICE SENSITIVITY ANALYSIS SUMMARY including the PRICE RANGE ANALYSIS SUMMARY.

For integer constrained problems the procedure also prints an INTEGER ITERATION LOG. The description of this LOG can be found in the **Details** section under **Integer Programming**.

When you request that the tableau be printed, the procedure prints the CURRENT TABLEAU. The description of this can be found in the **Details** section under **The Reduced Costs, Dual Activities, and the CURRENT TABLEAU**.

A problem data set can contain a set of constraints with several right-hand sides and several objective functions. LP considers combination right-hand side and objective function as defining a new linear programming problem and solves each, performing all sensitivity analysis on each problem. For each problem defined, LP prints a new sequence of output sections. **Example 1** in the next section discusses each of these elements.

The LP procedure produces the following printed output by default:

The PROBLEM SUMMARY includes:

1. type of optimization and the name of the objective row (as identified by the ID variable)
2. name of the SAS variable that contains the right-hand-side constants
3. name of the SAS variable that contains the type keywords
4. density of the coefficient matrix (the ratio of the number of nonzero elements to the number of total elements) after the logical variables have been appended
5. number of each type of variable in the mathematical program
6. number of each type of constraint in the mathematical program.

The SOLUTION SUMMARY includes:

1. termination status of the procedure
2. objective value of the current solution
3. number of phase 1 iterations that were completed
4. number of phase 2 iterations that were completed
5. number of initial basic feasible variables identified
6. time used in solving the problem excluding reading the data and printing the solution
7. number of inversion of the basis matrix
8. current value of several of the options.

The VARIABLE SUMMARY includes:

1. column number associated with each structural and logical variable in the problem.
2. name of each structural and logical variable in the problem. (LP gives the logical variables the name of the constraint ID for which the logical variable is either the slack or surplus. If no ID variable is specified, the procedure names the logical variable _OBSn_, where n is the observation which describes the constraint.)
3. variable's status in the current solution. The status can be BASIC, DEGEN, or ALTER, depending upon whether the variable is a basic variable, a degenerate variable, or can be brought into the basis to define an alternate optimal solution.
4. kind of variable—whether it is logical or structural, and, if structural, its bound type.
5. value of the objective coefficient associated with each variable.
6. activity of the variable in the current solution.
7. variable's reduced costs in the current solution.

The CONSTRAINT SUMMARY includes:

1. constraint row number and its ID
2. the kind of constraint—whether it is an LE, EQ, GE, RANGELE, RANGEEQ, RANGEGE, or FREE row
3. number of the slack or surplus variable associated with the constraint row

4. value of the right-hand-side constant associated with the constraint row
5. current activity of the row (excluding logical variables)
6. current activity of the dual variable (shadow price) associated with the constraint row.

The INFEASIBLE INFORMATION SUMMARY includes:

1. name of the infeasible row
2. right-hand side and current activity for the row
3. name of each nonzero and nonmissing variable in the row
4. activity and upper and lower bounds for the variable
5. all the rows in the problem for which the variable has nonzero and nonmissing coefficients.

The RHS SENSITIVITY ANALYSIS SUMMARY includes:

1. value of φ_{min}
2. leaving variable when $\varphi=\varphi_{min}$
3. objective value when $\varphi=\varphi_{min}$
4. value of φ_{max}
5. column number and name of each logical and structural variable
6. activity of the variable when $\varphi=\varphi_{min}$
7. activity of the variable when $\varphi=\varphi_{max}$.

The PRICE SENSITIVITY ANALYSIS SUMMARY includes:

1. value of φ_{min}
2. entering variable when $\varphi=\varphi_{min}$
3. objective value when $\varphi=\varphi_{min}$
4. value of φ_{max}
5. entering variable when $\varphi=\varphi_{max}$
6. objective value when $\varphi=\varphi_{max}$
7. column number and name of each logical and structural variable
8. price of the variable when $\varphi=\varphi_{min}$
9. variable's reduced cost when $\varphi=\varphi_{min}$
10. price of the variable when $\varphi=\varphi_{max}$
11. variable's reduced cost when $\varphi=\varphi_{max}$.

EXAMPLES

Two Simple Problems: Example 1

Consider the two problems

$$\max \quad y$$

$$\text{subject to:} \quad x + y \leq 1.9 \qquad (lp(1a))$$
$$x + 2y \geq -.5$$

$$-.3 \leq x \leq 1$$
$$-.4 \leq y$$

and

$$\min \quad 2x + y$$

$$\text{subject to:} \quad x + y \leq 1.9$$
$$x + 2y \geq -.5$$

$$-.3 \leq x \leq 1$$
$$-.4 \leq y \quad .$$

(lp(1b))

Since they differ only in objective function, if both problems are defined in one data set, PROC LP can solve them in one invocation. The DATA step to construct this multiple problem data set is

```
DATA EX_1;
   INPUT X Y _TYPE_ $ _RHS_ ;
   CARDS;
0    1   MAX        .
2    1   MIN        .
1    1   <=       1.9
1    2   >=       -.5
1    .   UPPERBD    .
-.3 -.4  LOWERBD    .
;
```

The statement

```
PROC LP;
```

is all that is needed to solve the two problems. Since the default names are used for the right-hand-side variable and the type identifier, no VAR, RHS, or TYPE statements are needed. This invocation of PROC LP results in the following page of PROBLEM SUMMARY output. Included in the summary is an identification of the objective, defined by the first observation of the problem data set; the right-hand-side variable, defined by the variable _RHS_; and the type identifier, defined by the variable _TYPE_. See **Output 5.1**.

Output 5.1   PROBLEM SUMMARY for Solving First of Two Problems with One
                 Invocation

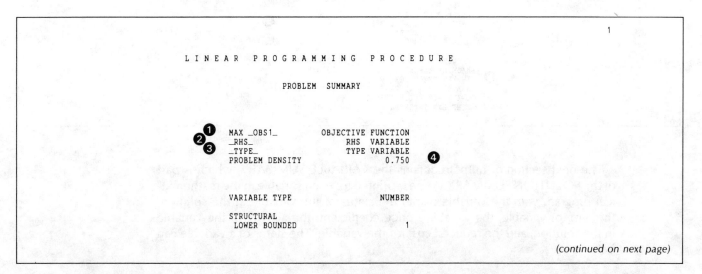

(continued on next page)

```
(continued from previous page)

                    UPPER AND LOWER BOUNDED        1

    ❺   LOGICAL
               SLACK                                1
               SURPLUS                              1

            TOTAL                                    4


            CONSTRAINT TYPE                    NUMBER
               LE                                    1
    ❻          GE                                    1
               FREE                                  2

            TOTAL                                    4
```

The next section of output contains the SOLUTION SUMMARY, which indicates whether or not a solution is found. In this example, the procedure terminates successfully (into an optimal solution), with 2.2 as the value of the objective function at optimality. Also included in this section of output is the number of phase 1 and phase 2 iterations, the number of variables used in the initial basic feasible solution, and the time used in solving the problem. If any options are specified in the PROC statement, the current option values are also printed. See **Output 5.2**.

Output 5.2   SOLUTION SUMMARY for Solving First of Two Problems with One Invocation

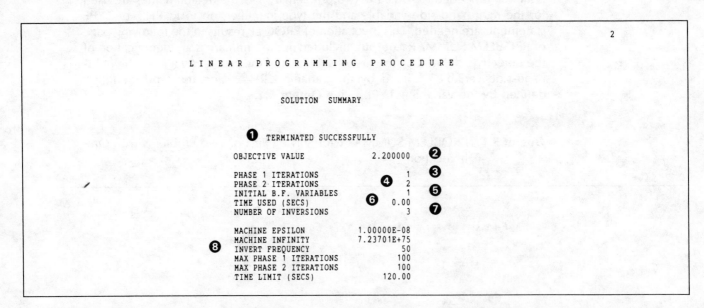

```
                                                                      2

            L I N E A R   P R O G R A M M I N G   P R O C E D U R E


                            SOLUTION  SUMMARY


            ❶   TERMINATED SUCCESSFULLY

            OBJECTIVE VALUE              2.200000        ❷

            PHASE 1 ITERATIONS                     1     ❸
            PHASE 2 ITERATIONS              ❹     2
            INITIAL B.F. VARIABLES                 1     ❺
            TIME USED (SECS)          ❻     0.00
            NUMBER OF INVERSIONS                   3     ❼

            MACHINE EPSILON             1.00000E-08
            MACHINE INFINITY            7.23701E+75
    ❽       INVERT FREQUENCY                      50
            MAX PHASE 1 ITERATIONS               100
            MAX PHASE 2 ITERATIONS               100
            TIME LIMIT (SECS)                 120.00
```

The next section of output contains the VARIABLE SUMMARY, which is part of the SOLUTION SUMMARY. A line is printed for each variable in the mathematical program with the variable name, the status of the variable in the solution, the type of variable, the variable's price coefficient, the activity of the variable in the solution, and the reduced cost for the variable. The status of a variable can be

BASIC   if the variable is a basic feasible variable in the solution.

DEGEN   if the variable is a basic feasible variable whose activity is at its lower bound.

ALTER   if the variable can be used to define an alternate optimal solution.

The TYPE column shows how LP interprets the variable in the problem data set. Types include:

NON-NEG   if the variable is a nonnegative variable with lower bound 0 and upper bound +INFINITY.

LOWERBD   if the variable has a lower bound specified in a LOWERBD observation.

UPPERBD   if the variable has an upper bound that is less than +INFINITY. This upper bound is specified in an UPPERBD observation.

UPLOWBD   if the variable has a lower bound specified in a LOWERBD observation and an upper bound specified in an UPPERBD observation.

INTEGER   if the variable is constrained to take integer values. If this is the case, then it must also be upper and lower bounded.

UNRSTRT   if the variable is an unrestricted variable having bounds of −INFINITY and +INFINITY.

SLACK   if the variable is a slack variable that LP has appended to a LE constraint. For variables of this type, the variable name is the same as the name of the constraint (given in the ID variable) for which this variable is the slack.

SURPLUS   if the variable is a surplus variable that LP has appended to a GE constraint. For variables of this type, the variable name is the same as the name of the constraint (given in the ID variable) for which this variable is the surplus.

The reduced cost associated with each nonbasic variable is the marginal value of that variable if it is brought into the basis. Basic variables always have a zero reduced cost. At optimality, for a maximization problem, nonbasic variables that are not at an upper bound have nonpositive reduced costs, for example X and _OBS3_. This shows the objective would decrease if they were to increase beyond their optimal value. Nonbasic variables at upper bounds have nonnegative reduced costs, showing that increasing the upper bound (if the reduced cost is not zero) increases the objective. For nonbasic variables at their upper bound, the reduced cost is the marginal value of increasing the upper bound, often called the *shadow price*. In this example, although X is a nonbasic upper-bounded variable, it is at its lower bound. Its negative reduced cost tells you that increasing it would decrease the objective.

For minimization problems, all signs are changed in the analysis. For example, at optimality the reduced costs of all nonupper-bounded variables are nonnegative, and the reduced costs of upper-bounded variables at their upper bound are nonpositive. See **Output 5.3**.

Output 5.3   VARIABLE SUMMARY for Solving First of Two Problems with One
Invocation

```
                                                                      3

              L I N E A R   P R O G R A M M I N G   P R O C E D U R E

                                 VARIABLE  SUMMARY
       ❶    ❷        ❸       ❹        ❺         ❻             ❼
            VARIABLE                                         REDUCED
      COL   NAME     STATUS   TYPE    PRICE     ACTIVITY      COST

       1 X                   UPLOWBD      0   -0.300000    -1.000000
       2 Y          BASIC LOWERBD        1    2.200000             0
       3 _OBS3_              SLACK       0           0    -1.000000
       4 _OBS4_     BASIC SURPLUS        0    4.600000             0
```

The next section of output contains the CONSTRAINT SUMMARY. For each
constraint row, free row, and objective row, a line is printed in the CONSTRAINT
SUMMARY. Included on the line are the constraint ID, the row type, the slack
or surplus variable associated with the row, the right-hand-side constant associated with the row, the activity of the row (not including the activity of the logical
variables), and the dual activity (shadow prices).

A dual variable is associated with each constraint row. At optimality the value
of this variable, the dual activity, tells you the marginal value of the right-hand-
side constant. For each unit increase in the right-hand-side constant, the objective changes by this amount. This quantity is also known as the *shadow price*.
For example, the marginal value for the right-hand-side constant of constraint
OBS3 is 1.0. See **Output 5.4**.

Output 5.4   CONSTRAINT SUMMARY for Solving First Two Problems with One
Invocation

```
                                                                      4

              L I N E A R   P R O G R A M M I N G   P R O C E D U R E

                                CONSTRAINT SUMMARY
       ❶                ❷     S/S ❸     ❹           ❺          ❻
      CONSTRAINT                                              DUAL
      ROW ID         TYPE     COL     RHS      ACTIVITY     ACTIVITY

       1 _OBS3_      LE         3    1.900000  1.900000    1.000000
       2 _OBS4_      GE         4   -0.500000  4.100000           0
       3 _OBS1_      OBJECTIVE       2.200000  2.200000           0
       4 _OBS2_      FREE            1.600000  1.600000           0
```

This completes the output for problem *lp(1a)*. Following is the output for the
second problem defined in the problem data, namely *lp(1b)*. The output of this
minimization is shown in **Output 5.5**.

Output 5.5 Summaries for Solving First of Two Problems with One Invocation

```
                                                                                 5

           L I N E A R   P R O G R A M M I N G   P R O C E D U R E

                         PROBLEM  SUMMARY



         MIN _OBS2_          OBJECTIVE FUNCTION
         _RHS_               RHS VARIABLE
         _TYPE_              TYPE VARIABLE
         PROBLEM DENSITY           0.750



         VARIABLE TYPE             NUMBER

         STRUCTURAL
           LOWER BOUNDED              1
           UPPER AND LOWER BOUNDED    1

         LOGICAL
           SLACK                      1
           SURPLUS                    1

         TOTAL                        4



         CONSTRAINT TYPE          NUMBER

         LE                          1
         GE                          1
         FREE                        2

         TOTAL                        4
```

```
                                                                                 6

           L I N E A R   P R O G R A M M I N G   P R O C E D U R E



                        SOLUTION  SUMMARY



                     TERMINATED SUCCESSFULLY

         OBJECTIVE VALUE          -0.700000

         PHASE 1 ITERATIONS             0
         PHASE 2 ITERATIONS             2
         INITIAL B.F. VARIABLES         2
         TIME USED (SECS)            0.00
         NUMBER OF INVERSIONS           1

         MACHINE EPSILON        1.00000E-08
         MACHINE INFINITY       7.23701E+75
         INVERT FREQUENCY              50
         MAX PHASE 1 ITERATIONS       100
         MAX PHASE 2 ITERATIONS       100
         TIME LIMIT (SECS)         120.00
```

```
                                                                        7
            L I N E A R   P R O G R A M M I N G   P R O C E D U R E
                           VARIABLE   SUMMARY

            VARIABLE                                        REDUCED
        COL NAME    STATUS  TYPE     PRICE    ACTIVITY        COST

          1 X               UPLOWBD      2   -0.300000     1.500000
          2 Y       BASIC LOWERBD        1   -0.100000            0
          3 _OBS3_  BASIC SLACK          0    2.300000            0
          4 _OBS4_        SURPLUS        0           0     0.500000
```

```
                                                                        8
            L I N E A R   P R O G R A M M I N G   P R O C E D U R E
                          CONSTRAINT SUMMARY

        CONSTRAINT          S/S                               DUAL
        ROW ID      TYPE    COL      RHS    ACTIVITY        ACTIVITY

          1 _OBS3_  LE       3   1.900000   -0.400000             0
          2 _OBS4_  GE       4  -0.500000   -0.500000      0.500000
          3 _OBS1_  FREE        -0.100000   -0.100000             0
          4 _OBS2_  OBJECTIVE   -0.700000   -0.700000             0
```

Analyzing the Sensitivity of the Solution to Changes in the Right-Hand-Side Constants: Example 2

This example demonstrates how LP can be used to examine the sensitivity of a solution to changes in the right-hand-side constants. It shows how to save the primal solution in a SAS data set. The problem is

$$\text{max} \quad x + y$$

$$\text{subject to:} \quad x + y \leq 2.5 \qquad\qquad\qquad (lp(2))$$

$$0 \leq x \leq 1$$
$$0 \leq y \leq 1 \quad .$$

Below is the SAS program to solve this problem and examine the sensitivity of the solution to changes in the right-hand-side value (2.5):

```
DATA EX_2;
   INPUT X Y TYPEID $ R1 RSEN;
   CARDS;
1 1 MAX      .   .
1 1 LE      2.5   1
1 1 UPPERBD .   .
;
PROC LP PRIMALOUT=SOLUTION;
   VAR X Y;
   TYPE TYPEID;
   RHS R1;
   RHSSEN RSEN;
```

Since by default PROC LP assumes that all variables have a lower bound of zero, there is no need to include an observation with TYPEID=LOWERBD. The variable RSEN contains the vector **r** that is used to modify the right-hand-side constants. In this example we examine the sensitivity of the optimal solution to changes in the right-hand-side constant of constraint

$$x + y \leq 2.5 \quad .$$

LP determines the range $[\varphi_{min}, \varphi_{max}]$ over which the optimal basis optimal in *(lp(2))* remains optimal in a new linear program having constraint

$$x + y \leq 2.5 + \varphi \quad .$$

The PROBLEM SUMMARY and SOLUTION SUMMARY for this example are shown in **Output 5.6**.

Output 5.6   PROBLEM SUMMARY and SOLUTION SUMMARY for Analyzing the Sensitivity of the Solution

```
                                                                         1

        L I N E A R   P R O G R A M M I N G   P R O C E D U R E

                       PROBLEM  SUMMARY


            MAX _OBS1_           OBJECTIVE FUNCTION
            R1                   RHS  VARIABLE
            TYPEID               TYPE VARIABLE
            PROBLEM DENSITY           1.000


            VARIABLE TYPE             NUMBER

            STRUCTURAL
              UPPER BOUNDED             2

            LOGICAL
              SLACK                     1

            TOTAL                       3


            CONSTRAINT TYPE          NUMBER

            LE                         1
            FREE                       1

            TOTAL                      2
```

```
                                                                                    2
        L I N E A R   P R O G R A M M I N G   P R O C E D U R E


                          SOLUTION   SUMMARY


                    TERMINATED SUCCESSFULLY

             OBJECTIVE VALUE              2.000000

             PHASE 1 ITERATIONS                  0
             PHASE 2 ITERATIONS                  1
             INITIAL B.F. VARIABLES              1
             TIME USED (SECS)              0.00
             NUMBER OF INVERSIONS               2

             MACHINE EPSILON           1.00000E-08
             MACHINE INFINITY          7.23701E+75
             INVERT FREQUENCY                  50
             MAX PHASE 1 ITERATIONS            100
             MAX PHASE 2 ITERATIONS            100
             TIME LIMIT (SECS)             120.00
```

```
                                                                                    3
        L I N E A R   P R O G R A M M I N G   P R O C E D U R E

                          VARIABLE   SUMMARY

             VARIABLE                                      REDUCED
        COL  NAME    STATUS  TYPE     PRICE   ACTIVITY      COST


         1 X                 UPPERBD      1   1.000000    1.000000
         2 Y                 UPPERBD      1   1.000000    1.000000
         3 _OBS2_  BASIC     SLACK        0   0.500000           0
```

```
                                                                                    4
        L I N E A R   P R O G R A M M I N G   P R O C E D U R E

                          CONSTRAINT SUMMARY

        CONSTRAINT        S/S                             DUAL
        ROW ID    TYPE    COL      RHS      ACTIVITY     ACTIVITY


         1 _OBS2_  LE        3   2.500000   2.000000          0
         2 _OBS1_  OBJECTIVE     2.000000   2.000000          0
```

The sensitivity analysis is reported in the next section of output. The report includes the maximum and minimum φ, namely φ_{min} and φ_{max}; the leaving variables; the objective function at optimality; and the variable activity for the right-hand side when $\varphi = \varphi_{min}$ and $\varphi = \varphi_{max}$. The leaving variables are the variables that would enter the basis if φ were to exceed these bounds. This summary is shown in **Output 5.7**.

Output 5.7   RHS SENSITIVITY ANALYSIS SUMMARY

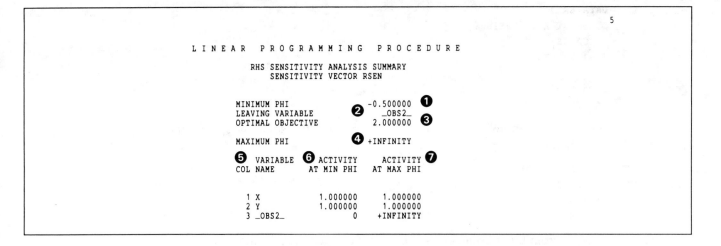

The SOLUTION data set contains three observations. See **Output 5.8**.

Output 5.8   Three Observations for Analyzing the Sensitivity of the Solution

OBS	_OBJ_ID_	_RHS_ID_	_TYPE_	_STATUS_	_VAR_	_VALUE_	_R_COST_	_PRICE_	_LBOUND_	_UBOUND_
1	_OBS1_	R1	UPPERBD	_UPPER_	X	1.0	1	1	0	1
2	_OBS1_	R1	UPPERBD	_UPPER_	Y	1.0	1	1	0	1
3	_OBS1_	R1	SLACK	_BASIC_	_OBS2_	0.5	0	0	0	.

Analyzing the Sensitivity of the Solution to Changes in the Objective Coefficients: Example 3

This example shows how LP can be used to examine the sensitivity of the solution to changes in the objective function coefficients. In this example an observation is added to the problem data set in order to define the change vector-**r**. LP identifies the range of parameter φ, namely $[\varphi_{min}, \varphi_{max}]$, over which the solution to $lp(2)$ is optimal in the new linear program:

$$\max \quad (1 + \varphi)x + (1 - \varphi)y$$

subject to: $\quad x + y \leq 2.5$ $\qquad\qquad\qquad$ (lp(2'))

$$0 \leq x \leq 1$$
$$0 \leq y \leq 1$$

The SAS program below appends the change vector to the problem:

```
DATA EX_3;
   INPUT X Y TYPEID $;
   CARDS;
1 -1 PRICESEN
;
DATA EX_3;
SET EX_2 EX_3;
```

To perform the sensitivity analysis without reprinting the solution, specify the NOPRINT option:

```
PROC LP NOPRINT;
   VAR X Y;
   TYPE TYPEID;
   RHS R1;
```

The output from this step includes the PROBLEM SUMMARY, the SOLUTION SUMMARY (including the VARIABLE SUMMARY and the CONSTRAINT SUMMARY), and the PRICE SENSITIVITY ANALYSIS SUMMARY. Since the PROBLEM and SOLUTION SUMMARY are the same as in **Example 2**, only the PRICE SENSITIVITY ANALYSIS SUMMARY is shown in **Output 5.9**.

Output 5.9   PRICE SENSITIVITY ANALYSIS SUMMARY

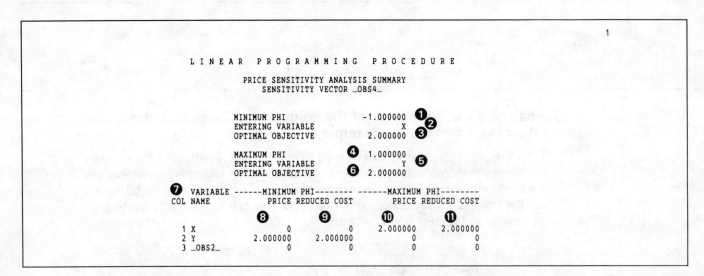

As with the sensitivity analysis of the right-hand-side constants, sensitivity analysis on the objective function results in a report of the minimum and maximum φ, the entering variables, and the objective function at optimality. Also included in the output are the modified price and modified reduced cost when φ is φ_{min} and φ_{max}. Note that the activity of the solution does not change for $\varphi\varepsilon[\varphi_{min},\varphi_{max}$

Finding a Minimum Cost Diet: Example 4

This example presents a somewhat larger problem than those in the last three examples. This is a demonstration of the use of the output data set defined by PRIMALOUT= to restart a problem that terminated because it exceeded the iteration limit. The form of the problem is inspired by one of the classic linear programming problems first solved by hand in 1947. In this application of linear programming, the goal is to identify a least-cost diet that satisfies recommended daily dietary requirements. The original problem contained seventy-seven food items and nine dietary constraints (Dantzig 1963).

In our example, we have chosen fifty-three food items from a USDA bulletin (number 72). For each of these items the USDA measured the amount of calories, protein, fat, carbohydrates, calcium, iron, vitamin A, thiamin, riboflavin, niacin, and vitamin C in a standard portion.

The SAS program that follows reads the data into a SAS data set in which variables are nutritional components and observations are foods. The data are then transformed to a data set defining a linear program that finds a minimum-cost, nutritionally sound diet. The recommended daily dietary requirements used to determine constraints for a sound diet are taken from the USDA bulletin; these define the right-hand-side constants.

```
DATA RAW;
    INPUT COST1 QUAN1 MEAS $ UP_BD NUMBER FOOD $ QUANTITY
    CALORIES PROTEIN FAT CARBO CALCIUM IRON
    VITAMINA THIAMIN  RIBO  NIACIN VITAMINC;
    CARDS;
15   1 CUP 4    1 MILK_W   245 160 9 9  12 288 .1  350 .07 .41  .2  2
                          .
                          .
                          .
132 1 CUP 1 568 CHOCOLAT 170 860 7 61 97 51  4.4  30 .02 .14  .9  0
44  4 OZ  2 581 PUDDING  193 260 2 2  59 31   .  120 .02 .06   .  4
;
PROC PRINT;


*-------------------------------------------------------------------;
* NORMALIZE THE RAW DATA SO ALL QUANTITIES ARE IN UNITS/GRAM,       ;
* THEN ADD AN UPPER BOUND ON THE AMOUNT OF ANY ONE FOOD THAT        ;
* WILL BE CONSUMED.                                                 ;
*-------------------------------------------------------------------;

DATA NORM;
   DROP I;
   SET RAW;
   ARRAY X(*) CALORIES - VITAMINC;
   DO I=1 TO DIM(X);
      X(I)=X(I)/QUANTITY;
      END;
   CONSUMD=1;
   UP_BOUND=UP_BD*QUANTITY;
   COST=COST1/QUANTITY;
   OUTPUT;


*-------------------------------------------------------------------;
* TRANSPOSE THE DATA SO THAT THE FOODS ARE THE INPUT VARIABLES.     ;
*-------------------------------------------------------------------;

PROC TRANSPOSE OUT=PROB1;
   VAR CALORIES-COST;
   ID FOOD;
```

```
*------------------------------------------------------------------;
* SORT THE DATA SET BY THE VARIABLE _NAME_.                        ;
*------------------------------------------------------------------;

PROC SORT;
   BY _NAME_;

*------------------------------------------------------------------;
* DEFINE THE TYPE IDENTIFIER AND THE RIGHT-HAND-SIDE CONSTANTS.    ;
* THE RHS'S ARE THE RECOMMENDED DAILY REQUIREMENTS OF THE SEVERAL  ;
* VITAMINS AND MINERALS FOR A MAN.                                 ;
*------------------------------------------------------------------;

DATA CONST;
   INPUT _NAME_ $ _TYPE_ $  MEN;
   CARDS;
CALORIES >=   2600
PROTEIN  >=     65
FAT      FREE    .
CARBO    FREE    .
CALCIUM  >=     .8
IRON     >=     10
VITAMINA >=   5000
THIAMIN  >=    1.3
RIBO     >=    1.7
NIACIN   >=     17
VITAMINC >=     60
CONSUMD  FREE    .
UP_BOUND UPPERBD .
COST     MIN     .
;

*------------------------------------------------------------------;
* SORT THE DATA SET BY THE VARIABLE _NAME_.                        ;
*------------------------------------------------------------------;

PROC SORT;
   BY _NAME_;

*------------------------------------------------------------------;
* MERGE THE TRANSPOSED RAW DATA WITH THE CONSTRAINT DATA           ;
* TO FORM THE PROBLEM DATA SET.                                    ;
*------------------------------------------------------------------;

DATA PROB;
   MERGE PROB1 CONST;
   BY _NAME_;

*------------------------------------------------------------------;
* PRINT THE PROBLEM DATA SET.                                      ;
*------------------------------------------------------------------;

PROC PRINT;
```

The first three pages of output contain the printouts from the two PROC PRINT statements. See **Output 5.10**.

Output 5.10 Minimum Cost Diet Printouts Generated by the PROC PRINT Statement

OBS	COST1	QUAN1	MEAS	UPBD	NUMBER	FOOD	QUANTITY	CALORIES	PROTEIN	FAT	CARBO	CALCIUM	IRON	VITAMINA	THIAMIN	RIBO	NIACIN	VITAMINC
1	15.0	1.0	CUP	4	1	MILK_W	245	160	9	9	12	288	0.1	350	0.07	0.41	0.2	2
2	15.0	1.0	CUP	4	3	MILK_S	245	145	10	5	15	352	0.1	200	0.10	0.52	0.2	2
3	19.0	1.0	OZ	4	13	CHEDDARC	28	115	7	9	1	213	0.3	370	0.01	0.13	0.0	0
4	64.0	1.0	CUP	2	16	COTTAGEC	245	260	33	10	7	230	0.7	420	0.07	0.61	0.2	0
5	23.0	1.0	OZ	4	25	SWISSC	28	105	8	8	1	262	0.3	320	0.00	0.11	0.0	0
6	66.0	1.0	CUP	2	71	YOGURT	245	125	8	4	13	294	0.1	170	0.10	0.44	0.2	2
7	6.7	1.0	EGG	4	73	EGGS	50	80	6	6	0	27	1.1	590	0.05	0.15	0.0	0
8	9.0	2.0	SLICES	5	77	BACON	15	90	5	8	1	2	0.5	0	0.08	0.05	0.8	0
9	35.0	3.0	OZ	3	80	HAMBURG	85	185	23	10	0	10	3.0	2	0.08	0.20	5.1	0
10	60.0	3.0	OZ	3	82	ROAST	85	375	17	34	0	8	2.2	70	0.05	0.13	3.1	0
11	83.0	3.0	OZ	3	86	STEAK	85	330	20	27	0	9	2.5	50	0.05	0.16	4.0	0
12	13.0	3.0	OZ	3	95	CHICKEN	85	115	20	3	0	8	1.4	80	0.05	0.16	7.4	0
13	28.0	3.0	OZ	3	113	PORK	85	245	18	19	0	8	2.2	0	0.40	0.16	3.1	0
14	11.0	2.0	SLICES	4	123	BOLOGNA	26	80	3	7	0	2	0.5	0	0.04	0.06	0.7	0
15	26.0	1.0	FRANK	4	126	FRANKFT	56	170	7	15	1	3	0.8	0	0.08	0.11	1.4	0
16	18.4	1.0	OZ	8	128	SALAMI	28	130	7	11	0	4	1.0	0	0.10	0.07	1.5	0
17	41.0	3.0	OZ	3	133	BLUEFISH	85	135	22	4	0	25	0.6	40	0.09	0.08	1.6	0
18	51.0	3.0	OZ	3	135	CLAMS	85	45	7	1	2	47	3.5	0	0.01	0.09	0.9	0
19	41.0	3.0	OZ	1	146	TUNA/OIL	85	170	24	7	0	7	1.6	70	0.04	0.10	10.1	0
20	15.0	1.0	CUP	2	149	NAVYBEAN	190	225	15	1	40	95	5.1	0	0.27	0.13	1.3	0
21	5.3	1.0	TBSP	4	160	PEANUTBU	16	95	4	8	3	9	0.3	0	0.02	0.02	2.4	0
22	18.4	4.0	SPEARS	4	164	ASPARAGU	60	10	1	0	2	13	0.4	540	0.10	0.11	0.8	16
23	27.3	1.0	CUP	2	168	BEANSNAP	125	30	2	0	7	63	0.8	680	0.09	0.11	0.6	15
24	5.8	2.0	BEETS	4	173	BEETS	100	30	1	0	7	14	0.5	20	0.03	0.04	0.3	6
25	25.4	1.0	STALK	2	177	BROCCOLI	180	45	6	1	8	158	1.4	4500	0.16	0.36	1.4	162
26	11.2	1.0	CUP	2	183	CABBAGE	145	30	2	0	6	64	0.4	190	0.06	0.06	0.4	48
27	14.4	1.0	CUP	2	190	CARROTS	145	45	1	0	10	48	0.9	15220	0.08	0.07	0.7	9
28	10.0	1.0	EAR	2	196	CORN	140	70	3	1	16	2	0.5	310	0.09	0.08	1.0	7
29	20.0	1.0	CUCK	1	199	CUCUMBER	207	39	1	0	7	35	0.6	0	0.07	0.09	0.4	23
30	89.0	1.0	HEAD	1	204	LETTUCE	220	30	3	0	6	77	4.4	2130	0.14	0.13	0.6	18
31	18.0	1.0	CUP	2	211	ONION	210	60	3	0	14	50	0.8	80	0.06	0.06	0.4	14
32	28.2	1.0	CUP	2	215	PEAS	160	115	9	1	19	37	2.9	860	0.44	0.17	3.7	33
33	9.8	1.0	POTATO	2	221	POTBAKED	99	90	3	0	21	9	0.7	0	0.10	0.04	1.7	20
34	8.0	10.0	PIECES	2	224	FR_FRIED	57	155	2	7	20	9	0.7	0	0.07	0.04	1.8	12
35	10.6	10.0	CHIPS	4	228	POTCHIPS	20	115	1	8	10	8	0.4	0	0.04	0.01	1.0	3
36	42.5	1.0	CUP	2	233	SPINACH	180	40	5	1	6	167	4.0	14580	13.00	0.25	1.0	50
37	9.5	1.0	POTATO	2	236	SWETPOT	110	155	2	1	36	44	1.0	8910	0.10	0.07	0.7	24
38	41.2	1.0	TOMATO	2	240	TOMATO	200	40	2	0	9	24	0.9	1640	0.11	0.07	1.3	42
39	26.0	1.0	APPLE	2	248	APPLE	150	70	0	0	18	8	0.4	50	0.04	0.02	0.1	3
40	23.0	1.0	BANANA	2	259	BANANA	175	100	1	0	26	10	0.8	230	0.06	0.07	0.8	12
41	31.2	1.0	ORANGE	2	294	ORANGE	180	65	1	0	16	54	0.5	260	0.13	0.05	0.5	66
42	7.2	1.0	SLICE	4	342	WHT_BRED	25	65	2	1	13	22	0.3	0	0.03	0.02	0.3	0
43	7.0	1.0	SLICE	4	350	RYE_BRED	25	60	2	0	13	19	0.4	0	0.05	0.02	0.4	0
44	4.4	1.0	SLICE	4	353	WIT_BRED	25	70	2	1	13	21	0.6	0	0.06	0.05	0.6	0
45	9.0	1.0	CUP	2	464	RICE	205	225	4	0	50	21	1.8	0	0.23	0.02	2.1	0
46	11.4	1.0	CUP	2	475	SPAGHETT	140	155	5	1	32	11	1.3	0	0.20	0.11	1.5	0
47	17.4	1.0	OZ	2	533	FUDGE	28	115	1	4	21	22	0.3	0	0.01	0.03	0.1	0

2

OBS	COST1	QUAN1	MEAS	UP_BD	NUMBER	FOOD	QUANTITY	CALORIES	PROTEIN	FAT	CARBO	CALCIUM	IRON	VITAMINA	THIAMIN	RIBO	NIACIN	VITAMINC
48	6	1.0	OZ	2	536	MARSHMLW	28	90	1	0	0	23	0.5	0	0.00	0.00	0.0	0
49	40	12.0	FL_OZ	4	553	BEER	360	150	1	0	14	18	0.0	0	0.01	0.11	2.2	0
50	47	1.5	FL_OZ	2	556	WHISKEY	42	110	0	0	0	0	0.0	0	0.00	0.00	0.0	0
51	39	12.0	FL_OZ	4	562	COLA	369	145	0	0	37	0	0.0	0	0.00	0.00	0.0	0
52	132	1.0	CUP	1	568	CHOCOLAT	170	860	7	61	97	51	4.4	30	0.02	0.14	0.9	0
53	44	4.0	OZ	2	581	PUDDING	193	260	2	2	59	31	0.0	120	0.02	0.06	0.0	4

3

OBS	_NAME_	MILK_W	MILK_S	CHEDDARC	COTTAGEC	SWISSC	YOGURT	EGGS	BACON	HAMBURG	ROAST	STEAK	CHICKEN	PORK
1	CALCIUM	1.176	1.437	7.607	0.939	9.357	1.200	0.540	0.1333	0.118	0.094	0.106	0.094	0.094
2	CALORIES	0.653	0.592	4.107	1.061	3.750	0.510	1.600	6.0000	2.176	4.412	3.882	1.353	2.882
3	CARBO	0.049	0.061	0.036	0.029	0.036	0.053	0.000	0.0667	0.000	0.000	0.000	0.000	0.000
4	CONSUMD	1.000	1.000	1.000	1.000	1.000	1.000	1.000	1.0000	1.000	1.000	1.000	1.000	1.000
5	COST	0.061	0.061	0.679	0.261	0.821	0.269	0.134	0.6000	0.412	0.706	0.976	0.153	0.329
6	FAT	0.037	0.020	0.321	0.041	0.286	0.016	0.120	0.5333	0.118	0.400	0.318	0.035	0.224
7	IRON	0.000	0.000	0.011	0.003	0.011	0.000	0.022	0.0333	0.035	0.026	0.029	0.016	0.026
8	NIACIN	0.001	0.001	0.000	0.001	0.000	0.001	0.000	0.0533	0.060	0.036	0.047	0.087	0.036
9	PROTEIN	0.037	0.041	0.250	0.135	0.286	0.033	0.120	0.3333	0.271	0.200	0.235	0.235	0.212
10	RIBO	0.002	0.002	0.005	0.002	0.004	0.002	0.003	0.0033	0.002	0.002	0.002	0.002	0.002
11	THIAMIN	0.000	0.000	0.000	0.000	0.000	0.000	0.000	0.0053	0.001	0.001	0.001	0.001	0.005
12	UP_BOUND	980.000	980.000	112.000	490.000	112.000	490.000	200.000	75.0000	255.000	255.000	255.000	255.000	255.000
13	VITAMINA	1.429	0.816	13.214	1.714	11.429	0.694	11.800	0.0000	0.024	0.824	0.588	0.941	0.000
14	VITAMINC	0.008	0.008	0.000	0.000	0.000	0.008	0.000	0.0000	0.000	0.000	0.000	0.000	0.000

OBS	BOLOGNA	FRANKFT	SALAMI	BLUEFISH	CLAMS	TUNA_OIL	NAVYBEAN	PEANUTBU	ASPARAGU	BEANSNAP	BEETS	BROCCOLI	CABBAGE	CARROTS
1	0.077	0.054	0.143	0.294	0.553	0.0824	0.500	0.5625	0.217	0.504	0.140	0.878	0.441	0.331
2	3.077	3.036	4.643	1.588	0.529	2.0000	1.184	5.9375	0.167	0.240	0.300	0.250	0.207	0.310
3	0.000	0.018	0.000	0.000	0.024	0.0000	0.211	0.1875	0.033	0.056	0.070	0.044	0.041	0.069
4	1.000	1.000	1.000	1.000	1.000	1.0000	1.000	1.0000	1.000	1.000	1.000	1.000	1.000	1.000
5	0.423	0.464	0.657	0.482	0.600	0.4824	0.079	0.3312	0.307	0.218	0.058	0.141	0.077	0.099
6	0.269	0.268	0.393	0.047	0.012	0.0824	0.005	0.5000	0.007	0.006	0.006	0.006	0.003	0.006
7	0.019	0.014	0.036	0.007	0.041	0.0188	0.027	0.0187	0.007	0.006	0.005	0.008	0.003	0.006
8	0.027	0.025	0.054	0.019	0.011	0.1188	0.007	0.1500	0.013	0.005	0.003	0.008	0.003	0.005
9	0.115	0.125	0.250	0.259	0.082	0.2824	0.079	0.2500	0.017	0.016	0.010	0.033	0.014	0.007
10	0.002	0.002	0.002	0.001	0.001	0.0012	0.001	0.0012	0.002	0.001	0.000	0.002	0.000	0.000
11	0.002	0.001	0.004	0.001	0.000	0.0005	0.001	0.0012	0.002	0.001	0.001	0.000	0.001	0.001
12	104.000	224.000	224.000	255.000	255.000	85.000	380.000	64.000	240.000	250.000	400.000	360.000	290.000	290.000
13	0.000	0.000	0.000	0.471	0.000	0.8235	0.000	0.0000	9.000	5.440	0.200	25.000	1.310	104.966
14	0.000	0.000	0.000	0.000	0.000	0.0000	0.000	0.0000	0.267	0.120	0.060	0.900	0.331	0.062

4

OBS	CORN	CUCUMBER	LETTUCE	ONION	PEAS	POT_BAKED	FR_FRIED	POT_CHIPS	SPINACH	SWEETPOTO	TOMATO	APPLE	BANANA	ORANGE
1	0.014	0.169	0.350	0.238	0.231	0.091	0.158	0.4000	0.928	0.400	0.120	0.053	0.057	0.300
2	0.500	0.188	0.136	0.286	0.719	0.909	2.719	5.7500	0.222	1.409	0.200	0.467	0.571	0.361
3	0.114	0.034	0.027	0.067	0.119	0.212	0.351	0.5000	0.033	0.327	0.045	0.120	0.149	0.089
4	1.000	1.000	1.000	1.000	1.000	1.000	1.000	1.0000	1.000	1.000	1.000	1.000	1.000	1.000
5	0.071	0.097	0.405	0.086	0.176	0.099	0.140	0.5300	0.236	0.086	0.206	0.173	0.131	0.173
6	0.007	0.000	0.000	0.000	0.006	0.000	0.123	0.4400	0.006	0.009	0.000	0.000	0.000	0.000
7	0.004	0.003	0.020	0.004	0.018	0.007	0.012	0.0200	0.022	0.009	0.004	0.003	0.005	0.003
8	0.007	0.002	0.003	0.002	0.023	0.017	0.032	0.0500	0.006	0.006	0.006	0.001	0.005	0.003
9	0.021	0.005	0.014	0.014	0.056	0.030	0.035	0.0500	0.028	0.018	0.010	0.000	0.006	0.006
10	0.001	0.000	0.001	0.000	0.001	0.000	0.001	0.0005	0.001	0.001	0.000	0.000	0.000	0.000
11	0.001	0.000	0.001	0.000	0.003	0.001	0.001	0.0020	0.072	0.001	0.001	0.000	0.000	0.001
12	280.000	207.000	220.000	420.000	320.000	198.000	114.000	80.0000	360.000	220.000	800.000	300.000	350.000	360.000
13	2.214	0.000	9.682	0.381	5.375	0.000	0.000	0.0000	81.000	81.000	8.200	0.333	1.314	1.444
14	0.050	0.111	0.082	0.067	0.206	0.202	0.211	0.1500	0.278	0.218	0.210	0.020	0.069	0.367

OBS	WHT_BRED	RYE_BRED	WIT_BRED	RICE	SPAGHETT	FUDGE	MARSHMLEW	BEER	WHISKEY	COLA	CHOCDLAT	PUDDING_	_TYPE_	MEN
1	0.880	0.760	0.840	0.102	0.079	0.7857	0.8214	0.05	0.000	0.00	0.300	0.161	>=	0.8
2	2.600	2.400	2.800	1.098	1.107	4.1071	3.2143	0.42	2.619	0.39	5.059	1.347	>=	2600.0
3	0.520	0.520	0.520	0.244	0.229	0.7500	0.0000	0.04	0.000	0.10	0.571	0.306	FREE	.
4	1.000	1.000	1.000	1.000	1.000	1.0000	1.0000	1.00	1.000	1.00	1.000	1.000	FREE	.
5	0.288	0.280	0.176	0.044	0.081	0.6214	0.2143	0.11	1.119	0.11	0.776	0.228	MIN	.
6	0.040	0.000	0.040	0.000	0.007	0.1429	0.0000	0.00	0.000	0.00	0.359	0.010	FREE	.
7	0.012	0.016	0.024	0.009	0.009	0.0107	0.0179	0.00	0.000	0.00	0.026	0.000	>=	10.0
8	0.012	0.016	0.024	0.010	0.011	0.0036	0.0000	0.01	0.000	0.00	0.005	0.000	>=	17.0
9	0.080	0.080	0.080	0.020	0.036	0.0357	0.0357	0.00	0.000	0.00	0.041	0.010	>=	65.0
10	0.001	0.001	0.002	0.000	0.001	0.0011	0.0000	0.00	0.000	0.00	0.001	0.000	>=	1.7
11	0.001	0.002	0.002	0.001	0.001	0.0004	0.0000	0.00	0.000	0.00	0.000	0.000	>=	1.3
12	100.000	100.000	100.000	410.000	280.000	56.0000	56.0000	1440.00	84.000	1476.00	170.000	386.000	UPPERBD	.
13	0.000	0.000	0.000	0.000	0.000	0.0000	0.0000	0.00	0.000	0.00	0.176	0.622	>=	5000.0
14	0.000	0.000	0.000	0.000	0.000	0.0000	0.0000	0.00	0.000	0.00	0.000	0.021	>=	60.0

The data are now in a form ready for PROC LP. An attempt to solve the problem is unsuccessful because the 5 iteration limit is not sufficient. Since an output data set was defined, the partial solution is saved in the data set PRIMAL.

```
PROC LP MAXIT2=5 PRIMALOUT=PRIMAL NOPRINT;
    VAR MILK_W-PUDDING;
    ID _NAME_;
    RHS MEN;
```

See **Output 5.11** for the PROBLEM SUMMARY and partial SOLUTION SUMMARY.

Output 5.11 PROBLEM SUMMARY and PARTIAL SOLUTION SUMMARY for Finding a Minimum Cost Diet

```
                                                                    5

                L I N E A R   P R O G R A M M I N G   P R O C E D U R E

                             PROBLEM  SUMMARY



            MIN COST           OBJECTIVE FUNCTION
            MEN                 RHS  VARIABLE
            _TYPE_              TYPE VARIABLE
            PROBLEM DENSITY              0.738


            VARIABLE TYPE               NUMBER

            STRUCTURAL
              UPPER BOUNDED              53

            LOGICAL
              SURPLUS                     9

            TOTAL                        62


            CONSTRAINT TYPE             NUMBER

            GE                           9
            FREE                         4

            TOTAL                       13
```

```
                                                                    6

                L I N E A R   P R O G R A M M I N G   P R O C E D U R E



                             SOLUTION  SUMMARY



            TERMINATE ON MAX PHASE 2 ITERATIONS

            OBJECTIVE VALUE             308.931

            PHASE 1 ITERATIONS              13
            PHASE 2 ITERATIONS               5
            INITIAL B.F. VARIABLES           0
            TIME USED (SECS)              0.07
            NUMBER OF INVERSIONS             3

            MACHINE EPSILON         1.00000E-08
            MACHINE INFINITY        7.23701E+75
            INVERT FREQUENCY                33
            MAX PHASE 1 ITERATIONS         100
            MAX PHASE 2 ITERATIONS           5
            TIME LIMIT (SECS)           120.00
```

Since the iteration limit was exceeded, the solution is not optimal. Also note that the MAXIT2= option changed the iteration limit from the default value of 100 to 5; these settings are included in the SOLUTION SUMMARY. The next step calls LP with PRIMAL as a PRIMALIN= data set, causing LP to start with the feasible solution previously found. Note that when using this option, care must be taken not to change the problem data set. These statements invoke the procedure:

```
PROC LP PRIMALIN=PRIMAL DATA=PROB;
   VAR MILK_W-PUDDING;
   ID _NAME_;
   RHS MEN;
```

These statements produce the following report. Note that the cost is in cents; consequently, the minimum-cost diet costs $1.58. See **Output 5.12**.

Output 5.12   Summaries for Finding a Minimum Cost Diet

```
                                                                    7

        L I N E A R   P R O G R A M M I N G   P R O C E D U R E

                          PROBLEM  SUMMARY



        MIN COST          OBJECTIVE FUNCTION
        MEN               RHS VARIABLE
        _TYPE_            TYPE VARIABLE
        PROBLEM DENSITY            0.738



        VARIABLE TYPE            NUMBER

        STRUCTURAL
          UPPER BOUNDED             53

        LOGICAL
          SURPLUS                    9

        TOTAL                       62



        CONSTRAINT TYPE         NUMBER

        GE                         9
        FREE                       4

        TOTAL                      13
```

```
                                                                    8

        L I N E A R   P R O G R A M M I N G   P R O C E D U R E



                         SOLUTION  SUMMARY



            TERMINATED SUCCESSFULLY

        OBJECTIVE VALUE           158.335

        PHASE 1 ITERATIONS              0
        PHASE 2 ITERATIONS             20
        INITIAL B.F. VARIABLES          9
        TIME USED (SECS)             0.09
        NUMBER OF INVERSIONS            3

        MACHINE EPSILON        1.00000E-08
        MACHINE INFINITY       7.23701E+75
        INVERT FREQUENCY               33
        MAX PHASE 1 ITERATIONS        100
        MAX PHASE 2 ITERATIONS        100
        TIME LIMIT (SECS)          120.00
```

L I N E A R   P R O G R A M M I N G   P R O C E D U R E

VARIABLE   SUMMARY

COL	VARIABLE NAME	STATUS	TYPE	PRICE	ACTIVITY	REDUCED COST
1	MILK_W		UPPERBD	0.0612245	0	0.0006155594
2	MILK_S	BASIC	UPPERBD	0.0612245	134.532	0
3	CHEDDARC		UPPERBD	0.678571	0	0.358535
4	COTTAGEC		UPPERBD	0.261224	0	0.165121
5	SWISSC		UPPERBD	0.821429	0	0.532449
6	YOGURT		UPPERBD	0.269388	0	0.216959
7	EGGS		UPPERBD	0.134	200.000	-0.003058
8	BACON		UPPERBD	0.6	0	0.168322
9	HAMBURG		UPPERBD	0.411765	0	0.243286
10	ROAST		UPPERBD	0.705882	0	0.398051
11	STEAK		UPPERBD	0.976471	0	0.700003
12	CHICKEN		UPPERBD	0.152941	0	0.043849
13	PORK		UPPERBD	0.329412	0	0.119116
14	BOLOGNA		UPPERBD	0.423077	0	0.195485
15	FRANKFT		UPPERBD	0.464286	0	0.242990
16	SALAMI		UPPERBD	0.657143	0	0.323931
17	BLUEFISH		UPPERBD	0.482353	0	0.367474
18	CLAMS		UPPERBD	0.6	0	0.553962
19	TUNA_OIL		UPPERBD	0.482353	0	0.337781
20	NAVYBEAN		UPPERBD	0.0789474	380.000	-0.00652583
21	PEANUTBU		UPPERBD	0.33125	64.000000	-0.074637
22	ASPARAGU		UPPERBD	0.306667	0	0.276582
23	BEANSNAP		UPPERBD	0.2184	0	0.193372
24	BEETS		UPPERBD	0.058	0	0.033991
25	BROCCOLI		UPPERBD	0.141111	0	0.103779
26	CABBAGE		UPPERBD	0.0772414	0	0.059250
27	CARROTS		UPPERBD	0.0993103	0	0.073756
28	CORN		UPPERBD	0.0714286	0	0.032403
29	CUCUMBER		UPPERBD	0.0966184	0	0.079632
30	LETTUCE		UPPERBD	0.404545	0	0.389380
31	ONION		UPPERBD	0.0857143	0	0.063838
32	PEAS		UPPERBD	0.17625	0	0.117645
33	POTBAKED		UPPERBD	0.0989899	0	0.034634
34	FR_FRIED		UPPERBD	0.140351	114.000	-0.046884
35	POTCHIPS		UPPERBD	0.53	0	0.144316
36	SPINACH		UPPERBD	0.236111	0	0.206970
37	SWETPOT		UPPERBD	0.0863636	220.000	-0.013493
38	TOMATO		UPPERBD	0.206	0	0.189128
39	APPLE		UPPERBD	0.173333	0	0.141067
40	BANANA		UPPERBD	0.131429	0	0.089458
41	ORANGE		UPPERBD	0.173333	0	0.146551
42	WHT_BRED		UPPERBD	0.288	0	0.107638
43	RYE_BRED		UPPERBD	0.28	0	0.112872
44	WIT_BRED		UPPERBD	0.176	100.000000	-0.030070
45	RICE		UPPERBD	0.0439024	410.000	-0.029739
46	SPAGHETT	BASIC	UPPERBD	0.0814286	18.406806	0
47	FUDGE		UPPERBD	0.621429	0	0.338515
48	MARSHMLW		UPPERBD	0.214286	0	0.001590984
49	BEER		UPPERBD	0.111111	0	0.080363
50	WHISKEY		UPPERBD	1.11905	0	0.945741
51	COLA		UPPERBD	0.105691	0	0.079689
52	CHOCOLAT		UPPERBD	0.776471	0	0.433160
53	PUDDING		UPPERBD	0.227979	0	0.135605
54	CALCIUM	BASIC	SURPLUS	0	759.933	0
55	CALORIES		SURPLUS	0	0	0.066172
56	IRON	BASIC	SURPLUS	0	15.425831	0
57	NIACIN	BASIC	SURPLUS	0	7.107038	0
58	PROTEIN	BASIC	SURPLUS	0	35.148492	0
59	RIBO		SURPLUS	0	0	10.394432
60	THIAMIN	BASIC	SURPLUS	0	0.641206	0
61	VITAMINA	BASIC	SURPLUS	0	15289.822	0
62	VITAMINC	BASIC	SURPLUS	0	13.098221	0

```
                                                                          10

          L I N E A R   P R O G R A M M I N G   P R O C E D U R E

                              CONSTRAINT SUMMARY

        CONSTRAINT           S/S                                    DUAL
        ROW ID      TYPE     COL      RHS      ACTIVITY           ACTIVITY

            1 CALCIUM   GE      54    0.800000    760.733              0
            2 CALORIES  GE      55   2600.000    2600.000       0.066172
            3 IRON      GE      56   10.000000    25.425831          0
            4 NIACIN    GE      57   17.000000    24.107038          0
            5 PROTEIN   GE      58   65.000000   100.148             0
            6 RIBO      GE      59    1.700000     1.700000     10.394432
            7 THIAMIN   GE      60    1.300000     1.941206          0
            8 VITAMINA  GE      61   5000.000    20289.822           0
            9 VITAMINC  GE      62   60.000000    73.098221          0
           10 CARBO     FREE           368.444    368.444            0
           11 CONSUMD   FREE          1640.939   1640.939            0
           12 COST      OBJECTIVE      158.335    158.335            0
           13 FAT       FREE          80.877030   80.877030          0
```

The dual variables (shadow prices) for the CALORIES and RIBO constraints are positive and tell you the marginal value of a unit of each right-hand-side constant. For example, an increase (decrease) in the recommended calorie requirement beyond 2600 would increase (decrease) the objective value by .066172 cents.

Range Analysis of the RHS: Example 5

This example demonstrates several features of the procedure. Suppose you want to perform right-hand-side range analysis on the diet problem solved in **Example 4**. To economize you do not want to resolve the problem. Moreover, you only want to print the results of the range analysis. To do this you invoke LP identifying the problem data set with the DATA= option and the primal solution with the PRIMALIN= option as you did in **Example 4**. To suppress printing you also specify PRINTLEVEL=−2. If you include RANGERHS on the PROC LP statement as

```
PROC LP PRIMALIN=PRIMAL DATA=PROB PRINTLEVEL=-2 RANGERHS;
```

nothing would be printed. To generate the right-hand-side range analysis while suppressing printing of other summaries, you specify the ENDPAUSE option. The procedure reads the data sets and performs the analysis but pauses before printing. At this point you reset the PRINTLEVEL= option to enable printing. Then you request the right-hand-side range analysis using the PRINT statement. The statements following show the sequence.

```
PROC LP PRIMALIN=PRIMAL DATA=PROB PRINTLEVEL=-2 ENDPAUSE;
   VAR MILK_W-PUDDING;
   ID _NAME_;
   RHS MEN;
RUN;


   RESET PRINTLEVEL=1;
   PRINT RANGERHS;
   QUIT;
```

Notice the last statement is QUIT. If you replace it with a RUN statement, then because PRINTLEVEL=1, the procedure prints the SOLUTION SUMMARY and an additional copy of the right-hand-side RANGE ANALYSIS SUMMARY. This program can be run either interactively or in batch. See **Output 5.13**.

Output 5.13 SOLUTION SUMMARY and RANGE SUMMARY

```
                    L I N E A R   P R O G R A M M I N G   P R O C E D U R E      1


                              SOLUTION   SUMMARY


                            CURRENT STATUS
                         TERMINATED SUCCESSFULLY

            OBJECTIVE VALUE            158.335

            PHASE 1 ITERATIONS              0
            PHASE 2 ITERATIONS             20
            INITIAL B.F. VARIABLES          0
            TIME USED (SECS)             0.09
            NUMBER OF INVERSIONS            3

            MACHINE EPSILON        1.00000E-08
            MACHINE INFINITY       7.23701E+75
            INVERT FREQUENCY              33
            MAX PHASE 1 ITERATIONS       100
            MAX PHASE 2 ITERATIONS       100
            TIME LIMIT (SECS)         120.00
```

```
                    L I N E A R   P R O G R A M M I N G   P R O C E D U R E      2

                              RHS RANGE SUMMARY

                 ----------MIN PHI---------- ----------MAX PHI----------
      ROW        RHS LEAVING OBJECTIVE       RHS LEAVING OBJECTIVE

      CALCIUM      -INF    .        .        760.733 CALCIUM   158.335
      CALORIES  2583.654 SPAGHETT 157.254   2832.308 SPAGHETT  173.708
      IRON         -INF    .        .        25.4258 IRON      158.335
      NIACIN       -INF    .        .         24.107 NIACIN    158.335
      PROTEIN      -INF    .        .        100.148 PROTEIN   158.335
      RIBO      1.470968 MILK_S   155.955   1.758621 SPAGHETT  158.945
      THIAMIN      -INF    .        .       1.941206 THIAMIN   158.335
      VITAMINA     -INF    .        .        20289.8 VITAMINA  158.335
      VITAMINC     -INF    .        .        73.0982 VITAMINC  158.335
```

Using Macro SASMPSX to Convert from IBM Format to LP Format: Example 6

This example shows how to use the SAS macro SASMPSX to convert a mathematical program stored in the CONVERT format as specified in Chapter 4 of the IBM MPSX Program Description Manual (number 5734-XM4) to the format expected by PROC LP. The SASMPSX macro (see **Appendix A** for a listing), which can be found in the sample library, assumes that the data to be transformed are in a SAS data set called RAW with variables FIELD1 to FIELD6 corresponding to the MPSX format fields. The data set produced by the SASMPSX macro has the MPSX column names as variable names in alphabetical order. The macro requires at most three changes to the problem data.

The problem in this example is to find an optimal product mix for a manufacturer who produces four items: a DESK, a CHAIR, a CABINET, and a BOOKCASE. Each item is processed in a stamping department (STAMP), an assembly department (ASSEMB), and a finishing department (FINISH). The time each item requires in each department is given in the input data. Because of resource limitations each department has an upper limit on the time available for processing. Furthermore, because of labor constraints the assembly department must work at least 300 hours. Finally, marketing tells you not to make more than 75 chairs, to make at least 50 bookcases, and to find the range over which the selling price of a bookcase can vary without changing the optimal product mix. The data shown in **Output 5.14** demonstrate how this example may appear for solution with MPSX.

Output 5.14   Sample Data for Using Macro SASMPSX to Convert from IBM Format to LP Format

```
                                                                               1

OBS                             CARD

  1     NAME          EXAMPLE6
  2     * THIS IS DATA FOR THE PRODUCT MIX PROBLEM.
  3     ROWS
  4      N  PROFIT
  5      L  STAMP
  6      L  ASSEMB
  7      L  FINISH
  8      N  CHNROW
  9      N  PRICE
 10     COLUMNS
 11         DESK       STAMP         3.00000    ASSEMB      10.00000
 12         DESK       FINISH       10.00000    PROFIT      95.00000
 13         DESK       PRICE       175.00000
 14         CHAIR      STAMP         1.50000    ASSEMB       6.00000
 15         CHAIR      FINISH        8.00000    PROFIT      41.00000
 16         CHAIR      PRICE        95.00000
 17         CABINET    STAMP         2.00000    ASSEMB       8.00000
 18         CABINET    FINISH        8.00000    PROFIT      84.00000
 19         CABINET    PRICE       145.00000
 20         BOOKCSE    STAMP         2.00000    ASSEMB       7.00000
 21         BOOKCSE    FINISH        7.00000    PROFIT      76.00000
 22         BOOKCSE    PRICE       130.00000    CHNROW       1.00000
 23     RHS
 24         TIME       STAMP       800.00000    ASSEMB    1200.0000
 25         TIME       FINISH      800.00000
 26     RANGES
 27         T1         ASSEMB      900.00000
 28     BOUNDS
 29      UP            CHAIR        75.00000
 30      LO            BOOKCSE      50.00000
 31     ENDATA
```

A program that converts these data to a SAS data set is shown below. The program expects that data be in a file with refname MPSDATA.

```
*---------------------------------------------;
* R_LIST: CONTAINS RAW DATA FOR A LISTING     ;
* RAW:    CONTAINS MODIFIED MPSX FORMAT DATA  ;
*---------------------------------------------;

%INCLUDE OR(SASMPSX);                          *LOAD  SASMPSX;

DATA RAW(DROP=CARD FIELD0)
   R_LIST(KEEP=CARD);
   INFILE MPSDATA;

   INPUT CARD $CHAR80. @;                      *FOR LISTING INPUT;
   OUTPUT R_LIST;
   INPUT FIELD0 $ 1 @;                         *FOR SKIPPING COMMENTS;
   IF FIELD0='*' THEN RETURN;

                                               *PLACE DATA IN FIELDS;
   INPUT FIELD1 $ 2-3   FIELD2 $ 5-12
         FIELD3 $ 15-22 FIELD4   25-36
         FIELD5 $ 40-47 FIELD6   50-61;
```

```
      OUTPUT RAW;

   PROC PRINT DATA=R_LIST;                    *PRINT INPUT DATA;

   %SASMPSX;                                  *INVOKE SASMPSX;

   DATA PROB;                                 *IDENTIFY OBJECTIVE ROW;
      SET PROB;                               *AND CHANGE ROW;
      IF    _ID_='PROFIT' THEN _TYPE_='MAX';
      ELSE IF _ID_='CHNROW' THEN _TYPE_='PRICESEN';

   PROC PRINT;                                *PRINT DATA IN LP FORMAT;
```

Several changes are made to the output from the SASMPSX macro in this program. The first change identifies the PROFIT row as the objective row to be maximized. The next change identifies the row labeled CHNROW as a change row for performing sensitivity analysis on the objective function.

The DATA step saves the modified MPSX format data in a SAS data set called RAW with variables FIELD1-FIELD6 and saves a SAS data set called R_LIST, which is used for printing the MPSX input data. In larger problems you may want to remove this code to avoid printing the input data set. At this point the SASMPSX macro is invoked to convert to the PROC LP format. After conversion, the data set is modified so that the type identifier variable _TYPE_ contains the keywords needed to identify the objective function and the change row. The SASMPSX macro places the problem in the output data set called PROB. The data set that results from execution of the code above is shown in **Output 5.15**.

Output 5.15   Data Set Produced after Making Changes to the SASMPSX Macro

OBS	_ID_	BOOKCSE	CHAIR	CABINET	DESK	TIME	_TYPE_	_RANGE_
1	_LO_	50	.	.	.	.	LOWERBD	.
2	_UP_	.	75.0	.	.	.	UPPERBD	.
3	ASSEMB	7	6.0	8	10	1200	LE	900
4	CHNROW	1	.	.	.	.	PRICESEN	.
5	FINISH	7	8.0	8	10	800	LE	.
6	PRICE	130	95.0	145	175	.	FREE	.
7	PROFIT	76	41.0	84	95	.	MAX	.
8	STAMP	2	1.5	2	3	800	LE	.

Note the variable named _RANGE_. This variable contains the row range information.

Now to solve the mathematical program, you call the LP procedure as

```
   PROC LP;
      RHS TIME;
```

Only the RHS statement is necessary since LP identifies the variable _TYPE_ as the default type variable, the variable _ID_ as the ID variable, and the remaining variables in the data set are identified as the structural variables in the mathematical program. The procedure produces **Output 5.16**.

Output 5.16 Solving the Mathematical Problem to Produce Summaries

```
                                                                         3

         L I N E A R   P R O G R A M M I N G   P R O C E D U R E

                       PROBLEM  SUMMARY



         MAX PROFIT         OBJECTIVE FUNCTION
         TIME                     RHS  VARIABLE
         _TYPE_                   TYPE  VARIABLE
         PROBLEM DENSITY               0.714



         VARIABLE TYPE                NUMBER

         STRUCTURAL
           NONEGATIVE                    2
           LOWER BOUNDED                 1
           UPPER BOUNDED                 1

         LOGICAL
           SLACK                         3

         TOTAL                           7



         CONSTRAINT TYPE              NUMBER

         LE                             3
         FREE                           2

         TOTAL                          5
```

```
                                                                         4

         L I N E A R   P R O G R A M M I N G   P R O C E D U R E



                       SOLUTION  SUMMARY


                     TERMINATED SUCCESSFULLY

         OBJECTIVE VALUE              8685.714

         PHASE 1 ITERATIONS                 2
         PHASE 2 ITERATIONS                 2
         INITIAL B.F. VARIABLES             2
         TIME USED (SECS)                0.00
         NUMBER OF INVERSIONS               3

         MACHINE EPSILON           1.00000E-08
         MACHINE INFINITY          7.23701E+75
         INVERT FREQUENCY                  50
         MAX PHASE 1 ITERATIONS           100
         MAX PHASE 2 ITERATIONS           100
         TIME LIMIT (SECS)             120.00
```

```
                                                                              5

            L I N E A R   P R O G R A M M I N G   P R O C E D U R E
                          VARIABLE   SUMMARY

            VARIABLE                                           REDUCED
     COL NAME     STATUS   TYPE     PRICE     ACTIVITY         COST

      1 BOOKCSE   BASIC  LOWERBD      76      114.286              0
      2 CHAIR            UPPERBD      41        0           -45.857143
      3 CABINET          NON-NEG      84        0            -2.857143
      4 DESK             NON-NEG      95        0           -13.571429
      5 ASSEMB    BASIC  SLACK         0      400.000             0
      6 FINISH           SLACK         0        0           -10.857143
      7 STAMP     BASIC  SLACK         0      571.429             0
```

```
                                                                              6

            L I N E A R   P R O G R A M M I N G   P R O C E D U R E
                          CONSTRAINT SUMMARY

     CONSTRAINT            S/S                                 DUAL
     ROW ID       TYPE     COL       RHS      ACTIVITY       ACTIVITY

      1 ASSEMB    RANGELE   5     1200.000     800.000            0
      2 FINISH    LE        6      800.000     800.000      10.857143
      3 STAMP     LE        7      800.000     228.571            0
      4 PRICE     FREE          14857.143    14857.143           0
      5 PROFIT    OBJECTIVE      8685.714     8685.714           0
```

```
                                                                              7

            L I N E A R   P R O G R A M M I N G   P R O C E D U R E
                     PRICE SENSITIVITY ANALYSIS SUMMARY
                       SENSITIVITY VECTOR CHNROW

            MINIMUM PHI              -2.500000
            ENTERING VARIABLE        CABINET
            OPTIMAL OBJECTIVE        8400.000

            MAXIMUM PHI             +INFINITY

            VARIABLE ------MINIMUM PHI-------- ------MAXIMUM PHI--------
     COL NAME         PRICE REDUCED COST         PRICE REDUCED COST


      1 BOOKCSE   73.500000          0        +INFINITY          0
      2 CHAIR     41.000000  -43.000000       41.000000    -INFINITY
      3 CABINET   84.000000          0        84.000000    -INFINITY
      4 DESK      95.000000  -10.000000       95.000000    -INFINITY
      5 ASSEMB            0          0                0          0
      6 FINISH            0  -10.500000                0    -INFINITY
      7 STAMP             0          0                0          0
```

An Infeasible Problem: Example 7

This example demonstrates a way the EPSILON= option affects the solution of
a linear program and shows an example of the INFEASIBLE INFORMATION SUM-
MARY that is printed when an infeasible problem is encountered. Consider the
following problem:

$$\max \quad r + s + t + u + v + w + x + y$$

$$\text{subject to:} \quad
\begin{aligned}
r + s + t + u + v + w + x + y &\leq 1.999999 \\
r &\geq 1.000000 \\
t &\geq 1.000000
\end{aligned}$$

$$r, s, t, u, v, w, x, y \geq 0$$

Examination of this problem reveals that it is infeasible within the accuracy of EPSILON, namely 1.0E-8. Consequently, PROC LP identifies it as infeasible. The following program attempts to solve it:

```
DATA;
   INPUT _ID_ $ R S T U V W X Y Z _TYPE_ $ _RHS_;
   CARDS;
OBJECT 1 1 1 1 1 1 1 1 1 MAX          .
CONST1 1 1 1 1 1 1 1 1 1 LE    1.999999
CONST2 1 0 0 0 0 0 0 0 0 GE           1
CONST3 0 0 1 0 0 0 0 0 0 GE           1

PROC LP;

PROC LP EPSILON=1.0E-5;
```

The results are shown in **Output 5.17**.

Output 5.17   Attempting to Solve an Infeasible Problem

```
                                                                            1

            L I N E A R   P R O G R A M M I N G   P R O C E D U R E

                           PROBLEM  SUMMARY


            MAX OBJECT          OBJECTIVE FUNCTION
            _RHS_               RHS  VARIABLE
            _TYPE_              TYPE VARIABLE
            PROBLEM DENSITY              0.389


            VARIABLE TYPE                NUMBER

            STRUCTURAL
              NONEGATIVE                     9

            LOGICAL
              SLACK                          1
              SURPLUS                        2

            TOTAL                           12
```

(continued on next page)

(continued from previous page)

CONSTRAINT TYPE	NUMBER
LE	1
GE	2
FREE	1
TOTAL	4

2

LINEAR PROGRAMMING PROCEDURE

SOLUTION SUMMARY

INFEASIBLE PROBLEM

OBJECTIVE VALUE	-0.000001
PHASE 1 ITERATIONS	3
PHASE 2 ITERATIONS	0
INITIAL B.F. VARIABLES	1
TIME USED (SECS)	0.00
NUMBER OF INVERSIONS	1
MACHINE EPSILON	1.00000E-08
MACHINE INFINITY	7.23701E+75
INVERT FREQUENCY	50
MAX PHASE 1 ITERATIONS	100
MAX PHASE 2 ITERATIONS	100
TIME LIMIT (SECS)	120.00

3

LINEAR PROGRAMMING PROCEDURE

VARIABLE SUMMARY

COL	VARIABLE NAME	STATUS	TYPE	PRICE	ACTIVITY	REDUCED COST
1	R	BASIC	NON-NEG	1	1.000000	0
2	S		NON-NEG	1	0	-1.000000
3	T	BASIC	NON-NEG	1	0.999999	0
4	U		NON-NEG	1	0	-1.000000
5	V		NON-NEG	1	0	-1.000000
6	W		NON-NEG	1	0	-1.000000
7	X		NON-NEG	1	0	-1.000000
8	Y		NON-NEG	1	0	-1.000000
9	Z		NON-NEG	1	0	-1.000000
10	CONST1		SLACK	0	0	-1.000000
11	CONST2		SURPLUS	0	0	-1.000000
12	CONST3		SURPLUS	0	0	-1.000000

4

LINEAR PROGRAMMING PROCEDURE

CONSTRAINT SUMMARY

	CONSTRAINT ROW ID	TYPE	S/S COL	RHS	ACTIVITY	DUAL ACTIVITY
1	CONST1	LE	10	1.999999	1.999999	1.000000
2	CONST2	GE	11	1.000000	1.000000	-1.000000
INF*	CONST3	GE	12	1.000000	0.999999	-1.000000
4	OBJECT	OBJECTIVE		1.999999	1.999999	0

```
                                                                        5

                L I N E A R   P R O G R A M M I N G   P R O C E D U R E

                          INFEASIBLE INFORMATION SUMMARY

                    INFEASIBLE ROW          RHS ❷  ACTIVITY
                ❶  CONST3              1.000000     0.999999
                                                  ❹
                       VARIABLE ACTIVITY  LOWERBD  UPPERBD
                   ❸  T        0.999999        0  INFINITY

      ROW_NAME COEFFICIENT ROW_NAME COEFFICIENT ROW_NAME COEFFICIENT ROW_NAME COEFFICIENT ROW_NAME COEFFICIENT
  ❺  CONST1      1.000000 CONST3      1.000000
                                                  ❹
                       VARIABLE ACTIVITY  LOWERBD  UPPERBD
                   ❸  CONST3          0        0  INFINITY

      ROW_NAME COEFFICIENT ROW_NAME COEFFICIENT ROW_NAME COEFFICIENT ROW_NAME COEFFICIENT ROW_NAME COEFFICIENT
  ❺  CONST3     -1.000000
```

Note the information given in the INFEASIBLE INFORMATION SUMMARY. For the infeasible row CONST3 the procedure identifies the variables with nonzero and nonmissing coefficients, namely T and CONST3 (the surplus variable for the constraint). It prints information about these variables in the current solution. For example, it prints that T has an activity of 0.999999, a lower bound of 0, and an upper bound of INFINITY. It also identifies all the constraints in the model that have nonzero and nonmissing coefficients for these variables. For example, it identifies that T is found in constraint CONST1 where it has a coefficient of 1 and in constraint CONST3 (the infeasible row) with a coefficient of 1.

Although the problem is infeasible, if you execute the same program but specify EPSILON as 1.0E−5, PROC LP terminates successfully within the accuracy of EPSILON. A note is printed on the SAS log informing you that the sum of the infeasibilities was within EPSILON:

```
NOTE: INFEASIBILITY=-1.0E-06 WITHIN EPSILON OF 0.
```

See **Output 5.18**.

Output 5.18 Solving an Infeasible Problem

```
                                                                        6

                L I N E A R   P R O G R A M M I N G   P R O C E D U R E

                              PROBLEM  SUMMARY


                  MAX OBJECT          OBJECTIVE FUNCTION
                  _RHS_                     RHS VARIABLE
                  _TYPE_                    TYPE VARIABLE
                  PROBLEM DENSITY             0.389
```

(continued on next page)

(continued from previous page)

VARIABLE TYPE	NUMBER
STRUCTURAL	
NONEGATIVE	9
LOGICAL	
SLACK	1
SURPLUS	2
TOTAL	12

CONSTRAINT TYPE	NUMBER
LE	1
GE	2
FREE	1
TOTAL	4

LINEAR PROGRAMMING PROCEDURE

SOLUTION SUMMARY

TERMINATED SUCCESSFULLY

OBJECTIVE VALUE	1.999999
PHASE 1 ITERATIONS	2
PHASE 2 ITERATIONS	1
INITIAL B.F. VARIABLES	1
TIME USED (SECS)	0.00
NUMBER OF INVERSIONS	4
MACHINE EPSILON	0.00001
MACHINE INFINITY	7.23701E+75
INVERT FREQUENCY	50
MAX PHASE 1 ITERATIONS	100
MAX PHASE 2 ITERATIONS	100
TIME LIMIT (SECS)	120.00

LINEAR PROGRAMMING PROCEDURE

VARIABLE SUMMARY

COL	VARIABLE NAME	STATUS	TYPE	PRICE	ACTIVITY	REDUCED COST
1	R	BASIC	NON-NEG	1	1.000000	0
2	S	ALTER	NON-NEG	1	0	0
3	T	BASIC	NON-NEG	1	0.999999	0
4	U	ALTER	NON-NEG	1	0	0
5	V	ALTER	NON-NEG	1	0	0
6	W	ALTER	NON-NEG	1	0	0
7	X	ALTER	NON-NEG	1	0	0
8	Y	ALTER	NON-NEG	1	0	0
9	Z	ALTER	NON-NEG	1	0	0
10	CONST1		SLACK	0	0	-1.000000
11	CONST2	ALTER	SURPLUS	0	0	0
12	CONST3	ALTER	SURPLUS	0	0	0

```
                                                                          9

              L I N E A R   P R O G R A M M I N G   P R O C E D U R E

                                CONSTRAINT SUMMARY

          CONSTRAINT               S/S                                DUAL
          ROW ID        TYPE       COL        RHS      ACTIVITY      ACTIVITY

               1 CONST1   LE        10     1.999999    1.999999     1.000000
               2 CONST2   GE        11     1.000000    1.000000            0
               3 CONST3   GE        12     1.000000    0.999999            0
               4 OBJECT   OBJECTIVE        1.999999    1.999999            0
```

A Goal-Programming Macro: Example 8

This example shows a simple macro that uses PROC LP to solve a linear goal-programming problem. Also, the macro shows how a SAS program can analyze a linear programming solution saved by PROC LP and then design a new linear programming problem based on this solution.

The macro assumes that the linear goal-programming problem is in canonical form. The macro can be modified easily to accommodate your particular needs. The canonical form is defined by a matrix of objective and constraint coefficients and a matrix containing additional information about the objectives, including the priority relationships among them. Formally, the problem is characterized by the linear systems:

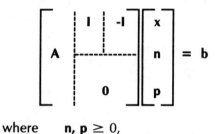

where $n, p \geq 0,$

and

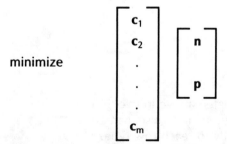

Here, the c_is are row vectors that complete the description of the objectives. The subscripts on the cs give the relative priority of each of the m objectives. For a complete discussion of this formulation of the linear goal-programming problem, see Ignizio (1976).

To demonstrate the macro, consider the following problem taken from Ignizio (1976). A small paint company manufactures two types of paint: latex and enamel.

In production the company uses 10 hours of labor to produce 100 gallons of latex and 15 hours of labor to produce 100 gallons of enamel. Without hiring outside help or requiring overtime, the company has 40 hours of labor available each week. Furthermore, each paint generates a profit at the rate of $1 per gallon. The company has the following objectives listed in decreasing priority:

- avoid the use of overtime
- achieve a weekly profit of $1000
- produce at least 700 gallons of enamel paint each week.

If x_1 denotes latex paint and x_2 denotes enamel paint, then the problem can be formulated in canonical form as:

$$
\begin{bmatrix}
10 & 15 & 1 & 0 & 0 & -1 & 0 & 0 \\
100 & 100 & 0 & 1 & 0 & 0 & -1 & 0 \\
0 & 1 & 0 & 0 & 1 & 0 & 0 & -1
\end{bmatrix}
\begin{bmatrix}
x_1 \\ x_2 \\ n_1 \\ n_2 \\ n_3 \\ p_1 \\ p_2 \\ p_3
\end{bmatrix}
=
\begin{bmatrix}
40 \\ 1000 \\ 7
\end{bmatrix}
$$

and

$$
\text{minimize}
\begin{bmatrix}
1 & 0 & 0 & 0 & 0 & 0 \\
0 & 0 & 0 & 0 & 1 & 0 \\
0 & 0 & 0 & 0 & 0 & 1
\end{bmatrix}
\begin{bmatrix}
p_1 \\ p_2 \\ p_3 \\ n_1 \\ n_2 \\ n_3
\end{bmatrix}
$$

where
$$x_1, x_2 \geq 0$$
$$n_i \text{ and } p_i \geq 0 \quad i=1,2,3 \quad .$$

The program that follows saves the problem as formulated above in two SAS data sets. The data set called OBJECT contains the first matrix; the data set named PRIOR contains the second matrix with the keyword MIN for each row type.

```
DATA OBJECT;
   INPUT _ID_ $ _RHS_ _TYPE_ $ LATEX= ENAMEL= N1=
      N2= N3= P1= P2= P3= ;
   CARDS;
OVERTIME   40   EQ LATEX=10 ENAMEL=15 N1=1 P1=-1
PROFIT   1000 EQ LATEX=100 ENAMEL=100 N2=1 P2=-1
E_SALES      7 EQ ENAMEL=1 N3=1 P3=-1
;
```

```
DATA PRIOR;
INPUT _TYPE_ $ P1= N2= N3=;
   CARDS;
MIN P1=1
MIN N2=1
MIN N3=1
;
```

Notice the use of named input. This type of input is particularly useful for storing sparse matrices, which often occur in linear programming applications.

To solve this linear goal programming problem, define a macro called GOALPROG (which can be found in the sample library) that has two arguments: the first identifies the first matrix of the canonical formulation, and the second identifies the second matrix. See **Output 5.19**.

Output 5.19   GOALPROG Macro Listing

```
                                                                       1
/*-------THIS MACRO SOLVES LINEAR GOAL PROGRAMS---------*/

%MACRO GOALPROG(OBJECT=,PRIOR=);

      /*----------------SET UP------------------*/

%LET ZSTAR = 0; %LET OPT=PRINTLEVEL=-2;

OPTION DQUOTE;
DATA PROB; SET &PRIOR;
   DROP N;
   RETAIN N 0; N=N+1; CALL SYMPUT('M',N);   * COUNT OBJECTIVES ;
   _ID_='OBJECT'||LEFT(PUT(_N_,$2.));
   _TYPE_='GE'; _RHS_=-9999999;

DATA PROB;
   SET &OBJECT PROB;

   /*--------LOOP FOR EACH OBJECTIVE-----------*/

%DO I=1 %TO &M;

  /*-CONSTRAIN PROBLEM TO ACHIEVE LAST OBJECTIVE-*/

   DATA PROB; SET PROB;
      IF _ID_="OBJECT%EVAL(&I-1)" THEN DO;
         PUT "NOTE: PRIORITY %EVAL(&I-1) OBJECTIVE ACHIEVED &ZSTAR .";
         _RHS_=&ZSTAR; _TYPE_='LE';
         END;

         /*---GET PRIMAL FEASIBILITY---*/

   %IF &I>1 %THEN %DO;
      PROC LP STARTPHASE=DUAL PRIMALIN=P PRIMALOUT=P PRINTLEVEL=-2;
      %END;

            /*---MODIFY OBJECTIVE---*/

   DATA PROB; SET PROB;
      IF      _ID_='CURR_OBJ' THEN DELETE;
      ELSE IF _ID_="OBJECT%EVAL(&I)" THEN DO;
         PUT "NOTE: SOLVING PRIORITY LEVEL &I OBJECTIVE.";
         OUTPUT; _ID_='CURR_OBJ'; _TYPE_='MIN';
         END;
      OUTPUT;

   %IF      &I=&M %THEN %LET OPT=PRIMALIN=P;
   %ELSE %IF &I>1 %THEN %LET OPT=PRIMALIN=P PRINTLEVEL=-2;

         /*---GET DUAL FEASIBILITY---*/

   PROC LP STARTPHASE=PRIMAL DUALOUT=D PRIMALOUT=P &OPT ;
```

(continued on next page)

```
(continued from previous page)

      /*--FIND CURRENT OBJECTIVE VALUE---*/

   DATA _NULL_; SET D;
      IF _ROW_ID_='CURR_OBJ' THEN CALL SYMPUT('ZSTAR',_RHS_);

   %END;


%MEND;
/*---------------END OF MACRO------------------------*/
```

For each observation in the PRIOR data set, the macro defines a linear program and solves it with PROC LP. The linear programs are defined so that the solution of a problem associated with one objective is binding on a problem with a lower priority objective. In this way the goal program is solved by a sequence of linear programs. To solve the sample problem, invoke the GOALPROG macro as follows:

    %GOALPROG(OBJECT=OBJECT,PRIOR=PRIOR);

The macro defines and solves three linear programs, one for each row in the PRIOR data set. The solution of the last linear program contains the solution to the linear goal program. See **Output 5.20**.

Output 5.20   GOALPROG Macro Summaries

```
                                                                    2

              L I N E A R   P R O G R A M M I N G   P R O C E D U R E

                          PROBLEM  SUMMARY


              MIN CURR_OBJ       OBJECTIVE FUNCTION
              _RHS_              RHS VARIABLE
              _TYPE_             TYPE VARIABLE
              PROBLEM DENSITY            0.258



              VARIABLE TYPE              NUMBER

              STRUCTURAL
                NONEGATIVE                 8

              LOGICAL
                SLACK                      2
                SURPLUS                    1

              TOTAL                       11


              CONSTRAINT TYPE           NUMBER

              LE                          2
              EQ                          3
              GE                          1
              FREE                        1

              TOTAL                       7
```

```
                                                                            3

            L I N E A R   P R O G R A M M I N G   P R O C E D U R E


                          SOLUTION   SUMMARY


                       TERMINATED SUCCESSFULLY

             OBJECTIVE VALUE            7.000000

             PHASE 1 ITERATIONS                0
             PHASE 2 ITERATIONS                2
             INITIAL B.F. VARIABLES            6
             TIME USED (SECS)              0.00
             NUMBER OF INVERSIONS              2

             MACHINE EPSILON          1.00000E-08
             MACHINE INFINITY         7.23701E+75
             INVERT FREQUENCY                 50
             MAX PHASE 1 ITERATIONS          100
             MAX PHASE 2 ITERATIONS          100
             TIME LIMIT (SECS)           120.00
```

```
                                                                            4

            L I N E A R   P R O G R A M M I N G   P R O C E D U R E

                          VARIABLE   SUMMARY

        VARIABLE                                            REDUCED
    COL NAME      STATUS  TYPE      PRICE    ACTIVITY         COST


      1 LATEX     BASIC  NON-NEG        0    4.000000             0
      2 ENAMEL    DEGEN  NON-NEG        0           0             0
      3 N1               NON-NEG        0           0      0.200000
      4 N2        BASIC  NON-NEG        0     600.000             0
      5 N3        BASIC  NON-NEG        1    7.000000             0
      6 P1        DEGEN  NON-NEG        0           0             0
      7 P2               NON-NEG        0           0      0.020000
      8 P3               NON-NEG        0           0      1.000000
      9 OBJECT1          SLACK          0           0      0.200000
     10 OBJECT2          SLACK          0           0      0.020000
     11 OBJECT3   BASIC  SURPLUS        0    10000006             0
```

```
                                                                            5

            L I N E A R   P R O G R A M M I N G   P R O C E D U R E

                          CONSTRAINT SUMMARY

    CONSTRAINT           S/S                                 DUAL
    ROW ID       TYPE    COL       RHS     ACTIVITY        ACTIVITY


      1 OVERTIME  EQ           40.000000   40.000000     -0.200000
      2 PROFIT    EQ            1000.000    1000.000      0.020000
      3 E_SALES   EQ            7.000000    7.000000      1.000000
      4 OBJECT1   LE     9             0           0     -0.200000
      5 OBJECT2   LE    10       600.000     600.000     -0.020000
      6 OBJECT3   GE    11      -9999999    7.000000             0
      7 CURR_OBJ  OBJECTIVE     7.000000    7.000000             0
```

The solution to the last linear program shows a value of 4 for the variable LATEX
and a value of 0 for the variable ENAMEL. This tells you that the solution to the
linear goal program is to produce 400 gallons of latex and no enamel paint.

The values of the objective functions in the three linear programs tell you
whether you can achieve the three objectives. The activities of the constraints
labeled OBJECT1, OBJECT2, and OBJECT3 tell you values of the three linear program objectives. Since the first linear programming objective OBJECT1 is 0, the

highest priority objective is accomplished, which is, to avoid using additional labor. However, because the second and third objectives are nonzero, the second and third priority objectives are not satisfied completely. This means that at optimality you cannot realize a weekly profit of $1000 or produce 700 gallons of enamel paint each week. More detailed information concerning these objectives can be obtained from the solutions to the intermediate linear programs.

A Simple Integer Program: Example 9

Recall the linear programming problem presented in the chapter "Introduction to SAS/OR™ Software." In that problem a firm produces two products, chocolates and gum drops, which are processed by four processes: cooking, color/flavor, condiments, and packaging. The objective is to determine the product mix that maximizes the profit to the firm while not exceeding manufacturing capacities. The problem is extended to demonstrate a use of integer constrained variables.

Suppose that you can only manufacture one of the two products and you must decide which one. In addition, there is a setup cost of 100 if you make the chocolates and 50 if you make the gum drops. To identify which product will maximize profit you define two zero-one integer variables, ICHOCO and IGUMDR and you also define two new constraints, CHO and GUM. The constraint labeled CHO requires ICHOCO to equal one when chocolates are manufactured. Similarly the constraint labeled GUM requires IGUMDR to equal one when gum drops are manufactured. Also, you include a constraint labeled ONLY_ONE that requires the sum of ICHOCO and IGUMDR to equal one. Since ICHOCO and IGUMDR are integer variables, this constraint eliminates the possibility of both products being manufactured. The objective coefficients of the integer variables ICHOCO and IGUMDR are the negatives of the setup costs for the two products. The following is the data set that describes this problem and the call to LP to solve it:

```
DATA;
   INPUT _ID_ $ CHOCO GUMDR ICHOCO IGUMDR _TYPE_ $ _RHS_;
   CARDS;
OBJECT     .25    .75   -100     -75 MAX         .
COOKING     15     40      0       0 LE      27000
COLOR        0  56.25      0       0 LE      27000
PACKAGE  18.75      0      0       0 LE      27000
CONDMNTS    12     50      0       0 LE      27000
CHO          1      0 -10000      0 LE          0
GUM          0      1      0  -10000 LE          0
ONLY_ONE     0      0      1       1 EQ          1
UPPER        .      .      1       1 UPPERBD     .
INT          .      .      1       2 INTEGER     .
;

PROC LP;
```

The solution shows that gum drops are produced. See **Output 5.21**.

Output 5.21 Summaries and an Integer Programming Iteration Log

```
                                                                        1

            L I N E A R   P R O G R A M M I N G   P R O C E D U R E

                         PROBLEM  SUMMARY


                MAX OBJECT        OBJECTIVE FUNCTION
                _RHS_                   RHS  VARIABLE
                _TYPE_                 TYPE  VARIABLE
                PROBLEM DENSITY        0.257


                VARIABLE TYPE          NUMBER

                STRUCTURAL
                  NONEGATIVE             2
                  INTEGER                2

                LOGICAL
                  SLACK                  6

                TOTAL                   10


                CONSTRAINT TYPE        NUMBER

                LE                       6
                EQ                       1
                FREE                     1

                TOTAL                    8
```

```
                                                                        2



            L I N E A R   P R O G R A M M I N G   P R O C E D U R E

                         INTEGER ITERATION LOG

       ITER PROBLEM  CONDITION OBJECTIVE BRANCHED VALUE SINFEAS ACTIVE


         1     +0      ACTIVE     397.5 ICHOCO    0.1     0.2      2
         2     +1    SUBOPTIMAL   285     .        .       0       1
         3     -1    FATHOMED     260     .        .       .       0
```

```
                                 SAS                                     3


            L I N E A R   P R O G R A M M I N G   P R O C E D U R E




                         SOLUTION  SUMMARY


                    OPTIMAL INTEGER SOLUTION

                OBJECTIVE VALUE        285.000

                PHASE 1 ITERATIONS          1
                PHASE 2 ITERATIONS          6
                PHASE 3 ITERATIONS         12
                INTEGER ITERATIONS          3
                INTEGER SOLUTIONS           1
                INITIAL B.F. VARIABLES      6
                TIME USED (SECS)         0.02
                NUMBER OF INVERSIONS        4
```

(continued on next page)

(continued from previous page)

```
MACHINE EPSILON            1.00000E-08
MACHINE INFINITY           7.23701E+75
INVERT FREQUENCY                    50
MAX PHASE 1 ITERATIONS             100
MAX PHASE 2 ITERATIONS             100
MAX PHASE 3 ITERATIONS        99999999
MAX INTEGER ITERATIONS             100
TIME LIMIT (SECS)               120.00
```

4

L I N E A R   P R O G R A M M I N G   P R O C E D U R E

VARIABLE   SUMMARY

COL	VARIABLE NAME	STATUS	TYPE	PRICE	ACTIVITY	REDUCED COST
1	CHOCO	DEGEN	NON-NEG	0.25	0	0
2	GUMDR	BASIC	NON-NEG	0.75	480.000	0
3	ICHOCO		INTEGER	-100	0	2475.000
4	IGUMDR	BASIC	INTEGER	-75	1.000000	0
5	COOKING	BASIC	SLACK	0	7800.000	0
6	COLOR		SLACK	0	0	-0.013333
7	PACKAGE	BASIC	SLACK	0	27000.000	0
8	CONDMNTS	BASIC	SLACK	0	3000.000	0
9	CHO		SLACK	0	0	-0.250000
10	GUM	BASIC	SLACK	0	9520.000	0

5

L I N E A R   P R O G R A M M I N G   P R O C E D U R E

CONSTRAINT SUMMARY

ROW	CONSTRAINT ID	TYPE	S/S COL	RHS	ACTIVITY	DUAL ACTIVITY
1	COOKING	LE	5	27000.000	19200.000	0
2	COLOR	LE	6	27000.000	27000.000	0.013333
3	PACKAGE	LE	7	27000.000	0	0
4	CONDMNTS	LE	8	27000.000	24000.000	0
5	CHO	LE	9	0	0	0.250000
6	GUM	LE	10	0	-9520.000	0
7	ONLY_ONE	EQ		1.000000	1.000000	-75.000000
8	OBJECT	OBJECTIVE		285.000	285.000	0

An Integer Program: Example 10

The following example is a pure integer program attributed to Haldi (Garfinkel and Nemhauser 1972) and used extensively in the literature as a test problem.

```
DATA HALDI;
  INPUT X1-X5 _TYPE_ $ _RHS_;
  CARDS;
  0  0  1  1  1 MAX      .
  2  3  1  2  2 LE       18
  3  2  2  1  2 LE       17
 -9  0  1  0  0 LE       0
  0 -7  0  1  0 LE       0
  1  1 10 10 10 UPPERBD .
  1  2  3  4  5 INTEGER .
  ;
```

Notice that the integer variables are bounded from above and below. This is a requirement of the LP procedure when solving integer problems. You can solve this problem by simply calling

```
PROC LP;
```

The output that follows shows an integer iteration log. The branch and bound tree can be reconstructed from the information contained in this log. The column labeled ITER numbers the integer iterations. The column labeled PROBLEM identifies the ITER number of the parent problem from which the current problem is defined. For example, ITER=5 has PROBLEM=−4. This means that problem 5 is a direct descendant of problem 4. Furthermore, since problem 4 BRANCHED on X2, you know that problem 5 is identical to problem 4 with an additional constraint on variable X2. The minus sign in the PROBLEM=−4 in ITER=5 tells you that the new constraint on variable X2 is a lower bound. Moreover, since VALUE=.125 in ITER=4, you know that X2=.125 in ITER=4 so that the added constraint in ITER=5 is X2≥⌈.125=1⌉. In this way the information in the log can be used to reconstruct the branch and bound tree. And in fact, when you save an ACTIVEOUT= data set it contains information in this format that is used to reconstruct the tree when you restart a problem using the ACTIVEIN= data set. See **Output 5.22**.

Output 5.22   Summaries and an Integer Programming Log

```
                                                                              1

        L I N E A R   P R O G R A M M I N G   P R O C E D U R E


                        PROBLEM  SUMMARY



            MAX _OBS1_           OBJECTIVE FUNCTION
            _RHS_                RHS VARIABLE
            _TYPE_               TYPE VARIABLE
            PROBLEM DENSITY            0.500


            VARIABLE TYPE              NUMBER

            STRUCTURAL
              INTEGER                     5

            LOGICAL
              SLACK                       4

            TOTAL                         9


            CONSTRAINT TYPE            NUMBER

            LE                          4
            FREE                        1

            TOTAL                       5
```

```
                                                                            2

         L I N E A R   P R O G R A M M I N G   P R O C E D U R E

                        INTEGER ITERATION LOG

   ITER PROBLEM  CONDITION OBJECTIVE BRANCHED VALUE SINFEAS ACTIVE


      1     +0     ACTIVE      9.6124 X1    .4922  1.36434     2
      2     -1     ACTIVE      8.8    X2    0.72   0.56        3
      3     +2  SUBOPTIMAL     7      .     .      0           2
      4     +1     ACTIVE      8.8125 X2    0.125  0.3125      3
      5     -4     ACTIVE      7.5    X5    7.5    0.5         4
      6     -5  INFEASIBLE     7      .     .      .           3
      7     +4     ACTIVE      8.5    X5    8.5    0.5         4
      8     -7  INFEASIBLE     8      .     .      .           3
      9     +7  SUBOPTIMAL     8      .     .      0           2
     10     -2  FATHOMED    8.33333   .     .    .666667       1
```

```
                                                                            3

         L I N E A R   P R O G R A M M I N G   P R O C E D U R E


                           SOLUTION  SUMMARY


                      OPTIMAL INTEGER SOLUTION

            OBJECTIVE VALUE            8.000000

            PHASE 1 ITERATIONS               0
            PHASE 2 ITERATIONS               5
            PHASE 3 ITERATIONS              18
            INTEGER ITERATIONS              10
            INTEGER SOLUTIONS                2
            INITIAL B.F. VARIABLES           4
            TIME USED (SECS)              0.03
            NUMBER OF INVERSIONS             2

            MACHINE EPSILON       1.00000E-08
            MACHINE INFINITY      7.23701E+75
            INVERT FREQUENCY               50
            MAX PHASE 1 ITERATIONS        100
            MAX PHASE 2 ITERATIONS        100
            MAX PHASE 3 ITERATIONS   99999999
            MAX INTEGER ITERATIONS        100
            TIME LIMIT (SECS)          120.00
```

```
                                                                            4

         L I N E A R   P R O G R A M M I N G   P R O C E D U R E

                          VARIABLE  SUMMARY

             VARIABLE                                      REDUCED
     COL NAME      STATUS   TYPE     PRICE    ACTIVITY       COST


       1 X1                 INTEGER      0           0     9.000000
       2 X2                 INTEGER      0           0     7.000000
       3 X3       DEGEN INTEGER          1           0            0
       4 X4       DEGEN INTEGER          1           0            0
       5 X5                 INTEGER      1    8.000000     1.000000
       6 _OBS2_   BASIC   SLACK         0    2.000000            0
       7 _OBS3_   BASIC   SLACK         0    1.000000            0
       8 _OBS4_           SLACK         0           0    -1.000000
       9 _OBS5_           SLACK         0           0    -1.000000
```

```
                                                                          5

              L I N E A R   P R O G R A M M I N G   P R O C E D U R E

                              CONSTRAINT SUMMARY

         CONSTRAINT           S/S                              DUAL
         ROW ID      TYPE     COL      RHS      ACTIVITY      ACTIVITY


             1 _OBS2_    LE      6    18.000000    16.000000         0
             2 _OBS3_    LE      7    17.000000    16.000000         0
             3 _OBS4_    LE      8          0            0     1.000000
             4 _OBS5_    LE      9          0            0     1.000000
             5 _OBS1_ OBJECTIVE       8.000000     8.000000         0
```

Alternative Search of the Branch and Bound Tree: Example 11

In this example we again solve the HALDI problem. However, here we use the modified PIP strategy discussed in the **Details** section.

```
PROC LP CANSELECT=OBJ IFEASIBLEPAUSE=1 DATA=HALDI;
RUN;
   RESET CANSELECT=LIFO IFEASIBLEPAUSE=9999999;
RUN;
```

Compare the number of integer iterations needed to solve the problem using this heuristic with the default strategy used in **Example 10**. Although in this example the difference is not profound, solution times can vary significantly with the search technique. See **Output 5.23**.

Output 5.23 Summaries and an Integer Programming Iteration Log: Using PIP Strategy

```
                                                                          1

              L I N E A R   P R O G R A M M I N G   P R O C E D U R E



                              PROBLEM  SUMMARY




            MAX _OBS1_        OBJECTIVE FUNCTION
            _RHS_                  RHS  VARIABLE
            _TYPE_                TYPE  VARIABLE
            PROBLEM DENSITY          0.500



            VARIABLE TYPE            NUMBER

            STRUCTURAL
              INTEGER                   5

            LOGICAL
              SLACK                     4

            TOTAL                       9



            CONSTRAINT TYPE          NUMBER

            LE                         4
            FREE                       1

            TOTAL                      5
```

```
                                                                          2

        L I N E A R   P R O G R A M M I N G   P R O C E D U R E

                         INTEGER ITERATION LOG

ITER PROBLEM  CONDITION OBJECTIVE BRANCHED VALUE SINFEAS ACTIVE


   1     +0    ACTIVE    9.6124 X1     .4922 1.36434    2
   2     +1    ACTIVE    8.8125 X2     0.125 0.3125     3
   3     -1    ACTIVE    8.8  X2        0.72  0.56      4
   4     +2    ACTIVE    8.5  X5        8.5   0.5       5
   5     +4 SUBOPTIMAL     8    .       .       0       4
```

```
                                                                          3


        L I N E A R   P R O G R A M M I N G   P R O C E D U R E

                         INTEGER ITERATION LOG

ITER PROBLEM  CONDITION OBJECTIVE BRANCHED VALUE SINFEAS ACTIVE

   6     -3   FATHOMED  8.33333    .        .666667    0
```

```
                                                                          4

        L I N E A R   P R O G R A M M I N G   P R O C E D U R E



                          SOLUTION  SUMMARY


                      OPTIMAL INTEGER SOLUTION

       OBJECTIVE VALUE              8.000000

       PHASE 1 ITERATIONS                  0
       PHASE 2 ITERATIONS                  5
       PHASE 3 ITERATIONS                 12
       INTEGER ITERATIONS                  6
       INTEGER SOLUTIONS                   1
       INITIAL B.F. VARIABLES              4
       TIME USED (SECS)                 0.02
       NUMBER OF INVERSIONS                2

       MACHINE EPSILON            1.00000E-08
       MACHINE INFINITY           7.23701E+75
       INVERT FREQUENCY                   50
       MAX PHASE 1 ITERATIONS            100
       MAX PHASE 2 ITERATIONS            100
       MAX PHASE 3 ITERATIONS       99999999
       MAX INTEGER ITERATIONS            100
       TIME LIMIT (SECS)              120.00
```

```
                                                              5

        L I N E A R   P R O G R A M M I N G   P R O C E D U R E

                       VARIABLE   SUMMARY

          VARIABLE                                     REDUCED
    COL   NAME    STATUS   TYPE     PRICE    ACTIVITY    COST

     1 X1      ALTER INTEGER        0         0          0
     2 X2            INTEGER        0         0       7.000000
     3 X3            INTEGER        1         0       1.000000
     4 X4      DEGEN INTEGER        1         0          0
     5 X5            INTEGER        1      8.000000   1.000000
     6 _OBS2_  BASIC SLACK          0      2.000000      0
     7 _OBS3_  BASIC SLACK          0      1.000000      0
     8 _OBS4_  DEGEN SLACK          0         0          0
     9 _OBS5_        SLACK          0         0      -1.000000
```

```
                                                              6

        L I N E A R   P R O G R A M M I N G   P R O C E D U R E

                      CONSTRAINT SUMMARY

     CONSTRAINT           S/S                              DUAL
     ROW  ID      TYPE    COL      RHS      ACTIVITY     ACTIVITY

      1 _OBS2_    LE       6    18.000000  16.000000        0
      2 _OBS3_    LE       7    17.000000  16.000000        0
      3 _OBS4_    LE       8        0          0            0
      4 _OBS5_    LE       9        0          0         1.000000
      5 _OBS1_    OBJECTIVE      8.000000   8.000000        0
```

REFERENCES

Bartels, R. (1971), "A Stabilization of the Simplex Method," *Numerical Mathematics*, 16, 414-434.

Bland, R.G. (1977), "New Finite Pivoting Rules for the Simplex Method," *Mathematics of Operations Research*, 2, 103-107.

Breau, R. and Burdet, C.A. (1974), "Branch and Bound Experiments in Zero-one Programming," *Mathematical Programming Study*, ed. M.L. Balinski, 2, 1-50.

Crowder, H., Johnson, E.L., and Padberg, M.W. (1983), "Solving Large-Scale Zero-One Linear Programming Problems," *Operations Research*, 31, 803-834.

Dantzig, G.B. (1963), *Linear Programming and Extensions*, Princeton: Princeton University Press.

Garfinkel, R.S. and Nemhauser, G.L. (1972), *Integer Programming*, New York: John Wiley & Sons.

Greenberg, H.J. (ed.) (1978), "Pivot Selection Tactics," in *Design and Implementation of Optimization Software*, Netherlands: Sijthoff & Noordhoff.

Hadley, G. (1962), *Linear Programming*, Reading, Massachusetts: Addison-Wesley.

Harris, P. (1975), "Pivot Selection Methods of the Devex LP Code," in *Mathematical Programming Study 4*, Amsterdam: North-Holland Publishing Co.

Ignizio, J.P. (1976), *Goal Programming and Extensions*, Lexington, Massachusetts: D.C. Heath and Company.

Reid, J.K. (1976), "A Sparsity-Exploiting Variant of the Bartels-Golub Decomposition for Linear Programming Bases," *Harwell Report CSS 20*, A.E.R.E., Didcot, Oxfordshire.

---------- (1976), "Fortran Subroutines for Handling Sparse Linear Programming Bases," *Harwell Report AERE-R 8269*, A.E.R.E., Didcot, Oxfordshire.

Taha, H.A. (1975), *Integer Programming*, New York: Academic Press.

210

Chapter 6

The NETFLOW
Procedure

Operating systems: All

ABSTRACT

The NETFLOW procedure finds the minimum cost flow in a network. Shortest path, maximum flow, and transshipment problems are easily stated in terms of finding the minimum cost flow in a network and can be solved with PROC NETFLOW.

INTRODUCTION

The NETFLOW procedure is used to find the minimum cost flow through a network. Networks are input to the procedure as a SAS data set. Each observation identifies one or more arcs and includes constraints on the allowable flow in each arc and on the supply and demand at the tail node and head node of each arc.

The procedure calculates the minimum cost flow that satisfies the supply and demand at each node without violating the minimum flow and capacity bounds on each arc. The procedure produces a SAS data set that contains all the variables in the input data set, the optimal flow across each arc in the network, and the value, at optimality, of a dual variable associated with each arc in the network. The dual variable gives the marginal cost of increasing the flow along each arc in the network that is at its upper or lower bound. Consequently, it is useful for analyzing the sensitivity of the network to flow changes.

The formal statement of the problem solved by PROC NETFLOW is

$$\min\ (\max)\ \Sigma_{\{(i,j)\varepsilon A\}} c_{ij} f_{ij}$$

subject to:

$$\Sigma_{\{i\,|\,(i,j))\varepsilon A\}}\ f_{ij}\ -\ \Sigma_{\{k\,|\,(j,k))\varepsilon A\}}\ f_{jk}\ \geq\ d_j\ \text{for } j\varepsilon J$$
$$\Sigma_{\{i\,|\,(i,j))\varepsilon A\}}\ f_{ij}\ -\ \Sigma_{\{k\,|\,(j,k))\varepsilon A\}}\ f_{jk}\ \leq\ s_j\ \text{for } j\varepsilon J$$

$$\ell_{ij}\ \leq\ f_{ij}\ \leq\ u_{ij}\ \text{for all } (i,j)\varepsilon A$$

where

    J   is the collection of nodes in the network

    A   is the collection of arcs in the network

    (i,j) is a directed arc from node i to node j

    c_{ij} is the cost per unit flow on arc (i,j)

    f_{ij} is the flow on arc (i,j)

    s_j is the supply at node j

    d_i is the demand at node i such that $d_i s_i = 0$

    ℓ_{ij} is the minimum feasible flow on arc (i,j)

    u_{ij} is the capacity of arc (i,j) .

Note that if node k has neither supply nor demand, then $s_k = d_k = 0$.

This problem is said to be infeasible if the total supply is less than the total demand; namely, if

$$\Sigma_{j\varepsilon J}\ s_j\ <\ \Sigma_{j\varepsilon J}\ d_j\ \ .$$

However, the ADDSUPPLY option tells the procedure to assume that the needed supply is available at each of the source nodes and to distribute the available supply optimally among them. This is a useful way to identify the optimal distribution of supply at each of the source nodes and the optimal flow from source to sink nodes. In particular, the supply constraints in the above formulation are replaced by

$$\Sigma_{\{i\,|\,(i,j)\varepsilon A\}}\ f_{ij}\ -\ \Sigma_{\{k\,|\,(j,k)\varepsilon A\}}\ f_{jk}\ \leq\ s_j + D - S\ \text{for } j\varepsilon K$$

where

    $\mathbf{K} = \{j\,|\,s_j \neq 0,\ j\varepsilon J\}$,

    $D = \Sigma_{j\varepsilon J}\ d_i$, and

    $S = \Sigma_{j\varepsilon J}\ s_i\ \ .$

SPECIFICATIONS

The following statements are used in PROC NETFLOW:

```
PROC NETFLOW options;
  BY variables;
  CAPACITY variables;
  COST variables;
  DEMAND variables;
  HEADNODE variable;
  MINFLOW variables;
  SUPPLY variable;
  TAILNODE variable;
```

The HEADNODE and TAILNODE statements are required.

PROC NETFLOW Statement

PROC NETFLOW options;

The options below can appear in the PROC NETFLOW statement:

ADDSUPPLY
> tells the procedure to provide additional supply at each of the source nodes if the total demand cannot be satisfied by the total supply.

ASINKNODE=sinknodename
> identifies a sink node. ASINKNODE= is useful if the network has only one sink node. *Sinknodename* should be the name of the sink node and must be a valid SAS name.

ASOURCENODE=sourcenodename
> identifies a source node. ASOURCENODE= is useful if the network has only one source node. *Sourcenodename* should be the name of the source node and must be a valid SAS name.

DATA=SASdataset
> names the SAS data set that contains the network specification. If DATA= is omitted, the most recently created SAS data set is used.

DEFCAPACITY=c
> requests that the default arc capacity be c. If this option is not specified, then c=99999.

DEFCOST=c
> requests that the default cost for a unit flow on each arc in the network is c.

DEFMINFLOW=m
> requests that the default minimum flow be m. If this option is not specified, then m=0.

DEMAND=value
> specifies the demand at the sink node specified by the NSINKNODE= or the ASINKNODE= option.

MAXFLOW
> specifies that NETFLOW solve a maximum flow problem. In this case NETFLOW finds the maximum flow from the source nodes to the sink nodes. When MAXFLOW is specified, NETFLOW ignores all cost data and attempts to maximize the flow through the network.

MAXIMUM

> specifies that NETFLOW find the maximum cost flow through the network.

NSINKNODE=*sinknodename*

> identifies a sink node. NSINKNODE= is useful if the network has only one sink node. *Sinknodename* should be the name of the sink node and must be numeric.

NSOURCENODE=*sourcenodename*

> identifies a source node. NSOURCENODE= is useful if the network has only one source node. *Sourcenodename* should equal the name of the source node and must be numeric.

OUT=*SASdataset*

> names the output data set. If OUT= is omitted, the procedure names the data set according to the DATA*n* convention. See "SAS Files" in the *SAS User's Guide: Basics* for more information.

SHORTPATH

> specifies that NETFLOW solve a shortest path problem. In this case NETFLOW finds the shortest path from the source node specified in the SOURCENODE= option to the the sink node specified in the SINKNODE= option.

SUPPLY=*value*

> specifies the supply at the source node specified by the NSOURCENODE= or the ASOURCENODE= option.

BY Statement

> BY *variables*;

A BY statement can be used with PROC NETFLOW to obtain separate analyses on observations in groups defined by the BY variables. When a BY statement appears, the procedure expects the input data to be sorted in order of the BY variables. If your input data set is not sorted, use the SORT procedure with a similar BY statement to sort the data.

CAPACITY Statement

> CAPACITY *variables*;

The CAPACITY statement identifies the variables in the input data set that contain the maximum feasible flow, or capacity, on the network arcs. These variables must be numeric, and the number of variables in the list must be the same as the number of variables in the HEADNODE statement.

COST Statement

> COST *variables*;

The COST statement identifies the variables in the input data set that contain the cost of a unit of flow on each arc, the profit from a unit flow on each arc, the length of each arc, or the time to traverse each arc. The solution of the network problem is independent of the interpretation of the variables specified in the COST statement. These variables must be numeric, and the number of variables in the list must be the same as the number of variables in the HEADNODE statement.

DEMAND Statement

DEMAND *variables;*

The DEMAND statement identifies the variables in the input data set that contain the demand at the arc headnodes. These variables must be numeric, and the number of variables in the list must be the same as the number of variables in the HEADNODE statement.

HEADNODE Statement

HEADNODE *variables;*

The HEADNODE statement specifies the variables in the input data set that contain the names of nodes on the heads of arcs. The variables specified can be either numeric or character. Since the procedure treats the variables symbolically, each variable can take any value as long as each node is defined uniquely.

MINFLOW Statement

MINFLOW *variables;*

The MINFLOW statement identifies the variables in the input data set that contain the minimum feasible flow on the network arcs. These variables must be numeric, and the number of variables in the list must be the same as the number of variables in the HEADNODE statement.

SUPPLY Statement

SUPPLY *variable;*

The SUPPLY statement identifies the variables in the input data set that contain the supply at the arc tailnodes.

TAILNODE Statement

TAILNODE *variable;*

The TAILNODE statement specifies the variable that contains the name of each node on the tail of an arc in the network. The variables specified can be either numeric or character. Since the procedure treats this variable symbolically, it can take any value as long as each node is defined uniquely.

DETAILS

Missing Values

The NETFLOW procedure treats missing values as missing when they occur in all variables except those listed in the TAILNODE and COST statements. Missing values for variables in these statements are in error and result in an error message.

Output Data Set

The output data set contains the network descriptor variables from the input data set and several new variables that describe the flow and the value of the dual variables at optimality. The flow variables are named _FLOW1_ to _FLOWn_, and the dual variables are named _DUAL1_ to _DUALn_, where n is the number of variables specified in the HEADNODE statement.

Dual Variables

The dual variables are identified with the capacity constraints

$$\ell_{ij} \leq f_{ij} \leq u_{ij}$$

on each arc $(i,j)\varepsilon\mathbf{A}$. For each arc that has flow at its upper or lower bound the dual activity, contained in the output data set, tells you the marginal cost of increasing the flow along the arc. For each arc with flow between its upper and lower bound, the dual variable is zero and has no meaningful economic interpretation. For example, if the problem is finding the minimum cost flow through a network, then an arc at a lower bound having a positive dual variable tells you that marginally increasing the flow through that arc marginally increases the total cost.

Solution Method

PROC NETFLOW uses the out-of-kilter algorithm developed by Ford and Fulkerson (1962). This algorithm finds the minimum cost flow only in circulation models (that is, models with no external source or sink nodes). NETFLOW imbeds the user-supplied model in an equivalent circulation model and then finds the minimum cost flow within the circulation model. The conversion to a circulation model is accomplished by appending an additional node to the network and then connecting all source and sink nodes to this new external node.

This should be kept in mind when interpreting the dual variables. For example, when the MAXFLOW option is specified, all arcs are assumed to have zero cost except the arc connecting the external node to the source node. That arc is assumed to have unit cost. Consequently, for a maximum flow problem, the dual variables have the following interpretation:

- +1 means that increasing flow on that arc (namely by increasing the arc capacity) increases flow through the network.
- 0 means that increasing flow on that arc may not increase the total flow through the network.
- −1 means that increasing flow in a direction opposite to the direction of the arc increases the flow through the network.

Remember, however, that the dual variables give information about the **marginal** changes to flow and cost.

When the SHORTPATH option is specified, PROC NETFLOW builds a circulation model by connecting the sinknode to the external node, and then connecting the external node to the sourcenode. The procedure forces one unit of flow through the network by placing upper and lower bounds of one on the arc connecting the external node to the source node. By interpreting the length of an arc as the cost of a unit of flow through the arc and minimizing the cost of flow through the network the procedure finds the shortest path through the network. It is identified by those arcs having unit flow.

EXAMPLES

Minimum Cost Flow: Example 1

This example shows how to use NETFLOW to find the minimum cost flow in a small, capacitated network shown in **Figure 6.1.**

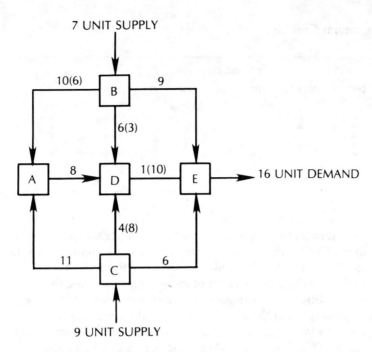

Figure 6.1   Finding Minimum Cost Flow: PROC NETFLOW

The letters in the nodes are the node names, the numbers on the arcs not enclosed in parentheses are the unit costs of flow, and the numbers on the arcs enclosed in parentheses are the arc capacities. The number of units supplied and demanded are as noted. The statements used to find the minimum cost flow produce the output data set that contains the solution in **Output 6.1.**

```
TITLE 'MINIMUM COST FLOW';

DATA;
   INPUT INNODE $ OUTNODE $ COST SUP DEM CAP;
   CARDS;
A D  8 .  .  .
B A 10 7  .  6
B D  6 .  .  3
B E  9 .  .  .
C A 11 9  .  .
C D  4 .  .  8
C E  6 .  .  .
D E  1 . 16 10
;

PROC NETFLOW;
   CAPACITY CAP;
   COST COST;
   DEMAND DEM;
   TAILNODE INNODE;
   HEADNODE OUTNODE;
   SUPPLY SUP;

PROC PRINT;
```

Output 6.1   Minimum Cost Flow

```
                              MINIMUM COST FLOW                                    1

        OBS    INNODE    OUTNODE    COST    CAP    SUP    DEM    _FLOW1_    _DUAL1_
         1       A          D        8       .      .      .        0         10
         2       B          A       10       6      7      .        0          1
         3       B          D        6       3      .      .        3         -1
         4       B          E        9       .      .      .        4          0
         5       C          A       11       .      9      .        0          5
         6       C          D        4       8      .      .        7          0
         7       C          E        6       .      .      .        2          0
         8       D          E        1      10      .     16       10         -1
```

The flows at optimality are contained in the variable _FLOW1_. The dual variable gives the marginal cost of increasing flow along each arc. For example, _DUAL1_ = 5 in observation 5. This tells you that the marginal cost of increasing flow along the arc from node C to node A is 5. Similarly, the -1 for the _DUAL1_ variable in observation 3 tells you the marginal cost of increasing flow along the arc from node B to node D. In this case, increasing flow **decreases** total cost. Since the solution is optimal, the flows in these two arcs are at their respective lower and upper bounds. The flow from node C to node A is 0, which is the minimum feasible flow for that arc, and the flow from node B to node D is 3, which is the capacity of that arc.

The minimum cost flow satisfying supply and demand is shown in **Figure 6.2.**

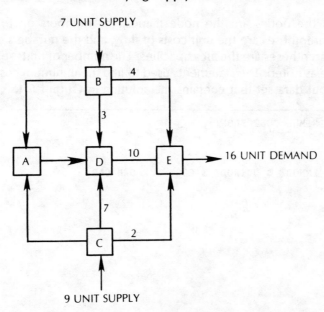

Figure 6.2   Minimum Cost Flow Satisfying Supply and Demand:
PROC NETFLOW

The cost at optimality is printed on the SAS log as:

```
NOTE: MINIMUM COST OF FLOW = 104.
```

Minimum Cost Flow: Example 2

This example shows how to represent the network shown in the first example in a more concise format. Rather than specifying a single arc in each observation, as in the last example, three arcs are specified in each observation. This is done by including a single TAILNODE variable and three HEADNODE variables in the data set. In Example 1, node A is the tail node for three arcs: one to node B, a second to node C, and a third to D. This information can be included in one observation. The program to solve the Example 1 network in this format along with the solution is saved by NETFLOW in the data set in **Output 6.2.**

```
TITLE 'MINIMUM COST FLOW' ;

DATA;
   INPUT INNODE $ (OUTNODE1-OUTNODE3) ($)
      SUP COST1-COST3 DEM1-DEM3 CAP1-CAP3;
   CARDS;
A D . .   0    8 . .    0 . .    . . .
B A D E   7   10 6 9    0 0 0    6 3 .
C A D E   9   11 4 6    0 0 0    . 8 .
D E . .   0    1 . .   16 . .   10 . .
;

PROC NETFLOW;
   TAIL INNODE;
   HEAD OUTNODE1-OUTNODE3;
   COST COST1-COST3;
   CAPACITY CAP1-CAP3;
   DEMAND DEM1-DEM3;
   SUPPLY SUP;

PROC PRINT;
```

Output 6.2   Minimum Cost Flow

MINIMUM COST FLOW   2

OBS	INNODE	OUTNODE1	OUTNODE2	OUTNODE3	COST1	COST2	COST3	CAP1	CAP2	CAP3	SUP	DEM1	DEM2	DEM3	_FLOW1_	_FLOW2_	_FLOW3_	DUAL1	DUAL2	DUAL3
1	A	D			8	.	.	.	.	.	0	0	.	.	0	.	.	10	.	.
2	B	A	D	E	10	6	9	6	3	.	7	0	0	0	0	3	4	1	-1	0
3	C	A	D	E	11	4	6	.	8	.	9	0	0	0	0	7	2	5	0	0
4	D	E			1	.	.	10	.	.	0	16	.	.	10	.	.	-1	.	.

The flows at optimality are contained in the variables _FLOW1_ to _FLOW3_. For example, the flow from node B to node E is found in observation 2 because that observation contains the arc that has B as its tail node and E as its head node. Since E is the value of OUTNODE3, the third HEADNODE variable, the flow along arc B to E is value of the third flow variable, namely, _FLOW3_. Note that the solution agrees with the solution in the first example.

Maximum Flow: Example 3

This example shows how you can use NETFLOW to solve the maximum flow problem. The problem here is to find the maximum flow from a source node to a sink node in a capacitated network. Consider the network in **Figure 6.3.**

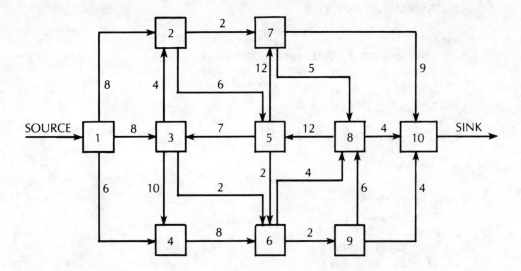

Figure 6.3   Solving the Maximum Flow Problem: PROC NETFLOW

Node 1 is the source node and node 10 is the sink node. The number beside each arc is the capacity of the arc.

To find the maximum flow from node 1 to node 10, include the MAXFLOW option on the PROC NETFLOW statement and specify the source and sink nodes. Since this example has only one source node and one sink node, you can identify them in the PROC NETFLOW statement using the NSOURCENODE= and NSINKNODE= options. The program finds the maximum flow and prints the solution shown in **Output 6.3.**

```
TITLE 'MAXIMUM FLOW';

DATA;
   INPUT IN OUT CAP;
   CARDS;
1 2    8
1 3    8
1 4    6
2 7    2
2 5    6
3 2    4
3 4    10
3 6    2
4 6    8
5 3    7
5 6    2
5 7    12
6 8    4
6 9    2
```

```
7  8    5
7  10   9
8  5    12
8  10   4
9  8    6
9  10   4
;

PROC NETFLOW MAXFLOW NSOURCENODE=1 NSINKNODE=10;
   TAILNODE IN;
   HEADNODE OUT;
   CAPACITY CAP;

PROC PRINT;
```

Output 6.3 Maximum Flow

```
                              MAXIMUM FLOW                              3

            OBS    IN    OUT    CAP    _FLOW1_    _DUAL1_

             1      1      2      8        8          0
             2      1      3      8        2          0
             3      1      4      6        4          0
             4      2      7      2        2          1
             5      2      5      6        6          1
             6      3      2      4        0          0
             7      3      4     10        0          0
             8      3      6      2        2          0
             9      4      6      8        4          0
            10      5      3      7        0         -1
            11      5      6      2        0         -1
            12      5      7     12        6          0
            13      6      8      4        4          1
            14      6      9      2        2          1
            15      7      8      5        0          0
            16      7     10      9        8          0
            17      8      5     12        0          0
            18      8     10      4        4          0
            19      9      8      6        0          0
            20      9     10      4        2          0
```

This program also produces the message:

```
NOTE: MAXIMUM FLOW = 14.
```

The _FLOW1_ variable shows the flow on each arc at optimality. Those arcs whose flow equals the arc capacity may or may not be critical in the sense of limiting the total flow through the network. The dual variable helps to differenti-ate between critical and noncritical arcs. In particular, a dual value of 1 tells you that increasing flow along that arc increases the flow through the network. This is not necessarily true for arcs that have dual values of 0 and are at capacity. Also, arcs with dual values of -1 are arcs along which a flow in the reverse direction would increase the total flow through the network.

Shortest Path: Example 4

This example shows how you can use NETFLOW to find the shortest path from a source node to a sink node. Consider the network in **Figure 6.4.**

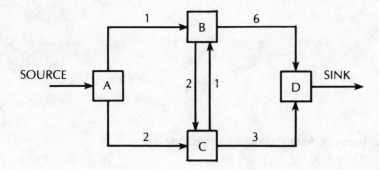

Figure 6.4   Finding the Shortest Path: PROC NETFLOW

The numbers on the arcs are the distances between nodes. To find the shortest path from node A to node D, invoke NETFLOW with the network definition as before, specify source and sink nodes, and tell NETFLOW that the problem is a shortest path problem with the SHORTPATH option in the PROC NETFLOW statement. The program to solve this problem produces **Output 6.4.**

```
TITLE 'SHORTEST PATH';

DATA;
   INPUT TAIL $ LENGTH HEAD $ ;
   CARDS;
A 1 B
A 2 C
B 2 C
C 1 B
B 6 D
C 3 D
;

PROC NETFLOW ASOURCENODE=A ASINKNODE=D SHORTPATH;
   COST LENGTH;
   HEADNODE HEAD;
   TAILNODE TAIL;

PROC PRINT;
```

Output 6.4   Shortest Path

```
                              SHORTEST PATH                                              4

          OBS     TAIL    HEAD    LENGTH    _FLOW1_    _DUAL1_

           1       A       B        1          0          0
           2       A       C        2          1          0
           3       B       C        2          0          1
           4       C       B        1          0          2
           5       B       D        6          0          2
           6       C       D        3          1          0
```

Since the arcs from A to C and from C to D have unit flow at optimality, these arcs are on the shortest path from node A to node D.

REFERENCES

Ford, L.R. and Fulkerson, D.R. (1962), *Flows in Networks*, Princeton: Princeton University Press.

Minieka, E. (1978), *Optimization Algorithms for Networks and Graphs*, New York: Marcel Dekker, Inc.

Papadumitriou, C.H. and Steiglitz, K. (1982), *Combinatorial Optimization: Algorithms and Complexity*, Englewood Cliffs, New Jersey: Prentice-Hall, Inc.

Chapter 7

The TRANS Procedure

Operating systems: All

ABSTRACT

The TRANS procedure is used to solve the transportation problem—meeting demands at destination nodes using available resources at source nodes while minimizing transportation costs.

INTRODUCTION

The TRANS procedure is used to find the minimum cost flow in a capacitated transportation network with *n* source nodes and *m* destination nodes. A network is capacitated if it has constraints on the amount of feasible flow on each arc. Consider the SAS data set in **Output 7.1**.

The first row gives the number of units demanded at each destination node, and the SUPPLY column gives the number of units supplied at each source node. If you exclude the first row and the SUPPLY column, the remaining entries represent the cost of shipping one unit between labeled cities. The transportation problem finds the minimum cost flow between supply points and destination points that satisfies the demand. PROC TRANS solves this problem and produces a SAS data set containing the number of units to ship between each supply and demand point.

Output 7.1 Uncapacitated Transportation Network

```
                                              SAS                                                        1

OBS  ATLANTA  CHICAGO  DENVER  HOUSTON  LOS_ANGE  MIAMI  NEW_YORK  SAN_FRAN  SEATTLE  WASHINGT  SUPPLY  CITY

 1     50       75       89       8        27      39      64       100        50        8       .
 2     20       58      121      70       193      60      74       213       218       54       10     ATLANTA
 3     58       20       92      94       174     118      71       185       173       57      150     CHICAGO
 4    121       92       20      87        83     172     163        94       102      149       90     DENVER
 5     70       94       87      20       137      96     142       154       189      122       27     HOUSTON
 6    193      174       83     137        20     223     245        34        95      230       80     LOS_ANGE
 7     60      118      172      96       233      20     109       259       273       92       26     MIAMI
 8     74       71      163     142       245     109      20       257       240       20       80     NEW_YORK
 9    213      185       94     164        34     259     257        20        67      244       25     SAN_FRAN
10    218      173      102     189        95     273     240        67        20      232        7     SEATTLE
11     54       59      149     122       230      92      20       244       232       20       15     WASHINGT
```

The formal statement of the problem solved by PROC TRANS is

$$\min\ (\max)\ \Sigma_{i=1}^{n}\ \Sigma_{j=1}^{m}\ c_{ij}x_{ij}$$

subject to:

$$\Sigma_{j=1}^{m}\,x_{ij} \leq s_i \quad \text{for}\ i = 1,...,n$$

$$\Sigma_{i=1}^{n}\,x_{ij} \geq d_j \quad \text{for}\ j = 1,...,m$$

$$\ell_{ij} \leq x_{ij} \leq u_{ij} \quad \text{for}\ i = 1,...,n\ \text{and}\ j=1,...,m,$$

where

c_{ij} is the cost per unit between nodes i and j,

x_{ij} is the amount shipped between nodes i and j,

s_i is the supply at node j,

d_j is the demand at node i,

ℓ_{ij} is the minimum allowable flow between nodes i and j, and

u_{ij} is the capacity of the arc between nodes i and j.

This problem is said to be infeasible if the total supply is less than the total demand, namely, if

$$\Sigma_{j=1}^{m}\ s_j < \Sigma_{i=1}^{n}\ d_i\ \ .$$

However, if you specify the ADDSUPPLY option, PROC TRANS assumes that the needed supply is available at each of the source nodes and optimally distributes the available supply among them. This is a useful way of identifying the optimal distribution of supply at each of the source nodes and the optimal flow from source to destination nodes. In particular, the supply constraints in the above formulation are replaced by

$$\Sigma_{j=1}^{m}\ x_{ij} \leq s_i +\ D -\ S \quad \text{for}\ i = 1,...,n$$

where

$$D = \Sigma_{j=1}^{m}\ d_j,\ \text{and}$$

$$S = \Sigma_{i=1}^{n}\ s_i\ \ .$$

SPECIFICATIONS

The following statements are used with PROC TRANS.

> **PROC TRANS** *options;*
>   **ID** *variable;*
>   **SUPPLY** *variable;*
>   **VAR** *variables;*

The ID and SUPPLY statements are required.

PROC TRANS Statement

PROC TRANS *options;*

These options can appear in the PROC TRANS statement:

ADDSUPPLY
> tells the procedure to provide additional supply at each of the source nodes if the total demand cannot be satisfied by the total supply.

CAPACITY=*SASdataset*
> names the SAS data set that contains the capacity on each arc in the transportation network. These data specify the maximum allowable flow on each network arc. If CAPACITY= is omitted, then the value of DEFCAPACITY is used for each arc in the network.

COST=*SASdataset*
> names the SAS data set that contains the cost, supply, and demand data for the transportation network. If COST= is omitted, the most recently created SAS data set is used.

DEFCAPACITY=*c*
> specifies the default capacity for the arcs in the network. The default value of *c* is 99999.

DEFMINFLOW=*s*
> specifies the default minimum flow for the arcs in the network. The default value of *s* is 0.

DEMAND=*d*
> gives the number of the observation that contains the number of units demanded at each destination node. The default is *d*=1.

MAXIMUM
> tells the procedure to maximize rather than minimize the objective function.

MINFLOW=*SASdataset*
> names the SAS data set that contains the minimum flow data for the transportation network. These data specify the minimum required flow on each arc in the network. If MINFLOW= is omitted, then the value of DEFMINFLOW is used for each arc in the network.

OUT=*SASdataset*
> specifies a name for the output data set. If OUT= is omitted, the SAS System creates a data set and names it according to the DATA*n* convention. See "SAS Data Sets" in the *SAS User's Guide: Basics* for more information.

ID Statement

ID *variable*;

The ID statement identifies the variable in all input data sets that names each of the source nodes. This variable is included in the output data set. The ID statement is required.

SUPPLY Statement

SUPPLY *variable*;

The SUPPLY statement identifies the variable in the COST= data set that contains the number of units of supply at each supply node. The SUPPLY statement is required.

VAR Statement

VAR *variables*;

The VAR statement identifies variables in the COST= input data set that contain the costs of transporting a unit of supply from a source node to a destination node. Each observation in the COST= data set is identified with a source node and each variable is identified with a destination node. The procedure associates variables in the MINFLOW= and CAPACITY= data sets with destination nodes.

DETAILS

Missing Values

Since the value of a cost variable is interpreted as the cost of a unit flow on an arc, a missing value for a cost variable is interpreted as a missing arc.

A missing value in the MINFLOW= and CAPACITY= data sets causes the procedure to assign the default capacity or default minimum flow to the corresponding arc.

Objective Value

If the problem is infeasible, a note to that effect is printed on the SAS log. Otherwise, the value of the objective function,

$$\Sigma_{j=1}^{m} \ \Sigma_{i=1}^{n} \ c_{ij}x_{ij}$$

at optimality is reported on the SAS log.

Demand

The demand at each destination node must also be specified. Since there are the same number of destination nodes as VAR statement variables, PROC TRANS assumes that the values of the first observation contain the number of units demanded at each destination node. If DEMAND=*d* is specified in the PROC TRANS statement, then observation *d* is assumed to contain the number of units demanded.

Output Data Set

The output data set contains the variables listed in the VAR statement, the variable listed in the ID statement, and an additional variable named _DUAL_. For each observation in the COST= data set that is associated with a source node, the output data set tells you:

- the optimal flow between the source and destination nodes
- the name of the source node as given in the ID variable
- the value of the dual variable associated with that source node.

The observation in the ouput data set corresponding to the demand observation in the input data set contains the dual variables at the destination nodes.

Dual Variables

The dual variables at the supply nodes tell you the marginal cost of increasing supply at those nodes. If a dual variable is negative, increasing the supply at that node decreases the total transportation costs. These variables are associated with the constraints

$$\sum_{j=1}^{m} x_{ij} \leq s_i \text{ for } i = 1,...,n \quad .$$

The dual variables at the demand nodes tell you the marginal cost of increasing demand at those nodes. A positive dual variable means that increasing the demand at that node increases total transportation costs. These variables are associated with the constraints

$$\sum_{i=1}^{n} x_{ij} \geq d_j \text{ for } j = 1,...,m \quad .$$

EXAMPLES

Uncapacitated Transportation Network: Example 1

The transportation problem described in the introduction is solved below. The cost data are stored in a SAS data set; in PROC TRANS you identify the COST variables and the SUPPLY variable. The solution is stored in a SAS data set as shown in **Output 7.2** and printed with PROC PRINT.

```
TITLE 'UNCAPACITATED TRANSPORTATION NETWORK';

DATA CST;
   INPUT ATLANTA CHICAGO  DENVER  HOUSTON  LOS_ANGE MIAMI
         NEW_YORK SAN_FRAN SEATTLE WASHINGT SUPPLY   CITY$;
   CARDS;
 50  75  89   8  27  39  64 100  50   8    .       .
 20  58 121  70 193  60  74 213 218  54   10    ATLANTA
 58  20  92  94 174 118  71 185 173  57  150    CHICAGO
121  92  20  87  83 172 163  94 102 149   90    DENVER
 70  94  87  20 137  96 142 154 189 122   27    HOUSTON
193 174  83 137  20 223 245  34  95 230   80    LOS_ANGE
 60 118 172  96 233  20 109 259 273  92   26    MIAMI
 74  71 163 142 245 109  20 257 240  20   80    NEW_YORK
213 185  94 164  34 259 257  20  67 244   25    SAN_FRAN
218 173 102 189  95 273 240  67  20 232    7    SEATTLE
 54  59 149 122 230  92  20 244 232  20   15    WASHINGT
```

```
                    ;
                    PROC TRANS COST=CST;
                       ID CITY;
                       VAR ATLANTA-WASHINGT;
                       SUPPLY SUPPLY;

                    PROC PRINT;
```

After this program executes, the following messages are printed on the SAS log:

```
    WARNING: OBSERVATION CONTAINING DEMAND HAS NOT BEEN SPECIFIED.
             IT IS ASSUMED TO BE 1.
    NOTE: MINIMUM COST ROUTING = 22928.
```

The warning tells you that observation 1 was assumed to contain the demand at the destination nodes. The second message gives the objective value at optimality. The job above produces the SAS data set in **Output 7.2.**

Output 7.2   Uncapacitated Transportation Network

UNCAPACITATED TRANSPORTATION NETWORK   2

OBS	CITY	ATLANTA	CHICAGO	DENVER	HOUSTON	LOS_ANGE	MIAMI	NEW_YORK	SAN_FRAN	SEATTLE	WASHINGT	_DUAL_
1	_DUAL_	71	33	105	48	165	109	20	179	186	20	.
2	ATLANTA	10	0	0	0	0	0	0	0	0	0	-51
3	CHICAGO	30	75	2	0	0	0	0	0	43	0	-13
4	DENVER	0	0	87	0	0	0	0	3	0	0	-85
5	HOUSTON	0	0	0	8	19	0	0	0	0	0	-28
6	LOS_ANGE	0	0	0	0	8	0	0	72	0	0	-145
7	MIAMI	0	0	0	0	0	26	0	0	0	0	-89
8	NEW_YORK	0	0	0	0	0	8	64	0	0	8	0
9	SAN_FRAN	0	0	0	0	0	0	0	25	0	0	-159
10	SEATTLE	0	0	0	0	0	0	0	0	7	0	-166
11	WASHINGT	10	0	0	0	0	5	0	0	0	0	-17

Since the first observation is associated with the demands, the ID value is _DUAL_, and the values of the VAR variables are the dual variables at the destination nodes, or the marginal costs of increasing demand at each node.

The second observation is associated with the supply at the source node called ATLANTA. The values of the VAR variables in this observation give the optimal flow between ATLANTA and each destination node. For example, to achieve the minimum cost, you must ship 10 units from ATLANTA to ATLANTA. No ATLANTA units are sent to any other destination. In contrast, the CHICAGO supply must be sent to 4 destinations: 30 units to ATLANTA, 75 units to CHICAGO, 2 units to SAN_FRAN, and 43 units to SEATTLE. The variable _DUAL_, the dual variable at the supply nodes, gives the marginal cost of increasing supply at each of those nodes. For example, the marginal cost of increasing supply at ATLANTA is -51. This means that a unit increase in supply in ATLANTA would decrease total transportation costs by $51.

Capacitated Transportation Network: Example 2

In this example the optimal flow is found on a capacitated transportation network. Suppose that there are upper bounds on the amount that can be shipped within each city. This can be interpreted as a limit on the available transportation within the cities. The following SAS program and output show how this capacity constraint is included in the model:

```
TITLE 'CAPACITATED TRANSPORTATION NETWORK';

DATA CAPCTY;
    INPUT ATLANTA CHICAGO DENVER HOUSTON LOS_ANGE MIAMI
        NEW_YORK SAN_FRAN SEATTLE WASHINGT CITY$;
    CARDS;
10  .   .   .   .   .   .   .   .   . ATLANTA
 .  60  .   .   .   .   .   .   .   . CHICAGO
 .  . 100   .   .   .   .   .   .   . DENVER
 .  .   .  10   .   .   .   .   .   . HOUSTON
 .  .   .   .  30   .   .   .   .   . LOS_ANGE
 .  .   .   .   .  20   .   .   .   . MIAMI
 .  .   .   .   .   .  75   .   .   . NEW_YORK
 .  .   .   .   .   .   .  25   .   . SAN_FRAN
 .  .   .   .   .   .   .   .  10   . SEATTLE
 .  .   .   .   .   .   .   .   .  10 WASHINGT
;
PROC TRANS COST=CST CAPACITY=CAPCTY;
    ID CITY;
    VAR ATLANTA-WASHINGT;
    SUPPLY SUPPLY;

PROC PRINT;
;
```

The SAS log contains:

```
WARNING: OBSERVATION CONTAINING DEMAND HAS NOT BEEN SPECIFIED.
         IT IS ASSUMED TO BE 1.
NOTE: 10 VARIABLES IN CAPACITY DATA SET MATCH VARIABLES IN THE
      COST DATA SET.
NOTE: MINIMUM COST ROUTING = 24036.
```

And the solution printed includes **Output 7.3**.

Output 7.3 Capacitated Transportation Network

```
                         CAPACITATED TRANSPORTATION NETWORK                                          3

OBS  CITY      ATLANTA  CHICAGO  DENVER  HOUSTON  LOS_ANGE  MIAMI  NEW_YORK  SAN_FRAN  SEATTLE  WASHINGT  _DUAL_

  1  _DUAL_       60       80      94      37       154      113      29       168       175       29        .
  2  ATLANTA       0        0       0       0         0       10       0         0         0        0      -53
  3  CHICAGO      44       60       3       0         0        0       0         0        43        0       -2
  4  DENVER        0        0      86       0         0        0       0         4         0        0      -74
  5  HOUSTON       0        0       0       8        18        1       0         0         0        0      -17
  6  LOS_ANGE      0        0       0       0         9        0       0        71         0        0     -134
  7  MIAMI         6        0       0       0         0       20       0         0         0        0        0
  8  NEW_YORK      0        8       0       0         0        0      64         0         0        8       -9
  9  SAN_FRAN      0        0       0       0         0        0       0        25         0        0     -148
 10  SEATTLE       0        0       0       0         0        0       0         0         7        0     -155
 11  WASHINGT      0        7       0       0         0        8       0         0         0        0      -21
```

Note that the optimal objective value is greater in the capacitated network (24036) than in the uncapacitated network (22928). Additional constraints can never decrease the objective value of a minimization problem at optimality. Also observe that the flow within CHICAGO, MIAMI, and SAN_FRAN are at their limits. The rerouting of flow within these cities accounts for the increase in cost.

Capacitated Transportation Network: Example 3

Suppose that we place a minimum on the flow within each city. Just as capacity restrictions can be interpreted as limits on available transportation, minimum flow restrictions can be interpreted as requirements to ship minimum quantities on certain routes, perhaps as a result of contractual agreements. The following program adds minimum flow requirements on four routes. Since the data set consists of mostly missing values, named input mode is used to input the data. The printed solution follows the program.

```
TITLE 'CAPACITATED TRANSPORTATION NETWORK';

DATA MINFLW;
   INPUT CHICAGO= DENVER=  SAN_FRAN= SEATTLE= CITY= $;
   CARDS;
CITY=CHICAGO CHICAGO=30 SAN_FRAN=40 SEATTLE=50
CITY=DENVER  DENVER=40
;
PROC TRANS COST=CST CAPACITY=CAPCTY MINFLOW=MINFLW;
   VAR ATLANTA—WASHINGT;
   ID CITY;
   SUPPLY SUPPLY;

PROC PRINT;
```

The SAS log contains:

```
WARNING: OBSERVATION CONTAINING DEMAND HAS NOT BEEN SPECIFIED.
         IT IS ASSUMED TO BE 1.
NOTE: 4 VARIABLES IN MINFLOW DATA SET MATCH VARIABLES IN THE
      COST DATA SET.
NOTE: 10 VARIABLES IN CAPACITY DATA SET MATCH VARIABLES IN THE
      COST DATA SET.
NOTE: MINIMUM COST ROUTING = 31458.
```

And the printed solution includes **Output 7.4**.

Output 7.4 Capacitated Transportation Network

```
                           CAPACITATED TRANSPORTATION NETWORK                                        4
 OBS  CITY      ATLANTA  CHICAGO  DENVER  HOUSTON  LOS_ANGE  MIAMI  NEW_YORK  SAN_FRAN  SEATTLE  WASHINGT  _DUAL_
   1  _DUAL_      202      173     101     155        38     231      148        52       20       148       .
   2  ATLANTA      10        0       0       0         0       0        0         0        0         0     -182
   3  CHICAGO       0       60       0       0         0       0        0        40       50         0     -153
   4  DENVER       11        8      71       0         0       0        0         0        0         0      -81
   5  HOUSTON       0        0       0       8         0      19        0         0        0         0     -135
   6  LOS_ANGE      0        0      18       0        27       0        0        35        0         0      -18
   7  MIAMI         6        0       0       0         0      20        0         0        0         0     -142
   8  NEW_YORK      8        0       0       0         0       0       64         0        0         8     -128
   9  SAN_FRAN      0        0       0       0         0       0        0        25        0         0      -32
  10  SEATTLE       0        7       0       0         0       0        0         0        0         0        0
  11  WASHINGT     15        0       0       0         0       0        0         0        0         0     -148
```

Note that the optimal objective value is greater in the minimum flow capacitated network than in the capacitated network. Additional constraints can never decrease the objective value of a minimization problem at optimality.

An Infeasible Problem: Example 4

This example shows what happens when the total demand exceeds the total supply. The data from the first example are used with the demand at ATLANTA increased to 100 units. Consequently, the demand exceeds the supply by 50 units. When the statements

```
PROC TRANS COST=CST;
    ID CITY;
    VAR ATLANTA-WASHINGT;
    SUPPLY SUPPLY;
```

are executed, the following message is printed on the SAS log:

```
WARNING: OBSERVATION CONTAINING DEMAND HAS NOT BEEN SPECIFIED.
         IT IS ASSUMED TO BE 1.
WARNING: DEMAND EXCEEDS SUPPLY BY 50 UNITS.
ERROR: THE PROBLEM IS INFEASIBLE.
```

However, if the ADDSUPPLY option is specified in the PROC TRANS statement, the procedure distributes the supply optimally among the source nodes. In that case the statements

```
TITLE 'USING THE ADDSUPPLY OPTION';

PROC TRANS DATA=CST ADDSUPPLY;
    ID CITY;
    VAR ATLANTA-WASHINGT;
    SUPPLY SUPPLY;

PROC PRINT;
```

produce the following messages on the SAS log and **Output 7.5**.

```
WARNING: OBSERVATION CONTAINING DEMAND HAS NOT BEEN SPECIFIED.
         IT IS ASSUMED TO BE 1.
WARNING: DEMAND EXCEEDS SUPPLY BY 50 UNITS. ADDITIONAL SUPPLY NEEDS
         WILL BE DISTRIBUTED OPTIMALLY AMONG THE SUPPLY POINTS.
NOTE: MINIMUM COST ROUTING = 12910.
```

The data set in **Output 7.5** is saved by PROC TRANS.

234   Chapter 7

Output 7.5   Using the ADDSUPPLY Option

```
                                      USING THE ADDSUPPLY OPTION                                              5
  OBS   CITY      ATLANTA  CHICAGO  DENVER  HOUSTON  LOS_ANGE  MIAMI  NEW_YORK  SAN_FRAN  SEATTLE  WASHINGT  _DUAL_

    1   _DUAL_       54       20      20      20        20      20       20        34        20       20        .
    2   ATLANTA      60        0       0       0         0       0        0         0         0        0      -34
    3   CHICAGO       0       75       0       0         0       0        0         0         0        0        0
    4   DENVER        0        0      89       0         0       0        0         0         0        0        0
    5   HOUSTON       0        0       0       8         0       0        0         0         0        0        0
    6   LOS_ANGE      0        0       0       0        27       0        0        25         0        0        0
    7   MIAMI         0        0       0       0         0      39        0         0         0        0        0
    8   NEW_YORK      0        0       0       0         0       0       64         0         0        8        0
    9   SAN_FRAN      0        0       0       0         0       0        0        75         0        0      -14
   10   SEATTLE       0        0       0       0         0       0        0         0        50        0        0
   11   WASHINGT     40        0       0       0         0       0        0         0         0        0        0
```

Appendix 1
SASMPSX Macro

This appendix contains the listing for the SASMPSX conversion macro discussed in **Example 6** of "The LP Procedure." You can also find the code for this macro in the SAS Sample Library. The macro converts a linear program that is in the CONVERT format as specified in Chapter 4 of the IBM MPSX Program Description Manual (number 5734-XM4) to the format expected by PROC LP. The macro assumes that the data to be transformed are in a SAS data set with the name RAW and the variables FIELD1 through FIELD6 as described in the MPSX manual. (See **Example 6** of "The LP Procedure" for more information.)

```
%MACRO SASMPSX;
*------------------------------------------------------------;
* COPYRIGHT (C) 1982 BY SAS INSTITUTE INC., CARY NC       ;
*                                                         ;
*               MPSX CONVERSION MACRO                     ;
*                                                         ;
*   CONVERTS AN LP PROBLEM IN THE FORMAT USED BY THE      ;
*   MPSX 'CONVERT' ROUTINE TO THAT USED BY PROC LP.       ;
*                                                         ;
*   THE INPUT DATA IS IN THE SAS DATA SET RAW.            ;
*   THE SAS DATA SET NAME CAN BE CHANGED USING THE        ;
*   MACRO FACILITY.                                       ;
*                                                         ;
*------------------------------------------------------------;
DATA ROWS     (KEEP=_ID_ _NAME_ _VALUE_)
     ROWSCAL (KEEP=_ID_ SCALE)
     COLSCAL (KEEP=_NAME_ SCALE)
     ROWTYPE (KEEP=_ID_ _TYPE_)
     ROWRANG (KEEP=_NAME_ _ID_ _RANGE_)
     ROWUBND (KEEP=_NAME_ _ID_ _VALUE_)
     ROWLBND (KEEP=_NAME_ _ID_ _VALUE_)
     ROWUNRS (KEEP=_NAME_ _ID_ _VALUE_)
     ROWINT  (KEEP=_NAME_ _ID_ _VALUE_)
     ROWNEW  (KEEP=ROW1 ROW2 ROWNEW COEFF1 COEFF2);
*------------------------------------------------------------;
*         SETUP FOR THE DATA STEP                         ;
*------------------------------------------------------------;
     LENGTH _ID_ _NAME_ _TYPE_ ROW1 ROW2 ROWNEW $ 8;
     LENGTH SCALE COEFF1 COEFF2 8;

     RETAIN INFINITY 7.2E75 INTFLAG 0;
     DROP INFINITY;
     GO TO NMERD; *---START PROCESSING DATA-;
*------------------------------------------------------------;
*            READ RAW DATA SUBROUTINE                     ;
*------------------------------------------------------------;
SETRAW: SET RAW;
     RETURN;
```

```
*------------------------------------------------------;
*          TERMINAL ERROR                              ;
*------------------------------------------------------;
ERROR: PUT 'ERROR: DATA IS NOT IN THE EXPECTED ORDER.';
       ABORT;
*------------------------------------------------------;
*          READ THE NAME SECTION                       ;
*------------------------------------------------------;
NMERD:LINK SETRAW;
      IF FIELD1¬='AM' THEN GO TO ERROR;
      PUT 'NOTE: CONVERT ' FIELD3 ' DATASET.';
      LINK SETRAW;
      IF FIELD1='OW' THEN GO TO ROWRD;
                      ELSE GO TO ERROR;


*------------------------------------------------------;
*          READ THE ROW SECTION                        ;
*------------------------------------------------------;
ROWRD:LINK SETRAW;
      IF FIELD3='''SCALE''' THEN DO;
         _ID_=FIELD2; SCALE=FIELD4; OUTPUT ROWSCAL;
         END;
      ELSE IF FIELD3='''MARKER''' THEN
         PUT 'NOTE: MARKER IN ROW ' FIELD2 ' IGNORED.';
      ELSE IF SUBSTR(FIELD1,1,1)='D' THEN DO;
         ROW1=FIELD3; ROW2=FIELD5; COEFF1=FIELD4;
         ROWNEW=FIELD2; COEFF2=FIELD6; OUTPUT ROWNEW;
         FIELD1=SUBSTR(FIELD1,2,1);
         END;
      IF FIELD1='N' THEN DO;
         _TYPE_='FREE';    _ID_=FIELD2; OUTPUT ROWTYPE;
         END;
      ELSE IF FIELD1='AX' THEN DO;
         _TYPE_='MAX ';    _ID_=FIELD2; OUTPUT ROWTYPE;
         END;
      ELSE IF FIELD1='IN' THEN DO;
         _TYPE_='MIN ';    _ID_=FIELD2; OUTPUT ROWTYPE;
         END;
      ELSE IF FIELD1='G' THEN DO;
         _TYPE_='GE ';     _ID_=FIELD2; OUTPUT ROWTYPE;
         END;
      ELSE IF FIELD1='E' THEN DO;
         _TYPE_='EQ ';     _ID_=FIELD2; OUTPUT ROWTYPE;
         END;
      ELSE IF FIELD1='L' THEN DO;
         _TYPE_='LE ';     _ID_=FIELD2; OUTPUT ROWTYPE;
         END;
      ELSE IF FIELD1='RI' THEN DO;
         _TYPE_='PRICESEN'; _ID_=FIELD2; OUTPUT ROWTYPE;
         END;
      ELSE IF FIELD1='OL' THEN GO TO COLRD;
      ELSE IF FIELD1='AN' THEN GO TO ERROR;
      ELSE IF FIELD1='OU' THEN GO TO ERROR;
      ELSE IF FIELD1='ND' THEN GO TO ERROR;
      GO TO ROWRD;
```

```
*-------------------------------------------------------;
*          READ THE COLUMN SECTION                      ;
*-------------------------------------------------------;
COLRD:LINK SETRAW;
      IF FIELD3='''SCALE''' THEN DO;
         _NAME_=FIELD2; SCALE=FIELD4; OUTPUT COLSCAL;
         END;
      ELSE IF FIELD3='''MARKER''' THEN DO;
         IF FIELD5='''INTORG''' THEN DO;
            IF INTFLAG=1 THEN DO;
               PUT 'ERROR: INTORG APPEARS BEFORE INTEND IN COLUMN '
                    FIELD2 '.'; ABORT;
               END;
            INTFLAG=1;
            END;
         ELSE IF FIELD5='''INTEND''' THEN DO;
            IF INTFLAG=0 THEN DO;
               PUT 'ERROR: INTEND APPEARS BEFORE INTORG IN COLUMN '
                    FIELD2 '.'; ABORT;
               END;
            INTFLAG=0;
            END;
         ELSE PUT 'NOTE: MARKER IN COLUMN ' FIELD2 ' IGNORED.';
         END;
      ELSE IF FIELD1='' THEN DO;
         IF FIELD3¬='' THEN DO;
            _ID_=FIELD3; _NAME_=FIELD2; _VALUE_=FIELD4; OUTPUT ROWS;
            IF INTFLAG=1 THEN LINK INTOUT;
            END;
         IF FIELD5¬='' THEN DO;
            _ID_=FIELD5; _NAME_=FIELD2; _VALUE_=FIELD6; OUTPUT ROWS;
            IF INTFLAG=1 THEN LINK INTOUT;
            END;
         END;
      ELSE IF FIELD1='HS' THEN GO TO RHSRD;
      ELSE IF FIELD1='AN' THEN GO TO ERROR;
      ELSE IF FIELD1='OU' THEN GO TO ERROR;
      ELSE IF FIELD1='ND' THEN GO TO ERROR;
      GO TO COLRD;
*----------OUTPUT INTEGER VARIABLE INFO----------------;
INTOUT:_ID_='_INT_'; _VALUE_=1;
      OUTPUT ROWINT;
      RETURN;
*-------------------------------------------------------;
*          READ THE RHS SECTION                         ;
*-------------------------------------------------------;
RHSRD:LINK SETRAW;
      IF FIELD1='' THEN DO;
         IF FIELD3¬='' THEN DO;
            _ID_=FIELD3; _NAME_=FIELD2; _VALUE_=FIELD4; OUTPUT ROWS;
            END;
         IF FIELD5¬='' THEN DO;
            _ID_=FIELD5; _NAME_=FIELD2; _VALUE_=FIELD6; OUTPUT ROWS;
            END;
         END;
```

```
        ELSE IF FIELD1='AN' THEN GO TO RANRD;
        ELSE IF FIELD1='OU' THEN GO TO BUNRD;
        ELSE IF FIELD1='ND' THEN STOP;
        GO TO RHSRD;
*----------------------------------------------------------;
*           READ THE RANGE SECTION                         ;
*----------------------------------------------------------;
RANRD:LINK SETRAW;
        IF FIELD1='' THEN DO;
            IF FIELD3¬='' THEN DO;
                _ID_=FIELD3; _NAME_=FIELD2; _RANGE_=FIELD4;
                OUTPUT ROWRANG;
                END;
            IF FIELD5¬='' THEN DO;
                _ID_=FIELD5; _NAME_=FIELD2; _RANGE_=FIELD6;
                OUTPUT ROWRANG;
                END;
            END;
        ELSE IF FIELD1='OU' THEN GO TO BUNRD;
        ELSE IF FIELD1='ND' THEN STOP;
        GO TO RANRD;
*----------------------------------------------------------;
*           READ THE BOUND SECTION                         ;
*----------------------------------------------------------;
BUNRD:LINK SETRAW;
        IF FIELD1='LO' THEN DO;
            _NAME_=FIELD3; _ID_='_LO_'; _VALUE_=FIELD4; OUTPUT ROWLBND;
            END;
        ELSE IF FIELD1='UP' THEN DO;
            _NAME_=FIELD3; _ID_='_UP_'; _VALUE_=FIELD4; OUTPUT ROWUBND;
            END;
        ELSE IF FIELD1='MI' THEN DO;
            _NAME_=FIELD3; _ID_='_LO_'; _VALUE_=-INFINITY; OUTPUT ROWUBND;
            END;
        ELSE IF FIELD1='FX' THEN DO;
            _NAME_=FIELD3; _ID_='_UP_'; _VALUE_=FIELD4; OUTPUT ROWUBND;
            _NAME_=FIELD3; _ID_='_LO_'; _VALUE_=FIELD4; OUTPUT ROWLBND;
             END;
        ELSE IF FIELD1='FR' THEN DO;
            _NAME_=FIELD3; _ID_='_UNRS_'; _VALUE_=1; OUTPUT ROWUNRS;
            END;
        ELSE IF FIELD1='ND' THEN STOP;
        GO TO BUNRD;
RUN;
*----------------------------------------------------------;
*  THIS SECTION SORTS DATASETS FOR LATER USE               ;
*----------------------------------------------------------;
PROC SORT DATA=COLSCAL; BY _NAME_ ;
PROC SORT DATA=ROWINT;  BY _NAME_ ;
PROC SORT DATA=ROWUBND; BY _NAME_ ;
PROC SORT DATA=ROWLBND; BY _NAME_ ;
PROC SORT DATA=ROWUNRS; BY _NAME_ ;
PROC SORT DATA=ROWS;    BY _NAME_ ;
RUN;
```

```
*-----------------------------------------------------;
*    THIS SECTION ADDS BOUNDING ROWS AND INTEGER ROWS,  ;
*            AND SCALES THE COLUMNS                      ;
*-----------------------------------------------------;
DATA ROWINT; SET ROWINT;
   IF _NAME_=LAG(_NAME_) THEN DELETE;
DATA ROWS;
   SET COLSCAL(IN=SCLFLG) ROWS ROWLBND ROWUBND ROWUNRS
       ROWINT;
     BY _NAME_ ;
   DROP SCALE S;
   RETAIN S;
   IF SCLFLG THEN DO; S=SCALE; DELETE; END;
   IF S¬=. THEN _VALUE_=_VALUE_/S;
RUN;


*-----------------------------------------------------;
*    TRANSPOSE ROWS DATASET INTO RECTANGULAR FORM       ;
*        AND SAVE IN PROB DATASET                       ;
*-----------------------------------------------------;
PROC SORT DATA=ROWS OUT=PROB(RENAME=(_NAME_=NAME));
   BY _ID_ _NAME_;
PROC TRANSPOSE DATA=PROB OUT=PROB(DROP=_NAME_);
   BY _ID_; ID NAME;
RUN;
*-----------------------------------------------------;
*    THIS SECTION SORTS DATASETS FOR LATER USE          ;
*-----------------------------------------------------;
PROC SORT DATA=PROB;    BY _ID_;
PROC SORT DATA=ROWTYPE; BY _ID_;
PROC SORT DATA=ROWSCAL; BY _ID_;
PROC SORT DATA=ROWRANG; BY _ID_;
RUN;
*-----------------------------------------------------;
* DEFINE NEW ROWS FROM LINEAR COMBINATIONS OF           ;
*                 OTHER ROWS                            ;
*-----------------------------------------------------;
PROC SORT DATA=ROWNEW;  BY ROW1 ;
DATA ROWAD1;
   MERGE ROWNEW(RENAME=(ROW1=_ID_) IN=INA) PROB; BY _ID_;
   ARRAY X(*) _NUMERIC_;
   RETAIN C1;
   C1=COEFF1;
   DROP C1 COEFF1 COEFF2 ROW2 _ID_ I;
   IF INA THEN DO;
      DO I=1 TO DIM(X);
         IF X(I)=. THEN X(I)=0; X(I)=X(I)*C1;
         END;
      OUTPUT;
      END;
PROC SORT DATA=ROWNEW;  BY ROW2 ;
DATA ROWAD2;
   MERGE ROWNEW(RENAME=(ROW2=_ID_) IN=INA) PROB; BY _ID_;
   ARRAY X(*) _NUMERIC_;
   RETAIN C2;
```

```
      C2=COEFF2;
      DROP C2 COEFF1 COEFF2 ROW1 _ID_ I;
      IF INA THEN DO;
         DO I=1 TO DIM(X);
            IF X(I)=. THEN X(I)=0; X(I)=X(I)*C2;
            END;
         OUTPUT;
         END;
PROC SORT DATA=ROWAD1; BY ROWNEW;
PROC SORT DATA=ROWAD2; BY ROWNEW;
DATA ROWADD;
   SET ROWAD1 ROWAD2; BY ROWNEW;
   ARRAY X(*) _NUMERIC_;
   DROP  Y I;
   DO I=1 TO DIM(X);
      Y=LAG(X(I));
      IF LAST.ROWNEW THEN X(I)=X(I)+Y;
      END;
   IF LAST.ROWNEW THEN OUTPUT;
RUN;
*---------------------------------------------------------;
* THIS SECTION SCALES THE ROWS, APPENDS THE TYPE          ;
* IDENTIFIER COLUMN, DOES SETUP FOR ROW RANGING,          ;
* AND MERGES NEW ROWS.                                    ;
*---------------------------------------------------------;
DATA PROB; MERGE PROB
                   ROWTYPE
                   ROWADD(RENAME=(ROWNEW=_ID_))
                   ROWRANG(DROP=_NAME_)
                   ROWSCAL(IN=SCLFLG KEEP=_ID_ SCALE);
            BY _ID_;
   ARRAY X(*) _NUMERIC_;
   IF SCLFLG=1 THEN DO I=1 TO DIM(X); X(I)=X(I)/SCALE; END;
   DROP SCALE I;
        IF _ID_='_UP_'   THEN _TYPE_='UPPERBD';
   ELSE IF _ID_='_LO_'   THEN _TYPE_='LOWERBD';
   ELSE IF _ID_='_UNRS_' THEN _TYPE_='UNRSTRCT';
   ELSE IF _ID_='_INT_'  THEN _TYPE_='INTEGER';
RUN;
%MEND;
```

Version 5 Changes and Enhancements to SAS/OR™ Software

NEW PROCEDURES

GANTT   prints Gantt charts on the line printer and high resolution graphics devices.

CHANGES TO EXISTING PROCEDURES

CPM   schedules projects subject to structural precedence constraints as before, but also subject to resource constraints and time constraints on each of the activities.

             summarizes resource utilization for the schedules it calculates in a SAS data set.

LP   handles integer and mixed-integer problems.

        performs parametric programming and range analysis.

        enables interactive control of solution process.

TIMEPLOT   is now part of the base SAS software product.

Additional changes have been made to:

- LINPROG matrix subroutine, which is no longer documented in this manual, and
- SASMPSX macro.

242

Operating System Notes

INTRODUCTION

This appendix provides a general description of the basic functions of an operating system and how the operating system and the SAS System interact to execute your SAS program. You will also learn about SAS features that relate to file access.

A detailed section for each operating system includes examples to illustrate these features.

To use SAS software products, you do not need to be an expert on operating systems; however, as you learn more about your operating system, you will be able to do more with SAS. After reading this material, you should have a better idea of how the operating system and the SAS System work together and where to find more information.

THE OPERATING SYSTEM

Your SAS programs execute in an environment controlled by a set of powerful programs called an *operating system*. The operating system controls all work done by the computer, such as allocating computer resources to run programs and storing data. Because an operating system oversees activities of the computer, it is sometimes called the *host environment*.

There are different operating systems for different types of computers. However, all operating systems are designed to handle certain basic tasks:

- accept jobs for execution
- store and retrieve data files
- manage terminal sessions
- allocate resources, such as internal memory, time, and disk space, to individual jobs
- control the action of peripheral equipment, such as printers, plotters, and disk and tape drives.

In the same way that you communicate with the SAS System using the SAS language, you communicate with an operating system using the operating system's language. We refer to operating system languages generally as *control languages*. **Table A3.1** lists the types of computers and operating systems under which the SAS System runs, and it gives the commonly used names of their control languages.

INTERACTIONS BETWEEN THE OPERATING SYSTEM AND THE SAS USER

Each time a SAS program executes, many interactions between the SAS System and the operating system occur. The amount of interaction that you need to be aware of depends on your program.

Consider the following example:

```
DATA WEATHER;
   INPUT TEMP PRECIP SUNHRS;
   CARDS;
85.5 0.00 12.33
84.2 0.09 12.31
79.5 0.10 12.30
;
PROC PRINT DATA=WEATHER;
   TITLE 'WEATHER INFORMATION';
```

Table A3.1 Computers, Operating Systems, and Control Languages

Computers	Operating Systems	Control Language Name
Data General ECLIPSE MV	AOS/VS	Command Line interpreter (CLI)
Digital VAX	VMS	Digital Command Language (DCL)
IBM and compatible mainframes*	OS	Job Control Language (JCL)
	TSO (OS interactive)	TSO Command Language
	CMS	CMS and CP Command Language
	VM/PC	CMS and CP Command Language
	VSE	Job Control Language (JCL)
	ICCF (VSE interactive)	ICCF Command Language
PRIME	PRIMOS	Command Procedure Language (CPL)

*The 370, 308X, and 4300 series are examples of IBM mainframes.
Amdahl 470 V6 is an example of an IBM-compatible mainframe.

Even in the simplest SAS execution, like this one, you need to be aware of two interactions:

1. *Invoking SAS.* You make a request to the operating system to use the SAS software.
2. *Receiving output.* The output from a SAS program is printed, displayed on a terminal, or written to a file.

Many of the SAS programs you write may involve no more interaction than our example. However, you need to be aware of two fairly common situations in SAS programming that require you to specify information to the operating system:

1. *Defining permanent files.* You can define a file when you want to read or write data that are stored independently from your SAS program.
2. *Rerouting output.* You can send output from a SAS program to the destination of your choice rather than to its default destination.

The following pages discuss each of these common situations in more detail.

Invoking the SAS System

In order to run a SAS program, you must issue a request to the operating system to use the SAS System. The request is made using the operating system's control language, for example, with the SAS command:

    SAS

When the request is received, the operating system executes a set of instructions that makes all the components of the SAS System (such as statements, procedures, formats, and functions) available to your SAS job. The operating system also provides space in the computer's main memory in which to execute the SAS program.

You can invoke SAS to execute in *batch mode, noninteractive mode,* or *interactive mode.* The mode determines how your program executes, as described below:

Batch Mode

Submit a group of control language statements and SAS statements to the operating system. The control language and SAS statements may be stored in a file or may be in a stack of cards. When you submit the job, the operating system schedules (enqueues) the job for execution. Once execution begins, you cannot alter the job or the execution process.

Noninteractive Mode

Create a file containing your SAS program only (with no control language). When you enter the command to invoke SAS from your terminal, you also enter the name of the file containing your SAS program. The operating system invokes SAS, locates the file, and executes the program. This mode is similar to batch in that once execution begins, you cannot alter the execution process. However, execution does proceed immediately; the job is not enqueued.

Interactive Mode

(also called *conversational* mode) Issue a command to invoke SAS from your terminal. One of two things happens:

- You will begin a *line-prompt session* in which SAS prompts you, usually with a line number and question mark, to enter your SAS program line by line. Your program executes one step at a time as you enter the statements.
- You will begin a *display manager session* in which you enter the SAS program on the program editor screen and issue the SUBMIT command to submit the code to SAS.

Whether your session is in line-prompt or display manager mode depends on the setting of the SAS system option DMS|NODMS and the kind of terminal you have. To use display manager, you must have a full-screen terminal and DMS must be in effect. Line-prompt mode occurs when your terminal is not full screen or when NODMS is in effect.

The **Details** section for your operating system illustrates how to invoke SAS. Also see the "SAS Display Manager" appendix of this book for information on executing SAS programs in a display manager session.

Receiving the Output

The set of instructions that the operating system executes when you invoke SAS includes requests telling the operating system where to send the output from the SAS job. This is called the *default destination.* SAS output consists of two main parts: 1) the SAS log, which contains the SAS statements used in the job, notes, and error messages; and 2) the SAS procedure output. All SAS jobs output a SAS log; however, not all SAS jobs produce procedure output.

The default destination of the SAS output depends on the execution mode:

- For a batch job the default destination is often a printer or a disk file.
- In noninteractive mode the SAS log and procedure output are displayed on the screen after the entire job executes.

- In interactive line-prompt mode, the SAS log and procedure output are displayed on the terminal screen as each step of your program executes instead of after the entire job executes.
- In interactive display manager mode, lines written to the SAS log appear on the SAS log screen; procedure output displays on the procedure output screen.

You can change the default destination for SAS output by using proper control language and SAS system options. (See **Re-routing SAS Output**, below). For more information on SAS output, refer to the chapter "Log and Procedure Output" in the *SAS User's Guide: Basics*.

Defining Files

In many SAS programs you will want to read or write a *permanent file* (a file that is stored for later use.) For example, you may want a SAS program to read a file of data that are stored on tape in order to create a SAS data set that can be printed by PROC PRINT, or you may want to enter new data after a CARDS statement and then store the data in a permanent disk file for later use.

A permanent file resides in a storage location managed by the operating system. Thus, the SAS System must interact with the operating system to access a permanent file. You allow this interaction to take place by *defining* the permanent file(s) needed by your program.

SAS programs use two general kinds of files: *SAS files* and *external files*. SAS files are specially structured files that can be created and processed only by the SAS System. SAS data sets are the most commonly used of the SAS files. External files can be created and processed by other programming languages, as well as by SAS. For the most part, SAS procedures use SAS files.

Following is a general description of how to define permanent SAS and external files. Refer to **Details** for your operating system for examples that illustrate how to define files for programs that read and create external files and SAS files.

External files   To define a permanent external file, associate a fileref (short for "file reference") with the complete name of the external file. You then specify the fileref in SAS statements to refer to the external file. For example, if you are reading an external file, specify the fileref in the INFILE statement. If you are creating an external file, specify the fileref in the FILE statement.

In most cases you must explicitly associate the fileref with the complete name of the external file.[1] The method used to associate the fileref with the file's name differs for each operating system, so be sure to see the **Details** section for your operating system.

SAS files   To define a permanent SAS file, associate a *libref* (short for "library reference") with a permanent library of SAS files, called a *SAS data library*.[2] The **Details** section for your operating system includes complete instructions on how to associate a libref with a SAS data library in your environment.

After the file is defined, you use the libref as the first-level name of the SAS file's complete two-level name in any SAS statement that requests the file. For example, the name could be specified in a PROC, DATA, or SET statement.

Once defined, a libref can be used repeatedly in SAS statements in that job or session to refer to any existing SAS file in the library or to add SAS files to the library.

In most cases librefs and filerefs must follow the rules for SAS names. Exceptions, if any, are given in **Details** for your operating system. For a general discussion of SAS files, their names, and SAS data libraries, see the chapter "SAS Files" in the *SAS User's Guide: Basics*.

SAS statements used to request files   The following list contains a brief description of the SAS statements that are used to request files. If you use one of these statements to request a permanent file, the file must also be defined. See the next section for a list of SAS statements used to define permanent files. All of these statements are fully described in the *SAS User's Guide: Basics*:

DATA   initiates the DATA step and allows you to create a SAS data set. If the data set is permanent, you must define the SAS library in which to store it unless your operating system is one that defines it for you (see **Details**).

FILE   specifies a fileref that refers to an external file. Subsequent PUT statements write to this file. Refer to **Details** for your operating system for information on how to define an external file.

%INCLUDE   specifies a fileref that refers to an external file containing SAS statements that you want to execute. Refer to **Details** for your operating system for information on how to define an external file.

INFILE   specifies a fileref that refers to an external file to be read by the SAS program. Refer to **Details** for your operating system for information on how to define an external file.

PROC   uses an option to refer to a SAS library or an external file that is to be read or created. For those procedures that can read and create files in the same execution, more than one option can be specified to refer to the appropriate SAS library or external file. When the procedure uses an entire SAS library, the value of the option is a libref. The value is a two-level permanent SAS file name when the procedure uses a SAS file within the library. If the procedure reads from or writes to an external file, the value of the option is a fileref.

SET
MERGE
UPDATE   read and manipulate observations in SAS data sets. If a data set being accessed by one of these statements is permanent, you must define the SAS library in which it is stored unless your operating system is one that defines the library for you (see **Details**).

SAS statements used to define files   The following list contains a brief description of the SAS statements that are used to define permanent files. Note that under some operating systems, only control language can be used to define a file, not SAS statements. Be sure to read the **Details** section for your operating system. All of these statements are fully described in the *SAS User's Guide: Basics*:

FILENAME   specifies a fileref with a complete file name, which includes a directory name and the name of a specific file in the directory. If the FILENAME statement does not precede a SAS statement that specifies a fileref, the SAS System uses a file in the current default directory.

LIBNAME   associates a libref with a directory name. This statement must precede a SAS statement that specifies the libref.[3]

> LIBSEARCH   establishes a search list of directories by specifying a list of librefs. Each libref listed must be associated with a directory in a LIBNAME statement. LIBSEARCH must follow LIBNAME statements that define the directories.[4]
>
> X   allows you to issue operating system commands from within your SAS program if executing in interactive or noninteractive mode.[5] If the X statement is used to issue an operating system command to define a permanent file, it must precede the statement that refers to that file (see **Details**).

Re-routing SAS Output

As discussed above, the default destination of SAS output is determined by the mode of execution. You can change the default destination with the proper control language or with SAS options. For example, if you are executing SAS in display manager mode, by default the SAS log appears on the log screen, and the procedure output appears on the output screen. You can copy the SAS log and procedure output with the PRINT command of display manager.

When you re-route output, you must override default output handling. This endeavor is both operating system- and site-specific. The method you use will also depend on what you want to do. For example, you can route your output to a particular printer or terminal, or you can even route it to a permanent file. Use the following sources of information to learn how to route output:

* *SAS User's Guide: Basics*. Look for SAS system options used to re-route output on your operating system.
* SAS Companion or Technical Report for your operating system. Look for options and control language used to re-route output.
* The SAS consultant at your site.

DETAILS FOR THE AOS/VS OPERATING SYSTEM

The SAS System running under the AOS/VS operating system is documented in "Changes and Enhancements in the Base SAS and SAS/GRAPH Products under AOS/VS," SAS Technical Report P-129.

Invoking the SAS System

Enter the SAS command after you receive the) prompt:

) SAS
or

) SAS/options
or

) SAS filename

If you enter *SAS* you will invoke the SAS System in interactive mode. Use the second method to specify valid *options* when you invoke SAS. For example, you can specify *SAS/FSDEVICE=devicename* to invoke SAS in display manager mode. With the third method, you can specify *SAS filename* to give the name of a file containing the SAS program to be executed. This method is called *noninteractive mode*.

Note that the SAS command is a CLI macro file that contains a set of control language instructions to invoke the SAS System.

Read more about the SAS command in SAS Technical Report P-129. For information on executing SAS in batch mode see P-129 and the *AOS/VS CLI User's Manual.*

Defining Files

How you define a file depends on whether the file is a SAS or non-SAS (external) file. The method that you use allows the SAS System to distinguish between SAS files and external files.

External files You can define an external file in one of the following two ways:

- with the CREATE/LINK command of the CLI control language before you invoke the SAS System
- in the FILENAME statement within your SAS program.

With either method you associate a *fileref* with a complete file name. The complete file name includes the directory name and the name of a specific file within the directory. You can also issue the CREATE/LINK command in the X statement, a SAS statement that allows you to enter CLI commands in your SAS program.

The fileref is then used in SAS statements, such as FILE and INFILE, to refer to the external file. If you specify a fileref in a SAS statement before you define the external file, the SAS System reads or creates a file in the current default directory with the following name:

```
:UDD:currentdefaultdirectory:fileref
```

where *fileref* is specified in the INFILE statement to give the name of the file that is read from the current default directory or where *fileref* is specified in the FILE statement to give the name of the file being created in the current default directory.

SAS files If you want to read or create a SAS file, you must define the appropriate directory with the LIBNAME statement. In the LIBNAME statement you associate a *libref* with a directory name only. The libref is then specified in SAS statements, such as DATA, SET, MERGE, and so on, to refer to the directory. Once you have defined a directory in the LIBNAME statement, you can use the associated libref to refer to any file in that directory.

If you do not specify the LIBNAME statement before you use the libref in a SAS statement, you will receive an error message that the directory to which you are referring cannot be found.

Note: discussion of SAS files in the following examples is limited to the most commonly used type, a **SAS data set**. A SAS data set is a SAS file containing observations and variables.

Methods for defining SAS data sets and external files are illustrated in the following sections.

Reading an External File

The following program reads an external file and includes a FILENAME statement to define the external file:

```
) SAS (invoke the SAS System)
SAS messages
1? FILENAME DAILY ':UDD:YOURDIR1:YOUR.RAW.DATA';
2? DATA WEATHER;
3?    INFILE DAILY;
more SAS statements
```

```
7? ENDSAS;
```

The FILENAME statement associates the fileref DAILY with the complete file name, and DAILY is then specified in the INFILE statement. Note that the complete file name includes a directory named YOURDIR1 and the file YOUR.RAW. DATA within the directory.

You can also use the CREATE/LINK to define the external file before you invoke the SAS System. For example:

```
CREATE/LINK DAILY :UDD:YOURDIR1:YOUR.RAW.DATA
```

If you use the CREATE/LINK command, you do not need the FILENAME statement. If you chose to define the file by issuing the CREATE/LINK command with the X statement, you can simply replace the FILENAME statement in the above program with the following SAS statement:

```
X 'CREATE/LINK DAILY :UDD:YOURDIR1:YOUR.RAW.DATA';
```

Since the X statement is a SAS statement, be sure to put a semicolon at the end.

If you do not define the external file, the SAS System will read (or attempt to read) a file from the current default directory with the following name:

```
:UDD:currentdefaultdirectory:DAILY
```

Reading a SAS Data Set

Use the LIBNAME statement to define the directory containing the SAS data set to be read, as shown in the following program:

```
) SAS (invoke the SAS System)
SAS messages
1? LIBNAME REPORT ':UDD:DIR2';
2? PROC PRINT DATA=REPORT.STATION;
3?    VAR A B C;
more SAS messages
4? ENDSAS;
```

The LIBNAME statement associates the libref REPORT with the directory :UDD:DIR2. REPORT is then used as the first level of the permanent SAS data set name REPORT.STATION in the PROC PRINT statement. When this program executes, the SAS System reads a SAS data set named STATION from the directory named :UDD:DIR2 and prints the values for variables A, B, and C.

If the LIBNAME statement is omitted or does not precede the PROC PRINT statement, you will receive an error message stating that the directory cannot be found.

Creating a SAS Data Set

Use the LIBNAME statement to define a directory in which to store a newly created SAS data set. The following program creates a SAS data set using an external file as input:

```
) SAS (invoke the SAS System)
SAS messages
1? FILENAME DAILY ':UDD:YOURDIR1:YOUR.RAW.DATA';
2? LIBNAME MAP ':UDD:YOURDIR2';
3? DATA MAP.WEATHER;
4?    INFILE DAILY;
more SAS statements and messages
```

```
5? ENDSAS;
```

The LIBNAME statement associates the libref MAP with YOURDIR2, the directory in which the SAS data set WEATHER is stored. MAP is then used as the first level of the permanent SAS data set name in the DATA statement. The FILENAME statement associates DAILY with the directory YOURDIR1 and the file YOUR. RAW.DATA, the input file.

If the LIBNAME statement is omitted, you will receive an error message stating that the directory cannot be found. If you do not specify the FILENAME statement, the SAS System will search the current default directory for a file named DAILY.

Creating an External File

Since the following program creates an external file, use the FILENAME statement to associate the fileref with the complete file name. The complete file name includes the directory name and the name of the file that is created within that directory. Since the following program uses a SAS data set as input, you must use a LIBNAME statement to define the appropriate directory:

```
) SAS (invoke the SAS System)
(SAS messages)
1? LIBNAME MAP ':UDD:DIR2'
2? FILENAME FREEZE ':UDD:DIR3:COLD.RAW.DATA';
3? DATA _NULL_;
4?    SET MAP.WEATHER;
5?    FILE FREEZE;
6?    IF TEMP < 32 THEN PUT TEMP;
more SAS statements and messages
9? ENDSAS;
```

The FILENAME statement associates FREEZE with the complete file name :UDD:DIR3:COLD.RAW.DATA. FREEZE is then specified in the FILE statement. You can also issue the CREATE/LINK command (before you invoke the SAS System or in the X statement) to define the external file.

If you do not define the external file for the above program, the SAS System will create a file in the current default directory with the following name:

```
:UDD:currentdefaultdirectory:FREEZE
```

DETAILS FOR THE CMS OPERATING SYSTEM

The SAS System running under the CMS operating System is documented in the *SAS Companion for the VM/CMS Operating System.*

Invoking the SAS System

Enter the SAS command after you receive the READY or R; prompt:

```
R;   (or READY)
SAS filename (options)
```

If your SAS program is stored in a file, specify the *filename* after the SAS command. Invoking the SAS System to execute in this way is called *noninteractive mode.* If you want to invoke SAS in interactive mode do not specify a filename. If you want to specify any of the valid *options* for the SAS command, enter a right parenthesis, followed by the options. The DMS | NODMS option and the type of terminal you are using determine whether you enter a line-prompt or display manager session. If you have a full-screen terminal and DMS is in effect, you enter display manager. If your terminal is not full screen or NODMS is in effect, you enter a line-prompt interactive session.

Note that the SAS command is a CMS command created by the SAS Institute that contains a set of control language instructions to invoke the SAS System.

Read more about the SAS command in the *SAS Companion for the VM/CMS Operating System*. To learn about running a SAS job in a CMS batch machine, refer to the *IBM Virtual/System Product: CMS User's Guide*.

Defining Files

The CMS command FILEDEF is used to define files for use in SAS programs. The FILEDEF command associates a *libref* with a SAS file or a *fileref* with an external (non-SAS) file. The libref or fileref is called a *DDname* in CMS terminology. The form of the FILEDEF command is

```
FILEDEF DDname device filename filetype filemode(options)
```

where

- *DDname* serves as a SAS file's libref or an external file's fileref
- *device* indicates the file's storage medium (usually DISK or TAPE)
- *filename* and *filetype* are the names by which CMS knows the file
- *filemode* is a letter (or letter/number combination) indicating the minidisk on which the file is stored (for disk files only)
- *options* are any of a number of CMS options for the FILEDEF command.

In most cases, you do not have to issue the FILEDEF explicitly to define a SAS file because the SAS System issues the FILEDEF automatically. You must explicitly issue the FILEDEF for an external file.

A FILEDEF can be issued before the SAS System is invoked or after SAS is invoked in an X or CMS statement. In any case, the FILEDEF must be issued before the SAS statement that references the file.

Special Naming Conventions

Although the SAS System allows you to use an underscore (_) in SAS names, CMS does not. Therefore, do not use an underscore character in a libref or a fileref.

Reading an External File

Issue a FILEDEF command to associate a fileref with the external file to be read. Then, use the fileref in the INFILE statement of your SAS program. For example, suppose you write a DATA step that reads the external disk file CLIMATE DATA, which is stored on your A-disk, and you want to use DAILY as the fileref:

```
R;
FILEDEF DAILY DISK CLIMATE DATA A
R;
SAS (invoke the SAS System)
(SAS messages)
1?
DATA WEATHER;
2?
INFILE DAILY;
3?
INPUT TEMP PRECIP SUNHRS;
```

```
4?
more SAS statements
```

The fileref DAILY points to the CMS file CLIMATE DATA A.

Reading a SAS Data Set

Under most circumstances you do not need to define a libref explicitly for a SAS file because SAS makes the association automatically. To access an existing SAS file on any minidisk, just use the file's two-level name in the appropriate SAS statement. SAS searches all accessed minidisks for the file you have specified and issues the appropriate FILEDEF when it finds the file. For example, suppose the SAS data set FOOD.PRICES is stored on your B-disk. When SAS reads this statement:

```
SET FOOD.PRICES;
```

it searches all accessed minidisks for a data set with filename PRICES and filetype FOOD. When it finds PRICES FOOD B, this FILEDEF is automatically issued:

```
FILEDEF FOOD DISK PRICES FOOD B
```

Note: if you have multiple SAS files with the same filename and filetype on different minidisks, SAS will find only the file on the minidisk that is first in the search order. For example, if you have a PRICES FOOD A and a PRICES FOOD B, SAS will find PRICES FOOD A. You must issue a FILEDEF for PRICES FOOD B explicitly if you want to access it.

Creating a SAS Data Set

Under most circumstances, you do not need to define a libref explicitly to create a SAS file because SAS makes the association automatically. When you are creating a new SAS file and you specify a two-level SAS name, SAS automatically issues a FILEDEF using the libref (first-level name) for the DDname parameter **and** for the filetype unless a FILEDEF with that DDname is already in effect. By default, the data set will be written to your A-disk. For example, suppose you are creating a SAS data set called FOOD.PRICES:

```
DATA FOOD.PRICES;
    INPUT ... ;
more SAS statements
```

When SAS reads the name FOOD.PRICES, it checks to see if a FILEDEF with DDname FOOD has been issued. If there is no such FILEDEF, SAS issues one automatically, using FOOD for both the DDname and filetype, PRICES as the filename, and A as the filemode:

```
FILEDEF FOOD DISK PRICES FOOD A
```

Note: do not use the same filetype for SAS files and external (non-SAS) files.

If you want a new SAS data set to be stored on a disk other than your A-disk, you must issue the appropriate FILEDEF explicitly. Specify the appropriate values for the DDname and filemode parameters. You can specify any value for filename and filetype; SAS will substitute the libref (first-level name) and data set name (second-level name) for filetype and filename, respectively. For example, if you want to store FOOD.PRICES on a B-disk, your FILEDEF could be:

```
FILEDEF FOOD DISK DUMMY DUMMY B
```

Notice that CMS and SAS identify the file by the same two names, but the order is reversed. For example, SAS calls the data set FOOD.PRICES, and CMS calls it PRICES FOOD.

Creating an External File

To create an external file in a SAS program, first issue a FILEDEF command to associate a fileref with the name of the external file to be created. Then use the fileref in the FILE statement of your SAS program. For example, suppose you write a DATA step that reads the external disk file CLIMATE DATA, (which is stored on your A-disk) and creates a second external file called COLD TEMPS A. You use the filerefs DAILY and FREEZE to reference the files:

```
R;
FILEDEF DAILY DISK CLIMATE DATA A
R;
FILEDEF FREEZE DISK COLD TEMPS A
R;
SAS
1?
DATA _NULL_;
2?
INFILE DAILY;
3?
INPUT TEMP PRECIP SUNHRS;
4?
FILE FREEZE;
5?
more SAS statements
```

DETAILS FOR THE OS OPERATING SYSTEM AND TSO

The SAS System running under the OS operating system is documented in the *SAS Companion for the OS Operating System and TSO.*

OS Batch

Invoking the SAS System　Use the EXEC statement in your JCL:

```
// EXEC SAS,OPTIONS='options'
```

In this case, the OS cataloged procedure named *SAS* contains all the job control language instructions to invoke the SAS System in batch mode. The *OPTIONS=* parameter can be used to specify valid SAS system options.

Read more about the SAS cataloged procedure in the *SAS Companion for OS Operating System and TSO.*

Defining files　Use the DD (Data Definition) statement to define permanent files, both SAS and external files. The DD statement associates a *fileref* with a permanent external file or a *libref* with a permanent library of SAS files. In OS terminology the fileref or the libref is called a *DDname.*

The external file can be an OS sequential data set or a partitioned data set (PDS). A sequential data set contains records stored in a sequence under a unique name. If the external file is a sequential data set, you associate a fileref with the sequential data set name in the DD statement, as follows:

```
//fileref DD DSN=external.file.name,DISP=disposition
```

The *fileref* is then specified in SAS statements, such as INFILE and FILE, to refer to the external file. For example,

```
INFILE fileref;
```

A PDS contains a group of data sets called members. The PDS has a name that identifies the group. Each member within the PDS has a unique name. You can identify one member by enclosing the member name in parentheses and including it as the last level of the PDS name. For example, if you want to define an external file that is a member of a PDS, you must specify the DD statement as follows:

```
//fileref DD DSN=external.file.name(member),DISP=disposition
```

In this case you only have access to the member specified. Then, you use the fileref in SAS statements, such as INFILE and FILE, to refer to that member.

To have access to all members of the PDS, use the PDS name only (without a member name) in the DD statement, as follows:

```
//fileref DD DSN=external.file.name,DISP=disposition
```

When you define the PDS in this way, you include the member name in parentheses after the fileref to refer to the specific member in the PDS. For example,

```
INFILE fileref(member1);
FILE fileref(member2);
```

The above statements refer to two members of the same PDS.

If you use a fileref in a SAS statement that is not associated with an external file in the DD statement, you will receive an error message indicating that the file to which you are referring has not been defined.

A group of SAS files is called a *SAS data library*. Once defined, all SAS files within the library are accessible. For example,

```
//libref DD DSN=SAS.library.name,DISP=disposition
```

Then use the *libref* in SAS statements, such as DATA, SET, and MERGE, to refer to the SAS library. You refer to a specific file within the library by including the SAS file name after the libref. The libref and the SAS file name are always separated by a period. For example,

```
DATA libref.SASname;
```

In some SAS statements, such as certain PROC statements, you use only the libref to refer to the entire SAS library. The utility procedure DATASETS is a good example:

```
PROC DATASETS LIBRARY=libref;
```

All of the SAS files in the library referred to by the libref are available to be processed by the DATASETS procedure.

A SAS library can contain several different types of SAS files. The discussion of SAS files in this section is limited to the most commonly used type, a **SAS data set**. A SAS data set is a SAS file that contains observations and variables.

If you use a libref in a SAS statement that is not associated with a SAS library in the DD statement, you will receive an error message indicating that the file to which you are referring has not been defined.

The DISP= parameter   Each of the DD statement examples includes a DISP= parameter. DISP= specifies a disposition (status) for the file at the beginning and end of the job. The disposition also implies an access method. (Refer to the *SAS Companion for OS Operating Systems and TSO* for details on specifying the DISP= parameter in the DD statement.) All of the examples in the following sections use existing files and, therefore, specify either DISP=OLD to obtain exclusive access to an existing file or DISP=SHR to obtain shared access to an existing file.

If your SAS program writes to an existing SAS library, you must specify DISP=OLD in the DD statement because you are updating the library. You must have exclusive access to a SAS library to update it. The need to specify DISP=OLD is noted for the following examples, where appropriate.

Methods for defining SAS libraries and external files are illustrated in the following sections.

Reading an external file   To read an external file you must include a DD statement in the JCL used to invoke the SAS System. In the following job:

```
//jobname JOB accountinginformation
// EXEC SAS
//DAILY DD DSN=YOUR.RAW.DATA(MON),DISP=SHR
//SYSIN DD *
DATA WEATHER;
   INFILE DAILY;
   INPUT TEMP PRECIP SUNHRS;
more SAS statements
```

the DD statement associates the fileref DAILY with the external file YOUR.RAW. DATA(MON). Notice that the external file is a PDS and the member MON is specified. DAILY is then used in the INFILE statement to refer to the external file.

Reading a SAS data set   You also use the DD statement to define a permanent SAS library. The DD statement in the following job associates the libref REPORT with the SAS library named YOUR.SAS.LIB. REPORT is then specified as the first level of a permanent SAS data set name in the PROC PRINT statement.

```
//jobname JOB accountinginformation
// EXEC SAS
//REPORT DD DSN=YOUR.SAS.LIB,DISP=SHR
//SYSIN DD *
PROC PRINT DATA=REPORT.STATION;
   VAR A B C;
```

The association is necessary to allow the SAS System to read a SAS data set named STATION from the SAS library YOUR.SAS.LIB. When the program executes, PROC PRINT locates STATION and prints the values of the variables A, B, and C.

Note: in the DD statement YOUR.SAS.LIB is an existing SAS library defined with DISP=SHR to allow for shared use of the SAS library that is being read.

Creating a SAS data set   The following program creates a SAS data set using an external file as input. Use the DD statement to define the existing SAS library in which to store the SAS data set created by this program. You must also define the external file in a DD statement:

```
//jobname JOB accountinginformation
// EXEC SAS
//DAILY DD DSN=YOUR.RAW.DATA(MON),DISP=SHR
//MAP DD DSN=YOUR.SAS.LIB,DISP=OLD
//SYSIN DD *
DATA MAP.WEATHER;
   INFILE DAILY;
more SAS statements
```

The first DD statement associates the fileref DAILY with the permanent external file named YOUR.RAW.DATA(MON). Notice that you again refer to a specific member of a PDS. The second DD statement associates the libref MAP with the existing SAS library named YOUR.SAS.LIB. MAP is then used as the first level of the permanent SAS data set name in the DATA statement. The SAS data set WEATHER created by this program is stored in YOUR.SAS.LIB.

Note: in contrast to the previous example, the SAS library must be defined with DISP=OLD because it is existing and because the SAS System will not allow you to write to a SAS library defined with shared access (DISP=SHR). Remember, if your program updates a SAS library, you must have exclusive access to the library.

Creating an external file   If your SAS program creates an external file, you must use a DD statement to define the file. The following program creates an external file using a SAS data set as input; therefore, you must include two DD statements in the JCL used to invoke the SAS System:

```
//jobname JOB accountinginformation
// EXEC SAS
//MAP DD DSN=YOUR.SAS.LIB,DISP=SHR
//FREEZE DD DSN=COLD.RAW.DATA,DISP=OLD
//SYSIN  DD  *
DATA _NULL_;
   SET MAP.WEATHER;
   FILE FREEZE(JAN);
   IF TEMP < 32 THEN PUT TEMP;
more SAS statements
```

In this case the libref MAP refers to a file named YOUR.SAS.LIB, and MAP is then used as the first level of the permanent SAS data set name in the SET statement. The fileref FREEZE refers to a PDS named COLD.RAW.DATA. The member of the PDS (JAN) created by this program is specified in the FILE statement. FREEZE is then used in the FILE statement. When this program executes, the PUT statement writes all TEMP values less than 32 to the external file COLD.RAW. DATA(JAN).

TSO (OS Interactive)

Invoking the SAS System   Enter the TSO command after you receive the READY prompt:

```
READY
SAS OPTIONS('options')
```

or

```
SAS INPUT('''filename''')
```

Enter *SAS OPTIONS('options')* to invoke SAS in interactive mode and specify valid SAS *options*. The DMS|NODMS option and the type of terminal you use determine whether you enter a line-prompt or display manager session. If you use a full-screen terminal and if DMS is in effect, you enter a display manager session. If your terminal is not full screen or if NODMS is in effect, you enter a line-prompt session.

Enter *SAS INPUT('''filename''')* to invoke SAS in noninteractive mode and specify *filename* to give the name of the file containing the SAS program to be executed.

The SAS command is a TSO CLIST (Command LIST) that contains a set of control language instructions to invoke the SAS System.

Defining files   Use the ALLOCATE command of TSO to define permanent files— SAS files and external files. The ALLOCATE command associates a *fileref* with a permanent external file or a *libref* with a permanent library of SAS files. In TSO terminology a libref or fileref is called a *DDname*.

The external file can be an OS sequential data set or a partitioned data set (PDS). A sequential data set contains records stored in a sequence under a unique name. If the external file to be defined is a sequential data set, you associate a fileref with the sequential data set name in the ALLOCATE command, as follows:

```
ALLOCATE FILE(fileref) DATASET('external.file.name') disposition
```

The *fileref* is then specified in SAS statements, such as INFILE and FILE, to refer to the external file. For example,

```
INFILE fileref;
```

A PDS contains a group of data sets called members. The PDS has a name that identifies the group. Each member within the PDS has a unique name. You can identify one member by enclosing the member name in parentheses and including it as the last level of the PDS name. For example, if you want to define an external file that is a member of a PDS, you must specify the ALLOCATE command as follows:

```
ALLOCATE FILE(fileref)DATASET('external.file.name.(member)') disposition
```

In this case you only have access to the member specified. Then you use the fileref in SAS statements, such as INFILE and FILE, to refer to that member.

To have access to all members, give the PDS name only (without a member name) in the ALLOCATE command, as follows:

```
ALLOCATE FILE(fileref) DATASET('external.file.name') disposition
```

When you use the fileref in SAS statements, such as INFILE and FILE, you include the member name in parentheses after the fileref to refer to a specific member in the PDS. For example,

```
INFILE fileref(member1);
FILE fileref(member2);
```

The above statements refer to two members of the same PDS.

If you use a fileref in a SAS statement that is not associated with an external file in the ALLOCATE command, you will receive an error message indicating that the file to which you are referring has not been defined.

A group of SAS files is called a *SAS data library*. Once defined, all SAS files within the library can be accessed. For example,

```
ALLOCATE FILE(libref) DATASET('SAS.library.name')disposition
```

Then use the *libref* in SAS statements, such as DATA, SET, and MERGE, to refer to the SAS library. You refer to a specific file within the library by including the SAS file name after the libref. The libref and the SAS file name are always separated by a period. For example,

```
DATA libref.SASname;
```

In some SAS statements, such as certain PROC statements, you use only the libref to refer to the entire SAS library. The utility procedure DATASETS is a good example:

```
PROC DATASETS LIBRARY=libref;
```

All of the SAS files in the library referred to by the libref are available to be processed by the DATASETS procedure.

A SAS library can contain several different types of SAS files. The discussion of SAS files in this section is limited to one type, **SAS data sets**. A SAS data set is a SAS file that contains observations and variables.

If you use a libref in a SAS statement that is not associated with a SAS library in the ALLOCATE command, you will receive an error message indicating that the file to which you are referring has not been defined.

The disposition operand   Each ALLOCATE command example includes a disposition operand. *Disposition* specifies the status of the file at the beginning and end of the job and also implies an access method. (Refer to the *SAS Companion for OS Operating Systems and TSO* for details on specifying the disposition operand.) All of the examples in this section use existing files and, therefore, specify either OLD to obtain exclusive access to an existing file or SHR to obtain shared access to an existing file.

If your SAS program writes to an existing SAS library, you must specify a disposition of OLD in the ALLOCATE command because you are updating the library. You must have exclusive access to a SAS library to update it. The need to specify OLD is noted for the following examples, where appropriate.

If your TSO CLIST invokes the SASCP command, you can also issue the ALLOCATE command from within your SAS program with the X or TSO statement. If you use the X or TSO statement, be sure to include it before the SAS statement that requests the file. For example, the X statement that issues an ALLOCATE command to define an input file must be specified before the INFILE statement.

If you do not define the permanent files requested by your SAS program, you will receive an error message.

Methods for defining SAS libraries and external files are illustrated in the following sections.

Reading an external file   You can enter the ALLOCATE command before you invoke the SAS System to define the file to be read by the following program:

```
ALLOCATE FILE(DAILY) DATASET('YOUR.RAW.DATA(MON)') SHR
SAS  (invoke the SAS System)
SAS messages
1? DATA WEATHER;
2?   INFILE DAILY;
more SAS statements
6? ENDSAS;
```

The ALLOCATE command associates the fileref DAILY with the permanent external file YOUR.RAW.DATA(MON). Notice that you are defining a specific member of a PDS. DAILY is then specified in the INFILE statement. You can also define the file by issuing the ALLOCATE command in the X statement, as follows:

```
X ALLOCATE FILE(DAILY) DATASET('YOUR.RAW.DATA(MON)') SHR;
```

The X statement must precede the INFILE statement in the above program; otherwise, you will receive an error message indicating that you are referring to a file that has not been defined.

Reading a SAS data set   Use the ALLOCATE statement to define a permanent SAS library to be used as input. In the following example the ALLOCATE command associates the libref REPORT with the SAS library named YOUR.SAS.LIB. REPORT is then used as the first level of the permanent SAS data set name in the PROC PRINT statement:

```
SAS  (invoke the SAS System)
SAS messages
```

```
1? TSO ALLOCATE FILE(REPORT) DATASET('YOUR.SAS.LIB') SHR;
2? PROC PRINT DATA=REPORT.STATION;
3?    VAR A B C;
SAS messages
4? ENDSAS;
```

In this case, the TSO statement (the equivalent of the X statement under TSO) is used to issue the ALLOCATE command. When this program executes, PROC PRINT locates the data set named STATION and prints the values of the variables A, B, and C.

Creating a SAS data set   The following program creates a SAS data set using a permanent external file as input. Therefore, you must issue the ALLOCATE command twice: once to define the external file to be used as input, and once to define the SAS library in which to store WEATHER, the SAS data set created by this program:

```
ALLOCATE FILE(DAILY) DATASET('YOUR.RAW.DATA(MON)') SHR
ALLOCATE FILE(MAP) DATASET('YOUR.SAS.LIB') OLD
SAS  (invoke the SAS System)
SAS messages
1? DATA MAP.WEATHER;
2?    INFILE DAILY;
3?    INPUT TEMP PRECIP SUNHRS;
more SAS statements and messages
6? ENDSAS;
```

The first ALLOCATE command associates the fileref DAILY with the external file YOUR.RAW.DATA(MON), a specific PDS member. DAILY is then used in the INFILE statement. The second ALLOCATE command associates the libref MAP with the SAS library YOUR.SAS.LIB. MAP is then used as the first level of the permanent SAS data set name in the DATA statement. When this program executes, the permanent SAS data set WEATHER contains observations with variables TEMP, PRECIP, and SUNHRS.

Note: this program creates a new SAS data set in the SAS library YOUR.SAS.LIB and thereby updates the library. Notice that the YOUR.SAS.LIB is defined in the ALLOCATE command with a disposition of OLD.

Creating an external file   The following program creates an external file using a SAS data set as input. As before, you must issue the ALLOCATE command twice: once to define the permanent external file created by the program and once to define the permanent SAS library that is used as input:

```
ALLOCATE FILE(MAP) DATASET('YOUR.SAS.LIB') SHR
ALLOCATE FILE(FREEZE) DATASET('COLD.RAW.DATA') OLD
SAS  (invoke the SAS System)
SAS messages
1? DATA _NULL_;
2?    SET MAP.WEATHER;
3?    FILE FREEZE(JAN);
4?    IF TEMP < 32 THEN PUT TEMP;
more SAS statements
8? ENDSAS;
```

The first ALLOCATE command associates the libref MAP with the SAS library named YOUR.SAS.LIB. MAP is then used in the SET statement as the first level in the permanent SAS data set name MAP.WEATHER. The second ALLOCATE command associates the fileref FREEZE with a PDS named COLD.RAW.DATA.

FREEZE is then used in the FILE statement along with the PDS member JAN that is created by this program. When the program executes, the SAS data set WEATHER is read from the SAS library YOUR.SAS.LIB and all TEMP values less than 32 are written to the external file COLD.RAW.DATA(JAN).

DETAILS FOR THE PRIMOS OPERATING SYSTEM

The SAS System running under the PRIMOS operating system is documented in "Changes and Enhancements in the Base SAS and SAS/GRAPH Products under PRIMOS," SAS Technical Report P-130.

Invoking the SAS System

Enter the SAS command after you receive the OK, prompt:

    OK, SAS

or

    OK, SAS -options

or

    OK, SAS filename

If you enter *SAS* you will invoke the SAS System in interactive mode. Use the second method to specify valid *options* when you invoke SAS. For example, you can specify *SAS -FSDEVICE=devicename* to invoke SAS in display manager mode. With the third method, you can specify *filename* to give the name of a file containing the SAS program to be executed. This method is called *noninteractive mode*.

Read more about the SAS command in SAS Technical Report P-130.

For information on executing SAS in batch mode, refer to P-130 and *PRIMOS Command Reference Guide*.

Defining Files

How you define a file depends on whether the file is a SAS or non-SAS (external) file. The method that you use allows the SAS System to distinguish between SAS files and external files.

External files   Use the FILENAME statement to define an external file. In the FILENAME statement you associate the *fileref* with a complete file name, which includes the directory name and a specific file within the directory. The FILENAME statement must be included in the SAS program before a SAS statement that refers to the permanent external file. For example, if your program uses an external file as input, the FILENAME statement that defines the file must precede the INFILE statement.

If you do not define the external file to be read or created by your program, the SAS System reads or creates a file in the current directory with the following name:

    <masterfiledirectory>currentdirectory>fileref

where *fileref* is specified in the INFILE statement to give the name of the file that is read from the current default directory or where *fileref* is specified in the FILE statement to give the name of the file being created in the current default directory.

SAS files   If you want to read or create a permanent SAS file, you must define the appropriate directory with the LIBNAME statement. In the LIBNAME statement you associate a *libref* with a directory name only. The libref is then used in SAS statements, such as DATA, SET, MERGE, and so on, to refer to the directory. Once you have defined a directory in the LIBNAME statement, you can use the associated libref to refer to any file in that directory.

The LIBNAME statement must precede a SAS statement that refers to the SAS files (that is, a statement that specifies the libref); otherwise, you will get an error message stating that the directory to which you are referring cannot be found.

Note: when you specify the directory name in the LIBNAME statement or the complete file name (directory name and specific file in the directory) in the FILENAME statement, consider including the master file directory name in the specification. For example,

```
LIBNAME libref '<MASTERDIR>YOURDIR';
FILENAME fileref '<MASTERDIR>YOURDIR2>INPUT.STUFF';
```

Although PRIMOS does not require this level of specification, including the name of the master file directory in a directory specification will ensure that you get the file you want.

Note: discussion of SAS files in the following examples is limited to the most commonly used type, a **SAS data set**. A SAS data set is a SAS file containing observations and variables.

Methods for defining SAS data sets and external files are illustrated in the following sections.

Reading an External File

Use the FILENAME statement in the SAS program to define the file to be read. The FILENAME statement associates the fileref DAILY with the complete file name <MFD>YOURDIR1>YOUR.RAW.DATA:

```
OK, SAS (invoke the SAS System)
SAS messages
1? FILENAME DAILY '<MFD>YOURDIR1>YOUR.RAW.DATA';
2? DATA WEATHER;
3?    INFILE DAILY;
more SAS statements
7? ENDSAS;
```

DAILY is then used in the INFILE statement. If you do not specify the FILENAME statement, the SAS System searches the current directory for the following file:

```
<masterfiledirectory>currentdirectory>DAILY
```

Reading a SAS data set

Use the LIBNAME statement to define the directory containing the SAS data set to be read:

```
OK, SAS (invoke the SAS System)
SAS messages
1? LIBNAME REPORT '<MFD>DIR2';
2? PROC PRINT DATA=REPORT.STATION;
3?    VAR A B C;
more SAS messages
4? ENDSAS;
```

In the above program the LIBNAME statement associates the libref REPORT with the directory named <MFD>DIR2. REPORT is then used as the first level of the permanent SAS data set name REPORT.STATION in the PROC PRINT statement. This association is necessary to allow PROC PRINT to locate a SAS data set named STATION in this directory and print the values of variables A, B, and C.

If the LIBNAME statement is omitted or is not included before the SAS statement that specifies the libref, the SAS System will issue an error message that the directory cannot be found.

Creating a SAS Data Set

The following program creates a permanent SAS data set named WEATHER. You must use the LIBNAME statement to define the directory in which to store WEATHER. This program also uses a external file as input:

```
OK, SAS (invoke the SAS System)
SAS messages
1? FILENAME DAILY '<MFD>YOURDIR1>YOUR.RAW.DATA';
2? LIBNAME MAP '<MFD>YOURDIR2';
3? DATA MAP.WEATHER;
4?    INFILE DAILY;
more SAS statements and messages
5? ENDSAS;
```

In this case LIBNAME associates the libref MAP with the directory <MFD>YOURDIR2. MAP is then used as the first level of the SAS data set name in the DATA statement.

If the LIBNAME statement is omitted, you will receive an error message stating that the directory cannot be found. If you do not specify the FILENAME statement, the SAS System will search the current directory for a file named DAILY.

Creating an External File

The following program creates an external file using a SAS data set as input. Use the FILENAME statement to associate the fileref with the complete file name. The complete file name will include the directory name and the name of a file to be created in that directory. Use a LIBNAME statement to define the directory containing the SAS data set to be read:

```
OK, SAS (invoke the SAS System)
SAS messages
1? LIBNAME MAP '<MFD>YOURDIR2'
2? FILENAME FREEZE '<MFD>DIR3>COLD.RAW.DATA';
3? DATA _NULL_;
4?    SET MAP.WEATHER;
5?    FILE FREEZE;
6?    IF TEMP < 32 THEN PUT TEMP;
more SAS statements and messages
9? ENDSAS;
```

The LIBNAME statement associates the libref MAP with <MFD>YOURDIR2, the directory containing the SAS data set WEATHER. MAP is then used as the first level of a permanent SAS data set name in the SET statement.

When this program executes, all TEMP values less than 32 in the SAS data set WEATHER are written to an external file named COLD.RAW.DATA. This file is located in the directory <MFD>DIR3. If the FILENAME statement is omitted, the SAS System writes the values to a file in the current directory with the following name:

*<masterfiledirectory>currentdirectory>*FREEZE

DETAILS FOR THE VM/PC OPERATING SYSTEM

The SAS System running under the VM/PC operating system is documented in the *SAS Companion for the VM/CMS Operating System.*

Invoking the SAS System

Enter the SAS command after you receive the READY or R; prompt:

```
R;   (or READY)
SAS filename (options)
```

If your SAS program is stored in a file, specify the *filename* after the SAS command. Invoking the SAS System to execute in this way is called *noninteractive mode.* If you want to invoke SAS in interactive mode do not specify a filename. If you want to specify any of the valid *options* for the SAS command, enter a right parenthesis, followed by the options. The DMS | NODMS option and the type of terminal you are using determine whether you enter a line-prompt or display manager session. If you are using a full-screen terminal and DMS is in effect, you enter a display manager session. If your terminal is not full screen or if NODMS is in effect, you enter a line-prompt session.

Note that the SAS command is a CMS command created by SAS Institute that contains a set of control language instructions to invoke the SAS System.

Read more about the SAS command in the *SAS Companion for the VM/CMS Operating System.*

Defining Files

The CMS command FILEDEF is used to define files for use in SAS programs. The FILEDEF command associates a *libref* with a SAS file or a *fileref* with an external (non-SAS) file. The libref or fileref is called a *DDname* in CMS terminology. The form of the FILEDEF command is

```
FILEDEF DDname device filename filetype filemode(options
```

where

- *DDname* serves as a SAS file's libref or an external file's fileref
- *device* indicates the file's storage medium (usually DISK)
- *filename* and *filetype* are the names by which CMS knows the file
- *filemode* is a letter (or letter/number combination) indicating the minidisk on which the file is stored (for disk files only)
- *options* are any of a number of CMS options for the FILEDEF command.

In most cases, you do not have to issue the FILEDEF explicitly to define a SAS file because the SAS System issues the FILEDEF automatically. You do have to issue the FILEDEF explicitly for an external file.

A FILEDEF can be issued before the SAS System is invoked or after SAS is invoked in an X or CMS statement. In any case, the FILEDEF must be issued before the SAS statement that references the file.

Special Naming Conventions

Although the SAS System allows you to use an underscore (_) in SAS names, VM/PC does not. Therefore, do no use an underscore character in a libref or a fileref.

Reading an External File

Issue a FILEDEF command to associate a fileref with the external file to be read. Then use the fileref in the INFILE statement of your SAS program. For example, suppose you write a DATA step that reads the external disk file CLIMATE DATA, which is stored on your A-disk, and you want to use DAILY as the fileref:

```
R;
FILEDEF DAILY DISK CLIMATE DATA A
R;
SAS (invoke the SAS System)
(SAS messages)
1?
DATA WEATHER;
2?
INFILE DAILY;
3?
INPUT TEMP PRECIP SUNHRS;
4?
more SAS statements
```

The fileref DAILY points to the CMS file CLIMATE DATA A.

Reading a SAS Data Set

Under most circumstances, you do not need to define a libref explicitly for a SAS file because SAS makes the association automatically. To access an existing SAS file on any minidisk, just use the file's two-level name in the appropriate SAS statement. SAS searches all accessed minidisks for the file you have specified and issues the appropriate FILEDEF when it finds the file. For example, suppose the SAS data set FOOD.PRICES is stored on your B-disk. When SAS reads this statement,

```
SET FOOD.PRICES;
```

it searches all accessed minidisks for a data set with filename PRICES and filetype FOOD. When it finds PRICES FOOD B, this FILEDEF is automatically issued:

```
FILEDEF FOOD DISK PRICES FOOD B
```

Note: if you have multiple SAS files with the same filename and filetype on different minidisks, SAS will find only the file on the minidisk that is first in the search order. For example, if you have a PRICES FOOD A and a PRICES FOOD B, SAS will find PRICES FOOD A. You must issue a FILEDEF for PRICES FOOD B explicitly if you want to access it.

Creating a SAS Data Set

Under most circumstances, you do not need to define a libref explicitly to create a SAS file because SAS makes the association automatically. When you are creating a new SAS file and you specify a two-level SAS name, SAS automatically issues a FILEDEF using the libref (first-level name) for the DDname parameter **and** for the filetype unless a FILEDEF with that DDname is already in effect. By default, the data set will be written to your A-disk. For example, suppose you are creating a SAS data set called FOOD.PRICES:

```
DATA FOOD.PRICES;
  INPUT ... ;
more SAS statements
```

When SAS reads the name FOOD.PRICES, it checks to see if a FILEDEF with DDname FOOD has been issued. If there is no such FILEDEF, SAS issues one automatically, using FOOD for both the DDname and filetype, PRICES as the file-name, and A as the filemode:

```
FILEDEF FOOD DISK PRICES FOOD A
```

Note: do not use the same filetype for SAS files and external (non-SAS) files. If you want a new SAS data set to be stored on a disk other than your A-disk, you must issue the appropriate FILEDEF explicitly. Specify the appropriate values for the DDname and filemode parameters. You can specify any value for filename and filetype; SAS will substitute the libref (first-level name) and data set name (second-level name) for filetype and filename, respectively. For example, if you want to store FOOD.PRICES on a B-disk, your FILEDEF could be:

```
FILEDEF FOOD DISK DUMMY DUMMY B
```

Notice that CMS and SAS identify the file by the same two names, but the order is reversed. For example, SAS calls the data set FOOD.PRICES, and CMS calls it PRICES FOOD.

Creating an External File

To create an external file in a SAS program, first issue a FILEDEF command to associate a fileref with the name of the external file to be created. Then use the fileref in the FILE statement of your SAS program. For example, suppose you write a DATA step that reads the external disk file CLIMATE DATA (which is stored on your A-disk) and creates a second external file called COLD TEMPS A. You use the filerefs DAILY and FREEZE to reference the files:

```
R;
FILEDEF DAILY DISK CLIMATE DATA A
R;
FILEDEF FREEZE DISK COLD TEMPS A
R;
SAS
1?
DATA _NULL_;
2?
INFILE DAILY;
3?
INPUT TEMP PRECIP SUNHRS;
4?
FILE FREEZE;
5?
more SAS statements
```

DETAILS FOR THE VMS OPERATING SYSTEM

The SAS System running under the VMS operating system is documented in "Changes and Enhancements in the Base SAS and SAS/GRAPH Products under VMS," SAS Technical Report P-128.

Invoking the SAS System

Enter the SAS command after you receive the $ prompt:

```
$ SAS
```

or

```
$ SAS/options
```

or

```
$ SAS filename
```

If you enter *SAS* you will invoke the SAS System in line-prompt mode. Use the second method to specify valid *options* when you invoke SAS. For example, you can specify *FSDEVICE=devicename* to invoke SAS in display manager mode. With the third method, you can specify *filename* to give the name of a file containing the SAS program to be executed. This method is called *noninteractive mode*.

Read more about the SAS command and how to execute SAS in batch mode in Technical Report P-128.

Defining Files

The method that you use to define a file depends on whether the file is a SAS or non-SAS (external) file. The method that you use allows the SAS System to distinguish between SAS files and external files.

External files   You can define an external file in one of the following two ways:

- with the ASSIGN command of the DCL control language before you invoke the SAS System
- in the FILENAME statement within you SAS program.

With either method you associate the *fileref* with a complete file name, which includes the directory name and the name of a specific file within the directory. You can also issue the ASSIGN command in the X statement, a SAS statement that allows you to enter DCL commands in your SAS program.

The fileref is then used in SAS statements, such as INFILE and FILE, to refer to external files. If you specify a fileref in a SAS statement before you define the external file, the SAS System reads or creates a file in the current default directory with the following name:

```
[currentdefaultdirectory]fileref.extension
```

where *fileref* is specified in the INFILE statement to give the name of the file that is read from the current default directory or where *fileref* is specified in the FILE statement to give the name of the file being created in the current default directory.

Extension is a part of the file name that indicates the type of information a file contains. You must include the extension in the complete file name when you define an external file. (Refer to SAS Technical Report P-128 for more information on extension names.)

SAS files   If you want to read or create a permanent SAS file, you must define the appropriate directory with the LIBNAME statement. In the LIBNAME statement you associate a *libref* with a directory name only. The libref is then used in SAS statements, such as DATA, SET, MERGE, and so on, to refer to the directory. Once you have defined a directory in the LIBNAME statement, you can use the associated libref to refer to any file in that directory.

If you do not include the LIBNAME statement in your program before a SAS statement that specifies the libref, you will get and error message stating that the directory to which you are referring cannot be found.

Note: discussion of SAS files in the following examples is limited to the most commonly used type, a **SAS data set**. A SAS data set is a SAS file containing observations and variables.

Methods for defining SAS data sets and external files are illustrated in the following sections.

Special Naming Conventions

Although the SAS System allows you to use an underscore (_) in SAS names, VMS does not. Therefore, do not use the underscore character in a libref or a fileref.

Reading an External File

You can use the FILENAME statement to define an external file. In the following program the FILENAME statement associates a fileref with a complete file name:

```
SAS (invoke the SAS System)
SAS messages
1? FILENAME DAILY '[YOURDIR1]YOURRAW.DAT';
2? DATA WEATHER;
3?    INFILE DAILY;
4?    INPUT TEMP PRECIP SUNHRS;
more SAS statements and messages
7? ENDSAS;
```

The FILENAME statement associates the fileref DAILY with the complete file name [YOURDIR1]YOURRAW.DAT. DAILY is then specified in the INFILE statement. Notice that the file name includes the directory name YOURDIR1 and the file YOURRAW within the directory DAT is the extension name.

You can also use the ASSIGN command to define the permanent external file before you invoke SAS. For example,

```
ASSIGN [YOURDIR1]YOURAW.DAT DAILY
```

Notice that the fileref DAILY is specified after the complete file name in the ASSIGN statement, which is opposite from the way you specify the FILENAME statement. If you chose to define the file by issuing the ASSIGN command with the X statement, you can simply replace the FILENAME statement in the above program with the following SAS statement:

```
X 'ASSIGN [YOURDIR1]YOURRAW.DAT DAILY';
```

Since the X statement is a SAS statement, be sure to put a semicolon at the end.

If you do not define the external file to be read by the above program, the SAS System will read (or attempt to read) a file from the current default directory with the following name:

```
[currentdefaultdirectory]DAILY.DAT
```

Reading a SAS Data Set

Use the LIBNAME statement to define the directory containing the SAS data set to be read, as shown in the following program:

```
SAS (invoke the SAS System)
(SAS messages)
1? LIBNAME REPORT '[DIR2]';
2? PROC PRINT DATA=REPORT.STATION;
3?    VAR A B C;
```

```
more SAS messages
4? ENDSAS;
```

The LIBNAME statement associates the libref REPORT with the directory [DIR2]. REPORT is then used as the first level of the permanent SAS data set name in the PROC PRINT statement. When this program executes, the SAS System reads a SAS data set named STATION from the directory named [DIR2], and PROC PRINT prints the values for the variables A, B, and C.

If you specify a libref that has not been associated with a directory in the LIBNAME statement, you will receive an error message that the directory cannot be found.

Creating a SAS Data Set

The following program creates a SAS data set using an external file as input. You must use the LIBNAME statement to define the directory in which to store the SAS data set. You must also use the FILENAME statement to associate a fileref with the complete file name [YOURDIR1]YOURRAW.DAT.

```
SAS (invoke the SAS System)
SAS messages
1? FILENAME DAILY '[YOURDIR1]YOURRAW.DAT';
2? LIBNAME MAP '[YOURDIR2]';
3? DATA MAP.WEATHER;
4?    INFILE DAILY;
more SAS statements and messages
5? ENDSAS;
```

The LIBNAME statement associates the libref MAP with the directory [YOURDIR2], the directory in which WEATHER is stored. MAP is then specified as the first-level name of the SAS data set in the DATA statement.

If the LIBNAME statement is not specified before a statement that specifies the libref, you will receive an error message that the directory cannot be found. If you do not specify the FILENAME statement, the SAS System will search the current default directory for a file named DAILY.DAT.

Creating an External File

When you are creating an external file, you can use the FILENAME statement or the ASSIGN command to define the complete file name. The following program uses a SAS data set as input to create an external file:

```
SAS (invoke the SAS System)
SAS messages
1? FILENAME FREEZE '[DIR3]COLDRAW.DAT';
2? LIBNAME MAP '[YOURDIR2]';
3? DATA _NULL_;
4?    SET MAP.WEATHER;
5?    FILE FREEZE;
6?    IF TEMP < 32 THEN PUT TEMP;
more SAS statements and messages
9? ENDSAS;
```

The FILENAME statement associates the fileref FREEZE with the complete file name [DIR3]COLDRAW.DAT, and the LIBNAME statement associates the libref MAP with the directory containing WEATHER, the SAS data set being used as input.

When this program executes, all TEMP values less than 32 are written to an external file named COLDRAW.DAT. This file is located in the directory [DIR3]. If you do not specify the FILENAME statement, the SAS System writes the values in a file in the current default directory. The file has the following name:

> [*currentdefaultdirectory*]FREEZE.DAT

DETAILS FOR THE VSE OPERATING SYSTEM AND ICCF

The *SAS Companion for the VSE Operating System* and "Enhancements and Updates for the VSE Operating System," SAS Technical Report P-132, give complete information on using the SAS System with the VSE operating system and ICCF.

The examples in this section use the word SAS to invoke the SAS System.

VSE Batch

Invoking the SAS System   Use the EXEC statement in your JCL:

> // EXEC PROC=SAS

In this case, a VSE batch procedure named *SAS* contains all the standard job control language required to invoke the SAS System in batch mode. Refer to the *SAS Companion for the VSE Operating System* for information on how to specify options at SAS invocation.

If your installation does not support a batch procedure to invoke the SAS System, your SAS consultant can tell you how to invoke SAS.

Defining files   To define files stored on disk use the following set of JCL statements: DLBL, EXTENT, and ASSGN. You must issue this set of statements for each disk file needed—SAS and non-SAS. (In this context non-SAS means an external file—a file that is not a SAS file.)

The DLBL statement associates a *fileref* with an external file or a *libref* with a library of SAS files. In VSE terminology the fileref or the libref is called a *filename*. The EXTENT statement provides information about disk space occupied by the file, names a disk volume, and assigns a logical unit. The ASSGN statement associates the logical unit with the disk volume.

For example, the following statements define an external file stored on disk:

> // DLBL *fileref*,'*external.file.name*',*expiry*
> // EXTENT *logicalunit*,*volumeserial*,*type*,*seq*,*begin*,*trks/blks*
> // ASSGN *logicalunit*,DISK,VOL=*volumeserial*,*disposition*

Use the following statements to define a library of SAS files stored on disk:

> // DLBL *libref*,'*SAS.library.name*',*expiry*
> // EXTENT *logicalunit*,*volumeserial*,*type*,*seq*,*begin*,*trks/blks*
> // ASSGN *logicalunit*,DISK,VOL=*volumeserial*,*disposition*

The *fileref* is then used in SAS statements, such as FILE and INFILE, to refer to a permanent external file, and the *libref* is then used in SAS statements, such as DATA, SET, MERGE, and so on, to refer to a permanent SAS library. Once defined the libref can be used repeatedly in SAS statements to read or create SAS files in the library.

These three statements must be specified in the order shown above. Notice that both DLBL statements show how to specify an expiration date (expiry), and the EXTENT statements show how to specify full extent information (type,seq, begin,trks | blks). These specifications are required when you are creating either a new SAS library or an external file, but they are not necessary for existing files. Example programs in the following sections use existing files.

Note: a SAS library can contain several different types of files. This discussion of SAS files is limited to one type, **SAS data sets**. A SAS data set is a SAS file containing observations and variables.

To define files stored on tape, use the TLBL, ASSGN, PAUSE, MTC, and UPSI statements. These statements are explained in the *SAS Companion for the VSE Operating System*, along with more detailed information on how to define tape and disk files.

If you use a libref or fileref in a SAS statement without having defined the file to which you are referring, you will receive an error message.

Special naming conventions The following information concerning fileref and libref naming conventions is summarized from the *SAS Companion for the VSE Operating System*:

- **Filerefs** or **librefs** specified in DLBL and TLBL statements must not exceed seven characters, although most SAS documentation states that as many as eight characters are allowed.
- The first letter of the **libref** specifies how the SAS library is accessed, that is, how the file is opened and whether you can write to it. Use one of the following letters as the first letter in a libref to indicate the appropriate access mode:

  W   to specify a work library assumed to be a temporary file.

  O   to create a new SAS library, not to be confused with writing a newly created SAS data set to an existing SAS library. The EXTENT statement must contain full extent information, as shown above.

  I or S   to read a SAS file from a SAS library; the file can be used for input only.

  U   (or any letter except W, O, S, or I) to specify read and write access to a SAS library.

- To access a permanent external file or SAS library stored on tape, you must use a libref or fileref ending with a 1-, 2-, or 3-digit number that matches the logical unit number specified in the control language.

These naming conventions are reflected in the following examples where appropriate. For more information on VSE naming conventions, please refer to the *SAS Companion for the VSE Operating System* and "Enhancements and Updates in SAS82.4 under VSE," SAS Technical Report P-132.

Methods for defining SAS libraries and external files are illustrated in the following sections.

Reading an external file In the following example, you must use the DLBL, EXTENT, and ASSGN statements to define the external file to be read:

```
* $$ JNM=jobname ...
* $$ LST LST= ...
* $$ LST LST= ...
// JOB jobname ...
// DLBL DAILY,'YOUR.RAW.DATA'
// EXTENT SYS050,VSE123
// ASSGN SYS050,DISK,VOL=VSE123,SHR
```

```
// EXEC  PROC=SAS
DATA WEATHER;
    INFILE DAILY RECFM=FB BLKSIZE=192 LRECL=1920;
    INPUT TEMP PRECIP SUNHRS;
more SAS statements
```

The DLBL statement associates the fileref DAILY with the file named YOUR.
RAW.DATA. DAILY is then used in the INFILE statement

Note: the INFILE statement, in addition to giving fileref DAILY, must also supply
the record format and block size. You must specify these two file characteristics
for any file that you are reading by using the SAS options RECFM= and BLK-
SIZE=. You must also give the logical record length (LRECL=) if the file's record
format is FB (fixed blocked) or VB (variable blocked).

Reading a SAS data set   Use DLBL, EXTENT, and ASSGN statements to define
a SAS library. In the following job, the DLBL statement associates the libref
REPORT with a SAS library named YOUR.SAS.LIB. REPORT is then used in the
PROC PRINT statement as the first level of the permanent SAS data set name:

```
* $$ JNM=jobname ...
* $$ LST LST= ...
* $$ LST LST= ...
// JOB jobname ...
// DLBL REPORT,'YOUR.SAS.LIB'
// EXTENT SYS050,VSE123
// ASSGN SYS050,DISK,VOL=VSE123,SHR
// EXEC  PROC=SAS
PROC PRINT DATA=REPORT.STATION;
    VAR A B C;
more SAS statements
```

When this program executes, the SAS data set named STATION is read from
the SAS library YOUR.SAS.LIB, and PROC PRINT prints all the values for variables
A, B, and C.

Note: if you specify a libref beginning with the letter I or S in this example,
you have read-only access to the SAS library. For example, if YOUR.SAS.LIB is
protected and allows only read access, you must specify IREPORT instead of
REPORT. Remember that a libref beginning with a letter other than W, I, S, or
O requests read and write access.

Creating a SAS data set   The following program creates a permanent SAS data
set using an external file as input. Therefore, you must use two sets of DLBL,
EXTENT, and ASSGN statements: one set to define the SAS library that will store
the newly created SAS data set and one to define the external file to be read.

```
* $$ JNM=jobname ...
* $$ LST LST= ...
* $$ LST LST= ...
// JOB jobname ...
// DLBL DAILY,'YOUR.RAW.DATA'
// EXTENT SYS050,VSE123
// ASSGN SYS050,DISK,VOL=VSE123,SHR
// DLBL MAP,'YOUR.SAS.LIB'
// EXTENT SYS067,ABC321
// ASSGN SYS067,DISK,VOL=ABC321,SHR
// EXEC  PROC=SAS
DATA MAP.WEATHER;
```

```
INFILE DAILY RECFM=recfmBLKSIZE=blksizeLRECL=lrecl;
   INPUT TEMP PRECIP SUNHRS;
 more SAS statements
```

The first DLBL statement associates the fileref DAILY with the permanent external file YOUR.RAW.DATA. DAILY is then used in the INFILE statement. The second DLBL statement associates the libref MAP with the SAS library YOUR.SAS.LIB. MAP is then used as the first level of the permanent SAS data set name in the DATA statement. When this program executes the new SAS data set WEATHER is stored in YOUR.SAS.LIB. Observations in WEATHER will contain the variables TEMP, PRECIP, and SUNHRS.

Creating an external file   The following program creates an external file using a SAS data set as input. Again, you must include one set of JCL statements to define the SAS library to be used as input and one set to define the external file that is created by this program.

```
* $$ JNM=jobname ...
* $$ LST LST= ...
* $$ LST LST= ...
// JOB jobname ...
// DLBL MAP,'YOUR.SAS.LIB'
// EXTENT SYS051,VSE123
// ASSGN SYS051,DISK,VOL=VSE123,SHR
// DLBL FREEZE,'COLD.RAW.DATA',99/365
// EXTENT SYS050,VSE123,1,0,5280,300
// ASSGN SYS050,DISK,VOL=VSE123,SHR
// EXEC  PROC=SAS
DATA _NULL_;
   SET MAP.WEATHER;
   FILE FREEZE;
   IF TEMP < 32 THEN PUT TEMP;
   more SAS statements
```

The first DLBL statement associates the libref MAP with the SAS library YOUR.SAS.LIB. MAP is then used in the SET statement as the first level of the permanent SAS data set name. The second DLBL statement associates the fileref FREEZE with the permanent external file COLD.RAW.DATA. FREEZE is then used in the FILE statement. When this program executes, all TEMP values less then 32 that are read from the SAS data set WEATHER are written to the file COLD.RAW.DATA. These values replace existing information in the file.

ICCF (VSE Interactive)

Invoking the SAS System   Enter the ICCF proc (short for procedure) after you receive the *READY prompt:

```
*READY
SAS
```

The ICCF proc (named *SAS*, in this case) contains the standard job control language used to invoke the SAS System. If you are using a full-screen terminal, display manager mode is default; otherwise, line-prompt mode is the default. Refer to the *SAS Companion for the VSE Operating System* for information on how to specify options at SAS invocation.

If your installation does not support a proc to invoke the SAS System, your SAS consultant can tell you how to invoke SAS.

Defining files   In the ICCF proc that is used to invoke the SAS System, you must include a /FILE statement to define each permanent file—SAS and non-SAS. In this context non-SAS means an external file—any file that is not a SAS file.

In the /FILE statement you associate a *fileref* with a permanent external file and a *libref* with a library of SAS files. In ICCF terminology the fileref or the libref is called a *filename*. For example, to define an external file include the /FILE statement in the ICCF proc:

```
/FILE NAME=fileref,ID'external.file.name',UNITS=logicalunit,
/    SERIAL=volumeserial,DATE=expiry,LOC=begin,trks/blks
```

The *fileref* is then used in SAS statements, such as FILE and INFILE, to refer to the external file.

To define a SAS data library, include the following /FILE statement in the ICCF proc:

```
/FILE NAME=libref,ID'SAS.library.name',UNITS=logicalunit,
/    SERIAL=volumeserial,DATE=expiry,LOC=begin,trks/blks
```

The *libref* is then used in SAS statements, such as DATA, SET, MERGE, and so on, to refer to the library of SAS files.

The /FILE statements shown above include parameters for specifying an expiration date (DATE=expiry), beginning tracks, and number of tracks or blocks used (LOC=begin,trks | blks). This information is required if you are creating a new SAS library or a new external file, but it is not necessary if you are using an existing library.

Note: UNITS must specify a logical unit that was assigned to the disk volume *volumeserial* in the ICCF start-up JCL. See your systems personnel for more information on logical units.

You cannot use tape files with the SAS System running under ICCF.

If you use a libref or fileref in a SAS statement without having defined the file to which you are referring, you will receive an error message.

Note: a SAS library can contain several different types of files. This discussion of SAS files is limited the most commmonly used type, a **SAS data set**. A SAS data set is a SAS file containing observations and variables.

Special naming conventions   The following information concerning fileref and libref naming conventions is summarized from the *SAS Companion for the VSE Operating System*:

- Filerefs or librefs specified in /FILE statements must not exceed seven characters, although most SAS documentation states that as many as eight characters are allowed.
- The first letter of the **libref** specifies how the SAS library is accessed, that is, how the file is opened and whether you can write to it. Use the following letters as the first letter in a libref to indicate the appropriate access mode:

  W   to specify a work library assumed to be a temporary file.

  O   to create a new SAS library, not to be confused with writing a newly created SAS data set to an existing SAS library. Remember to include the DATE= and LOC= parameters in the /FILE statement, as shown above.

  I or S   to read a SAS file from a SAS library; the file is used for input only.

U   (or any letter except W, O, S, or I) to specify read
and write access to a SAS library.

These naming conventions are reflected in the following examples where appropriate. For more information on VSE naming conventions, please refer to the *SAS Companion for the VSE Operating System* and "Enhancements and Updates in SAS82.4 under VSE," SAS Technical Report P-132.

Methods for defining SAS libraries and external files are illustrated in the following sections.

Reading an external file   If your SAS program reads an external file, you must define that file by including the /FILE statement in the ICCF proc. Assume that the file to be read is an existing file named YOUR.RAW.DATA. Include the following statement:

```
/FILE NAME=DAILY,ID'YOUR.RAW.DATA',UNITS=SYS050,SERIAL=VSE123
```

The /FILE statement associates the fileref DAILY with the external file YOUR. RAW.DATA, an existing file.

Now, invoke the SAS System and enter your program. You will use the fileref DAILY in the INFILE statement to refer to the external file:

```
SAS (invoke the SAS System)
SAS messages
*ENTER DATA?
DATA WEATHER;
*ENTER DATA?
INFILE DAILY RECFM=recfm BLKSIZE=blksize LRECL=lrecl;
*ENTER DATA?
INPUT TEMP PRECIP SUNHRS;
more SAS statements and messages
*ENTER DATA?
ENDSAS;
```

Note: the INFILE statement, in addition to fileref DAILY, must also supply the record format and block size. You must specify these two file characteristics for any file that you are reading by using the SAS options RECFM= and BLKSIZE=. You must also give the logical record length (LRECL=) if the file's record format is FB (fixed blocked) or VB (variable blocked).

Reading a SAS data set   The following program reads a SAS data set from an existing SAS library. You must define the library by including a /FILE statement in the ICCF proc:

```
/FILE NAME=REPORT,ID'YOUR.SAS.LIB',UNITS=SYS050,SERIAL=VSE123
```

The /FILE statement associates the libref REPORT with the SAS library named YOUR.SAS.LIB.

You are now ready to invoke the SAS System and enter the program:

```
SAS (invoke the SAS System)
SAS messages
*ENTER DATA?
PROC PRINT DATA=REPORT.STATION;
*ENTER DATA?
VAR A B C;
        more SAS messages
*ENTER DATA?
ENDSAS;
```

The libref REPORT is used in the PROC PRINT statement as the first level of the permanent SAS data set name. When this program executes the SAS data set named STATION is read from the SAS library YOUR.SAS.LIB, and PROC PRINT prints all values for variables A, B, and C.

Note: if you specify a libref beginning with the letter I or S, you have read-only access to the SAS library. For example, if you specify IREPORT instead of REPORT in this example, you have read-only access to YOUR.SAS.LIB. Remember that a libref beginning with a letter other than W, I, S, or O requests read and write access.

Creating a SAS data set   The following program creates a SAS data set using an external file as input. Therefore, you include two /FILE statements in the ICCF proc: one to define the SAS library that will store the newly created SAS data set and one to define the external file to be used as input:

```
/FILE NAME=DAILY,ID'YOUR.RAW.DATA',UNITS=SYS050,SERIAL=VSE123
/FILE NAME=MAP,ID'YOUR.SAS.LIB',UNITS=SYS067,SERIAL=ABC321
```

The first /FILE statement associates the fileref DAILY with the permanent external file YOUR.RAW.DATA. The second /FILE statement associates the fileref MAP with the permanent SAS data library YOUR.SAS.LIB, an existing SAS library.

You are now ready to invoke the SAS System and enter the program statements:

```
SAS (invoke the SAS System)
SAS messages
*ENTER DATA?
DATA MAP.WEATHER;
*ENTER DATA?
INFILE DAILY RECFM=recfm BLKSIZE=blksize LRECL=lrecl;
*ENTER DATA?
INPUT TEMP PRECIP SUNHRS;
more SAS statements and messages
*ENTER DATA?
ENDSAS;
```

DAILY is used in the INFILE statement to refer to the external file. MAP is used as the first level of the permanent SAS data set name in the DATA statement. When this program executes, it creates the new SAS data set WEATHER in YOUR.SAS.LIB. Observations in WEATHER will contain the variables TEMP, PRECIP, and SUNHRS.

Creating an external file   The following program creates an external file using a SAS data set as input. Again, in the ICCF proc you must include one /FILE statement to define the SAS library to be used as input and another /FILE statement to define the external file that is created by this program:

```
/FILE NAME=MAP,ID'YOUR.SAS.LIB',UNITS=SAS051,SERIAL=VSE123
/FILE NAME=FREEZE,ID'COLD.RAW.DATA',UNITS=SYS050,SERIAL=VSE789
```

The first /FILE statement associates the libref MAP with an existing SAS library, YOUR.SAS.LIB. The second /FILE statement associates the fileref FREEZE with the external file COLD.RAW.DATA, also existing.

You are now ready to invoke the SAS System and enter the program:

```
SAS (invoke the SAS System)
SAS messages
*ENTER DATA?
DATA _NULL_;
*ENTER DATA?
```

```
SET MAP.WEATHER;
*ENTER DATA?
FILE FREEZE;
*ENTER DATA?
IF TEMP < 32 THEN PUT TEMP;
more SAS statements and messages
*ENTER DATA?
8? ENDSAS;
```

The libref MAP is used as the first level of the permanent SAS data set name in the SET statement. The fileref FREEZE is used in the FILE statement. When this program executes, all TEMP values less then 32 that are read from the SAS data set WEATHER are written to the file COLD.RAW.DATA. These values replace existing information in the external file.

NOTES

1.   **AOS/VS, PRIMOS, and VMS**: If you do not define the external file to be read or created by your SAS program, the SAS System uses a file in the current default directory with the following name:

```
AOS/VS   :UDD:currentdefaultdirectory:fileref
PRIMOS   <masterdirectory>currentdirectory>fileref
VMS      [currentdefaultdirectory]fileref.DAT
```

2.   **AOS/VS, PRIMOS, and VMS**: A SAS data library is a logical concept, not a physical entity. All permanent SAS files in a directory belong to the same SAS data library.

CMS and VM/PC: A SAS data library is a logical concept, not a physical entity. All SAS files with the same filetype and filemode make up a logical SAS data library.

OS and VSE: A SAS data library is a physical data set— an OS or VSE data set that contains one or more SAS files.

3.   **AOS/VS, PRIMOS, and VMS**: The LIBNAME statement is available if you are running the SAS System under one of these operating systems.

4.   **AOS/VS, PRIMOS, and VMS**: The LIBSEARCH statement is available if you are running the SAS System under one of these operating systems.

5.   **CMS and OS**: Under TSO you can use the SAS TSO statement to issue TSO commands from within your SAS program. Under CMS you can use the SAS CMS statement to issue CMS commands from within your SAS program. The X statement is used like a CMS statement under CMS and like a TSO statement under TSO.

Full-Screen Editing

INTRODUCTION

This appendix shows you how to enter information if you are using the SAS System with a full-screen terminal. Use the editing features described here with the SAS Display Manager System for entering SAS program statements. These editing features can also be used to enter text in other full-screen SAS software products, for example, to enter FSLETTER text in the SAS/FSP software product or to compose screen applications with the SAS/AF software product. You can also set your terminal keys to convenient functions with the SAS user profile facility.

The display manager examples below illustrate full-screen editing capabilities that are available wherever you need them in the SAS System.

```
Command ===>                                              SAS Log   00:00




















-----------------------------------------------------------------------
Command ===>                                              Program Editor

00001     PROC PRINT DATA=A;
00002     RUN;
00003
00004 /* MOVING TEXT AROUND ON THE SCREEN
00005 IS EASY.  IF YOU ARE ENTERING A SAS PROGRAM,
00006 FIRST TYPE YOUR STATEMENTS ON THE
00007 NUMBERED LINES LIKE THIS: */
00008
```

Screen A4.1   Entering Text

```
Command ===>                                              SAS Log   00:00




















-----------------------------------------------------------------------
Command ===>                                              Program Editor

I0001     PROC PRINT DATA=A;
00002     _
00003     RUN;
00004
00005 /* TO ENTER ANOTHER LINE BETWEEN THE TWO LINES OF
00006 YOUR PROGRAM, YOU CAN ENTER THE CHARACTER I ON
00007 ONE OF THE LINE NUMBERS ON THE LEFT AND PRESS
00008 THE ENTER KEY.  I (INSERT) IS CALLED A LINE COMMAND.
00009 LINE COMMANDS USUALLY AFFECT ONLY ONE LINE OR A BLOCK
00010 OF SPECIFIED LINES. */
```

Screen A4.2   Inserting Lines with a Line Command

```
Command ===>                                      SAS Log   00:00




---------------------------------------------------------------
Command ===> CAPS ON                              Program Editor
00001    PROC PRINT DATA=A;
00002       TITLE 'RESEARCH FUNDS ACCOUNT BALANCE';
00003    RUN;
00004
00005 /* TO CAUSE ALL TEXT ENTERED OR ALTERED AFTER THE
00006 COMMAND IS EXECUTED TO BE TRANSLATED INTO UPPERCASE,
00007 YOU CAN TYPE A CAPS ON COMMAND ON THE COMMAND LINE
00008 IN THE AREA FOLLOWING THE ARROW AND PRESS THE ENTER
00009 KEY. THIS IS CALLED A COMMAND-LINE COMMAND.  COMMAND-
00010 LINE COMMANDS APPLY TO THE ENTIRE FILE. */
```

Screen A4.3   Translating Text into Uppercase with a Command-Line Command

```
Command ===>                                      SAS Log   00:00




---------------------------------------------------------------
Command ===>                                      Program Editor

00001    PROC PRINT DATA=A;
00002       TITLE 'RESEARCH FUNDS ACCOUNT BALANCE';
00003    RUN;
00004
00005 /* IF YOU WANT TO CHANGE THE WORD 'FUNDS' TO 'FUND'
00006 IN THE TITLE STATEMENT, YOU WILL NEED TO USE THE
00007 DELETE KEY.  THIS IS ONE OF DISPLAY MANAGER'S EDITING
00008 KEYS. THESE ARE THE EDITING KEYS THAT THE SAS SYSTEM
00009 SETS FOR YOUR CONVENIENCE.  IF YOU ALSO NEED TO USE
00010 YOUR TERMINAL'S OWN EDITING KEYS, YOU NEED TO REFER
00011 TO THE MANUAL THAT CAME WITH THE TERMINAL. */
```

Screen A4.4   Deleting Characters with an Editing Key

```
Command ===>                                    SAS Log   00:00
```

```
-------------------------------------------------------------------
Command ===> SUBMIT                              Program Editor

00001    PROC PRINT DATA=A;
00002       TITLE 'RESEARCH FUND ACCOUNT BALANCE';
00003    RUN;
00004
00005 /* WHEN YOU ARE READY TO RUN YOUR PROGRAM, YOU
00006 CAN TYPE THE SUBMIT COMMAND ON THE COMMAND LINE
00007 AND PRESS THE ENTER KEY. */
00008
```

Screen A4.5 Submitting SAS Program Statements

```
Command ===>                                    SAS Log   00:00
```

```
-------------------------------------------------------------------
Command ===> KEYS                                Program Editor
00001 /* THE EXAMPLES SO FAR HAVE SHOWN YOU HOW TO USE LINE
00002 COMMANDS, COMMAND-LINE COMMANDS, AND THE EDITING
00003 KEYS.  YOU CAN ALSO SET EACH FUNCTION
00004 KEY ON YOUR TERMINAL TO ANY OF THE SAS FULL-SCREEN
00005 LINE OR COMMAND-LINE COMMANDS VALID IN THE DISPLAY
00006 MANAGER OR FULL-SCREEN PROCEDURE SCREEN YOU ARE USING.
00007 TO FIND OUT THE CURRENT SETTINGS, TYPE THE WORD
00008 KEYS ON THE COMMAND LINE AND PRESS THE ENTER KEY. */
```

Screen A4.6 Function Key Settings

The result of the KEYS command is shown below. These are the default function key settings for the program editor screen that SAS Institute provides to your site; yours may be different from those shown.

```
                FUNCTION KEY DEFINITIONS
Command ===>
KEY     COMMAND
01      help
02      split
03      submit
04      recall
05      rfind
06      rchange
07      backward
08      forward
09      output
10      left
11      right
12      cursor
13      help
14      split
15      submit
16      recall
17      rfind
18      rchange
19      backward
20      forward
21      output
22      left
23      right
24      cursor
```

Screen A4.7   Function Key Definition Screen

Notice that one of the function keys is set to execute the SUBMIT command. Instead of typing the word SUBMIT on the command line and pressing ENTER as you did above to submit your program statements, simply press the function key set to execute the SUBMIT command.

EDITING KEYS

The editing keys you can use with display manager and the procedures that allow full-screen editing are shown below. You can use these same keys when editing text on data lines and commands on command lines. In general, you use an editing key to make a change to one character or one line of an unprotected field and a function key to search or scroll an entire file. The editing keys you can use in full-screen editing are listed and defined in **Figure A4.1**.

Note: the words or symbols on the editing keys described in **Figure A4.1** may not be the same as those on the terminal you are using.[1]

 The INSERT key allows you to insert characters within a line. Press the key and position the cursor where you want to insert text. Characters are shifted to the right to make room for new text. *

---

* IBM users: On a 3270 series terminal, press the RESET key to discontinue the insert.
Minicomputer users: Press the INSERT key again to discontinue the INSERT.

The DELETE key erases the character either preceding the cursor position or in the current cursor position, depending on the terminal keyboard you are using.

 The ERASE EOF (End-of-Field) key deletes or erases all the characters from the cursor position to the end of either a data entry line or, on some screens, the end of a field.

 The HOME key moves the cursor to the first column of the first unprotected field on the screen, the entry area of the command line on most screens. *

 The REFRESH key redisplays the contents of the screen line-by-line. It removes messages from the operating system and is especially useful for removing unwanted characters input since the last time you pressed ENTER or a function key. **

 The NEW LINE key moves the cursor to the first unprotected field of the next line. Use the NEXT FIELD key to move the cursor from the line number to the data entry area.

 The PRIOR FIELD key moves the cursor to the previous unprotected field.

 The NEXT FIELD key moves the cursor to the next unprotected field.

 The ENTER key executes commands entered on a command line or on a line number.

Figure A4.1   Editing Keys

---

* **IBM users**: Press the ALT and Home keys.

** **CMS, OS, and VM/PC**: Press ALT PA2.
VSE: Press ALT CLEAR.

COMMANDS

Command Conventions

SAS full-screen editing commands follow these conventions:

COMMAND OPTION | *option* [| **OPTION** | *option* | ...]

where

bold CAPS
> indicates a **KEYWORD**; use exactly the same spelling and form as shown.

lowercase italic
> indicates you supply the actual value.

vertical bar |
> means *or* use only one of the terms separated by vertical bars.

brackets [ ]
> indicate optional information or keywords.

three periods (...)
> mean that more than one of the terms preceding ... can be optionally specified.

For example, in the FIND command

FIND *characterstring* [**PREFIX** | **SUFFIX** | **WORD**]

FIND
> is the command **KEYWORD**.

characterstring
> is a user-defined option. You supply the value of the string of characters you want to locate. It is not in brackets so you know you are required to specify a character string.

[**PREFIX** | **SUFFIX** | **WORD**]
> are three system-defined option **KEYWORDS** that appear in bold uppercase letters, enclosed by brackets [ ], separated by vertical bars |; the bold uppercase letters indicate that each is entered exactly as written; the brackets indicate that these options are allowed but not required; the vertical bars indicate that you can specify only one of the three.

Line Commands

You can use line commands to perform such tasks as moving, copying, inserting, and deleting lines or blocks of lines, and designating target locations for moved, copied, and inserted lines. As an example, a list of line commands that you can use for full-screen editing in the text editor in SAS software products follows. See "SAS Display Manager" appendix for the line commands available in the display manager program editor.

SINGLE COMMANDS:

> A,B   target position, A (after) or B (before), of an M, MM, C, CC, or COPY command.

C	copy a line to the location indicated either by an A (after) or B (before) line command. To copy more than one line, see the CC line command below.
D[*n*]	delete one or more lines.
I[*n* | A[*n*] | B[*n*]]	insert one or more lines immediately following or preceding an I command.
M	move a line to the location indicated either by an A or B line command. To move more than one line, see the MM line command below.
MASK	enter the mask to be used for newly inserted lines.
O	a target position command that overlays the contents of one or more lines with moved or copied lines.
R[*n*]	repeat a line *n* times immediately following that line.
TF[*n*]	flow lines of text, deleting trailing blanks. You can follow TF with some number *n* to specify the right margin.
TS[*n*]	insert one or more blank lines within a line of text.

BLOCK COMMANDS:

CC	copy block of lines designated by CC on the first and last lines.
DD	delete block of lines designated by DD on the first and last lines.
MM	move block of lines designated by MM on the first and last lines.
RR	repeat block of lines designated by RR on the first and last lines.

SPECIAL SHIFT COMMANDS:

>*n*	shift data *n* columns to the right.
<*n*	shift data *n* columns to the left.
>>*n*	shift data on block of lines *n* columns to the right.
<<*n*	shift data on block of lines *n* columns to the left.

Command-Line Commands

You can use command-line commands to perform many editing and file management tasks. As an example, the command-line commands that you can use in the SAS text editor are listed below by function:

Scrolling Commands

AUTOADD	LEFT
BACKWARD	*n*
FORWARD	RIGHT
TOP	HSCROLL
BOTTOM	VSCROLL

File Management Commands

COPY	END	INCLUDE

General Editing Commands

CHANGE	CAPS
RCHANGE	CPRO
DES	CUNPRO
FILL	CURSOR
FIND	NULLS
RFIND	NUMS
BOUNDS	PREVCMD
CANCEL	RESET

Help, Function Keys, and Host-level Commands

HELP	KEYS	X command

Many of these commands can also be used in other screens in SAS full-screen procedures, as well as in display manager. See "SAS Display Manager" appendix for a list and glossary of display manager commands.

USING COMMANDS: MORE EXAMPLES

Entering Commands Directly

Both command-line commands and line commands can be entered directly or executed with function keys. To execute a command with a function key, you need to know the function key settings. In some procedures you can alter function key settings and then permanently store the new settings. See the **Function Keys** section for a discussion of executing commands with function keys.

Entering command-line commands directly   To enter a command-line command directly, type the command on the command line and press the ENTER key. For example, to scroll backward the default vertical scroll amount, type

    BAC

on the command line and press ENTER. The BAC command is an example of the most basic kind of command to enter; it requires only that you type a keyword and press ENTER. The examples below include commands that allow options and commands that require cursor placement.

Command-line commands with options   The BAC command allows options to be specified. For example, to scroll backward the maximum amount, type

    BAC MAX

on the command line and press ENTER.

Entering line commands directly   To enter a line command directly, type the command over a line number and press the ENTER key. In the text editor screens of most full-screen procedures, unlike the program editor screen in display manager, the numbering facility is OFF by default. To number the data entry lines, use the NUMS ON command-line command. Type NUMS ON on the command line and press ENTER.

Examples below include single line commands, line commands with options, line commands requiring target commands and positioning of the cursor, and block commands. Note the underscore (_) marking the cursor position in several of the examples.

Single line command   As an example, to insert a new line for entering text, type I, the insert line command, on any part of a line number

```
00I001 data line one
000002 data line two
000003 data line three
```

and press ENTER. One new line, the default, is inserted between the first and second lines.

```
000001 data line one
000002 _
000003 data line two
000004 data line three
```

Line command with option   Some line commands, the I line command, for example, allow you to specify an option for which you supply the value, such as some number n. To specify how many lines to insert, follow the I line command with some number n, such as 3, and a blank space

```
I3 001 data line one
000002 data line two
000003 data line three
```

and press ENTER. Three new lines are inserted between the first and second lines.

```
000001 data line one
000002 _
000003
000004
000005 data line two
000006 data line three
```

Line command requiring cursor position   The TS (text split) line command requires that you enter the command, then position the cursor before pressing ENTER. Enter the TS command on a line number, position the cursor,

```
TS0001 Split this line after the semicolon;_then add new copy
```

and then press ENTER. A new line is inserted:

```
000001 Split this line after the semicolon;_
000002
000003                                        then add new copy.
```

Line command requiring a target command   The following example shows how to use the M (move) and A (after) line commands:

```
M00001 Move this line
A00002 after the second line
000003 with the M (move) and A (after) line commands.
```

The first line becomes the second line:

```
000001 after the second line
000002 Move this line
000003 with the M (move) and A (after) line commands.
```

Block line command   You can also use line commands to affect blocks of lines. For example,

```
MM0001 Move the first two lines
MM0002 after the third line
A00003 with the M (move) and A (after) line commands.

000001 with the M (move) and A (after) line commands.
000002 Move the first two lines
000003 after the third line
```

See **Command Conventions** earlier in this appendix for a description of command conventions.

Executing line commands without line numbers   If your data lines are not numbered, you can still execute line commands without having to use the NUMS ON command to display line numbers. Type the line command, preceded by a colon (:), on the command line, position the cursor on the line you want to be affected by the line command, and press ENTER. For example, to execute the TS (text split) line command from the command line, type :TS on the command line, position the cursor, and press ENTER.

You can also execute a line command with a function key even when line numbers are not displayed. Position the cursor where you want the command to take effect, and press a function key set to execute that line command. See **Altering Settings: the Function Key Definition Screen** for setting a function key to execute a line command.

Entering Multiple Commands

You can enter a series of commands on the command line by separating the commands with semicolons. For example, you can type the BACKWARD MAX scroll command and the FIND command on the command line, separate them with a semicolon,

```
BACKWARD MAX; FIND 'DATA ONE'
```

and execute both by pressing the ENTER key once.

FUNCTION KEYS

Executing Commands with Function Keys

To execute a command with a function key can be as simple as pressing the function key instead of typing a command on the command line and pressing ENTER. To use a function key to execute a command with an option, you can either assign that function key the command with the option, such as BACKWARD MAX, or you can type the option MAX on the command line and press the BACKWARD function key. You can execute a command that requires cursor placement, such as SPLIT, by positioning the cursor before pressing the SPLIT function key.

Function keys and multiple commands   You can also combine the use of function keys and the submission of multiple commands. For example, if you set a function key to execute the command and option BACKWARD MAX followed by a semicolon,

```
BACKWARD MAX;
```

then you can enter

```
FIND 'DATA ONE'
```

on the command line and execute both by pressing the key you set to execute BACKWARD MAX; . The procedure executes the BACKWARD MAX command first and then the FIND command.

Altering Settings: the Function Key Definition Screen

You can alter the function key settings to execute any commands that are valid for the particular screen in the SAS full-screen software product that you are using. Use the KEYS command to display the function key definition screen for the screen you are currently using. Twenty-four function keys with settings are listed although some terminals may have only twelve function keys.

You can assign any valid command-line command or line command to any function key on your terminal. Precede line commands with a colon (:). You can use editing keys such as EOF and DELETE, or simply type over a function key setting to alter it. On the function key definition screen, you can use the following commands:

```
BACKWARD
CANCEL
FORWARD
END
```

You can use any of these commands by pressing a function key set to execute it or by typing it on the command line and pressing the ENTER key. You can scroll backward and forward to view the entire list of key settings; you can cancel any changes made; you can use the END command, or a key assigned to execute the END command, to save your altered settings and return to the screen on which you executed the KEYS command. Altered function key settings remain in effect until you exit from the procedure or until you alter the settings again. The next time you enter the procedure, the original default settings will be in effect again.

To keep your altered function key settings from one session to another, you must store them in your own user profile catalog. At the beginning of each SAS session, use the appropriate operating system commands to make your user profile catalog available. See the sections **User Profile** and **Access to Your PROFILE Catalog**.

SAS USER PROFILE

Installation Profile

Each installation of the SAS System receives a special SAS data library that contains information used by SAS software to control various aspects of your SAS session. For example, in base SAS software, a catalog in the installation profile library contains the default function key settings for the SAS Display Manager System and PROC DATASETS; similiar information for additional SAS software products is contained in other catalogs within that same library. In some cases, these default settings can be tailored to your site by your SAS installation representative.

Keep in mind that any changes made to the installation profile library are universal for your site. That is, the default settings stored in the catalogs in this library are for everyone using the SAS System at your installation. If these default settings are not suitable for your own applications, you can set up your own user profile. See **User Profile** below.

User Profile

A user profile catalog is available for customizing default function key settings to meet individual needs and preferences. When looking for current function key settings, for example, the SAS System searches the user profile for function key settings stored under the appropriate names before it looks in a catalog in the installation profile library.

Your own user profile information is stored in either a permanent catalog named SASUSER.PROFILE or a temporary catalog named WORK.PROFILE.[2] SASUSER is a reserved libref and PROFILE is a reserved SAS catalog name. The PROFILE catalog stores the function key settings for a particular screen or procedure each time you enter the function key definition screen and save the settings. You create a function key definition screen in your user profile catalog each time you use the KEYS command to display a function key definition screen and then save that screen by exiting it with the END command. By default, any function key definition screen that you create in this way is automatically stored under the appropriate name in the PROFILE catalog. For example, in base SAS software, you can have different function key settings for each display manager screen and PROC DATASETS because the system assigns a reserved name to each function key definition screen when it stores it in the user profile catalog. When you are using a particular display manager screen or full-screen procedure, the system looks for your function key setting information stored under a particular name for that screen or procedure only.

The user profile catalog is intended to be a personal catalog and cannot be accessed by more than one SAS user. Normally, an individual's profile is associated with an individual's user id.[3] It should not be stored in a SAS data library that is shared by a number of users.

Access to Your PROFILE Catalog

The individual user profile information is stored in a catalog named PROFILE in a SAS data library.[4] You should have access to your own user profile. In some cases, the reserved libref and catalog name SASUSER.PROFILE is used in a command procedure and automatically accessed when you invoke the SAS System at your site. In other cases, you may need to make the catalog SASUSER.PROFILE available to your session each time you execute the SAS System.

If you do not make the catalog SASUSER.PROFILE available to your session, WORK.PROFILE is opened and any function key definition screens you create are stored there. As with SAS data sets placed in temporary storage, your function key definition screens placed in the catalog WORK.PROFILE are available only for that session.

The library referenced by SASUSER, unlike the library containing the profile information for the entire installation, does not exist until you create it. (You can, however, reference an existing SAS data library using the libref SASUSER.) You must use a host operating system command to create a file or data set to contain a SAS data library that is associated with the reserved libref SASUSER. The system creates a PROFILE catalog automatically the first time you make a library referenced by SASUSER available to your session. Note that you must have write access to this SAS data library.

NOTES

1. If you are using one of the terminals listed below, use **Table A4.1** to determine the keys that have been assigned special editing functions in SAS full-screen procedures and display manager. See **Figure A4.1** for a description of the functions of these editing keys. If you are using a terminal other than one of those listed below that does not have keys matching the words or symbols shown in **Figure A4.1**, consult your SAS representative. If you are using an IBM terminal in the 3270-series, you can disregard this section.

Table A4.1   Full-Screen Editing Functions Assigned to Terminal Keys

Full-Screen Editing Key	PT45 Key	PST100 Key	PT25 Key
a (INSERT)	ichar or shift/del	insert or backspace	shift/del
a (DELETE)	dchar or backspace	delete or del	backspace
ERASE EOF	line feed	erase	shift/f8
HOME	home	home	home
REFRESH	control/clear	pf10	control/erase
NEW LINE	return or enter	return or enter	new line or enter
NEXT FIELD	f13	f2	shift/f5
PRIOR FIELD	f14	f3	shift/f6
ENTER	f3 or f15	f1 or pf13	f3 or shift/f7
MOVE CURSOR UP	↑	↑	↑
MOVE CURSOR DOWN	↓	↓	(not available)
MOVE CURSOR LEFT	←	←	←
MOVE CURSOR RIGHT	→	→	→

continued on next page

Table A4.1 *continued*

Full-Screen Editing Key	TEK4105 Key	VT100 Key	DASHER Key
⌃a (INSERT)	backspace	backspace	C1
⌃a (DELETE)	rub out	delete	DEL
ERASE EOF	line feed	line feed	erase EOL
HOME	- (minus sign on numeric keypad)	- (minus sign on numeric keypad)	home
REFRESH	, (on numeric keypad)	, (on numeric keypad)	erase page
NEW LINE	return	return	new line or enter
NEXT FIELD	. (on numeric keypad)	. (on numeric keypad)	C4
PRIOR FIELD	0 (on numeric keypad)	0 (on numeric keypad)	C3
ENTER	enter	enter	CR
MOVE CURSOR UP	F1	↑	↑
MOVE CURSOR DOWN	F2	↓	↓
MOVE CURSOR LEFT	F3	←	←
MOVE CURSOR RIGHT	F4	→	→

2. **CMS and VM/PC**: The SAS System automatically creates SASUSER.PRO-FILE for you on your A-disk the first time you enter display manager or a SAS full-screen procedure. The SASUSER.PROFILE catalog remains on your A-disk for use in different SAS sessions. Disregard all references to explicitly making SASUSER.PROFILE available to your session.

3. **CMS and VM/PC**: The SASUSER.PROFILE catalog is stored on your own A-disk. This catalog is created automatically by the SAS System. You need not issue any CMS commands to use it.

4. **CMS and VM/PC**: Skip the section **Access to Your PROFILE Catalog**.

SAS® Display Manager

INTRODUCTION

The SAS Display Manager System is a full-screen facility that allows you to interact with all parts of your SAS job—program statements, log, and procedure output. It provides you with a full-screen editor for inputting and preparing your SAS statements and data, displays the SAS log created when you run a SAS job, and displays the output produced by your SAS program statements. Display manager has three primary screens:

- the program editor screen where you input, edit, and save SAS source files and submit SAS program statements
- the log screen where you can browse the SAS log
- the output screen where you can browse output from your SAS jobs.

You also have access to special screens, such as the function key definition screen, and to SAS HELP, an on-line help facility where you can browse information about the entire SAS System.

```
Command ===>                                          SAS Log   11:14



Copyright (c) 1984 SAS Institute Inc., Cary, N.C. 27511, U.S.A.
NOTE: XXXXX Version of SAS Release X.XX at SAS Institute Inc.(00000000).
NOTE: LICENSED CPUID MODEL = XXXXXXX, SERIAL = 00000000.







--------------------------------------------------------------------
Command ===>                                          Program Editor

00001 __
00002
00003
00004
00005
00006
00007
00008
```

Screen A5.1   Program Editor/Log Screen

The display manager first shows you the screen shown in **Screen A5.1**. The bottom half is a program entry and edit area for your SAS statements; the top half of this split screen displays the SAS log.

Program Editor Screen

You type SAS statements in the program editor, review, make changes, and submit the statements for execution. In a SAS line-prompt session your program statements are submitted to the SAS System each time you enter a line; in a display manager session, you can delete and insert lines, enter, edit, and re-edit your SAS program statements and then submit them to SAS all at one time.

Log Screen

The top half of **Screen A5.1** is the log screen. Statements submitted to the SAS System from the program editor produce the SAS log that, together with any notes or error messages, is displayed in the display manager log screen. Except for entering commands on the command line, you cannot alter any text displayed in the log screen. As statements and messages build up in the SAS log, lines scroll off the top of the screen. Scrolling commands, which can be executed from the command line as well as with function keys, are available for browsing text in the log screen.

Output Screen

When you submit SAS program statements containing a PROC step that produces printed output, you can view that output in the output screen. The display manager displays the first page of the output and then allows you to see the rest of the output, one page at a time, or to skip to the last page of output. After the last page of requested output has been displayed, you can choose to return to the program editor/log screen or to browse the output in page-browse or line-browse mode. You can use function keys to scroll in page-browse mode; you can use function keys and execute command-line commands in line-browse mode.

TERMINALS, KEYS, AND COMMANDS

Function Keys

The SAS Display Manager System defines function keys for you to use to prepare your SAS program statements, to scroll information displayed on each screen, and to move from one screen to another. Some keys on your terminal keyboard, therefore, take on new meanings when you enter display manager. The default function key settings for display manager that were provided to your SAS site are described in this appendix. To set your own function keys, see the appendix on "Full-Screen Editing" for a discussion of the user profile facility.

Function keys on each screen   The set of function keys that is available to you depends on the display manager screen with which you are working. In addition to entering commands directly on the command line or on line numbers, you can use function keys to execute commands. See the appendix on "Full-Screen Editing" for a discussion of

- using function keys to execute commands
- viewing the default settings
- altering the settings

• storing your altered settings.

Editing Keys

You can continue using some of your terminal's own editing keys with display manager, such as enter, insert, delete, and cursor movement keys. Ask someone knowledgeable at your site if you need help getting started with these keys.

The editing keys you use with display manager are shown below. You can use these same keys when editing program statements in the program editor or when entering commands on the command line of the program editor, log, or output screens. You can use these keys in all **unprotected fields**. In general, you choose an editing key to make a change to one character or one line of an unprotected field on the screen, whereas you choose a function key to search or scroll an entire file.

Note: the words or symbols on the editing keys described in **Figure A5.1** may not be the same as those on the terminal you are using.[1]

 Press the INSERT key once to turn it on, and position the cursor where you want to insert a character. The next key you press inserts its character before the cursor position, shifting characters to the right to make room.*

 The DELETE key erases the character either preceding the cursor position or in the current cursor position, depending on the terminal you are using.

 The ERASE EOF (End-of-Field) key deletes or erases all the characters from the cursor position to the end of either a data entry line or, on some screens, the end of a field.

 The HOME key moves the cursor to the first column of the first unprotected field on the screen, the entry area of the command line on most screens.**

 The REFRESH key redisplays the contents of the screen line-by-line. It removes messages from the operating system and is especially useful for removing unwanted characters input since the last time you pressed ENTER or a function key.***

 The NEW LINE key moves the cursor to the first unprotected field of the next line. Use the NEXT FIELD key to move the cursor from the line number to the data entry area.

---

* **IBM users:** On a 3270 series terminal, press the RESET key to discontinue the INSERT.
Minicomputer users: Press the INSERT key again to discontinue the INSERT.

** **IBM users:** Press the ALT and Home keys.

*** **CMS, OS and VM/PC:** Press ALT PA2.
VSE: Press ALT CLEAR.

The PRIOR FIELD key moves the cursor to the previous unprotected field.

 The NEXT FIELD key moves the cursor to the next unprotected field.

 The ENTER key executes a command entered on a command line or on a line number. Do not confuse the ENTER key with the SUBMIT key. This key executes commands; the SUBMIT key submits SAS statements to the SAS System from the data lines of the program editor screen.

Figure A5.1 Editing Keys

Commands

Most of the commands you use with display manager are *command-line commands* entered on the command line of each screen. Notice in **Screen A5.1** that both screens in the program editor/log screen have a command line in the top left corner. You can also add a command line to the output screen.

Another type of command, called a *line command*, is used for editing SAS program statements and is available only in the program editor screen. See the appendix on "Full-Screen Editing" for a discussion of both kinds of commands, their execution, and command definitions. Commands you can use in display manager are listed according to screen in the sections that follow. Command definitions appear at the end of this appendix.

A COMPLETE EXAMPLE

This section uses an education example to go through a SAS display manager session step-by-step. This example illustrates a simple SAS program that you can use display manager to execute. You can enter your DATA and PROC statements in the program editor screen, use the log screen to view your SAS log, and use the output screen to view your output.

Suppose your company encourages employees to continue their education by taking night courses at a local college, weekend seminars, and so on. You have available for each person in your department:

- his or her name
- the number of credit hours he or she completed in the past year at the college
- the number of hours he or she spends in other educational activities
- the number of years he or she has been in your department.

You want to find out whether people who have been in your department for a short time participate more in continuing education than those with several years' seniority. You can:

1. create a data set, giving it a two-level name if you want to store it
2. identify your variables, the employee's name, the number of education

hours spent in regular courses, the number of hours spent in special educational activities, the total number of education hours (the regular course hours multiplied by the number of weeks in the semester plus the hours spent in special educational activities), and the number of years employed

3. enter your data
4. print a chart showing employee names, educational activities, and the number of years employed
5. print a graph to examine the relationship between the hours spent in educational activities and the number of years employed.

To begin, log on to your system, and, after receiving the operating system prompt, invoke the SAS System by executing the command

    SAS

Under some operating systems, you are required to identify the type of terminal you are using when you execute the SAS command.[2]

If the cursor is on the command line press the NEXT FIELD key twice to move the cursor to the data entry area. You are now ready to enter the SAS statements and data lines.[3]

Enter the statements and data lines for the DATA step. Remember that SAS statements can begin in any column and that you can split a statement between two lines or enter several statements on one line. You may find your programs easier to read if you follow our convention of beginning DATA, PROC, and global statements in column 1 and indenting other statements. **Screen A5.2** shows the program editor after you have filled in all the lines.

When you have filled in the last line on the program editor, press the FORWARD function key to scroll more lines into view. To control the forward and backward scroll amount, enter

    VSCROLL n

(where *n* is the number of lines) on the command line of the program editor and press the ENTER key. You can also set the vertical scroll amount to HALF or PAGE for scrolling a half or a whole page at a time. HALF is the default vertical scroll amount.

Scroll forward each time you fill in the lines in the program editor screen until you have entered all statements and data lines for the DATA step.

You can scroll back through the example to check for errors. When you are ready to run the DATA step, use the SUBMIT command or function key.

The SAS System displays messages indicating completion of the DATA step in the log screen.[4] Move the cursor to the log screen with the UP or DOWN cursor key or the HOME key, and press the FORWARD or BACKWARD function key to scroll through the log. You can alter the vertical scroll amount by entering the command VSCROLL and the scroll amount on the command line of the log screen, just as you did in the program editor.

Notice that the program editor is now empty so you can enter more statements. To see the statements you entered before, browse the log. To rerun those statements, first return the cursor to the program screen and use the RECALL command or function key; the previously submitted lines are displayed in the program editor. Use the SUBMIT command or function key to submit these program statements to the SAS System for execution again.

Now enter the PROC PRINT and PROC PLOT steps in the program editor. Precede the PROC PRINT statement with the OPTIONS statement specifying the DATE and NUMBER options if you want the date and page number to appear at the top of your output.

```
Command ===>                                          SAS Log   11:14


Copyright (c) 1984 SAS Institute Inc., Cary, N.C. 27511, U.S.A.
NOTE: XXXXX Version of SAS Release X.XX at SAS Institute Inc.(00000000).
NOTE: LICENSED CPUID MODEL = XXXXXX, SERIAL = 00000000.







------------------------------------------------------------------------
Command ===>                                          Program Editor

00001 data educatn;
00002     input name $ credhrs othered yrsexp;
00003     toted=(credhrs*16)+othered;
00004     cards;
00005 aiken 0 16 3
00006 barker 2 0 3
00007 faulkner 3 8 2
00008 house 3 16 2 _
```

Screen A5.2   Entering Your Program Statements

```
Command ===>                                          SAS Log   11:14


Copyright (c) 1984 SAS Institute Inc., Cary, N.C. 27511, U.S.A.
NOTE: XXXXX Version of SAS Release X.XX at SAS Institute Inc.(00000000).
NOTE: LICENSED CPUID MODEL = XXXXXX, SERIAL = 00000000.




------------------------------------------------------------------------
Command ===>                                          Program Editor

00009 mailer 0 16 4
00010 noble 0 0 5
00011 parker 2 0 2
00012 radner 3 4 1
00013 restin 3 0 3
00014 rusk 3 4 2
00015 silver 0 8 5
00016 smith 0 0 4
00017 tate 3 8 2
00018 tucker 0 0 4
00019 volker 0 8 5
00020 ;
00021 run;
```

Screen A5.3   Scrolling to Enter More Program Statements

```
Command ===>                                           SAS Log   11:14


NOTE: THE DATA SET WORK.EDUCATN HAS 15 OBSERVATIONS AND 5 VARIABLES.
   20 ;








-----------------------------------------------------------------------
Command ===>                                           Program Editor

00001 _
00002
00003
00004
00005
00006
00007
00008
```

Screen A5.4   Messages in the Log Screen

```
Command ===>                                           SAS Log   11:14


NOTE: THE DATA SET WORK.EDUCATN HAS 15 OBSERVATIONS AND 5 VARIABLES.
   20 ;








-----------------------------------------------------------------------
Command ===>                                           Program Editor

00001 options date number;
00002 proc print;
00003 run;
00004 proc plot;
00005    plot yrsexp*toted;
00006 run;
00007
00008
```

Screen A5.5   Entering More Program Statements

When you use the SUBMIT command or function key, the SAS System executes your program statements. Because these statements contain PROC steps that produce printed output, the program editor/log screen is removed, and the output screen appears, displaying the results of the PRINT procedure.

Output A5.1   PRINT Procedure Output

```
                        11:44 FRIDAY, JANUARY 18, 1985    1

OBS     NAME      CREDHRS    OTHERED    YRSEXP    TOTED

  1     AIKEN        0         16         3         16
  2     BARKER       2          0         3         32
  3     FAULKNER     3          8         2         56
  4     HOUSE        3         16         2         64
  5     MAILER       0         16         4         16
  6     NOBLE        0          0         5          0
  7     PARKER       2          0         2         32
  8     RADNER       3          4         1         52
  9     RESTIN       3          0         3         48
 10     RUSK         3          4         2         52
 11     SILVER       0          8         5          8
 12     SMITH        0          0         4          0
 13     TATE         3          8         2         56
 14     TUCKER       0          0         4          0
 15     VOLKER       0          8         5          8
```

When the PRINT procedure produces only one page of output, as in this example, you will hear a beep from the terminal when that one page has been displayed. Press the END function key to view the output of the PLOT procedure. (By default, function keys number 3 and 15 on the output screen are set to execute the END command.)

Output A5.2   PLOT Procedure Output

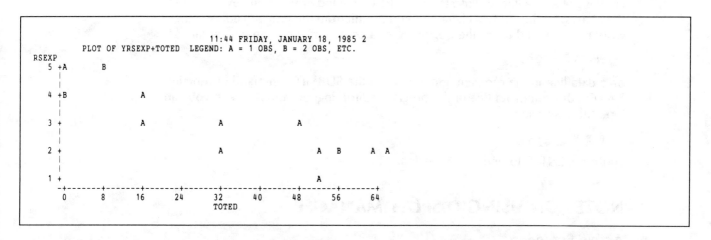

You will hear another beep from the terminal, signifying that all output produced by the PLOT procedure has been displayed. You can then browse the output in page-browse mode, enter line-browse mode, or return to the program editor/log screen. Press the COMMAND function key to enter line-browse mode. (By default, function keys number 2 and 14 are set to execute the COMMAND command.) A command line then appears at the top of the output screen. Use the END command or function key to return to the program editor/log screen.

When you return to the program editor/log screen, you see the most recent SAS statements and messages about your job in the log screen. You can view the earlier statements by scrolling backward.

```
┌─────────────────────────────────────────────────────────────────────┐
│ Command ===>                                            SAS Log  11:14 │
│                                                                       │
│      24    PLOT YRSEXP*TOTED;                                          │
│      25 RUN;                                                           │
│                                                                       │
│                                                                       │
│                                                                       │
│                                                                       │
│                                                                       │
│                                                                       │
│                                                                       │
│                                                                       │
│ ─────────────────────────────────────────────────────────────────── │
│ Command ===> _                                         Program Editor  │
│                                                                       │
│ 00001                                                                 │
│ 00002                                                                 │
│ 00003                                                                 │
│ 00004                                                                 │
│ 00005                                                                 │
│ 00006                                                                 │
│ 00007                                                                 │
│ 00008                                                                 │
└─────────────────────────────────────────────────────────────────────┘
```

Screen A5.6   SAS Statements and Messages in the Log Screen

You can leave your SAS session in one of several ways. Enter /* in the first two columns of a data line and use the SUBMIT command or function key. Note that the /* must be the last two characters you submit from the program editor; otherwise, it is assumed to be the beginning of a comment. You can also enter

ENDSAS;

on a data line in the program editor and use the SUBMIT command or function key. On the command line of the program editor, log, or output screen you can type the command

BYE

and press ENTER to end a SAS session.

NOTES ON USING DISPLAY MANAGER

Active Screen

On the program editor/log screen, only one screen is active at a time. The active screen is defined by display manager as the screen that the cursor is on. When you press ENTER or a function key, only the screen active at that time is affected.

Protected and Unprotected Areas

In display manager screens, protected areas are areas of the display that you are allowed to view but not alter in any way. Unprotected areas are those in which you are allowed to enter and alter text. For example, in the program editor screen, you can type commands in the entry area of the command line, line commands over the line numbers, and data in the data entry area that follows the line numbers; most of the program editor screen is unprotected. On the other hand, the log and output screens and the help facility are browsing screens. Most of the areas on these screens are protected; you are not allowed to enter or alter any text. The only area on these screens that is unprotected is the entry area of the command line. You can type and edit commands on the command lines of these screens.

The boxed areas below mark the unprotected areas of the program editor/log screen:

```
Command ===> [                              ]        SAS Log   11:14


Copyright (c) 1984 SAS Institute Inc., Cary, N.C. 27511, U.S.A.
NOTE: XXXXX Version of SAS Release 5.xx at SAS Institute Inc.(00000000).
NOTE: LICENSED CPUID MODEL = XXXXXX, SERIAL = 00000000.




--------------------------------------------------------------------

Command ===> [_                             ]        Program Editor

00001 [                                                        ]
00002
00003
00004
00005
00006
00007
00008
```

Screen 5.7   Unprotected Areas of the Program Editor/Log Screen

Color and Highlighting Attributes

If you are using a color terminal that has extended color and highlighting attributes in an environment that supports them, you can use the following display manager commands to set and change colors and highlighting:

CBANNER   to change the color or highlighting of the border, the line numbers, and screen description.

CPROT   to change the color or highlighting of all protected areas other than the banner. See CBANNER above.

CSOURCE   to change the color or highlighting of SAS source lines in the log screen.

CUNPROT   to change the color or highlighting of unprotected areas.

The colors and highlighting you can use are determined by the features of your terminal. See the *SAS/GRAPH User's Guide* and the *SAS/GRAPH Guide to Hardware Interfaces* for the colors available for your terminal.

Color   Use the following abbreviations to specify color attributes in display manager commands:

B   blue
R   red
P   pink
G   green
C   cyan
Y   yellow
W   white

Highlighting   Use the following abbreviations to specify highlighting attributes in display manager commands:

H   highlight
U   underline
R   reverse video
B   blinking

Setting both color and highlighting   You can assign an appropriate highlighting attribute at the same time you set a color attribute. Follow the color code with a highlighting code. For example, to set the color attribute of unprotected fields to yellow and the highlighting attribute to underline, use the command

```
CUNPROT Y U
```

To turn off the highlighting attribute, reissue the same color command and specify only a color code. For example, execute

```
CUNPROT Y
```

to allow the color of the unprotected areas of the screen to remain yellow but to remove the underlining.

Function Key Definition Screen

You can display the function key definition screen for the screen you are currently using by executing the KEYS command. You can view the current function key settings, or you can alter a key setting by typing the name of another valid command over the current one. On the function key definition screen you can use the following commands or function keys set to execute these commands:

BACKWARD
CANCEL
FORWARD
END

You can scroll backward and forward to view the entire list of key settings; you can cancel any changes made; you can use the END command, or a function key assigned to execute the END command, to save your altered settings and return to the screen on which you executed the KEYS command.

Note that the function key settings displayed on the screen are those currently active. If you want to execute a command that a function key is not currently set to execute, you must enter the command on the command line. For example, on the program editor and log screens there is no END function key by default because there is no END command for these screens. Execute the END command from the command line to save your settings and exit the function key definition screens of the program editor and log screens.

Entering Multiple Commands

You can enter a series of commands on the command line by separating the commands with semicolons. For example, you can type the BACKWARD MAX scroll command and the FIND command on the command line, separating them with a semicolon, and execute them in order by pressing the ENTER key once.

```
BACKWARD MAX; FIND 'DATA ONE'
```

Function keys and multiple commands   You can also combine the use of function keys and the submission of multiple commands. For example, if you set a function key to the command and option BACKWARD MAX followed by a semicolon,

```
BACKWARD MAX;
```

then you can enter

```
FIND 'DATA ONE'
```

on the command line and execute them in order by pressing the key you set to execute BACKWARD MAX; . The procedure executes the BACKWARD MAX command first and then the FIND command.

As a general rule, when you assign commands that do not allow any options to a function key, you may want to follow that command keyword with a semicolon. On the function key definition screen of the program editor screen, for example, you may want to place semicolons after the following commands:

```
BOTTOM;
RECALL;
SPLIT;
TOP;
```

Executing Display Manager Commands Stored in External Files

Executing command list at initialization time   You can execute a list of display manager commands stored in an external file automatically at initialization time. When you enter display manager, the system looks for a file, a sequential data set, or a member of a partitioned data set assigned the reserved fileref SASEXEC. If you have assigned SASEXEC to an external file containing a list of display manager commands, those commands are automatically executed. If the system finds no such file, no action is taken, and all default settings are used when you enter display manager.

By executing a series of commands stored in an external file, you can save time and decrease the possibility of errors. Suppose there is a series of commands you want executed each time you enter display manager. You can:

- alter the default active screen
- alter the default colors of protected and unprotected areas of the screen
- execute host-level commands that make SAS data libraries, external files, or data sets available to your session
- copy and submit SAS statements that take you directly into a full-screen procedure.

Using the AUTOEXEC command   You can execute a list of display manager commands stored in an external file at any time during your display manager session by executing the AUTOEXEC command. You can follow the AUTOEXEC command with any fileref assigned to a file or data set containing a list of display manager commands. If you do not specify a fileref, the system looks for a file assigned the fileref SASEXEC by default. Because you can specify a fileref other than SASEXEC, you can use the AUTOEXEC command to execute more than one file of display manager commands during your session. The syntax and definitions of the AUTOEXEC and AUTOSHOW commands are shown below.

When you execute the AUTOEXEC command and specify the fileref of a file containing a list of display manager commands, the first command is then executed from the command line of the active screen, which is the screen from which you executed the AUTOEXEC command. You can send commands to all of the display manager screens, one at a time, by including commands that change the active screen. For example, if you issue the AUTOEXEC command from the program editor, the first command is sent to that command line to be executed. Use the LOG command to make the log screen active; all following commands are executed on the log screen. Similarly, you can use the OUTPUT command to make the output screen active and the PROGRAM command for the program editor.

An invalid command   If an invalid command is encountered during the execution of your file of commands, an error message is displayed, and the AUTOEXEC processing stops.

Display of executing commands   By default these commands are not displayed as they are executed. The command AUTOSHOW ON causes each command to be displayed on the appropriate command line just before execution. AUTOSHOW OFF turns off the display of the AUTOEXEC commands as they are being executed.

The AUTOEXEC and AUTOSHOW commands   Enter the AUTOEXEC command to send a list of commands stored in an external file to one or more command lines in display manager. The list of commands is sent to the command line of the screen from which you enter the AUTOEXEC command.

You are not required to specify SASEXEC to execute commands stored in a file associated with the fileref SASEXEC; SASEXEC is the default. If you specify another fileref, the display manager commands stored in the file assigned that fileref are then executed.[5]

Use the AUTOSHOW command with the OFF or ON option to specify whether the commands are to be displayed on the command line as they are executed. AUTOSHOW OFF is the default.

Creating your file of display manager commands   The commands you want to be executed from a display manager command line, whether at initialization time or with the AUTOEXEC command, must be stored in an external file, **not** a SAS data set. You can store them in a file, a sequential data set, or a member of a partitioned data set.

Here are some general rules to follow when entering a list of commands to be executed at initialization time or with the AUTOEXEC command:

1. Enter only one command on each line and follow each command with a semicolon. Note: when you are working in display manager and entering commands on the command line directly, one at a time, you do not need to end a command with a semicolon.
2. Do not type beyond the 80th column.[6]
3. You can send commands to each display manager screen one at a time. Use the commands PROGRAM, LOG, OUTPUT, and HELP to designate which screen you want to be active and, therefore, the one on which the following commands will be executed.[7]

4. After you designate the active screen, list only commands that are valid on that screen.
5. The file in which the list of commands is stored **must** be assigned the reserved fileref SASEXEC if you want it to be executed automatically when you enter display manager.[8]

A sample list of stored commands   Below is a sample list of commands that you can store in an external file and execute with the AUTOEXEC command or at initialization time:

PROGRAM;
INCLUDE MYFILE;
SUBMIT;
CBA G;
LOG;
CURSOR 5;
SPLIT;
CSO B;
VSCROLL PAGE;
OUTPUT;
CPRO;
PROGRAM;
OUTPUT OFF;
VSCROLL PAGE;

These commands are explained in detail below:

PROGRAM designates that the active screen is the program editor; therefore, all commands that follow this command are sent to the command line of the program editor screen to be executed **until** you specify that another screen is active. In a file executed at initialization time, you are not required to specify PROGRAM because the program editor is the active screen by default.

INCLUDE MYFILE brings the contents of the external file identified by the fileref MYFILE to the data lines of the program editor screen.[5] This file contains a series of SAS program statements that you want submitted from the program editor to the SAS System. It could, for example, make some SAS data sets available to your session by containing X statements that make fileref assignments through host-level commands; it may also be used to enter an OPTIONS statement.

SUBMIT submits the program statements that you brought into the data lines of the program editor with the INCLUDE command.

CBA G sets the color of the banner on the program editor screen to green.

LOG activates the log screen. All commands that follow the LOG command are sent to the command line of the log screen to be executed **until** you make another screen active.

CURSOR 5 positions the cursor five lines below its default position, the command line of the log screen. This

	command positions the cursor in preparation for the execution of the next command.
SPLIT	tells the screen to split at the cursor location. Because you just positioned the cursor five lines below the command line of the log screen, you have altered the default location of the split between the program editor and log screens.
CSO G	sets the color of the source lines on the log screen. CSO G sets the color of the source lines to green.
VSCROLL PAGE	alters the vertical scroll amount of the log screen and sets it to the full depth of the log screen. HALF is the default.
OUTPUT	activates the output screen in page-browse mode. All commands that follow are now sent to the output screen.
CPRO B	sets the color of the protected text in the output screen. CPRO B sets the color of the protected text to blue.
PROGRAM	activates the program editor screen. All commands that follow are now sent to the command line of the program editor screen.
OUTPUT OFF	indicates that you do not want output produced during your session automatically displayed in the output screen.
VSCROLL PAGE	alters the vertical scroll amount of the program editor screen and sets it to the full depth of the screen. The default is HALF.

This list is just a sample of the kind of commands you may want to store and execute from an external file.

PROGRAM EDITOR SCREEN

Notes on Using the Program Editor Screen

Submitting SAS source lines from the program editor   You can think of the program editor as being entirely separate from the SAS System since SAS does not see the lines entered until you are ready to submit your job with the SUBMIT command or function key. After the job has executed, you can resume working in the program editor, entering commands, using editing keys and functions keys, and entering and editing program statements or data.

Program editor screen line length   When you submit SAS program statements for execution from the program editor screen, the data lines are broken into lengths of 80 columns. It is recommended that you not submit source lines longer than 80 columns. If you do submit longer source lines, do not continue a word from the 80th to the 81st column; it will be divided when submitted.[9]

Executing line commands without line numbers   You can execute line commands even if you have set NUMS OFF. You can position the cursor where you want the line command to be executed and then press a function key set to execute a line command. For example, you can position the cursor where you want a line to split and then press a function key set to execute :TS (the text split line command preceded by a colon). You can also execute a line command from the command line by preceding it with a colon, just as you do when you set a function key. You can type :TS on the command line, position the cursor, and then press the ENTER key.

Line Commands

The line commands available in the program editor screen of display manager are listed below. You can use line commands to move, copy, repeat, insert, and delete lines or blocks of lines; and to designate target locations for moved, copied, and inserted lines. In display manager you can use line commands only on the program editor screen. The log screen, whether you are using it to view the SAS log or SAS HELP, and the output screen are browsing screens; therefore, you cannot use line commands to alter text. Below is a list of line commands. Complete definitions appear at the end of this appendix.

Single commands

A[n],B[n]
C[n]
COLS
D[n]
I[n | A[n] | B[n]]
M[n]
MASK
O[n]
P[n]
R[n]
TF
TS

Block commands

CC
DD
MM
OO
PP
RR[n]

Special shift commands

>[n]
<[n]
>>[n]
<<[n]
)[n]
([n]
))[n]
(([n]

Command-Line Commands

You can use the command-line commands listed below on the command line of the program editor screen. Definitions of all commands you can use with display manager appear at the end of this appendix.

ASSIGN*
AUTOADD*
AUTOEXEC
AUTOSHOW
BACKWARD
BOTTOM
BYE
CAPS
CBANNER
CHANGE
CPRO(T)
CUNPRO(T)
CURSOR
FIND
FORWARD
HELP
HSCROLL
INCLUDE
KEYS
LEFT
LINESIZE
LOC
LOG
NODMS**
NULLS
NUMBER
OUTPUT
PRINT
PROGRAM
RCHANGE
RECALL
RESET
RFIND
RIGHT
RULE*
SAVE
SCREEN*
SPLIT
SUBMIT
TOP
VSCROLL
X***

LOG SCREEN

Notes on Using the Log Screen

Line length   The length of data lines on the log screen is sensitive to the value of certain line size options that you can specify with the OPTIONS statement.[10] You can scroll RIGHT to view data lines longer than the line length of your terminal screen.

---

* not in IBM versions.
** not in IBM versions.
*** not available under VSE.

Command-Line Commands

You can use the command-line commands listed below on the command line of the log screen. Definitions of all commands you can use with display manager appear at the end of this appendix.

ASSIGN*
AUTOEXEC
AUTOSHOW
BACKWARD
BOTTOM
BYE
CAPS
CBANNER
CPROT
CSOURCE
CUNPROT
CURSOR
FIND
FORWARD
HELP
HSCROLL
KEYS
LEFT
LOC
OUTPUT
PRINT
PROGRAM
RFIND
RIGHT
RULE*
SAVE*
SCREEN*
SPLIT
TOP
VSCROLL
X**

OUTPUT SCREEN
Notes on Using the Output Screen

When the output screen displays output resulting from any procedures you have executed, the procedure displays the first page of output and then waits for your prompt to go to the next page. To display each succeeding page of output, press the ENTER key or any function key **except** the END key.

If you have many pages of output and do not want to wait for the procedure to display them all, one by one, you can press the END key to cause the display manager to skip over all the intervening pages and display only the last page of output. All output is produced whether or not you choose to view each page. The terminal emits a beep when the last page of output is displayed.

When the last page of output is displayed and you receive the audible signal from the terminal, you are in page-browse mode. Now that you have entered page-browse mode, you have three choices; you can:

---

* not in IBM versions.
** not available under VSE.

1. use the function keys operable in page-browse mode to browse the output
2. return to the program editor/log screen by pressing the END key
3. enter line-browse mode by pressing the COMMAND function key. A command line then appears at the top of the screen, and you can either use function keys or enter commands that are operable in line-browse mode.

Browsing more than one set of output   If your submitted statements included more than one PROC step that produced output, you cannot return to the program editor/log screen from the last page of the first set of output by pressing the END key. You must reach the last page of the last set of output produced before you can exit the output screen.

When you reach the last page of the first set of output, you can press the COMMAND key to put a command line on the screen and to take you into line-browse mode for browsing that set of output; or you can proceed to the first page of the next set of output by pressing the END key. If you enter line-browse mode, pressing the END key also takes you to the first page of the next set of output. If you do not want to view all pages of a set of output, press the END key again to display the last page of that set of output. At this point, you have the same choices described above. You can browse the output in page-browse mode, browse it in line-browse mode by pressing the COMMAND key, or press the END key to return you to the program editor/log screen.

Using function keys in page-browse mode   Because there is no command line available to you in page-browse mode of the output screen, you must use function keys to execute commands. The same function key settings apply to the output screen in both page-browse and line-browse mode. You cannot view the function key definition screen from page-browse mode unless you have a function key for the output screen defined to execute the KEYS command. Use the COMMAND function key to create a command line to take you into line-browse mode where you can execute the KEYS command to view the function key settings for the output screen. (By default function keys number 2 and 14 are set to execute the COMMAND command.) Use the END function key to take you to the next procedure's output or to exit the output screen. (By default function keys number 3 and 15 are set to execute the END command.)

You can also view the function key settings of the output screen by executing the following commands in sequence from the command line of the program editor or the log screen:

```
OUTPUT; KEYS
```

The OUTPUT command takes you to the OUTPUT screen; the KEYS command then displays the function key definition screen of the output screen.

Linesize on output screen   The maximum line length depends on the operating system under which you are using the SAS System.[11]

Command-Line Commands in Line-Browse Mode

When viewing the output screen, you must enter line-browse mode to be able to enter commands directly. After hearing a beep from the terminal, which signifies that all of the output has been displayed and that you have entered page-browse mode, press the COMMAND function key to create a command line on the output screen and to enter line-browse mode. Then you can use the command-line commands listed below. Definitions of all commands you can use with display manager appear at the end of this appendix.

ASSIGN*
AUTOEXEC
AUTOSHOW
BACKWARD
BOTTOM
BYE
CAPS
CBANNER
COMMAND
CPROT
CUNPROT
CURSOR
FIND
FORWARD
HELP
HSCROLL
KEYS
LEFT
LOC
LOG
PRINT
PROGRAM
RFIND
RIGHT
RULE**
SAVE*
SCREEN*
SPLIT*
TOP
VSCROLL
X***

COMMAND GLOSSARY

Line Commands

A[n],B[n]   A line command that marks the target position of a *source* line(s), a line or lines being moved or copied with a C, M, P, CC, MM, PP, or INCLUDE command. Indicate an A (after) on the line number of the line you want the source line(s) to follow. Use a B (before) to mark the line you want the source line(s) to precede. After the A or B, you can specify the number of times you want the source line or lines to be duplicated. Follow A or B with some number *n* and a blank space. **CMS, OS, VM/PC, and VSE**: You cannot use the target commands with the INCLUDE command.

C[n]   A line command that copies one or more lines to another location in the file, indicated by a target line

---

* not in IBM versions.
** not in IBM versions.
*** not available under VSE.

command. Indicate C on the line number of the line to be copied. Then indicate an A on the number of the line you want the copied line to follow, a B on the number of the line you want it to precede, or an O or OO on the line or lines you want it to overlay. You can also specify n number of lines to be copied. Follow C with some number n and a blank space.

CC   A line command that copies a block of lines to another location in the file, indicated by a target line command. Indicate CC on the line numbers of the first and last lines of the block of lines to be copied.

COLS   A line command that creates a special line indicating the column numbers across your display screen. The column indicator line appears above the line on which you execute the COLS command. The COLS line is a special line that is not submitted when you submit program statements from the program editor. Use the RESET key or command or delete the line to remove the COLS line.

D[n]   A line command that deletes one or more lines. Indicate D on the line number of the line to be deleted. By default, one line is deleted. To delete more than one line, follow D with some number n and a blank space.

DD   A line command that deletes a block of lines. Indicate DD on the line numbers of the block of lines to be deleted.

I[n]   This line command is used to insert one or more new lines. By default one line is inserted after the line on which you execute the I command. To insert more than one line, follow I with some number n and a blank space. See also the IA and IB commands below. See the MASK command to insert lines with a defined content other than a blank line. See the TS (text split) command to insert space within a line of text.

IA[n]   Use this line command to insert one or more lines after the line on which you enter the IA (insert after) command. By default only one line is inserted. See also the I and IB commands.

IB[n]   Use this line command to insert one or more lines before the line on which you enter the IB (insert before) command. By default only one line is inserted. See also the I and IA commands.

M[n]   A line command that moves one or more lines to another location in the file, indicated by a target line command. Indicate M on the line number of the line to be moved. If you move more than one line, follow M with some number n and a blank space. Then specify an A on the line number of the line you want the moved line to follow, a B on the line you want it to precede, or an O on the line you want the moved line or lines to overlay.

MASK A line command that defines the initial contents of a new line. Type MASK on any line number and press ENTER. Then type on that line whatever characters you want to be repeated and press ENTER again. After you define a MASK, a line with the contents of the MASK line is inserted when you use the I (insert) line command.

The MASK remains in effect throughout the session. To redefine it, simply repeat the steps described above. To return to the default, a blank line, use the same process and leave the line blank.

MM A line command that moves a block of lines to another location in the file, indicated by a target line command. Indicate the block to be moved with an MM line command on the first and last line numbers of the block.

> [n] A line command that shifts data one or more spaces to the right. Indicate > or > followed by some number *n* and a blank space on the line number of the line to be shifted. Note that a **data** shift command allows no loss of data. The default is one space.

< [n] A line command that shifts data one or more spaces to the left. Indicate < or < followed by some number *n* and a blank space on the line number of the line to be shifted. Note that a **data** shift command allows no loss of data. The default is one space.

> > [n] A line command that shifts a block of lines one or more spaces to the right. Indicate >> or >> followed by some number *n* and a blank space on the line number of the first line of the block to be shifted and another >> or >>*n* on the last line number of the block. Note that a **data** shift command allows no loss of data. The default is one space.

< < [n] A line command that shifts a block of lines one or more spaces to the left. Indicate << or << followed by some number *n* and a blank space on the line number of the first line of the block to be shifted and another << or <<*n* on the last line number of the block. Note that a **data** shift command allows no loss of data. The default is one space.

)[n] A line command that shifts columns of data one or more columns to the right. Indicate) or) followed by some number *n* and a blank space on the line number of the line to be shifted. Note that a **column** shift command, unlike a **data** shift command, can cause loss of data. The default is one column.

([n] A line command that shifts columns of data one or more columns to the left. Indicate (or (followed by some number *n* and a blank space on the line number of the line to be shifted. Note that a **column** shift command, unlike a **data** shift command, can cause loss of data. The default is one column.

))[*n*]   The column shift line command shifts a block of lines one or more columns to the right. Indicate)) or)) followed by some number *n* and a blank space on the line number of the first line of the block to be shifted and another)) or))*n* on the last line number of the block. Note that a **column** shift command, unlike a **data** shift command, can cause loss of data. The default is one column.

(([*n*]   A line command that shifts a block of lines one or more columns to the left. Indicate ((or ((followed by some number *n* and a blank space on the line number of the first line of the block to be shifted and another ((or ((*n* on the last line number of the block. Note that a **column** shift command, unlike a **data** shift command, can cause loss of data. The default is one space.

O[*n*]   A line command that marks the target position of a C, M, P, CC, MM, or PP line command. Indicate the O (overlay) line command on the line number of the line you want the contents of the *source line*, the moved or copied line, to overlay. Characters from the source line overlay blank or null spaces on the *target line*, the line marked with the O line command. After the O line command you can specify the number of target lines you want the source line or lines to overlay. Follow O with some number *n* and a blank space.
If any characters occupy the same positions on the source and target lines, the characters on the target line remain, and characters from the source line do not appear. If you are executing the M (move) command, you receive an error message, and the line intended to be moved remains in its original position.

OO   A line command that marks a block of lines, identified by an OO on the line numbers of the first and last lines of the block, as the target position of source lines, lines marked with the C, M, P, CC, MM, or PP line commands. See the O line command.

P[*n*]   A line command that copies or overlays one or more lines to another location in the file, indicated by a target line command. The P (pattern) line command is similiar to the C (copy) line command; the difference is that the system remembers the line marked with the P line command and copies it to the new location each time you enter a target line command until you remove the P line command. You can remove it with the RESET key or command or by using any of the editing keys you normally use to erase or remove characters, such as the EOF key, the character delete key, or the space bar. Indicate P on the line number of the source line, the line you want to copy. Then indicate an A on the number of the line you want the source line to follow, a B on the number of the line you want it to precede, or an O or OO on the line or lines you want it to overlay. You can also specify *n* number of lines to be copied. Follow P with some number *n* and a blank space.

PP   A line command that copies a block of lines to another location in the file, indicated by a target line command. The PP (pattern block) command is similiar to the CC line command; the difference is that the system remembers the block of lines marked with the PP line command and copies it to the new location each time you enter a target line command until you remove the PP line command. You can remove it with the RESET key or command or by using any of the editing keys you normally use to erase or remove characters, such as the EOF key, the character delete key, or the space bar. Indicate PP on the first and last line numbers of the block of lines you want to designate as the source lines, the lines you want to copy. Then indicate an A on the number of the line you want the source lines to follow, a B on the number of the line you want them to precede, an O or OO on the first and last lines of the block you want the source lines to overlay.

R[*n*]   A line command that repeats a line one or more times immediately following. Indicate R on the line number of the line to be repeated. To repeat a line more than once, follow R with some number *n* and a blank space.

RR[*n*]   A line command that repeats a block of lines immediately following that block. Indicate RR on the line numbers of the first and last lines of the block of lines to be repeated. You can also specify how many times you want the block of lines repeated; follow RR with some number *n* and a blank space. You can specify *n* on the first or last RR command or on both.

TF   A line command that flows a paragraph or an indicated block of text by removing trailing blanks from each line. You can use the TF (text flow) line command to move text into wasted space left at ends of lines, especially after performing insertions and deletions.

TS   A line command that inserts a blank line for inserting new text. Either type TS (text split) on a line number, position the cursor where you want the text to split, and press ENTER, or position the cursor and press the :TS function key. See the I (insert) command for inserting space between lines rather than within the text of a line.

Command-Line Commands

Command-line commands that are available in display manager screens are defined below:

ASSIGN *'filename' fileref*

  AOS/VS, PRIMOS, and VMS only: Use the ASSIGN command to assign a fileref to an external file. You can specify a fully qualified file name, according to the requirements of the operating system you are using, or just an individual file name (and type under VMS) if it is in a directory to which you currently have access. For example, to assign the fileref PROG1 to an AOS/VS, PRIMOS, or VMS fully-qualified file name, you can execute the ASSIGN command in the form

```
ASSIGN ':UDD:youruserdir:PROG.SAS' PROG1
```

```
ASSIGN '[yourdir]PROG.SAS' PROG1
```

```
ASSIGN '<masterfiledirectory>userfiledirectory>PROG.SAS'
```

See the INCLUDE and SAVE commands.

CMS, OS, and VM/PC: You can execute host-level commands before entering display manager or after entering display manager with the X command or statement.

VSE: You can place a /FILE statement, an ICCF control language statement, in the ICCF procedure that invokes the SAS System. You cannot use the X command or statement in the ICCF environment. See the INCLUDE and SAVE commands.

AUTOADD [ON | OFF]

AOS/VS, PRIMOS, and VMS only: The AUTOADD ON command adds data entry lines to the bottom of the screen each time you scroll forward so that you do not have to use an INSERT command to insert new lines for entering new data or text. If line numbers are on (NUMS ON), these lines are numbered each time you scroll foward. If you execute AUTOADD OFF, the editor does not add new lines for data entry each time you scroll foward.

AUTOEXEC [SASEXEC | fileref]

Enter the AUTOEXEC command to send a list of commands stored in an external file to one or more command lines in display manager. The first command in the list is sent to the command line of the screen from which you enter the AUTOEXEC command.

If you do not specify a fileref that you assigned to an external file through a host-level command, the procedure looks for a file assigned the fileref SASEXEC by default. If you specify another fileref, the display manager commands stored in file associated with that fileref are then executed.

AUTOSHOW OFF | ON

Use the AUTOSHOW command with the OFF or ON option to specify whether commands being executed from an external file are to be displayed on the command line as they are executed. AUTOSHOW OFF is the default.

BACKWARD [n | MAX]

In addition to using a function key, you can scroll toward the top of the screen with the BAC command. The amount of scroll is controlled by the VSCROLL command.

You can specify a particular number of lines to scroll backward by entering BAC n (n being the number of lines you want to scroll backward). You can scroll the maximum amount by entering BAC MAX or BAC M. The scroll value specified with the BAC command, either n or MAX, is operative only for that scroll; it temporarily overrides but does not alter the default scroll value or the one set by the VSCROLL command.

BOTTOM

Use the BOTTOM or BOT command to scroll the last line of text to the bottom of the screen.

BYE

You can use the BYE command to end a SAS session. You can execute the BYE command from the command line of the log or program editor screen.

CAPS OFF | ON

When you execute CAPS ON, all text entered, as well as text on lines that have been modified, is translated into uppercase letters when you press ENTER or a function key. All text is left as entered when CAPS OFF is in effect. The CAPS command affects only the screen on which it is entered and is in effect for the remainder of the SAS session or until changed by another CAPS command. The default is CAPS ON in minicomputer versions and CAPS OFF in IBM versions.

CBANNER *color* [*highlight*]

The CBA command changes the color or color and highlighting attributes of the banner lines. These lines are the borders, line numbers if any, and command line. Specifying CBA affects only the screen on which the command is entered and is in effect for the remainder of the SAS session or until changed by another CBA command.

CHANGE *string1* *string2* [**NEXT | FIRST | LAST | PREV | ALL**]
                          [**WORD | SUFFIX | PREFIX**]

Use the CHANGE command to change one or more occurrences of *string1* to *string2*. Follow the CHANGE command with string of characters to be changed, a space, and then the new string, or type the strings on the command line and press the CHANGE function key.

You can specify on the CHANGE command that the system search for and alter the NEXT occurrence of the specified string after the current cursor location; the FIRST occurrence of the string in the file, regardless of your current cursor location; the LAST occurrence of the string in the file; or the PREVious occurrence. If you specify ALL, you receive a message that reports how many times the string occurs in the entire file, and each occurrence is changed. By default, the CHANGE command searches for and changes the NEXT occurrence of the specified string after the current cursor location.

You can also specify one of the following options: PREFIX, SUFFIX, or WORD. If you do not specify one of these, *string1* is changed to *string2*, regardless of context.

In the CHANGE command, as in the FIND command, a WORD is one or more symbols preceded and followed by a delimiter. A delimiter is any symbol other than an uppercase letter, a lowercase letter, a digit, or an underscore.

Remember to use single quotes to enclose strings with special characters or embedded blanks. Single word strings require no quotation marks. For example,

```
C YOUR MY
C 'YOUR DATA SET' 'MY DATA SET'
```

Also enclose your string in single quotes if CAPS are ON and you do not want lowercase letters in the string translated into uppercase letters.

If your string contains a single quotation mark, such as

```
C "Bob's" "Bill's"
```

enclose it in double quotation marks.

You can combine the use of the CHANGE command and RFIND function key (or command). For example, after you enter a CHANGE command, you can press the RFIND function key to locate the next occurrence of *string1* before pressing RCHANGE to change it to *string2*.

Also see the RCHANGE, FIND, and RFIND commands.

COMMAND

Use the CMD command, assigned to a function key, in page-browse mode of the procedure output screen to put a command line at the top of the screen, taking you into line-browse mode. Execute the command again to remove the command line and return you to page-browse mode.

CPROT *color* [*highlight*]

The CPROT command changes the color or color and highlighting attributes of protected fields on the log or output screen to those specified for the remainder of the SAS session or until changed by another CPROT command. This color or color and highlighting attributes become the default for the protected fields only for the screen on which you enter the command.

The CPROT command has no effect on the program editor screen since its protected areas are governed by the CBANNER command.

CSOURCE *color* [*highlight*]

The CSO command changes the color or color and highlighting attributes of SAS source line on the log screen to those specified. The CSO command is in effect for the remainder of the SAS session or until changed by another CSO command.

CUNPROT *color* [*highlight*]

The CUN command changes the color or color and highlighting attributes of unprotected fields to those specified for the remainder of the SAS session or until changed by another CUN command. This color or color and highlighting attributes become the default for all unprotected fields that are not otherwise defined by color or highlighting attribute commands. Note: the CUNPROT command affects the unprotected fields only for the screen on which it is executed.

CURSOR [*rownumber*] | [*rownumber colnumber*]

The CURSOR command, without any options specified, is designed to be executed with a function key. Press the CURSOR key to return the cursor to the command line of whatever screen you are currently using.

Specifying options with the CURSOR command is especially useful when executing a list of commands stored in an external file. (See the AUTOEXEC command.) You can use the CURSOR command to position the cursor in preparation for the execution of a following command. For example, if you execute

```
CURSOR 10
```

on the command line of the log screen and then execute the SPLIT command, you can alter the location of the split between the program editor and the log screens. Note: do not move the cursor outside the boundaries of the screen from which you want the next command to be executed.

END

In line-browse mode of the procedure output screen, the END command either returns you to the program editor/log screen or takes you to the first page of the next procedure's output. In page-browse mode, it takes you to the next page of output or, if you are already viewing the last page, returns you to the program editor/log screen.

FIND *characterstring* [**NEXT | FIRST | LAST | PREV | ALL**]
[**PREFIX | SUFFIX | WORD**]

Use the FIND command to search for a specified string of characters. Remember to enclose the string in single quotes if it contains embedded blanks or special characters. You can execute the FIND command by entering it directly or by typing the character string on the command line and pressing the FIND function key.

You can specify in the FIND command that the system search for the NEXT occurrence of the specified string after the current cursor location; the FIRST occurrence of the string in the file, regardless of your current location; the LAST occurrence of the string in the file; or the PREVious occurrence. If you specify ALL, you receive a message that reports how many times the string occurs in the entire file. By default, the FIND command searches for the NEXT occurrence of the specified string after the current cursor location.

You can also specify one of the following options: PREFIX, SUFFIX, or WORD. If you do not specify one of these options, the system searches for each occurrence of the string, regardless of context.

In the FIND command, a WORD is one or more symbols preceded and followed by a delimiter. A delimiter is any symbol other than an uppercase letter, a lowercase letter, a digit, or an underscore. For example,

```
ABC123
```

is a WORD, but

```
ABC$123
```

is two WORDs separated by the delimiter $. A PREFIX or SUFFIX is treated just as its grammatical definition. In the first example, ABC123, you could specify ABC as a PREFIX and 123 as a SUFFIX. In the second example, ABC$123, ABC and 123 are WORDs, not a PREFIX and a SUFFIX.

Remember to use single quotes to enclose strings with special characters or embedded blanks. For example,

```
F YOUR
F 'YOUR DATA SET'
```

Also enclose your string in single quotes if CAPS are ON and you do not want lowercase letters in the string translated into uppercase letters.

If your string contains a single quotation mark, such as

```
F "Bob's"
```

enclose it in double quotation marks.

See also the CHANGE, RCHANGE, and RFIND commands.

FORWARD [*n* | **MAX**]

In addition to using a function key, you can scroll toward the bottom of the screen with the FOR *n* command. The amount of scroll is controlled by the VSCROLL command.

You can specify a particular number of lines to scroll forward by entering FOR *n* (*n* being the number of lines you want to scroll foward). You can scroll the maximum amount by entering FOR MAX or FOR M. The scroll value specified with the FOR command, either *n* or MAX, is operative only for that scroll; it temporarily overrides but does not alter the default scroll value or the one set by the VSCROLL command.

HELP [*topic*]

When you enter the HELP command, SAS HELP, an on-line help facility, appears on your display screen. You can specify a topic at the same time that you execute the HELP command. If you do not specify a topic, a list of allowed topics is displayed.

   CMS, OS, VM/PC, and VSE: You can execute HELP from any of the three display manager screens. SAS HELP is then displayed, occupying the entire display area. Use the END command or function key to return display manager to the screen.

   AOS/VS, PRIMOS, and VMS: You can execute HELP from any of the three display manager command lines, but SAS HELP is always displayed in the upper portion of the program editor/log screen. You can browse help information by using the same commands and function keys that are available in the log screen. If you execute HELP from the output screen, you must return to the program editor/log screen to view the help information. After viewing the help information, you can return the SAS log to the log screen by entering the LOG command or submitting at least one statement from the program editor.

HSCROLL HALF | **PAGE** | *n*

The HSCROLL command sets the horizontal scroll amount, the amount the active screen scrolls when you press the LEFT or RIGHT scrolling keys. If you specify PAGE, the scroll amount is equal to the entire width of the display area. If you specify HALF, the scroll amount is one-half of the display area. HALF is the default.

INCLUDE *fileref* | *fileref(membername)*
INCLUDE *fileref* | *'filename'*
INCLUDE *singlelinenumber* | *firstline lastline*

The INCLUDE command allows either an entire external file or lines from the log screen to be displayed in the program editor screen. When including lines from the log screen, you can specify particular lines. The included lines are inserted at the bottom of the list of SAS source statement lines or wherever you specify with the A, B, or O line command. When specifying lines on the log screen, you can optionally use a hyphen or a colon between your first and last line specifications.

   CMS, OS, and VM/PC: If you are working with an external file, you should use a host-operating system command to assign it a fileref. You can execute it before invoking SAS or from display manager with an X command.

   AOS/VS and VMS: You can bring an external file to the program editor screen with the INCLUDE command in one of four ways. The *filename* can be a fully qualified filename, according to the conventions of the operating system you are using, or the name (and type under VMS) of a file in a directory to which you currently have access.

1. Assign a fileref to a file name with a host-level command either before invoking SAS or from display manager with an X command.
2. Assign a fileref to a file name with the display manager ASSIGN command.
3. Specify an actual file name by enclosing it in single quote. In AOS/VS, the file name specified must be in your current working directory; in VMS, it must be specified in your home directory. Under VMS, you must include the file type.
4. Specify an unassigned fileref; the system then assigns that specified fileref to an existing file of the name *fileref*.SAS in your current working directory.

PRIMOS: See the note above for AOS/VS and VMS. You can use all but the first method listed.

VSE: You can place a /FILE statement, an ICCF control language statement, in the ICCF procedure that invokes the SAS System. You cannot use the X command or statement in the ICCF environment.[5]

KEYS

Use the KEYS command to display the function key definition screen. You can view the current settings or alter them and store your new ones. You can scroll forward and backward on the function key definition screen; use the END command or function key to return to the previous screen.

LEFT [*n* | MAX]

This command scrolls the screen *n* spaces to the left. By default the screen scrolls half of its width. To override the scroll amount temporarily, enter LEFT and the number of spaces you want the screen to scroll. Enter LEFT MAX to scroll the screen to the left boundary.

LINESIZE *n*

Use the LINESIZE command to alter the line length of data lines on the program editor screen; *n* can be any number between the width of your screen minus 1 and 256. The LINESIZE command allows you to use the INCLUDE command to display files of long data lines in the program editor for editing, for example, saved SAS output files. Note: if you specify a LINESIZE shorter than your current line length, your data lines will be truncated.

   AOS/VS, PRIMOS, and VMS: The maximum line length of the program editor is 256 columns.

   CMS, OS, VM/PC, and VSE: The maximum line length of the program editor is 80 columns.

LOC *n*

Use the LOC or LOCATE command, followed by some line number *n*, to scroll that line to the top of the display screen.

LOG

The LOG command moves the cursor to the command line of the log screen and makes it the active screen.

AOS/VS, PRIMOS, and VMS only: You can also use the LOG command to return the SAS log to the upper portion of the program editor/log screen, replacing the output screen or help information.

NODMS

AOS/VS, PRIMOS, and VMS only: The NODMS command takes you from display manager to line mode and turns off the SOURCE option. The screen is cleared, and you receive the SAS prompt. The SAS System is then ready to receive your next SAS statement. Leaving display manager does not close the file that is currently open or end your SAS session. When you leave display manager and enter line mode, all of your current WORK data sets are still available to you.

NULLS ON | OFF

When you execute NULLS ON, all data lines are padded with nulls instead of blanks. Turning NULLS ON allows you to use the INSERT editing key to insert characters between text already entered on a line.

If you execute NULLS OFF, the data lines are padded with blanks. To use the INSERT editing key, you must first use the EOF editing key to turn those blanks into nulls.

The effect of the NULLS command on how a file is saved with the SAVE command depends on the host operating system you are using.

AOS/VS, PRIMOS, and VMS: If NULLS are ON when you save the file, the file is saved with no trailing blanks. If NULLS are OFF, trailing blanks are saved.

CMS, OS, VM/PC, and VSE: If you are saving a file in a sequential or partitioned data set with a fixed block record format, the setting of the NULLS command has no effect. If you are saving to a data set with a variable block record format, NULLS ON causes no trailing blanks to be saved, and NULLS OFF causes the trailing blanks to be saved.

NUMBER ON | OFF
NUMS ON | OFF

AOS/VS, PRIMOS, and VMS: Use the NUMS ON command to create line numbers for data lines on your screen. If your screen already contains text, all data are shifted to the right, and the line numbers appear on the left. Execute NUMS OFF to remove line numbers and shift text back to the left. NUMS ON is the default on the display manager program editor screen. If the data line numbers are displayed, you can type line commands directly over line numbers. If you set NUMS OFF, you can still execute line commands by entering them from the command line or by using a function key. Precede the line command with a colon when executing it on the command line rather that on a line number. For example, type :TS (text split) or :I (insert) on the command line, position the cursor, and then press ENTER. When using a function key, position the cursor, and then press the function key set to execute :TS.

OUTPUT
OUTPUT [ON | OFF]
OUTPUT [TOP]

The OUTPUT command, executed with no option specified, replaces the program editor/log screen with the output screen.

The OUTPUT command followed by ON or OFF specifies whether procedure output is displayed in the output screen immediately while the procedure is executing (ON) or held for later viewing (OFF). If OUTPUT OFF is in effect, specify OUTPUT to view your output. The default is OUTPUT ON.

AOS/VS, PRIMOS, and VMS only: The OUTPUT TOP command replaces the log screen in the upper portion of the program editor/ log screen with the output screen.

PRINT [PROGRAM | RECALL | LOG | OUTPUT]
[fileref | fileref(membername)]

CMS, OS, VM/PC and VSE only: You can use the PRINT command to print the entire information stream of a display manager screen, not just what is currently displayed.

You can print the stream of information in the program editor by specifying the PROGRAM option; print all statements previously submitted from the program editor with the RECALL option; the stream of information in the log screen with the LOG option; and all procedure output with the OUTPUT option.

Under OS and VSE, the information is sent to the default system printer unless you specify a fileref. Under CMS and VM/PC, assign a fileref to a printer, and then specify it with the PRINT command.

You can also send the contents to an external file by specifying its previously assigned fileref or fileref followed by a member name.

PRINT [ALL]

AOS/VS, PRIMOS, and VMS only: With the PRINT command, you can print what is currently showing in the screen on the default system printer. By specifying ALL, you can print the entire contents of the current screen, not just what is visible at the time you enter the PRINT command.

PROGRAM

The PROGRAM command moves the cursor to the command line of the program editor screen and makes it the active screen.

RCHANGE

Use the RCHANGE or RC command to continue to FIND and CHANGE a string of characters previously specified in a FIND or CHANGE command.

See also the CHANGE, FIND, and RFIND commands.

RECALL

Use the RECALL command to bring back to the program editor screen any lines you have submitted to SAS since you entered display manager. The system adds the recalled lines to the top of the program editor screen in front of any other nonblank lines already entered. After you have used the RECALL command to recall the most recently submitted block of statements, you can enter it again to recall the next most recent block.

RESET

You can use the RESET command on the program editor screen to remove any pending line commands, any conflicting line commands, and the COLS and MASK lines.

RFIND

Use the RFIND or RF command to continue the search for a string of characters previously specified in a FIND or CHANGE command.

See also the FIND, CHANGE, and RCHANGE commands.

RIGHT [*n* | **MAX**]

This command scrolls the screen *n* spaces to the right. By default the screen scrolls half of its width. To override the scroll amount temporarily, enter RIGHT and the number of spaces you want the screen to scroll. Enter RIGHT MAX to scroll the screen to the right boundary.

RULE OFF | ON

AOS/VS, PRIMOS, and VMS only: You can use the RULE ON command to display a ruler on the message line beneath the command line. The ruler marks vertical columns and moves with the data lines as you scroll right and left.

The ruler is temporarily overridden by any message that SAS displays on the message line, but the ruler returns when the message is removed. The default is RULE OFF.

SAVE *fileref* | *fileref(membername)*

CMS, OS, and VM/PC: The SAVE command writes all program lines in the program editor screen into a file that you designate with a fileref (DDname).

See also the NULLS command.

VSE: The SAVE command writes all program lines in the program editor screen into a file that you designate with a fileref (DDname).[5]

SAVE *fileref* | *'filename'*

AOS/VS, PRIMOS, and VMS: The SAVE command writes the entire information stream of the display manager screen from which you execute the SAVE command into a file that you designate with a fileref or an actual file name. You can use a host operating system command to assign a fileref to a sequential file **before** you enter display manager (except under PRIMOS), or you can use the SAS display manager command ASSIGN once you have entered display manager. If you specify an unassigned fileref, the system writes the information stream into a file named *fileref*.SAS in your current working directory. If you specify an actual file name, enclose it in single quotes. The *filename* can be either a fully qualified file name, according to the conventions of the operating system you are using, or just the name (and type under VMS) of a file in a directory to which you currently have access.

See also the NULLS command.

SCREEN OFF | ON

AOS/VS, PRIMOS, and VMS only: You can use the SCREEN command to store the contents of the display manager screen in an external file, **not** a SAS data set or catalog. After you have entered the SCREEN ON command, a file is immediately created with the exact contents of what is displayed on the physical screen. Each time you press ENTER, SUBMIT, or any function key thereafter, another file is created. Each external file containing the contents of a screen is given a file name in the form SCRNnnnn.SCR.

The first file created is given the name SCRN0001, and each file is given the extension SCR. The screen file is stored in your current working directory.

Each time you begin a SAS session, the system begins numbering screen files with SCRN0001.SCR. If SCRN0001.SCR already exists, the newly created one is written over the existing one.

Enter the SCREEN OFF command when you no longer want the contents of the screen copied to external data files. The default is SCREEN OFF.

SPLIT

You can indicate where you want the screen to split between the log and program editor screens with the SPLIT command. Enter SPLIT on the command line, position the cursor where you want the split to occur, and press ENTER; or position the cursor and press the SPLIT function key. Note: you **must** position the cursor within the boundaries of the screen on which you entered the SPLIT command. Moving the cursor into the area of another screen activates the command line of that screen.

SUBMIT ['*SAS statement;'*]

Use the SUBMIT key or command with no option specified to submit SAS program statements from the data lines of the program editor screen

Optionally, you can submit a SAS program statement directly from the command line with the SUBMIT command. You can type the command, one or more SAS statements, each followed by a semicolon, on the command line and press ENTER, or you can type just the statements with semicolons on the command line and press the SUBMIT function key.

TOP

Use the TOP command to scroll the first line of text to the top of the screen.

VSCROLL HALF|PAGE|*n*

The VSCROLL command sets the vertical scroll amount, the amount the active screen scrolls when you press the FORWARD or BACKWARD scrolling function keys. If you specify PAGE, the scroll amount is the number of data lines currently displayed. If you specify HALF, the scroll amount is one-half of the display area. If you specify *n*, the scroll amount is *n* lines. HALF is the default.

X *hostcommand*
X '*hostcommand'*

You can issue many host commands by entering an X on the command line followed by one or more host commands. Note that in minicomputer environments, the host command or string of commands **must** be enclosed in single quotation marks if it contains special characters; in IBM environments you are not allowed to enclose the host command in single quotes.

See the documentation available for SAS under the operating system you are using for any restrictions on the execution of host operating system commands.

VSE: The X command is not currently supported.

NOTES

1.   If you are using one of the terminals listed below in **Table A5.1**, use the following charts to determine the keys that have been assigned special editing functions in SAS full-screen procedures and display manager. See **Figure A5.1** for a description of the functions of these editing keys. If you are using a terminal other than one of those listed below that does not have keys matching the words

or symbols shown in **Figure A5.1**, consult your SAS representative. If you are using an IBM terminal in the 3270-series, you can disregard this section.

Table A5.1   Full-Screen Editing Functions Assigned to Terminal Keys

Display Manager Editing Key	PT45 Key	PST100 Key	PT25 Key
$\hat{a}$ (INSERT)	ichar or shift/del	insert or backspace	shift/del
$\not{a}$ (DELETE)	dchar or backspace	delete or del	backspace
ERASE EOF*	line feed	erase	shift/f8
HOME	home	home	home
REFRESH	control/clear	pf10	control/erase
NEW LINE	return or enter	return or enter	new line or enter
NEXT FIELD	f13	f2	shift/f5
PRIOR FIELD	f14	f3	shift/f6
ENTER	f3 or f15	f1 or pf13	f3 or shift/f7
MOVE CURSOR UP	↑	↑	↑
MOVE CURSOR DOWN	↓	↓	(not available)
MOVE CURSOR LEFT	←	←	←
MOVE CURSOR RIGHT	→	→	→

Continued on next page

* The PRIME computer does not accept the LINEFEED key. When using any of the terminals above under PRIMOS, use the TAB key to execute the display manager function ERASE EOF.

Table A5.1 *Continued*

Display Manager Editing Key	TEK4105 Key	VT100 Key	DASHER Key
$\hat{a}$ (INSERT)	backspace	backspace	C1
ϗ (DELETE)	rub out	delete	DEL
ERASE EOF*	line feed	line feed	erase EOL
HOME	- (minus sign on numeric keypad)	- (minus sign on numeric keypad)	home
REFRESH	, (on numeric keypad)	, (on numeric keypad)	erase page
NEW LINE	return	return	new line or enter
NEXT FIELD	. (on numeric keypad)	. (on numeric keypad)	C4
PRIOR FIELD	0 (on numeric keypad)	0 (on numeric keypad)	C3
ENTER	enter	enter	CR
MOVE CURSOR UP	F1	↑	↑
MOVE CURSOR DOWN	F2	↓	↓
MOVE CURSOR LEFT	F3	←	←
MOVE CURSOR RIGHT	F4	→	→

2.   If you are using one of the terminals listed in **Table A5.1**, you must identify it to the SAS System. If you have already invoked the SAS System, you can use the statement

```
OPTIONS DMS;
```

and then receive a prompt, asking you to identify the devicename. When invoking the SAS System, you can specify the devicename with the FSDEVICE= (FSD=) option. For example

AOS/VS	SAS/FSD=D1
PRIMOS	SAS -FSD=PT25
VMS	SAS/FSD=VT100

Table A5.2   Devices to Be Identified with the FSDEVICE= Option

TERMINALS:

Manufacturer	Model No.	Devicename
Data General	6052	DG6052 D1 (alias)
	6053	DG6053 D2 (alias)
	6093	DG6093 D3 (alias)
	D100	D100
	D200	D200
	D210	D210
	D211	D211
	D400	D400
	D410	D410
	D450	D450
	D460	D460
	D470C	D470C
	G300	G300
	G500	G500

Note: devicename DG605X is an alias for all Data General terminals.

Manufacturer	Model No.	Devicename
Digital Equipment	VT52	VT52
	VT100	VT100
	VT125	VT125
	VT131	VT131
	VT132	VT132
	VT220	VT220
	VT240	VT240
	VT241	VT241
Prime Computer (PRIME)	PT25	PT25
	PT45	PT45
	PST100	PST100
Tektronix	4105	TEK4105

3.   **AOS/VS, PRIMOS, and VMS:** By default the program editor translates all
characters into uppercase. If you want to prevent the translation, execute the

CAPS OFF command on the program editor screen either from the command line or with a function key before entering program statements.

CMS, OS, VM/PC, and VSE: By default the program editor does not translate all characters into uppercase. Execute the CAPS ON command if you want text entered or lines altered after you execute the command to be translated into uppercase.

4. **AOS/VS, PRIMOS, and VMS:** A message indicating the use of computer resources is also displayed in the log screen unless you previously specified the NOSTIMER option.

5. **VSE:** If the file referred to is a sequential file, you must use a /FILE statement in the ICCF procedure. If it is a member of an ICCF library, you are not allowed to use a /FILE statement in the ICCF procedure. Instead, specify the actual ICCF member name.

6. **AOS/VS, PRIMOS, and VMS:** The display manager editor breaks information into 80-column lengths; a command that exceeds 80 columns is divided and may not be properly executed.

CMS, OS, VM/PC, and VSE: Any characters typed beyond the 80th column are truncated.

7. **CMS, OS, VM/PC, and VSE:** You can specify only PROGRAM, LOG, and OUTPUT to indicate an active screen.

8. **AOS/VS, PRIMOS, and VMS:** SASEXEC.SAS can be the actual file name and file type. As long as you have access to the directory in which SASEXEC.SAS is stored, you do not have to assign it a fileref. **Do not** give another file the name SASEXEC.

9. **CMS, OS, VM/PC, and VSE:** 80 columns is the maximum line length in the program editor.

AOS/VS, PRIMOS, and VMS: 256 columns is the maximum line length in the program editor.

10. **AOS/VS, PRIMOS, and VMS:** The length of the data line on the log screen is sensitive to the value of the LINESIZE= option in the OPTIONS statement. The maximum line length on the log screen is 256 columns.

CMS, OS, VM/PC, and VSE: The length of the data line on the log screen is sensitive to the value of the TLS= option in the OPTIONS statement. The maximum line length on the log screen is 132 columns.

11. **AOS/VS, PRIMOS, and VMS:** The maximum line length on the output screen is 256 columns.

CMS, OS, VM/PC, and VSE: The maximum line length on the output screen is 132 columns.

336

Index

X

SAS/OR™ User's Guide, Version 5 Edition

Judith K. Whatley edited the *SAS/OR User's Guide, Version 5 Edition*. **Kathryn A. Council** was contributing editor. **David D. Baggett** and **Betty Fried** were copy editors. **Gigi Hassan, Frances A. Kienzle,** and **James K. Hart** provided editorial services. **Gail C. Freeman** and **Blanche Weatherspoon** provided text composition.

Craig R. Sampson and **Pamela A. Troutman** wrote the Text Composition Program. **Arlene B. Drezek** and **Sarah M. Richardson** provided composition and production. **Elisabeth C. Smith** and **Michael J. Pezzoni** provided the line illustrations.

Your Turn

If you have comments about SAS software or the *SAS/OR™ User's Guide, Version 5 Edition*, please let us know by writing your ideas in the space below. If you include your name and address, we will reply to you.

Please return this sheet to the Publications Division, SAS Institute Inc., SAS Circle, Box 8000, Cary, NC 27511-8000.